STATE OF INNOVATION
THE U.S. GOVERNMENT'S ROLE
IN TECHNOLOGY DEVELOPMENT

edited by
Fred Block and Matthew R. Keller

Routledge
Taylor & Francis Group

LONDON AND NEW YORK

First published 2011 by Paradigm Publishers

Published 2016 by Routledge
2 Park Square, Milton Park, Abingdon, Oxon OX14 4RN
711 Third Avenue, New York, NY 10017, USA

Routledge is an imprint of the Taylor & Francis Group, an informa business

Library of Congress Cataloging-in-Publication Data

State of Innovation : the U.S. government's role in technology development / edited by Fred Block and Matthew R. Keller
    p. cm.
  Includes bibliographical references and index.
  ISBN 978-1-59451-823-2 (hardcover : alk. paper)
  ISBN 978-1-59451-824-9 (paperback : alk. paper)
  1. Technological innovations—Government policy—United States. 2. Technological innovations—Economic aspects—United States. 3. Techology and state—United States. 4. Industrial policy—United States. I. Block, Fred L. II. Keller, Matthew R.
  HC110.T4S73 2010
  338'.0640973—dc22

                                                                      2010014738

Designed and Typeset by Straight Creek Bookmakers.

ISBN 13 : 978-1-59451-823-2 (hbk)
ISBN 13 : 978-1-59451-824-9 (pbk)

Contents

State of Innovation

The U.S. Government's Role in Technology Development

Peter Evans

What makes the appearance of *State of Innovation* an important event—both for future theorizing on the dynamics of economic growth and for progress in the direction of more effective policies? Anyone with even a cursory acquaintance with U.S. history is aware of the U.S. government's central role in fostering the country's exceptional economic growth, from Hamiltonian tariff policy to canals to agricultural research. Likewise, no one familiar with the history of contemporary innovation would gainsay the central role of government initiatives from DARPA to the National Nanotechnology Initiative.

Of course government agencies and government support for private actors play an absolutely essential role in fostering innovation. Only someone trapped in ideological amber would expect otherwise. Private entrepreneurship is also a central part of the story. Who would expect otherwise in the country that epitomized late-twentieth-century capitalism? The scholars who put together this book are not interested in rehearsing stale state-versus-market debates built on nineteenth-century theorizing. They are interested in figuring out how to realize the twenty-first-century potential for innovations that will enable human capabilities to flourish and prevent the planet from turning into a hostile biosphere.

This is an important book precisely because it is not an argument for a bigger government role. It is an argument for looking at how innovation is actually organized and how it might be organized better. It helps us to understand how networks, organizations, and institutional arrangements worked across the conventional public-private divide to produce an impressive array of innovations in late-twentieth-century America. Starting with careful histories of what actually worked, it goes on to derive general analytical lessons that will help guide future experiments in building innovation-fostering institutional structures.

The critical question is how to create positive synergies between public support and private initiative, between government action and markets, between networks and corporate organizations to produce the innovations we need and want. The book attacks this question in two ways. First it offers concrete histories of how innovations happened.

Fresh, well-documented narratives give readers a chance to reconsider the usefulness of conventional prior accounts. Second, it offers new analytic frames, new conceptualizations, and new propositions regarding which institutional designs work and why.

The history is the crucial foundation. The book's contributors chronicle systematically and thoroughly a range of projects and policy arenas in which diversely structured synergies have emerged among government agencies, businesses, and scientists and engineers. One of the revelations of the book is that precisely in the period since Ronald Reagan's election in 1980, when the political rhetoric regarding growth and innovation was almost purely "free market," the U.S. government was carefully and quietly developing new capacity to carry out effective innovation policies in collaboration with the private sector. As Block and Keller show in their chapter, in 2006, seventy-seven out of eighty-eight award-winning innovations benefited from some federal support. Similarly, in their chapter, Vallas, Kleinman, and Biscotti provide evidence that most of the blockbuster new pharmaceuticals developed by U.S. firms over the last twenty years drew heavily on governmental support.

If the book offered only historical narrative it would be a signal contribution, but the same chapters also make theoretical contributions. It is the combination of theory and history that makes the book so exceptionally valuable. *State of Innovation* digs further to analyze the mechanisms by which these government innovation policies in the United States—and in several comparative cases—have been able to achieve consistent results.

The argument is that these programs have adapted to a new era of networked production in which both innovation and production increasingly take place in complex collaborations among different firms and, often, nonprofit entities. As Whitford and Schrank put it, "the activities most likely to be targeted by industrial policy are increasingly governed by decentralized production networks rather than competitive markets or vertically integrated corporations." Nor are decentralized production networks seen as a panacea. Networked production is constantly threatened by "network failures," and the public sector programs are often able to provide participants with the institutional resources they need to avoid these failures.

State of Innovation is intended to make contributions to history and theory, and it succeeds, but its aspirations clearly go further. It is also designed to sustain policies effective in the past and generate even better policy in the future. It deserves success in achieving this goal as well. Read carefully and dispassionately, *State of Innovation* could be a kind of manual for how effective synergies can be created between public agencies and private firms. Moving from intellectual to political success is not, however, something the authors take for granted.

U.S. politicians and policymakers are the most obvious targets (admirable chapters on Ireland and China notwithstanding), but they are hardly soft targets. Even while the projects recounted here were delivering an impressive array of practical results, public political discourse remained mired in old Manichean visions of markets fighting to free themselves from stifling government. Old ideological tropes forced the successes chronicled here to remain largely "below the radar" in public discussions of the politics of innovation rather than being openly celebrated.

This book should help legitimate the state and private managers who are pursuing innovation "below the radar" and give them courage to continue. Nonetheless, it may not be U.S. policymakers who take the fullest advantage of the book's lessons, but rather policymakers in other countries less hobbled by the persistence of old ideological habits.

Late-twentieth-century efforts by U.S. policymakers to use their political and economic leverage to push governments around the world to embrace a "Washington Consensus" have faltered. Policymakers and managers and entrepreneurs searching for ways to accelerate innovation in countries such as China, Brazil, and India are now freer to pursue more complex and eclectic strategies. *State of Innovation* could be a source of inspiration. Ironically, it may not be the official U.S. model but the unacknowledged model embedded in U.S. practice that turns out to be America's contribution to twenty-first-century global economic progress. If this does happen, those who put together *State of Innovation* will deserve some of the credit.

Acknowledgments

This volume would not exist without the insight and support of Leonardo Burlamaqui of the Ford Foundation. It was Leonardo who initially suggested investigating the developmental activities of the U.S. government, and he provided multiple years of funding that made this project possible. He was also an active participant in the various workshops and conferences that culminated in this volume. We are also grateful to Antonio Barros de Castro and Ana Celia Castro for initially facilitating this connection.

We have incurred many other debts during the long gestation of this book. Patricia McFate, also at the Ford Foundation, has provided financial support from the start. We are particularly grateful to the labor of the authors of the various chapters for their years of work in researching and revising their contributions. There are, however, many others who have contributed important ideas along the way—too numerous for us to mention them each by name. But we do want to thank those who participated in the various workshops and conferences that helped move this project along. These include Rob Atkinson, Robert Berdahl, Nicole Biggart, Kelly Bradfield, David Douglas, Gary Dymski, Peter Evans, Neil Fligstein, Glenn Fong, Marion Fourcade, Ron Hira, Victor Hwang, John Irons, Lucas Kirkpatrick, Jan Kregel, Michael McQuarrie, Jock O'Connell, Robert Pollin, Andrew Revkin, Daniel Sarewitz, Michael Shellenberger, James Shoch, Michael Peter Smith, Marc Stanley, Eddy U, Linda Weiss, and Nick Ziegler. We also want to publicly thank all of the participants in the innovation community who shared their knowledge and insights with us.

Along the way, valuable research assistance was provided by Dina Biscotti, Athmeya Jayaram, Matt Khoury, John Kincaid, Jason Logan, and Katie Wilmes. Janet Firshein provided key assistance for the Washington, D.C., event. We received logistical support from Lori Dana and the staff at the UC Davis Institute of Government Affairs and from the UC Washington Center. Laura Keller provided indispensable artistic assistance. Penny Kramer and Susan Weiss did terrific editorial work to improve the chapters. We are also grateful to Jennifer Knerr, Jessica Priest, Chrisona Schmidt, Kay Mariea, and others at Paradigm Publishers for their work on this book.

Fred would like to thank Carole Joffe for her patience and support through this book's long development. He is also deeply grateful to Judith and Miriam Joffe-Block for their continuing help with this project. Margaret Somers has been unfailingly supportive even when this project has diverted attention from their own collaboration.

Matthew would like to express his warmest thanks to Laura Keller for her tireless support, and to his son Brodie, whose ever-present enthusiasm has been a recurrent source of inspiration.

CHAPTER 1

Innovation and the Invisible Hand of Government

Fred Block

The long, deep U.S. recession of 2007–2009 seems very different from earlier economic downturns; it suggests a possible turning point in the nation's economic trajectory. Unemployment has been worse and more persistent in this downturn, and many venerable economic institutions, from Merrill Lynch and Bear Stearns to General Motors and Chrysler, have disappeared or undergone dramatic reorganization; many other firms have had to make fundamental changes in their business models. The crisis has also forced a sharp retreat from the governing philosophy that had been in place since the election of Ronald Reagan in 1980. That philosophy—market fundamentalism—insists that "government is the problem, not the solution," and its preferred remedies for economic problems are tax cuts, relaxed regulation of business and finance, and greater reliance on markets to solve economic and social problems (Block 2007).[1] George W. Bush, who had long championed this approach, had to make a U-turn in the fall of 2008. In the face of a financial collapse, he unleashed an unprecedented government rescue of Wall Street through hundreds of billions of dollars of direct support for firms like Citibank, Bank of America, AIG, Morgan Stanley, and Goldman Sachs (Wessel 2009).

Bush's successor, Barack Obama, continued these extensive government efforts to rescue and reshape major financial institutions, and he has proposed an ambitious program of new regulations for the financial industry. Obama has loaned billions to two out of three of the major automobile firms, reorganized their top management, and guided them through a dramatic reorganization in bankruptcy court. In its early days, the new administration pushed through a huge government stimulus bill devoting billions of dollars to shifting the U.S. economy from oil and coal to alternative energy sources, and the administration continues to pursue plans to reorganize the health care industry and the energy sector.

Moreover, the new administration understands that even as it attempts to pull the economy back from crisis and recession, it faces a number of deeper long-term challenges. One of the most important is the chronic weakness of the U.S. international trade position. For a generation, this trade balance has been strongly negative because of the U.S. appetite for both foreign oil and cheap manufactured imports from Asia.

Because of its huge trade deficit, the United States has relied for many years on foreign borrowing to finance its balance of payments deficit, a pattern that many observers think is unsustainable (Obstfeld and Rogoff 2007; Mann and Pluck 2007).

The seriousness of the trade problem is indicated by a measure of the U.S. trade balance in high-tech products, which has also turned negative in recent years (data available at www.census.gov/foreign-trade/Press-Release/current_press_release/ft900 .pdf).[2] Historically, the U.S. surplus in global trade for technologically sophisticated products helped offset the deficit for raw materials and basic manufactured goods such as small appliances and apparel. But if the United States is starting to import more high-tech goods than it exports, then the prospects for a significant improvement in the trade balance are even dimmer.

Two other long-term challenges reinforce this focus on the economy's capacity for innovation. The first is the imminent threat of global climate change resulting from rising levels of carbon dioxide in the atmosphere. Without significant shifts away from burning fossil fuels in the United States and other countries, the globe faces rising oceans and increasingly disruptive weather patterns. And it is now widely recognized that progress in this direction requires significant technological advances to bring down the prices for several different sources of renewable energy (Weiss and Bonvillian 2009). The final challenge is the one of assuring new domestic employment opportunities as the economy recovers from the recession. With many jobs moving abroad in both the manufacturing and the service sectors, the administration's political success rests on its ability to bring about vigorous employment growth at home.

For all three of these reasons, the new administration has strongly emphasized strengthening the U.S. economy's capacity for innovation. This focus is particularly clear in the stimulus bill—the American Recovery and Reinvestment Act—passed in January 2009. The idea is that if the United States can capitalize on its scientific and engineering resources to produce a continuous stream of new high-tech products and services, including "green" energy technologies, this would strengthen U.S. exports and expand domestic employment. Just as the U.S. global leadership in computer hardware and software and in biotechnology helped sustain the U.S. economy over the past three decades, it is hoped that building new high-tech and green industries will improve the U.S. competitive position. Moreover, innovations in new energy technologies, in particular, would strengthen the trade balance by reducing U.S. imports of foreign oil (Executive Office of the President 2009) while also reducing the production of greenhouse gases.

But in prioritizing the U.S. innovation economy, the Obama administration faces a series of difficult questions. How does innovation actually work in the current U.S. economy? What are the respective contributions of the private sector and the public sector in facilitating innovation? What policies can and should the government use to accelerate innovation in the private sector?

This book is intended to provide answers to these questions. Each chapter is based on careful, in-depth research on how the innovation economy actually works both in the United States and in other nations. Through a series of detailed case studies—of particular industries and of specific government technology programs—the chapters are designed to illuminate the landscape of effective innovation and suggest the lessons that have been learned from recent innovation efforts.

This introductory chapter is designed to set the stage for the more detailed arguments of the following chapters by tracing out the history of innovation policies in the United States and by providing an overview of the complex institutional structure of the current innovation system in the United States. The introduction will elaborate the key finding that emerges from the chapters—that the United States, particularly over the past three decades, has developed a sophisticated and complex innovation system in which the government plays an absolutely central role. The current administration in Washington does not have to begin from scratch; it has the opportunity to refine and improve a system that has been developing for some time.

The introduction will also explore the intersection between the book's findings and the question of governance philosophy with which the current administration and the larger society are currently wrestling. The severity of the 2007–2009 financial and economic crisis and the fact that it was precipitated by significant regulatory failures in the financial sector has discredited the market fundamentalist views that have dominated U.S. politics since the 1980s. But the new administration has not yet advanced an alternative governing philosophy. On the contrary, the president has repeatedly affirmed his commitment to the free market and has argued that the measures he is taking are simply designed to make markets work more effectively. Obama has repeatedly invoked his commitment to pragmatism—a search for solutions unconstrained by any ideological commitments.

However, there are many reasons for doubting that pragmatism will be sufficient to guide the nation through a series of difficult transitions. It is a basic law of politics that you cannot beat something with nothing. When opponents endlessly recycle the familiar claims of market fundamentalism that government must get out of the way of the private economy, the administration has to explain that these are stale and outmoded ideas. But it is very difficult to do that without articulating an alternative governing philosophy and a roadmap of where the country is headed.

This is where the innovation economy looms large. The historical experience with the innovation economy provides powerful arguments against the core assumptions of market fundamentalism. For many technologies, it has not been Adam Smith's invisible hand, but the hand of government that has proven decisive in their development. Moreover, the innovation economy depends on a series of principles that are at fundamental variance with market fundamentalism. In fact, careful study of the innovation economy helps us see some of the outline of a new governance philosophy that could provide a durable foundation for prosperity in the United States in the twenty-first century.

The introduction will address these different tasks in three parts. The first shows how the dramatic changes in the innovation economy of the last thirty years have been built on top of a set of institutions that have a much longer history. The second part describes how the different elements of the current innovation system fit together. The third part extracts the principles of governance on which this innovation economy rests.

Historical Overview

From World War II to the early 1970s, theorists of market fundamentalism were largely on the margins of economic and political debates in the United States (Block 2007; Leopold 2009). The prevailing Keynesian consensus insisted that government had a fundamental role in guiding the economy and maintaining high levels of investment and employment. However, as the U.S. economy experienced growing economic difficulties in the 1970s, the market fundamentalist critique of Keynesianism and "big government" gained traction. Starting with the election of Ronald Reagan in 1980, market fundamentalists returned to power and their ideas dominated policy debates in the United States until the financial crisis in 2008.

Market fundamentalists argue that the best policy is to rely to the greatest extent possible on allegedly self-regulating markets while keeping the government's economic activity to a minimum. The thinkers who were most important in popularizing these ideas, particularly Milton Friedman, George Stigler, and other figures from the Chicago School of Economics, long insisted that the United States had taken a wrong turn during Franklin Roosevelt's New Deal in the 1930s, when the government role in the economy was significantly expanded through both increased regulation of business and expanded public provision through old age and unemployment assistance.

These thinkers wanted to go back to the pre–New Deal regime of limited government, and they argued that the dynamic economic growth that the country enjoyed for most of the century and a half from the founding of the Republic to the start of the New Deal was a direct consequence of reliance on markets and small government (Friedman and Friedman 1990). Their vision of a halcyon American past meant that they had to ignore or downplay the poverty, misery, and mass unemployment that was widespread as industrialization progressed during the course of the nineteenth century (Katz 1986; Keyssar 1986).

But even more importantly, they had to create a fictive American past in which the substantial economic role played by government—from the founding—was made to disappear. The history of the United States is no different from that of other modern countries; fighting wars and preparing for wars have been an absolutely critical spur to economic growth and development (Roland 2003; Ruttan 2006). Many of the key industrial and organizational breakthroughs of the late eighteenth and nineteenth centuries came in industries that were developing weapons or other supplies, such as ships or uniforms, that were being procured on a large scale by the military (Smith 1985; Ruttan 2006). Starting with the Revolutionary War, continuing with the War of 1812, the wars against the Native Americans, and the Civil War, some of the most important innovations in production and organizational technologies came in the manufacture of guns and other weapons. In fact, the rifle figures prominently in manufacturing history as one of the first instances of the use of interchangeable parts to facilitate expanded production (Hounshell 1984; Ruttan 2006; Smith 1977). Moreover, the machine tools developed for weapons production then migrated to industries producing sewing machines, bicycles, and ultimately automobiles (Rosenberg 1963; Ruttan 2006).

The government began to invest in technological expertise for military purposes in the first years of the Republic (Angevine 2004). The Army Corps of Engineers was created in 1802, and military academies such as West Point, the Naval Academy, and the Citadel were the earliest instances of government investment in higher education. As early as the 1820s and 1830s, army engineers were at work building canals and lighthouses, and improving river navigation—projects that had both military and commercial implications (Shallat 1994).

This same pattern, of course, continued into the present century. World War I dramatically accelerated the development of automobiles, airplanes, and radio. The government directly mobilized the research laboratories of major corporations for the war effort, and important scientists and engineers, drawing on the wartime experience, began to argue in the 1920s for the creation of a national research endowment through which the U.S. government would adopt a permanent role in financing key scientific and technological research. While that idea gained little political traction, the government did establish the Naval Research Laboratory in 1923, which was the military's first venture in creating a permanent peacetime laboratory (Wise 1985).

But the market fundamentalist version of the pre–New Deal past also has to ignore a very long history of deliberate state initiatives that did not have an immediate military justification.[3] This goes back to Alexander Hamilton's famous *Report on Manufactures* (1791) that insisted, against the laissez-faire orthodoxy of that day, that the young Republic needed to use policies such as tariffs and government procurement contracts to nurture new industries to make the nation competitive with the advanced nations of Europe (Bourgin 1989; Chang 2008). While Hamilton's report was never fully implemented, it still provided valuable arguments for those eager to use the state to pursue industrial ends, and U.S. industrialization proceeded behind high tariff walls through the nineteenth century.

Hamiltonian ideas helped inspire the aggressive role of state governments in building canals and railroads in the first half of the nineteenth century. Sometimes these efforts were directly financed out of state funds and sometimes state governments would organize and subsidize newly created private entities to do the work (Angevine 2004; Dobbin 1994). Either way, these transportation innovations played an important role in driving economic growth in the antebellum period.

With Lincoln's presidency and the start of the Civil War, the initiative in economic policy shifted definitively toward the federal government. Lincoln launched the building of the intercontinental railroad, which probably ranked at the time among the most ambitious efforts in human history (Ambrose 2000). Lincoln also presided over the creation of the Department of Agriculture and the start of the land grant colleges, which were conceived as efforts to modernize society's dominant economic sector—farming. In fact, the first permanent government laboratory was established in the 1860s in the Department of Agriculture to do research on plant and animal diseases and soil quality (Harding 1947). Lincoln also recognized the growing role of scientific knowledge when he signed the legislation for the National Academy of Sciences—a nonprofit organization designed so that the organized scientific community could provide continuous input and advice to the government (Kleinman 1995).

The steps taken in the Civil War period laid the foundation for rapid economic growth and the creation of an integrated national economy in the last three decades of the nineteenth century. But the volatility and other dangers generated by this new industrial economy produced a new wave of federal initiatives in the first years of the twentieth century. In search of greater stability, Progressive Era reformers extended the reach of the national government. The first federal laboratory with expertise in the physical sciences was started in 1901 in the newly created National Bureau of Standards. This bureau was created to emulate what the USDA had done for agriculture—to promote expertise that would accelerate industrial development. The NBS (later renamed the National Institute of Standards and Technology, or NIST) played an important role in radio and telephony (Allen and Sriram 2000; Needell 2000).

A series of new federal regulatory institutions were also created in this period. The Pure Food and Drug Act of 1906 created the agency that would ultimately become the Food and Drug Administration (1906), and the Federal Reserve Board (1913) and the Federal Trade Commission (1914) were also products of this period. These agencies came to play a dual role. On the one side, they acted as regulatory police to prevent businesses from pursuing strategies that could be economically destructive. On the other, they often acted as partners or collaborators helping businesses to stabilize markets, maintain competition, and adopt more effective business practices (Hilts 2003; Greider 1987; Berk 2009). Berk (2009) conceptualizes this approach as "regulated competition" and gives Louis Brandeis much of the credit for bringing this idea into the policy arena.

In short, the market fundamentalist history of the U.S. economy before the New Deal is basically fanciful. Leaving warfare and armaments out of the history of U.S. industry is like the proverbial production of Hamlet without the prince. But even beyond that, economic development in the nineteenth century and in the first decades of the twentieth depended on an ongoing partnership between the government and business. Government provided necessary infrastructure such as roads, canals, railroads, and harbors, and helped train the labor force and build the society's technological capabilities; government agencies worked to facilitate the diffusion of productive innovations in agriculture, industry, and services.

But if this government-business partnership has been a constant of U.S. history since the founding of the Republic, there is no question that the intensity and importance of the government role in driving innovation has intensified dramatically over the past seven decades. Three key turning points significantly tilted the curve toward a heightened role for the federal government. These are each points of inflection where the impact of government innovation activity became even more central to the organization of the U.S. economy. But there is a great deal of continuity across these different periods, and each one builds on the previous ones in important ways.

The First Turning Point: World War II and the Rise of a Science State

While the market fundamentalists emphasize FDR's New Deal measures as the critical turning point, in reality World War II was far more important for innovation policies. Some of the newly created New Deal agencies played the same role that earlier regulatory agencies had played—helping to facilitate innovation through regulated competition. For example, the Federal Housing Authority helped real estate developers by creating a set of standards for the building of new residential subdivisions (Weiss 1987). But the real sea change came with World War II, which saw a dramatic expansion in the government's technological capacities. Since there was an almost immediate transition to the Cold War, these new capacities became institutionalized on a permanent basis.

The first aspect of the shift was that during World War II and the early Cold War years, the government's scientific and technological capacity was expanded through the creation of an elaborate network of permanent federal laboratories staffed with highly trained scientists and engineers (Hooks 1991; Kleinman 1995; Westwick 2003). To be sure, the roots of this government capacity go back to the creation of the Army Corps of Engineers and the first laboratories at the Department of Agriculture and the Bureau of Standards. However, the Manhattan Project created the system of atomic laboratories, including Los Alamos, Lawrence Berkeley, Oak Ridge, and Sandia, that still exists almost seventy years later (Westwick 2003). As indicated in Schrank (Chapter 5) and Block and Keller (Chapter 8), this system of laboratories has become central to the current U.S. innovation system.

World War II also made the federal government the principal source of funding for foundational scientific research. This shift was consolidated in the early Cold War years with the creation of the National Science Foundation in 1950 (Kleinman 1995). The experience of the Manhattan Project, when physicists went to the government to instruct policymakers about the military implications of a new technology, marked an historical turning point. From that moment onward, the federal government exercised sufficient oversight over the scientific community through funding that it could anticipate which new technologies might have military applications. As Shelley Hurt shows (Chapter 2), even before scientists had made the key breakthroughs in combining DNA to produce new organisms, policymakers in the Nixon administration were keenly aware that developments in genetic engineering could produce new generations of biological weaponry as well as new commercial products.

Another aspect of the shift that began in World War II was that a significant cadre of government officials took more direct responsibility for pushing forward the technological frontier. Some did this by running government laboratories and motivating scientists and engineers to solve specific technological problems. Others did this in their capacity as providers of funding for research going on in the private sector and in universities or as people responsible for procurement who insisted that vendors provide products that accomplish certain technical objectives. But in all these cases, nurturing innovation became an important part of the job description for a substantial number of government workers. This also represented a significant historical shift.

Sometimes, to be sure, these officials spent large sums of money on technological dead ends or white elephants that had little durable value (Alic 2007). But it is still important that for the first time in U.S. history, a group of people were empowered by their society to direct the process of technological development in particular directions. This represented a significant change from reliance during peacetime on the creativity of scientists and engineers working in university and corporate laboratories.

Even so, it remains difficult to assess the costs and benefits of the shift that started during World War II. If we think of the years from Pearl Harbor in 1941 until the Soviet launch of Sputnik in 1957 as a single period, the technological achievements are quite spectacular. This newly created military-industrial complex built thousands of planes and tanks, developed the atomic bomb, the hydrogen bomb, civilian nuclear power, the computer, the transistor, the semiconductor, made major advances in airplane, radar, and missile technology, and completed much of the preparatory work for the laser. On the other hand, spending on technology of this period was at historically unprecedented levels, and there was unquestionably an enormous amount of waste in this system (Alic 2007). Whether or not the technological gains were proportionate with the increased spending is a debate that will not soon be resolved.

The Second Turning Point: 1957 and the Move to Greater Decentralization

Two separate events that happened in 1957 established another inflection point in the development of the innovation system in the United States. The first was the Soviet Sputnik launch in October 1957. This created considerable panic in U.S. policy circles over the loss of U.S. technological advantage relative to its Cold War enemy. Washington rushed to make adjustments, including the reorganization of the space program through the creation of NASA and the passage of the National Defense Education Act to strengthen U.S. education, particularly in math and science. But for our purposes, the most significant change was the creation in 1958 of the Defense Advanced Research Projects Agency (DARPA) in the Defense Department (Roland 2002; Bonvillian 2009).[4] Up until the creation of DARPA in 1958, all military R&D dollars were controlled by the military services themselves. The idea behind DARPA was to devote some portion of military spending to "blue sky thinking"—beyond the horizon ideas—that might not produce anything usable for another ten or twenty years. Freed from the constraints of weapons procurement, DARPA was able to experiment with new strategies for accelerating the development of innovative technologies. The agency made a huge contribution to the development of the computer industry in the 1960s and 1970s by funding the creation of computer science departments, providing early research support to some of the most promising start-up firms, supporting key research on semiconductors and on the human computer interface, and ultimately overseeing the earliest incarnation of the Internet (NRC 1999; Waldrop 2001).

The second key event was the 1957 revolt by a group of scientists and engineers who were working for a firm started by William Shockley, the Nobel Prize–winning physicist who had developed the first transistor at Bell Labs (Lecuyer 2006). The rebels, labeled for all history as the "traitorous eight," broke away to start a new firm with the support of Fairchild Camera and Instrument Company. The new firm made significant advances in semiconductor technology and helped establish the engineer-run spin-off as a viable business model for pushing the technological envelope.[5]

Several of the eight went on to found Intel and other firms. One of them, Eugene Kleiner, started Kleiner Perkins, the pioneering venture capital firm which demonstrated that substantial money could be made by those willing to invest and support these engineer-run spin-offs. But most importantly, the Fairchild pioneers helped to establish a new paradigm where economic growth depended not so much on the consolidation of giant corporations, but rather on a process of economic fission that was constantly spinning off new economic challengers. Sometimes these new firms were started by defectors from established firms and sometimes by researchers in university and government laboratories, but the consequence was the same—to expand the number of ideas that were moving from laboratory to marketplace.

These two separate events achieved a convergence in the 1960s as DARPA's program officers began to exploit the possibilities of this new innovation environment. With standard defense contracting, the leverage of government officials to generate rapid technological advances was somewhat limited. Once they had a contract, big defense firms could use their political muscle on Capitol Hill to protect them from what they perceived to be excessive demands for innovation. Even when procurement officers tried to use competition among firms for the initial contract as a means to achieve ambitious technological breakthroughs, leverage was restricted because the number of firms with the appropriate competence was limited and those firms had a common interest in pushing back when they were pressured to take chances on risky, unproven technological pathways.[6]

However, DARPA's program officers came to see that things could work differently in industries where there were already some ambitious new start-up firms and the potential for more. This kind of environment made it much easier for program officers to generate real competition among different groups of researchers since those running the startup firms understood that their firm's future viability rested on meeting ambitious benchmarks. Moreover, this leverage could be had with much smaller dollar amounts than were needed to influence the decisions of giant defense contractors; a few million dollars, while insignificant for a multibillion-dollar firm, could look like a huge amount of money to a newly formed firm.

Moreover, as the possibility of creating spin-offs became institutionalized, established firms also had to adapt to the new environment. Large firms had to worry that their best scientists and engineers might leave to pursue their research interests in another setting. This meant that when DARPA expressed interest in providing funding to a research group at established firms such as IBM or Xerox, management had strong reasons to endorse the project even if it did not fit with the firm's priorities. Consequently DARPA had the ability to mobilize effort by technologists in the most common research settings—big firms, small firms, and university and government laboratories.

Since DARPA gave its program officers a great deal of discretion and avoided the elaborate grant writing and refereeing procedures used by NSF and NIH, its program officers were able to take maximum advantage of this enhanced leverage. With less paperwork, they could get the money flowing quickly, but they also had no hesitation in cutting off funding for research groups that were unable to make progress in meeting technological benchmarks. They also used their funding networks to accelerate the flow of knowledge across competing research groups. They brought their funded researchers together for periodic workshops to share ideas and find out which technological pathways had been identified as dead ends by other groups.

When DARPA officers were working with start-ups or with university researchers who had not yet created a firm, they used their network ties to help move the particular technology to the marketplace. This might mean connecting a professor with an entrepreneur who was willing to build a new firm, linking a start-up firm to venture capitalists who could provide both capital and technical assistance, locating a larger company that was willing and eager to commercialize the technology, or helping the firm get a government procurement contract that would support the commercialization process.

In addition, DARPA officers often intervened to expand the pool of scientists and engineers working on a particular problem. They did this in the 1960s by financing the creation of new computer science departments at a series of different universities. By multiplying the number of researchers with the specific expertise that was needed to improve computer programming or develop faster microprocessors, they could accelerate the pace of technological change for an extended period of time.

One particular example illustrates how effectively the DARPA model worked in synchrony with a more open and decentralized model of technological development. In the second half of the 1970s, it became apparent that the fabrication of new computer chips had become a major bottleneck for technological development. Many people, including some graduate students in computer science, had the capacity to design new chips, but getting a design into a prototype was expensive and only the more established actors were able to persuade firms to make this investment. DARPA stepped in and financed a laboratory, affiliated with the University of Southern California, whose mission was to fabricate chips from anybody who claimed to have a superior design. By taking on this expense, the agency opened the way for more participants in the effort to produce faster and better microchips (Roland 2002).

The Third Turning Point: The 1980s and More Agencies Enter the Picture

The third turning point is a bit more complicated because it coincided with the resurgence of free market rhetoric during the Reagan administration. The conventional wisdom is that during the administration of Ronald Reagan those who argued that the United States should embrace an active "industrial policy" to deal with the competitive threat from foreign firms were decisively defeated (Graham 1992) as the government, instead, chose to rely on private markets. But under Reagan, the government took a number of major steps to build on DARPA's successes in pursuing a highly decentralized form of industrial policy. While this turning point has been largely overlooked, it has proven hugely consequential for the development of U.S. innovation capacity.

The choices made in the Reagan years flowed logically from three converging trends that dated back to the 1960s and intensified in the 1970s. The first was the continuing problem in the U.S. international trade balance. For the first two decades after the end of World War II, the United States exported much more than it imported. But as

Japanese and Western European producers began to catch up with U.S. producers in a number of major industries, including automobiles, U.S. imports of manufactured goods rose, pushing the United States toward a deficit position (Block 1977; Hughes 2005). Starting in the Nixon administration and continuing in the Carter administration, there was much high-level debate about how the United States could use its scientific and technological leadership to reestablish its advantage in international trade (Hughes 2005). As early as the Nixon administration, policymakers were conceptualizing new forms of public-private partnership to address this problem (Hurt, Chapter 2).

Second, as the trade deficit worsened during the 1970s, there were increasingly vocal calls for the United States to embrace an industrial policy that followed the model that Japan had used to transform itself into an advanced industrial economy (Graham 1992; Hughes 2005). Proponents argued that the creation of a centralized industrial policy agency could help the United States both to revitalize declining industries such as auto and steel and to provide the capital and incentives required to seed the growth of new industries based on cutting-edge technologies. When the Carter administration loaned Chrysler Motors billions of dollars to avoid bankruptcy, some observers saw this as a bold first step in the direction of the Japanese model (Hughes 2005).

A third trend cut in a different direction. Over the course of the 1970s, policymakers became increasingly aware of DARPA's successes in pursuing decentralized industrial policy initiatives. It was during the 1970s that the personal computer emerged, with Apple introducing its first model in 1976. This brought a great deal of attention to the dramatic growth of the computer industry in Silicon Valley and to DARPA's critical role in setting the context for the explosive growth of personal computing (Fong 2001).

But the big developments in biotechnology in the 1970s were also critical for persuading policymakers that the computer industry was not a unique case. The founding of Genentech in 1976 showed that university-based scientists could be persuaded to transform their academic research into new businesses and that government agencies could help accelerate this process by targeting research funding and helping these academic entrepreneurs overcome the obstacles to successful commercialization of their ideas (Collins 2004; Vallas, Kleinman, and Biscotti, Chapter 3).

In the final years of the Carter administration, several steps were taken to accelerate this decentralized vision of technological development by mobilizing the government's research assets. The National Science Foundation began to experiment with the creation of industry-university research centers that would focus the energies of a group of scientists, often at multiple institutions, on the concrete technological problems faced by a particular industry (Turner 2006).

In 1980 Congress passed the Stevenson-Wydler Technology Innovation Act, which encouraged the network of federal laboratories to engage in direct collaboration with state and local governments, universities, and private industry on research efforts. It also mandated that the laboratories spend funds on technology transfer activities. The more famous Bayh-Dole Act in the same year encouraged universities and small businesses to pursue commercial exploitation of technological breakthroughs that resulted from federally funded research. While there is dispute as to how much difference this legislation has actually made (Lowe, Mowery, and Sampat 2004), the new legislation served an important symbolic function in legitimating close cooperation between university researchers and industry.

When the Reagan administration began in 1981, its free market ideology ruled out any consideration of planning or industrial policy on the Japanese model. However, the administration proved much more pragmatic when it came to building on the DARPA model of decentralized industrial policy. In fact, the Reagan administration significantly accelerated the implementation of policy ideas that had been generated by the Nixon and Carter administrations (Block 2008; Slaughter and Rhoades 2002). In 1982 Reagan signed the Small Business Innovation Development Act that built on a pilot program initiated by the National Science Foundation during the Carter administration. Under this Small Business Innovation Research (SBIR) program, government agencies with large research budgets were required to devote a fraction, initially 1.25 percent of their research funding, to support initiatives that came from small, independent, for-profit firms. The program provided small Phase I awards of $50,000 that could be followed by larger Phase II awards of $500,000 as firms met benchmarks for turning ideas into marketable products. As shown in Chapter 8, over the last quarter century, this program has supported many highly innovative start-up firms.

Legislation passed in 1984 created a blanket antitrust exemption for private firms to engage in cooperative research efforts to develop new products. It created the legal foundation to establish industrywide research consortia that shared funding and information on "precompetitive" research. The Reagan administration followed up on this in 1987 by helping to fund SEMATECH—a research collaboration that helped U.S. semiconductor firms meet increasingly intense competitive pressure from Japan. A 1986 bill established the legal framework for cooperative research and development agreements (CRADAs) between federal laboratories and private firms that would give firms the right to commercially exploit research findings that originated at those laboratories.

Finally, the Omnibus Trade and Competitiveness Act of 1988 created two new programs that were designed to improve U.S. competitiveness. The Advanced Technology Program provided a federal matching grant for private sector research efforts designed to commercialize promising new technologies. Its potential recipients included both big businesses and small (Negoita, Chapter 4). The manufacturing extension program was developed on the analogy with agricultural extension. It created a decentralized program to provide expertise at the local level to help manufacturers make use of advanced technologies (Hallacher 2005).

After Reagan

The twenty years from 1989 to 2008 saw an incremental evolution of the various technology initiatives that had been put in place through the Reagan years. Spending for many of the programs expanded and an increasing number of government agencies gained experience in employing the tools that DARPA had initially developed to accelerate the commercialization of new technologies. There was also substantial growth in the network of new institutions at the state and local levels that worked in cooperation with federal programs to make a decentralized system of technology incubation effective. For example, state and local governments funded organizations that helped aspiring entrepreneurs figure out how to make effective applications to the SBIR program to fund their projects.

There were, however, some intense political fights over this newly emergent innovation system (Hughes 2005). The most intense fight centered on the Advanced Technology Program (ATP) in the Department of Commerce (Negoita, Chapter 4). The ATP program provided federal matching funds to help firms—both small and big—overcome technological barriers across all industrial sectors. When Bill Clinton became president in 1993, he had ambitious plans to expand the ATP program, and he brought in a veteran of DARPA to direct this expanded effort.[7] However, Republicans opposed these plans, arguing that what ATP was doing was "industrial policy" and hence illegitimate. As Negoita (Chapter 4) shows, what made ATP vulnerable to this argument is that it did not have a mission justification, unlike the defense agencies or the National Institutes of Health that had a mission to fight disease. Nor could it be defended like the SBIR program on the grounds that it was solely a supporter of small business, since some of its funds went to large corporations.

When the Republicans gained control of Congress in 1994, they tried to eliminate the program by cutting its funding, and George W. Bush tried to do the same in successive budgets. The program was finally phased out in 2007 because it could not overcome its history as a lightning rod for criticism from the right. But what is really important about this story is how unique the political attack on ATP was. The manufacturing extension program enjoyed bipartisan support through this period (Hallacher 2005), and there are few complaints about technology initiatives at the National Science Foundation or at the Department of Energy. George W. Bush's budgets continued to increase funding for the National Institutes of Health up through 2006, and Bush also expanded funding for the National Nanotechnology Initiative designed to help develop new materials constructed at the atomic or molecular level that can be used by a wide range of different industries (Appelbaum et al., Chapter 11).

What is most striking about this recent period is that, with the exception of the fights over ATP, there is a discrepancy between the growing importance of these federal initiatives and the absence of public debate or discussion about them. By the decade of the 2000s, most important innovations in the U.S. economy were receiving support from these federal initiatives, and even many historically low-tech industries were taking advantage of new scientific breakthroughs nurtured by this system (Block and Keller, Chapter 8). Yet journalists rarely report on these programs, few academics write about them, and most politicians ignore them.

The contrast is particularly dramatic with the SBIR program (Wessner 2008a). It serves as one of the central linchpins of this new innovation system because it is the first place that many technological entrepreneurs go for funding. Providing more than $2 billion per year in direct support to high-tech firms, the program has nurtured new enterprises and moved hundreds of new technologies from the laboratory to the marketplace. And yet the program receives little attention from journalists; the *New York*

Times mentioned it only about eight times in its first twenty-five years of existence. This lack of visibility became a real problem between 2008 and 2010 when SBIR's normally routine reauthorization was jeopardized by congressional proposals that could have severely undermined the program's effectiveness. In short, the program is so obscure that even many in Congress do not recognize its value and importance.

The Obama Administration and a Possible Fourth Turning Point

The Obama administration took office in January 2009 when the U.S. economy was in free fall from the financial crisis that had begun with the meltdown of the mortgage finance system. The administration quickly pushed for a major stimulus bill that was designed to put a floor under the economy by supporting aggregate demand. Much of this bill was devoted to tax cuts and relief to state governments so that they would not have to make huge new cuts in the face of declining tax revenues. But the new administration also included a significant amount of money that was designed to finance innovation and the rebuilding of infrastructure.

More specifically, the American Recovery and Reinvestment Act allocated tens of billions of dollars to the Department of Energy to support the development of a series of alternative energy technologies as well as efforts to retrofit existing structures to reduce energy waste. Two aspects of this initiative are particularly noteworthy. First, the scale of the funding represents an unprecedented expansion of government efforts to shape innovation in the civilian economy. Newly allocated funds, as well as loan programs that had been authorized but barely used in previous legislation, mean that the Department of Energy can ramp up its efforts across the entire technological life course. At the same time, a newly funded program called ARPA-E, deliberately patterned on the Defense Department model, has allowed DOE to fund "blue sky" energy ideas that might take twenty years or longer to reach fruition. Recently the Department of Energy signaled its seriousness by funding forty-six new energy frontier research centers with $777 million over five years, thirty-one of which would be based at universities and another twelve at federal laboratories, with the remainder at nonprofits and one at a corporation.

Second, the scale of the funding means that the Department of Energy is also empowered to move mature technologies into the stage of broad production and deployment. Through matching funds and loan programs, the department is providing firms with hundreds of millions of dollars to build productive facilities for solar panels, a new generation of batteries for electric cars, and large-scale demonstration projects for biofuels made from materials that do not compete with food production. Other programs are specifically designed to overcome the obstacles to the widespread deployment of photovoltaics on the rooftops of homes and businesses.

The DOE initiatives represent an effort to overcome what has been the key weakness in the U.S. innovation system—a failure to provide government support during the critical period when a new technology has to be ramped up for mass production or mass deployment. That weakness accounts for the fact that after inventing the Internet, the United States slipped to fifteenth in the world in citizen access to high speed connections to the web. The same thing happened with the United States declining to eighth in the world in the deployment of photovoltaics to generate electricity (Knight, Chapter 9). Yet another example of this process happened with flat panel displays; while the United States pioneered the key technological breakthroughs, production quickly moved to East Asia since the U.S. government was unwilling to help domestic firms solve the problems of mass production (Block 2008).

The DOE is trying to break this pattern by providing direct assistance to firms building production facilities in the United States for the batteries needed to power a new generation of plug-in hybrid cars. And similar efforts are in motion to build U.S. productive capacity for solar energy, wind energy, and biofuels. To be sure, the success of these efforts cannot be assumed, and the resources made available through the 2009 stimulus will be exhausted within a couple of years. So it remains an open question as to whether the Obama administration will preside over a fourth turning point in the development of the U.S. government's capacity to support innovation across the civilian economy.

One factor in determining whether 2009 represents a fourth inflection point will be the success of the Obama administration in explaining to the public how its innovation policies build on government capacities that have been expanding for decades. That requires explaining how the system is organized and the principles on which it is based.

Institutional Design: How the Innovation System Is Organized

Explaining what the innovation system that has evolved since the Reagan years looks like is not easy because the system is highly decentralized and comprises a lot of overlapping elements. This complexity is, in part, intentional because the innovation process is highly uncertain; even the best scientists and engineers spend a lot of time wandering down false pathways. Moreover, overlap and redundancy increase the chances that somebody with an unorthodox but promising idea will have a chance to persuade some funding agency to support his or her efforts.

Yet a schematic diagram can be a useful aid in understanding the different parts of the system; the figure can be thought of as two intersecting mushrooms (see Figure 1.1). There are four key elements—the two stems and the two tops. While all four elements are critical for the system to work, the most important innovation activities take place in the significant area where the two tops intersect. The stem on the left represents academic scientists working in university departments to push forward the frontiers of science. Most of their research activity is funded by the government through long-established agencies such as the National Science Foundation and the National Institutes of Health. The research going on here is focused on solving scientific puzzles, but as we have learned repeatedly, this core scientific work can have unexpected practical and commercial applications.

Figure 1.1 Evolution of the Innovation System

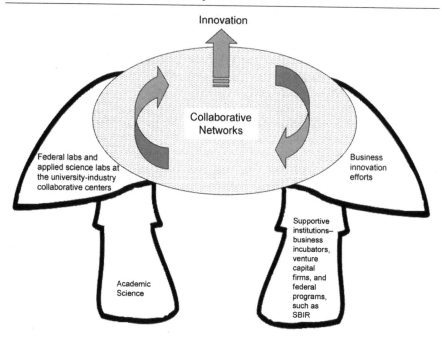

The idea is that the stem on the left provides the necessary supports for the research work that goes on in the left top. The left top represents laboratory settings where government and university scientists and engineers are using their knowledge to solve more concrete problems, such as developing effective vaccines against HIV or upholding Moore's Law by again doubling the capacity of a microchip (Fuchs, Chapter 7). The two main types of institutions here are the network of federal laboratories and hundreds of university-based centers and laboratories with a focus on specific issues that often cut across a number of scientific fields. The federal labs range from the giant nuclear facilities such as Lawrence Berkeley, Los Alamos, and Oak Ridge to the various laboratories at the National Institutes of Health, and dozens of small, specialized laboratories in both defense and nondefense agencies. Most of these federal laboratories are multidisciplinary, so they can easily bring scientists from diverse fields to bear on particular problems.

Some of these laboratories have taken aggressive steps to encourage their scientists and engineers to start new firms to commercialize their discoveries (Schrank, Chapter 5). Consequently they have become engines of regional economic growth, spinning off a series of new firms that have created an agglomeration of new high-tech industries. But many of the federal laboratories have also become sites for nonlocal collaborations. Business firms, both small and large, increasingly come to these laboratories for help in solving their technological problems. This may mean using the facilities of the laboratories to run their experiments or developing a cooperative research and development agreement to work on a project with laboratory scientists; sometimes it involves Work for Others, where the business firm pays the lab to do research.[8]

The network of atomic laboratories evolved out of an earlier institutional structure—the university-based laboratory that relied on outside funding to hire a permanent staff—much of which was separate from academic departments. The Lawrence Berkeley National Laboratory had been founded back in 1931 as the Radiation Laboratory, and parallel institutions such as the MIT Radiation Laboratory had a long history of support from the military (Westwick 2003). Through the Cold War years, the military services funded dozens of these specialized laboratories or research centers on university campuses to focus the attention of scientists and engineers on particular technological challenges.

The big change that started in the late 1970s was the systematic effort by the federal government to expand this model to include industry. The purest model is represented by NSF's program for industry-university collaborative research centers. These are awarded like other NSF grants on a competitive basis, but the academic entrepreneur who gets the grant has to recruit an industry advisory committee with the idea that the center could eventually become self-supporting with industry participants making annual support payments (Geiger and Sa 2008). The centers also build bridges to other academic institutions to mobilize collaborative efforts of other experts in that specific field. The center is intended to become a collaborative public space where industry and university technologists work in close cooperation to solve key technological problems (Lester and Piore 2004), ideally creating enough intellectual excitement to attract graduate students to focus their energy on this particular set of issues.

NSF-funded centers now represent a small fraction of all the specialized university-based centers and laboratories that actively include business partners. Some of these are now being initially funded by business groups, some get their funding from state and local governments, some are funded through congressional earmarks, and new ones are constantly being created by both military and civilian government agencies.

It is in this left mushroom top where much of the society's effort at technological development is now occurring. Most of the large corporations have been cutting back internally funded research operations and are now depending on these sites for key technological breakthroughs (Block and Keller, Chapter 8). But the central point is that the old dividing line between public and private has become increasingly fuzzy and indistinct in these settings. Whether in federal laboratories or university-industry centers, publicly funded scientists and engineers are often working side by side with scientists and engineers from industry. They can even be the same people, since a university-based researcher might also be the CEO of a firm that is trying to commercialize some of his or her key discoveries.

The mushroom top on the right contains the for-profit business firms, small, medium, and large, that take these new technologies through the final stages of preparation for commercial use. Almost all of these firms depend on work that has been done in the mushroom on the left, and most of the important innovation work now occurs in the area where the two mushrooms intersect—active collaboration between technologists from different organizations. Many traditional large corporations have embraced the idea of "open innovation" that involves a recognition that some of the most valuable new ideas will come to them from the outside (Chesbrough, Vanhaverbeke, and West 2006). Firms of all sizes are engaged in a process of searching out the new technologies that are being developed elsewhere.

The enthusiasm for open innovation reflects a remarkable shift that has occurred over the last three decades; much of the private sector scientific effort has migrated from large firms to smaller firms with 500 or fewer employees. NSF data shows that by 2003, fully half of all Ph.D.'s employed by the private sector worked for firms with 500 or fewer employees (Block and Keller, Chapter 8). But this figure understates the trend because those figures measure only employees; there are also tens of thousands of additional Ph.D. scientists and engineers who are self-employed as consultants or as the proprietors of their own small businesses.[9]

The small businesses that now employ the majority of private sector Ph.D.'s depend heavily on government programs for their survival. The SBIR program is the largest single example, but there are thousands of other small firms that are kept alive by research and development funding from a wide variety of government agencies as well as government procurement contracts. To be sure, many of these small firms also work with larger firms that provide research support and subcontracts, but it is often the public sector support that provides a stable economic base.

One of the most interesting business models is a growing population of firms that are essentially private research and development laboratories that deliberately keep their size below 500 employees to remain eligible for SBIR grants that provide some of their core funding. But they combine this with working under contract with other firms and government agencies on specific projects. When the firm develops a new technology with commercial potential, the usual practice is to sell the technology or spin off a new firm to exploit it. These private R&D laboratories tend to be located in close proximity to major universities or federal laboratories to facilitate cooperation, and a number of them are employee owned, which is a way to signal their strong commitment to the ethic of scientific discovery (one example is Physical Sciences in Andover, Massachusetts).

The stem on the right is the network of support institutions that have evolved to facilitate the commercialization of new technologies. This includes the technology transfer offices at federal laboratories and universities that assist scientists and engineers in the six-foot mushroom to find uses for their discoveries. It includes an increasingly rich mixture of local, state, and nonprofit programs that serve as technology incubators providing a variety of services and supports for start-up firms, including counseling on government grants and business problems. It also includes federally funded programs such as the manufacturing extension program and the National Technology Transfer Center that was founded in 1989 to facilitate partnerships between industry and university and government laboratories.

This stem also includes state-level and private financing sources that invest in these small high-tech firms. While private sector venture capital gets much of the attention, private venture capital firms are generally reluctant to invest in firms that are still years away from having a commercial product. Angel investors, who are willing to take greater risks over a longer period of time, play a greater role in supporting early stage firms as do university endowments, as do venture funds set up by nonprofits and state governments (Keller, Chapter 6). The shortage of patient, long-term capital for these start-up firms continues to be one of the major weaknesses of this whole innovation system.

The federal government can be thought of as the soil in which these mushrooms grow. Federal agencies are responsible for most of the funding of the activity in the left mushroom and they also provide significant funding to the other side. Moreover, federal agencies are increasingly active in overcoming the network failures that are endemic to this decentralized innovation system (Whitford and Schrank, Chapter 13). Because both laboratory breakthroughs and the extended process of transforming those breakthroughs into commercial products depend on cooperation across organizational lines—involving complex networks of collaboration—there is a continuing danger that participants will be unable to find trustworthy and competent collaborators.

As detailed in the following chapters, government agencies help scientists, engineers, and entrepreneurs to overcome these network failures in a wide variety of ways. In the model pioneered by DARPA, funders bring together groups of technologists working on the same problems so they can share ideas and generate new insights. Government funders also use their own contact networks to help firms connect to the types of support and expertise that they need, for example, early-stage financing, introductions to potential business partners, or a group of highly specialized researchers at a particular laboratory or university. Officials also validate the competence of particular firms and scientists by awarding them research grants or SBIR funding. Programs such as the Manufacturing Extension Program, the Advanced Technology Program, and the university-industry cooperative research centers work to upgrade the skill levels of industry participants, helping them to master technologies at the cutting edge so they can be competent network partners.

The missing element from this graphic is the citizenry that funds government with its taxes and that purchases—either directly or indirectly—the technologies produced by this innovation system. But the public has been mostly kept in the dark about the workings of this innovation system, especially when it comes to recognizing the role that government plays in this system. There are multiple explanations for this lack of knowledge, but one of the most important is that this system does not fit with the claims of market fundamentalism. The reality is very different from the fables that market fundamentalists tell about self-regulating markets and the inherent limitations of public sector employees who are not continuously disciplined by market calculations.

This lack of public knowledge or understanding is a problem for three reasons. The first is that without public understanding, both the funding and the legitimacy of this system are in constant danger. Demands on the federal budget are intense and the financing for innovation programs always competes with other worthy programs. Moreover, without public understanding and support, ambitious government efforts such as the initiatives by the Department of Energy to accelerate the deployment of carbon-free energy are vulnerable to political attack by market fundamentalists as wasteful, incompetent, and unnecessary. Second, without knowledge, the public cannot push for spending that meets its own priorities. For example, innovation programs at the Department of Agriculture have often prioritized the needs of corporate agriculture over the needs of consumers. Finally, and most importantly, the public in many cases is not just a passive recipient of new technologies; it has to be an active partner in making those technologies effective. For example, the diffusion of the personal computer and the Internet over the past twenty years or the ongoing challenge of improving public health necessarily involved public learning. With the computer, millions and millions of people had to figure out how to boot up a computer and how to manipulate various programs; sometimes they were trained at work but sometimes they had to struggle on their own. Similarly, with health, people have to learn about diet and exercise and what kinds of warning signs indicate the need for immediate medical attention; those with chronic conditions have to master protocols to keep those conditions under control.

This is the point that John Alic elaborates in his chapter: important innovation tends to be a widely diffused process that rests on significant amounts of learning by many people (Alic, Chapter 12). It is not just about something that goes on in laboratories and start-up corporations. Creating the kind of society that is able to take advantage of the innovations that improve people's quality of life requires that the citizenry be an active part of the process. As explained in the book's final chapter (Newfield, Chapter 14), the whole society needs shared narratives about technological possibilities and this requires including the public in the conversation from an early stage.

Organizing Principles and a New Governance Philosophy

The last task of this introduction is to explain the organizing principles of this new innovation system in order to elaborate its implications for a new governance philosophy for the U.S. economy. This is inevitably a task of interpretation, since the current system is far from coherent; it contains discordant and even contradictory elements. Nevertheless, there are three principles that are quite visible in the current system and one that follows logically from the others, even though current practices have not yet embraced this final principle.

Coordinated Decentralization

The most important feature of this system is that high levels of initiative are left to actors on a widely dispersed basis in recognition that overcoming technological barriers cannot be centrally directed. As with science itself, the core idea is that progress is likely to be greatest if different teams of technologists working in different locations have the freedom to experiment with different ways to solve technological puzzles. This is a strategy designed both to prevent the waste of large sums on scientific "white elephants" that lead nowhere (Alic 2007) and to encourage the greatest level of creativity among independent teams of innovators. Decentralization also helps to partially insulate the innovation system from shifts in the balance of partisan advantage and managerial orientation in the nation's capital. As Whitford and Schrank (Chapter 13) argue, it is precisely the advantages of technological decentralization that have transformed the decentralized structure of American politics from a liability to an asset.

However, it is also important to recognize that effective decentralization can co-exist with certain forms of central coordination. For example, agricultural extension services were delivered at the local level so that extension agents could compile the particular types of knowledge that were relevant to the crops, climate, and soil issues of a specific place. However, this was consistent with the Department of Agriculture setting standards of best practices for extension agents and attempting to build a sense of professional identity that unified extension agents in different parts of the country. Central coordination can also involve processes of "road mapping" in which government agencies assemble widely dispersed groups of experts to identify the key transitions that have to occur for a particular technology to become commercially viable. And most importantly of all, actors at the center can assure that competing technology groups are aware of each other's successes and failures in meeting key goals (Fuchs, Chapter 7).

Ó Riain (Chapter 10) and Appelbaum and colleagues (Chapter 11) show that Ireland and China are also struggling to achieve the proper balance between decentralization of efforts and centralized coordination. In the Irish case, there is evidence that excessive centralization weakened the initiatives that had been successful in nurturing technological startups. In China, the regime appears to be using the division of labor among different levels of government as a way to counteract excessive centralization.

Public-Private Partnership

What happens on a decentralized basis is a high level of cooperation between public entities and private entities. This is reflected most obviously in the initiatives that involve cost sharing, as when ATP or the Department of Energy matches the funds put up by private firms to cover the research required to overcome a technological barrier. But it is also present when private firms provide support for the NSF's industry-university collaborative research centers or pay the federal labs through Work for Others to tackle a particular problem. And even when the government is providing most of the funding, as with the SBIR program or the public sector venture capital initiatives, both parties still have a very substantial stake in a successful outcome.

Sometimes one side does not live up to the expectations of partnership. When DARPA, for example, pulls back from funding a research project because of insufficient progress, there is bound to be bitterness on the other side. And there have been visible instances where business firms have basically "gamed" their government partners. For example, when the Clinton administration funded the Partnership for a New Generation of Vehicles, the intention was to engage the Big Three automakers in a project of developing fuel-efficient vehicles (Sperling 2001). But the auto companies took the money while continuing to place low priority on the development of hybrid and electric vehicles.

But even when the norms of partnership are violated, it is clear to everyone that partnership implies reciprocity—an obligation to recognize and be sensitive to the legitimate needs of the partner. Government actors, on the one side, recognize that business firms must ultimately figure out a way to survive in the marketplace, while the business firms need to help their funders look good to others in the agency and ultimately to Congress.

Cooperative Sharing of Expertise

The core paradox of innovation is that while firms have strong incentives to keep their knowledge of technical processes a secret from the rest of the world, such secrecy impedes the flow of information among different groups of experts that appears necessary for breakthroughs to happen (Hargadon 2003; Lester and Piore 2004). So firms are constantly trying to figure out how they can protect potentially lucrative "intellectual property" while overcoming the technical barriers to development of a viable commercial product. In short, one of the classic network failures (Whitford and Schrank, Chapter 13) is that a firm's network partner walks away with a key idea that someone else then exploits.

This is precisely why public agencies and publicly funded scientists and engineers loom so large in this new innovation system. First, when a firm brings a problem and shares information with technologists at a federal lab or a university, the risk of commercially consequential loss of proprietary information is relatively small. Even though these scientists and engineers are being strongly encouraged to commercialize their discoveries by starting their own firms, few of them have the stomach or resources to do that while waging a legal battle over intellectual property with an existing firm. Moreover, professional ethics militate against selling a key idea to an interested third party.

Second, the public agencies often serve as a kind of honest broker to encourage firms to behave cooperatively in dealing with each other's intellectual property. In some cases, this is quite explicit. For example, some of the agencies involved with the SBIR program, especially in the military, work hard to connect its awardees with the large contractors that put together the ships, planes, and other weapons systems. Since the SBIR firm has to disclose information about its new technology to persuade Boeing or Northrop Grumman to include it as a subcontractor, it puts itself at risk of the bigger firm assigning its engineers to replicate the small firm's invention. However, the Pentagon treats the SBIR application and reports as certification of the firm's intellectual property, and it makes clear to prime contractors that it will not tolerate taking ideas without compensation.

In other cases, the mechanism is less formal but no less important. As Lester and Piore (2004) have argued, government agencies create "collaborative public spaces" in which technologists from different settings are able to talk freely without worrying about the consequences for future ownership of intellectual property. As Fuchs shows in her chapter, DARPA brings its funded scientists and engineers, some of whom work for industry, to regular workshops to share their ideas to accelerate the flow of knowledge. The funder's presence ensures that everybody behaves cooperatively by disclosing information; a grantee who sought to exploit the situation by absorbing everyone else's ideas while keeping its own progress secret would likely risk losing any future funding. A similar dynamic appears to work in the industry consortia that are funded by government agencies or in the NSF-funded industry-university collaborative research centers.

Fuchs (Chapter 7) also describes certain "platform technologies" (Tassey 2007) that might not develop at all without a government role in forging cooperation across a large number of industry actors. The problem is that the initial investment in these platform technologies is too great and too risky for any one firm or even several firms to do on their own. Her example is the shift to silicon photonics as the next strategy for developing future generations of even tinier microchips which was dependent on DARPA forging a high degree of cooperation and consensus across the entire technological community, both scientists and engineers working for industry and those working in universities and federal labs.

Gain Sharing

Partnership and cooperation logically imply that future gains should be shared among the partners, and it is here that present arrangements fall significantly short. Despite the extraordinarily important role that public agencies play in funding and supporting this innovation system, they derive no direct returns from their successful investments. The algorithm or "secret sauce" that made Google so successful as a search engine was initially funded by an NSF grant (Battelle 2005), but the only benefit that NSF received was the indirect one that Google's growth and large payroll expanded the government tax revenues that help fund NSF and other innovation agencies.

However, this is an inadequate mechanism because there are intense conflicts over how each additional federal tax dollar is spent, and the federal government has been struggling with deficits for the past decade. In this environment, it has been difficult to maintain existing levels of federal spending on research and development. With limited resources, fierce and unproductive battles have broken out that pit biological scientists against physical scientists and supporters of basic research against the advocates for programs designed to accelerate commercialization of new technologies. In short, without a mechanism to ensure that taxpayers share in the gains from the innovations that they have helped to foster the future of the current innovation system is at risk.

Moreover, the danger is compounded by the society's systematic underinvestment in education from kindergarten through university level. Ultimately, the innovation system depends on a well educated population (Alic, Chapter 12), and budget cutting, especially at the state level, over the last generation has weakened public schools and reduced access to higher education. A better system of gain sharing is necessary to ensure that we can finance the kind of high-quality, inclusive education system that is indispensable for an innovation society (Newfield 2008).

A poignant example of the violation of the principle of gain sharing is discussed by Vallas, Kleinman, and Biscotti (Chapter 3). A new pharmaceutical that brings in more than $1 billion per year in revenue is a drug marketed by Genzyme. It is a drug for a rare disease that was initially developed by scientists at the National Institutes of Health. The firm set the price for a year's dosage at upward of $350,000. While legislation gives the government the right to sell such government-developed drugs at "reasonable" prices, policymakers have not exercised this right. The result is an extreme instance where the costs of developing this drug were socialized, while the profits were privatized. Moreover, some of the taxpayers who financed the development of the drug cannot obtain it for their family members because they cannot afford it.

Conclusion

The combination of these principles—coordinated decentralization, private-public partnership, cooperative sharing of expertise, and gain sharing—gives us the framework for the current innovation system and also provides a broader alternative to market fundamentalism. Whereas market fundamentalism insists that only institutions that are governed by the logic of the marketplace can be trusted to use resources efficiently, this alternative governing philosophy recognizes that our society has long been effectively pluralistic. Other institutions such as universities, government laboratories, public agencies, and the military have found ways to motivate people to be creative and effective without appealing to the maximization of individual income. Moreover, the very plurality of individual motivations is a source of strength since people are different and they respond to different incentives.

The logic of this argument has been elaborated most clearly by Michael Walzer in *Spheres of Justice* (1983), in which he argues for a society based on the principle of complex equality. Walzer's framework is relevant precisely because he recognizes that the different parts of society such as the government, the economy, the scientific community, and the universities cannot be kept separate from each other but are intertwined and interdependent. Walzer would dismiss market fundamentalism as utopian because it imagines that the government can somehow be removed from its extensive involvement in the economy. But as Viviana Zelizer (2006) has argued at length, just because things are intertwined does not mean that they have to be organized on a unitary basis. Walzer's critical insight is that each of these intertwined spheres needs to be true to its own organizing principles.

Walzer's starting point is a critique of the old egalitarianism which sought to ensure that everybody got the same or roughly equal income and life chances. Walzer sees that goal as unrealistic and argues that the different realms of society need to have their own distinct distributional principles. In the sphere of the market, it is appropriate that the one who builds a better mousetrap should earn greater rewards. In science, recognition and glory goes to those who make the most important discoveries. In the realm of health care, however, justice dictates that those with greater medical needs should receive more assistance, and in the sphere of politics, those with the greater capacity to win votes of their fellow citizens should be rewarded with a greater share of political power. The core idea of complex equality is that society needs to take steps to protect the integrity of each sphere. This means creating mechanisms to block the tendency for advantage in one sphere to spill over into others. Hence, those with political power should not be able to translate that power into economic wealth, and similarly those with economic wealth should not be able to translate that directly into political power. This is necessary to ensure that distribution in each of the different spheres is consistent with the principle of justice relevant to that sphere.

In short, complex equality is the foundation for an innovation society in which the different actors are able to coordinate despite having different goals and different values. The entrepreneur can work together with the scientist who is driven by the need to solve puzzles and with the public agency official who seeks to serve his or her country by accelerating technological progress. In fact, it is precisely because they have different immediate goals that it is easier for them to cooperate. If they were all seeking to maximize income, the coordination we have been describing would be impossible.

Of course, this moral and intellectual division of labor leaves room for people to change their minds and their institutional positions. The scientist or engineer can decide to become an entrepreneur, while the entrepreneur might decide to take a turn as a government technology officer. But it is also critical that the society construct ethical boundaries between these different spheres, so as to minimize conflicts of interests and to ensure that the values of science or public service not be undermined by the quest for profits (Biscotti et al. 2009).

More broadly, complex equality points to a pluralistic politics that would strengthen democratic governance. None of us want to live in a society that is dominated by any one of these groups; rule by the captains of industry and finance is as deeply offensive as is the rule of a narrow self-perpetuating political elite or a scientific meritocracy. But with each of these groups having a separate sphere of influence and power, the ongoing contestation creates a political space in which the people get to decide the most important questions. A true innovation society requires both complex equality and "government of the people, by the people, and for the people."

Notes

John Alic, Shelley Hurt, Matthew R. Keller, and Andrew Schrank provided valuable criticisms of earlier drafts of this chapter, but they cannot be blamed for any remaining errors or defects.

1. Market fundamentalism is characterized by a discrepancy between its antistate ideology and its use of state power to accomplish its goals. As Karl Polanyi (2001 [1944], 146) wrote, "The road to the free market was opened and kept open by an enormous increase in continuous, centrally organized and controlled interventionism."

2. There are, however, reasons to believe that the Commerce Department series might understate U.S. high-tech exports. In particular, some of the software and other computer

services that originate in the United States but are downloaded to computers overseas might not be counted, particularly because U.S. firms gain tax advantages from attributing the income they earn on these transactions to overseas subsidiaries (O'Connell 1999).

3. The complexity, of course, is that any economic development initiative can almost always be justified in military terms. If the United States is at a technological disadvantage in a particular area, it could weaken the U.S. ability to prevail in military conflicts. This logic is not unique to the Cold War period; it has prevailed throughout the history of the nation.

4. The official name of the agency has fluctuated between ARPA and DARPA (Defense Advanced Research Projects Agency). Both names are used in the literature, but they refer to the same agency.

5. The high-tech spin-off model probably predated the actions of the traitorous eight (Hyde 2003), but this incident is often singled out because of its direct connection to firms, such as Intel, that are still key players in Silicon Valley. The pattern of new firm creation by spin-offs from existing firms has been common to industrial districts for centuries (Piore and Sabel 1984). What is distinctive about the Fairchild and related cases are that the people forming the new firms are highly trained scientists and engineers.

6. The exception to this pattern in the pre-DARPA period was Pentagon support for research at the premier corporate laboratories such as Bell Labs and the IBM laboratories because researchers in these laboratories were effectively insulated from commercial considerations.

7. Although it has been largely forgotten, Clinton also pushed the Technology Reinvestment Program, which was designed to strengthen the industrial base in the post–Cold War era. Managed initially by DARPA, the program was cut short once the Republicans gained control of the Congress in 1994 (Cohen 1998).

8. For recent data on the number and dollar value of the CRADA and Work for Others at the Department of Energy laboratories, see Government Accountability Office 2009.

9. The available data make it difficult to discern trends in the organization of the scientific labor force. For example, some of the Ph.D.s who list themselves as self-employed or as proprietors on tax forms could also be employees, most likely at universities or government laboratories.

PART I

Telling the Stories

What Are the Instruments and How Have They Been Deployed in Different Parts of the Economy?

It has been difficult for scholars to develop an adequate map of the innovation initiatives of the U.S. government. The issue is not, primarily, a lack of transparency. Most of the government's technology-focused programs release some details concerning their work, and they face periodic assessments, many of which are available to the public. Moreover, critical programs such as the Defense Advanced Research Projects Agency (DARPA), the Small Business Innovation Research program (SBIR), and the Advanced Technology Program (ATP) have received some attention from the scholarly community.

The problem is that the vastness, diversity, and ever-changing shape of federal R&D-related programs resist easy categorization. Overlaps and networked relations among the panoply of agencies, programs, and subprograms involved in R&D are virtually impossible to plot on an organizational chart or encapsulate as comprising a coherent, analytically consistent set of policy approaches or core principles. Programs are spread across multiple agencies, they employ different operating procedures and purposes, and they are usually uncoordinated. Nor is there a central data repository that captures their collective activities, even though such a repository would provide greater transparency and allow program officers to identify common interests, assess promising technology directions pursued by other research programs, and avoid technological dead ends.

Not only does the system's decentralization render it opaque, but the internal pieces of the system are also in flux. Strategies and tactics evolve as programs learn from past successes and failures as well as from other programmatic models. They also adjust to meet changing technical hurdles involving key networks of researchers and industrial partners. In some cases their mandates can be reconfigured or their operations transformed or eliminated by the passage of a new law or an administrative directive. While these attributes of the system can be frustrating for analysts, they can also be conceptualized as strengths of a new innovation paradigm. Programs based on centralized planning and standards have helped nations catch up, but they rarely, if ever, offer a sustainable means to generate cutting-edge innovations. A decentralized system with complex and changing network ties is better suited for the unpredictable world of innovation precisely because it offers opportunities for multiple technical pathways to be pursued simultaneously. If one agency denies a grant application for a particular technology, another may well accept it. If the peer review methodology adopted in one part of the system tends to stifle transformative, "outside the box" projects, more adventurous, higher-risk strategies pursued in another agency might take on the risk. If a collaboration between a federal agency and U.S. automakers for generating new battery technologies fails to generate desired advances, a small firm supported by the Small Business Innovation Research program might well generate a key breakthrough. If one program is focused on short-term, incremental innovation, another might be pushing forward revolutionary new platform technologies.

In short, these potential strengths of the U.S. government's role in the innovation system arise from a decentralized set of agencies that are (1) embedded in multiple networks, (2) adaptable to new political conditions and industrial requirements and able to learn from past mistakes, (3) loosely coupled and flexible in their approaches to technological development. The system closely resembles what Seán Ó Riain (2004a) has described as a "developmental network state" that has generated rapid and sustained development in technology-intensive industries in places like Ireland, Israel, and Taiwan (see also Breznitz 2007).

Yet the U.S. model has several unique aspects. First, it took its current shape in the early 1980s, when market fundamentalism began to dominate American political rhetoric. In a political climate in which state actions were characterized as necessarily "distorting" the beneficent outcomes of unfettered markets, highly visible civilian programs were subjected to intense scrutiny and repeated political challenges. Other agencies deliberately kept a low profile to minimize political attacks. Consequently, public awareness of and confidence in the government's role in the economy was undermined, further reinforcing the dominant market-centered ideology. Development efforts were effectively hidden.

A second result was to reinforce the military and national security dimension of the U.S. innovation regime. High-profile, better-resourced, and often more innovative research and development strategies typically either developed in or migrated to agencies that could legitimate their activities as related to national security—a justification that has long retained a special status even among the most vociferous advocates of market liberalism. Indeed, as chapters in this section show, it has typically been the defense and intelligence agencies and the former nuclear laboratories that have been at the forefront of developmentalism within the U.S. polity.

These elements will be starkly apparent in this initial section of the book, which attempts to capture the depth, breadth, and dynamic quality of the U.S. developmental state. The chapters identify key agencies, operating strategies, and the types of collaborative relationships that have been forged among government programs, private firms, and university researchers in developing cutting edge technologies at the core of the U.S. economy. Shelley Hurt draws on archival research to document the high-level debates within the Nixon administration that gave rise to systematic efforts by both the Department of Defense and the National Institutes of Health to advance the commercial possibilities of breakthroughs in biotechnology. Steven Vallas, Daniel L. Kleinman, and Dina Biscotti continue the biotechnology story by showing the magnitude of NIH involvement in most of the successful new pharmaceuticals developed by biotech firms.

Marian Negoita's discussion of the now defunct Advanced Technology Program (ATP) in the Department of Commerce traces the agency's successes and failures in forging collaborative networks with industrial partners and the consequences of the limits imposed on this politically targeted agency over the course of its operations. Andrew Schrank provides an illuminating account of the evolving strategies employed by the managers of the Sandia National Laboratory as it sought to develop and deepen the linkages between Sandia researchers and private industry to enhance American competitiveness. Matthew R. Keller describes how the CIA became the key exemplar in the government's embrace of a public sector venture capital model for nurturing new technologies. Erica Fuchs's account of the Defense Advanced Research Projects Agency (DARPA) shows how this path-breaking agency altered its approach to forging collaborative networks in an attempt to meet new challenges in pursuing Moore's Law.

Though each chapter describes a different agency and a different approach to innovation policy, they also stress a series of common attributes and features of these federal initiatives. Certainly these programs provide funding for research and development. But they also forge new technology trajectories by coordinating dynamic linkages among potential—and sometimes reluctant—collaborators in the research, design, and development of technologies. They provide third-party certification of promising individual researchers, firms, or avenues of research for public agencies and private investors. They develop road maps around which industrial and university researchers congeal research programs and partnerships. In sum, successful agencies have found ways to forge new network ties and reduce uncertainty and risk in the necessarily unpredictable quest to realize innovative ideas and technologies.

The chapters also underscore unique elements of the U.S. economic and political context, which have shaped the emergence, development, and depth of the contemporary U.S. government's role in the economy. Shelley Hurt's chapter sheds new light on the Nixon's administration's understanding of the need for robust mechanisms for public-private collaboration. Though not fully realized during his time in office, the internal policy debates and tentative steps toward the creation of a new relationship between government agencies, industry, and universities laid the groundwork for many developmental initiatives that would follow under the Carter and Reagan administrations.

If Hurt's account provides new insights into the origins of the third turning point in U.S. innovation policy (Block, Chapter 1), each of the other chapters provides an account of how the system consolidated and responded to new political and economic conditions. Negoita, for instance, shows how the ATP's operations were perpetually disrupted and renegotiated as the agency became a lightning rod for conservative criticism during the 1990s. While President Clinton envisioned ATP as a critical component of a civilian technology portfolio aimed at strengthening American competitiveness, the Republican architects of the Contract with America who swept to power in the 1994 congressional elections saw the program as an archetypal example of the distorting and destructive effects of government intervention in the economy.

This bleak tale of the constant pressure faced by a prominent civilian-oriented technology initiative is counterbalanced by several accounts of robust experimental-ism and expansion of R&D programs affiliated with national security interests, which has unquestionably been the single most powerful justification for U.S. technology initiatives under a market fundamentalist political climate. The chapters by Fuchs, Schrank, and Keller show how the managers of agencies like DARPA, the former nuclear-affiliated labs operated by the Department of Energy, and even the CIA have had far more leeway to explore novel strategies for developing, commercializing, and integrating new technologies. While these programs have experienced mixed results, they provide rich grounds for assessing a range of policy options, oriented to different parts of the research and development process, that are available to policymakers.

Finally, the chapters in this section speak to the virtual ubiquity of federal technology policies and programs in core success stories of the U.S. economy—even as a market fundamentalist ideology reigned in the political sphere. While the federal role in the development of the Internet and the semiconductor industries are well-known, the chapter by Vallas, Kleinman, and Biscotti uses new data to underscore the critical role that government programs have played in the development of blockbuster drugs within the pharmaceutical industry. The authors show that the fingerprints of government can be seen not only in the indirect role played by a favorable intellectual property regime and the construction of an innovation environment that has favored the industry's growth, but also in the nearly ubiquitous role of government researchers and govern-ment financing in the discovery and development of best-selling pharmaceuticals. As the authors suggest, this largely neglected story of federal involvement in the networks of firms at the heart of the biotechnology industry has important consequences for how we understand an industry that is typically characterized as relying upon private sector dynamism. Andrew Schrank's chapter also reveals the importance of the de-velopmental state in driving local and regional development, and in altering political landscapes—in this case, in helping to forge new political coalitions and a new balance of power in a New Mexico long dominated by "oil patch" interests.

These chapters are meant to be illustrative; there are literally hundreds of other federal technology initiatives that are not covered by these case studies. For example, we were not able to include documentation of the Small Business Innovation Research program, the Department of Energy's initiatives in support of energy conservation and new energy technologies, or the industry-university collaborative research centers funded by the National Science Foundation. The point, however, is simply to convey that under the surface of market fundamentalist rhetoric, the scope of developmental initiatives pursued by the U.S. government has been both broad and deep.

CHAPTER 2

The Military's Hidden Hand
Examining the Dual-Use Origins of Biotechnology in the American Context, 1969–1972
Shelley L. Hurt

Basic research is our comparative advantage in the world. In time, a lot of countries will be able to manufacture as well as the Japanese. We're different in being able to create wealth with science.

Frank Press

During the past thirty years, the American biotechnology sector's rise to dominance ostensibly epitomizes America's shift to an information-based economy. This shift is described as emerging from scientific innovations during the 1970s, which were subsequently exploited by business in the 1980s. Contrary to the conventional wisdom, this chapter argues that the commercial biotechnology sector emerged as a result of President Richard M. Nixon's decision to convert the nation's biological warfare program into the biological research program in 1969. Even though the circumstances surrounding this decision are little understood, Nixon's conversion decision entailed a massive redirection of resources, including institutional and legal innovations to harness the biological research program to meet national goals. These proactive federal science policy decisions laid the foundation for the renowned legislative and judicial decisions of 1980, which accelerated the commercialization of biotechnology already under way in the early- and mid-1970s as a result of the conversion process.

Hence this chapter serves as both complement and challenge to the accompanying chapter in this volume on biotechnology by Steven P. Vallas, Daniel Lee Kleinman, and Dina Biscotti. On the one hand, my chapter agrees with these contributors' assertion that "state initiatives" from above contributed mightily to the emergence and growth of the biotechnology industry. The striking absence of this fact in popular historical narratives of American scientific innovation, particularly biotechnology, remains all too plentiful. On the other hand, this chapter argues that the strategic industrial policy that comprised these particular state initiatives surrounding the commercialization of biotechnology were much more centralized than these authors acknowledge. Certainly America's federal science policy does not approximate the state directives found in Japan and France, yet U.S. policymakers were keenly aware of biotechnology's potential to serve as a strategic national resource in both economic and military terms. Consequently the executive branch exercised a great deal of leverage over federal science policy to ensure the country harnessed this vital resource. Indeed, the geopolitical imperatives of the Cold War confrontation shaped perceptions about exploiting molecular biology's full dual-use potential just as it had in numerous areas of science and technology policy. As Robert L. Paarlberg has correctly noted, the Cold War is best characterized as a "science race" rather than an arms race (Paarlberg 2004, 150).

This chapter contributes to the literature in two ways. First, it reperiodizes the onset of biotechnology a full decade before the heyday of commercial activity blossomed in the 1980s. It serves as a corrective to the dominant historical narratives about 1980 representing the initial impetus behind commercializing biotechnology. Rather, I argue that the *Diamond v. Chakrabarty* Supreme Court case of 1980 as well as the Bayh-Dole and Stevenson-Wydler Acts of 1980 should be viewed as representing the culmination of state-driven policies that had been debated and acted upon in both the executive and legislative branches for over a decade. Second, the chapter highlights the military underpinnings of the industrial policy launched in the wake of the nation's largest-ever disarmament decision. In other words, it shows the militaristic roots behind a key shift in American-style industrial policy. These twin purposes illuminate the critical role of the state, particularly senior policymakers in the executive branch who were determined to maximize molecular biology's potential as a new strategic national resource.

This unearthed historical narrative directly confronts the prevalent viewpoint that the U.S. government is neither interested in nor capable of exercising state power to spur innovation. Even though this viewpoint dominates discussions of American state weakness in the domestic realm, this chapter foregrounds policymakers' success in forging a bipartisan commitment to wield influence over the nation's R&D enterprise. Thus the chapter demonstrates how the government's strength derives from deploying federal science policy in a federalist system that "allow[s] a stronger state to masquerade as a weak one" (O'Mara 2005). Consequently the scope and breadth of federal science policy in shaping U.S. economic competitiveness and military superiority is little understood. The persistent myth of America's weak state rests uneasily alongside the country's extraordinary dominance in the cutting-edge fields of twenty-first century science, such as biotechnology, nanotechnology, and informatics. While these dual-use scientific fields are championed for their promise to solve intractable social ills, such as disease and hunger, they are also the wellspring of a new generation of military weapons (NAS 2004; Armstrong and Warner 2003; Tucker 2002; Martin 2002). While these burgeoning scientific fields blossomed after decades of federal investments in basic research during the Cold War, few recognize that the origins of this durable foundation sprang from the national security lessons of World War II.[1]

Indeed, common perceptions of most contemporary scientific advances are completely unhinged from their World War II moorings. This break with science's military past has led to a misunderstanding about the political forces that gave rise to the knowledge-based economy in which biotechnology and other scientific fields are closely identified. Shedding science's relationship to its military past came about in the wake of Vietnam when Americans were skeptical about the relationship between science and war (Mendelsohn 1994). Once the Vietnam era began fading in the mid-1970s, Americans started associating scientific change with technological progress, with scientists as entrepreneurs, and with the inexorable march of industrialism (Plein 1991; Wright 2001; Wright 1990a). These positive associations sanitized science, cleansing it of any connotation of warfare. At the same time, the American developmental state went into hiding as policymakers altered past institutional patterns of funding, regulating, and mobilizing science while remaining committed to the World War II national security lesson of prioritizing technological superiority above all else.

In order to bolster these strong claims, this chapter concentrates on two institutional innovations and one legal innovation to showcase the enormous impact the conversion process had on fostering the market-friendly conditions that led to the judicial and legislative changes in 1980 discussed above. The two institutional innovations dealt directly with the fallout from university scientists' opposition to Vietnam. As will be shown in more detail below, senior Nixon administration officials sought to shift federal support of university research from military agencies, such as the Department of Defense, to civilian agencies, such as the National Science Foundation, to placate university scientists who wanted a wider variety of funding options from the government. The second institutional innovation dealt with encouraging and expanding technology transfer between the public and private sectors by replacing the post–World War II military-university partnership with an industry-university partnership. Finally, the legal innovations involved major patent law reforms, by granting exclusive licenses to industry for the first time and by facilitating an expansion of process patents, which were critically important for the biotechnology industry. These aspects of patent law reform contributed to achieving the first two federal science policy goals, since patent law reforms enabled industry to capture publicly funded inventions for commercialization more easily. These three state-led innovations did not remove the military from its historic and influential role in spurring R&D but moved it into the shadows to continue its support of federal science policy, yet without inviting the animosity of university students and scientists.

While these institutional and legal reforms unfolded throughout the 1970s, the sweeping cultural changes of the decade have led students of American politics to marginalize the military from their assessments of the knowledge-based economy's origins.[2] Nevertheless, and somewhat ironically, given the decade's identification with ushering in an era of neoliberalism and government retrenchment, Daniel Bell perceptively noted in *The Coming of Post-Industrial Society* in 1973 that future federal science policy would be subjected to increasing levels of centralization due to the high stakes involved in perpetuating government's relationship with science (Bell 1973). Indeed, contrary to conventional wisdom, Bell correctly predicted that the pressures to sustain this relationship after the upheavals of the 1960s would lead to "the reality of a new bureaucratic-technological order that is meshed with a centralized political system struggling to manage a complex and fractionated society." In other words, this chapter in American political history needs to be relearned for informing possible trajectories of science and technology in the twenty-first century while illuminating the American state's hidden developmental characteristics.

The chapter is divided into four sections that highlight distinct stages in the evolution of molecular biology from one closely associated with war to one associated with peace and profit. The first section briefly evaluates the impetus behind President Nixon's decision to convert the nation's biological warfare program into the biological research program. The second and third sections examine the specific policies surrounding the institutional and legal innovations that arose out of the conversion process. This section concentrates on the linkages between Nixon's strategic industrial policy and the judicial and legislative changes that were implemented in 1980. My conclusion reflects on the implications of reframing the historical narrative of biotechnology's emergence along the lines of a renewed emphasis on the politics of state intervention and the state's capacity to spark innovation.

Nixon's Decision and Debates over Conversion

Despite the tremendous impact at home and abroad of Nixon's conversion decision, a dearth of scholarship exists on both the reasons behind it and the consequences of it.[3] While space constraints do not permit a full explanation of the president's reasoning, I do want to highlight the primary cause of his decision, which has remained obscure.[4] The overriding reason stemmed directly from the geopolitical implications of the biological revolution in molecular genetics, which had been gaining steam throughout the 1950s and 1960s. By the mid-1960s, "a former high-level defense department official" told journalist Seymour M. Hersh, "There's a revolution in the biological sciences, just as there was in the physical sciences in the 1920s. It [genetics] is analogous to quantum theory. A huge area of science is in ferment—and it may have military implications and advantages for us" (Hersh 1968, 280). At the same time, the National Science Foundation released its annual report, exclaiming, "We are now immersed ... in a biological revolution, the 'molecular or genetic revolution,' which will undoubtedly have social and cultural impact of far-reaching consequences" (Appel 2000, 209). These exuberant views mirrored a parade of headlines in major newspapers across the country, leading to congressional hearings on the topic throughout the decade.[5] By 1970, Dr. Jacob Bronowski, a fellow at the Salk Institute and founder of the newly formed Council for Biology in Human Affairs, stressed that "over the last 10 years ... the action in the sciences has shifted from physics to biology" (Blakeslee 1970, 11).

In many respects, this revolution benefited tremendously from the exorbitant increases in federal science funding in the wake of Sputnik in 1957. By 1963 the budget allocations for all federal R&D spending neared $12.5 billion (Wright 1994, 24). Honing in on an exact percentage of this total increase for the biological sciences is difficult due to "the politics of numerical data," which includes distinguishing between basic and applied research (Appel 2000, 142). However, three aspects of the budget are clear. First, the share of the federal budget for the life sciences increased over fivefold during this period (Appel 2000, 142). Second, the National Science Foundation expended more money on the biological sciences than the NIH, which will become an important issue later on in the chapter (Appel 2000, 146). Finally, the share for the biological warfare program tripled in the early 1960s, increasing even more over the long run.[6] From the early 1950s to 1969, controlling for inflation, the budget allocation for the chemical and biological warfare (CBW) program increased by more than 2,000 percent from $10 million to $352 million, with most of the change coming during the Kennedy administration (Wright 1990b, 33). Accordingly, historian Susan Wright describes the impact of these huge federal outlays in generating a vast R&D "network extending far beyond the boundaries of Fort Detrick [the nation's principal BW lab] ... to contractors in approximately 300 universities, research institutes and corporations." Needless to say, American scientists and policymakers were not the only ones enthralled with the promising breakthroughs of molecular biology.

U.S. government officials became increasingly concerned about Soviet geneticists making rapid advances in the biological sciences after the Soviet authorities officially put an end to the Lysenko period. Consequently, George B. Kistiakowsky, President Eisenhower's science adviser, traveled to Russia in 1967 with a National Academy of Sciences delegation. They found that "genetics and molecular biology [were] making a swift comeback" (Sullivan 1967, 1). According to these high-ranking U.S. officials, Soviet genetics had "reached parity with research in American, British and West European laboratories." The prospect of Soviet competition in the biological sciences, particularly biological weapons, contributed mightily to Nixon's decision.

Indeed, a Presidential Science Advisory Committee assessment, prepared for Nixon during the first several months of his term, argued the Soviet Union was making major advances in exploiting the biological sciences, putting the United States at risk. According to a top-secret memo about this assessment, Lee A. DuBridge, Nixon's science adviser, informed Henry A. Kissinger, adviser to the president for national security affairs, "The conclusion regarding our capabilities is very important and should be taken into full account during policy formulation since it appears that we are weak in absolute terms, as well as relative to the Soviet Union."[7] Such a consideration prompted DuBridge to suggest that the administration follow the Department of Defense's recommendations within "NSSM-59 to forgo the further development of an offensive BW capability while maintaining R&D programs on defensive measures and to an extent that would avoid technological surprise by an enemy." By shifting the country's research emphasis from offensive to defensive development, DuBridge hoped "a 'new start' might be generated in this heretofore controversial area."

With these geopolitical considerations in mind, on November 25, 1969, President Nixon called on Congress to ratify the Geneva Protocol of 1925, stating his intention to "reinforce our continuing advocacy of international constraints on the use of these weapons" (Nixon 1969). Nevertheless, President Nixon had no intention of letting the United States fall behind in this critical scientific area as nations throughout the world pursued the myriad possibilities of the biological revolution. Therefore, while Nixon's unilateral decision on the U.S. biological warfare program is hailed as one of the most significant accomplishments in disarmament policy during the twentieth century, it should not be viewed as the nation's abandonment of this fertile site of R&D. Senior policymakers in both branches of government aggressively pursued programs to secure U.S. dominance in the biological sciences while simultaneously gaining credit for arms control.[8]

The Makings of a Strategic Industrial Policy

On December 10, 1969, just days after Nixon's decision, DuBridge warned Nixon about the danger of relinquishing American dominance in science and technology at such a critical juncture in world politics. He wrote to the president about the critical necessity of "maintaining the momentum in science," sharing with the president his concerns: "While many other countries in the world are continuing to increase their budgets for the support of basic science and technology, the U.S. effort is declining. The U.S. leadership, built up so successfully over the past 20 years, is therefore threatened in a number of very important areas such as high energy physics, optical and radio astronomy, chemical biology and other fields."[9] In a later assessment, DuBridge emphasized his alarm about this decline, which "occurred at the very time that other nations, conspicuously the Soviet Union and Japan and West Germany, have been rapidly increasing their scientific and technological efforts."[10] These warnings about America's deteriorating relative position in the world motivated the White House into action.

At the same time, senior congressional lawmakers recognized the necessity of thoroughly reforming the nation's R&D enterprise to reflect rapidly changing conditions at home and abroad. Lawmakers argued that the federal government must take a more proactive role in federal science policy to overcome the widespread dissatisfaction among the nation's top scientists, whose participation and commitment in scientific innovation were critical to the country's competitiveness. These concerns led Representative Emilio Q. Daddario (D-CT), chairman of the Subcommittee on Science, Research, and Development, to hold "extensive hearings" on the immediate priority of greatly expanding the "centralization of federal science activities" (Barfield 1973a, 409). According to Daddario, "the scientific community [was] divided and uncertain about the necessity for wholesale restructuring and moving drastically from the existing decentralized, pluralistic system." Nevertheless, Daddario expressed the sentiments of many congressmen when he declared that the nation could not continue on its present course without a "formalized science policy to guide it" (Lyons 1970; Cohn 1970, 9). Hence Daddario's subcommittee announced its main recommendation to the administration for turning the deteriorating situation around by "immediately draft[ing] a master plan for science policy." This master plan sought to address the myriad challenges for the nation in harnessing the biological revolution.

Since the mid-1960s, Congress held numerous hearings about the risks and opportunities stemming from the rapid developments in molecular biology. For instance, Daddario's subcommittee first began addressing the need for technology assessment in this area in 1965, introducing a bill in 1967 to establish a technology assessment board, which the *New York Times* described as the biggest congressional addition since the General Accounting Office had been established in 1921. Eventually this bill evolved into the legislation that launched the Office of Technology Assessment in 1974. Throughout the mid to late 1960s, Daddario heard testimony from scientists and engineers who were intensely interested in the consequences of so much dramatic technological change. Even though the technology assessment agenda contained several items, policymakers and scientists showed particular interest in the critical area of "genetic engineering and other ramifications of recent discoveries in biology" (Wilford 1970). Alongside this demonstration of congressional intent for the master plan, Congress allocated $10 million in 1970 for a newly created genetic task force "to coordinate genetics research, identify areas of imminent clinical application, and set priorities for federal funding" (*New Scientist* 1970, 564).

Hence the conversion process opened wide the possibility of mobilizing the country under newfound auspices that were separate from militarization and warfare; it simultaneously provided Congress and the White House with an opportunity to centralize authority over the nation's R&D enterprise for ushering in the new scientific era. Despite policymakers' determination to move forward aggressively with the conversion process, White House officials remained concerned with reversing the prevalent antiscience and antitechnology mood in the country. This political hot potato pervaded public and private remarks by policymakers who were searching for ways to remedy Americans' loss of confidence in science's contribution to society. The problem had become so acute that Nixon administration officials began drafting presidential speeches on the "present attack on science and technology."[11] These debates even spilled into the White House's inner circle after Edward E. David, Nixon's second science adviser, publicly hailed the biological sciences to a group of assembled science journalists. He warned them of the dangers over America's growing "timidity" about scientific experimentation, especially in the area of biology (P.M.B. 1971, 875). David told the sympathetic audience that "we must not place limitations on biological experiments," no doubt reflecting the dominant viewpoint within the administration. Nevertheless, David's public remarks, which were reprinted in the press, drew fierce criticism from Patrick Buchanan, special assistant to the president for speechwriting, who immediately recognized the political firestorm that would likely erupt if the public were to believe David's remarks were officially condoned. Buchanan blasted a memo off to John Ehrlichman, assistant to the president for domestic affairs, arguing, "One recalls there were no limits on 'biological experiments' in Germany from 1932 [sic] to 1945."[12] Buchanan demanded that David issue a public apology to signal that his remarks did not reflect the administration's position.

While these politically sensitive issues were being debated, White House officials began lamenting the slow pace of the conversion process, insisting the country would suffer peril if it failed to grasp this opportunity. In February, David shared his concern with presidential assistant Peter M. Flanigan about the need to pursue this goal much more aggressively:

> We have not been able to convert manpower and laboratory work rapidly and effectively enough to civilian purposes. The reason is that most civilian agencies of government do

not have the traditions or people for a vital R&D program. This may be cured in part by the reorganization, but emphasis is needed in our reorganization proposals on establishing viable R&D in the new Departments.[13]

The reasons for establishing R&D capabilities stemmed from the growing recognition that the federal government would need to exert considerable leverage to convert these massive military resources and personnel toward civilian and commercial ends. Internal documents show that the White House was intent on ensuring that "the application of science and technology [would] improve U.S. competitiveness in international markets."[14] With this national goal in mind, Nixon enthusiastically acknowledged an observation made by Paul W. McCracken, member of the Council of Economic Advisers, about the high rates of return on federal investments on R&D. McCracken told the president, "There is broad agreement in the evidence on the payoffs to R&D that the rate of return to such activity has been high, perhaps on the order of twice as high as the return to investment in physical capital."[15] Nixon underlined this sentence in the memo and wrote in the margins, "George–Peter–E–*note!*"[16]

The New Technology Opportunities Program

In early 1970, soon after Nixon made his conversion decision, the National Science Foundation predicted that the 1970s would become known as the "Decade of Biology" (Appel 2000, 243). This prescient enthusiasm for the promises of the new scientific era permeated White House deliberations over a strategic industrial policy that would succeed in exploiting the myriad benefits of molecular biology. Senior policymakers considered the stakes so high that they determined to exercise greater direct control over the nation's R&D enterprise to accomplish their goals. Edward E. David has noted the importance senior White House officials placed on molecular biology's relationship to the national interest: "It was with regard to biomedical research that we first heard (in Lyndon Johnson's day) the opinion that administration and planning of research were too important to be left to scientists" (David 1980, 55). In facing the mammoth challenges of the conversion process, Nixon administration officials acknowledged that they would be required to centralize authority over federal science policy in order to affect the necessary institutional and legal changes that would enable the country to reap the benefits of the biological revolution.

In the summer of 1971, after the White House and Congress had debated various policies for carrying out the conversion process, the Nixon administration initiated the New Technologies Opportunities (NTO) program, the vehicle for launching a massive strategic industrial policy. To get the NTO program off the ground, Edward J. Burger Jr., member of the Office of Science and Technology in the Nixon administration, recalls in his memoir that Ehrlichman sent a notice on July 1, 1971, to "nearly all of the cabinet secretaries plus the heads of certain other executive branch agencies" about the administration's plan for "mounting a study to determine opportunities for directing extra attention and money to areas of technology in behalf of selected national problems" (Burger 1980, 111). In fact, the archival record shows that Ehrlichman's memo identified four specific issues that the president hoped all participating departments and agencies would address when contributing to this program:

1. Long-term budget impacts. 2. *Hard estimate* on cost, manpower and timing of implementation before any new technology programs can be considered. 3. A fix from private industry on their potential financial support for new projects. 4. Assuming a cluster of programs meet the above criteria, what kind of organization (Government/private/mix) should be created (if any) or redirected to carry out these programs.[17]

To begin assessing the various dimensions of these four issues, Burger describes the administration's erecting "a management superstructure ... to sift and analyze the many ideas collected" (Burger 1980, 112). The NTO program eventually incorporated "some 300 people in more than 14 agencies" (Wade 1971b, 386). The centrality of the conversion process in this enormous endeavor became immediately apparent to outside observers. For instance, *Science* magazine described the NTO program as an "attempt to square the swords-into-plowshares idea with the national economic situation" (Wade 1971b, 386).

The New Technology Opportunities program's ambitions were characterized at the time as so far-reaching that citizens writing letters to the White House compared the program to the Manhattan Project and the Apollo Program.[18] The *New York Times* declared, "If the program comes to fruition, it could represent a major step toward making the Government a virtual partner for the first time in industries outside of aerospace and defense" (Wilford 1971, 1). Indeed, NTO's initiators aimed for precisely that. Throughout the summer and fall, a flurry of activity consumed the White House as plans were devised for a dramatically increased federal role in providing incentives to stimulate the economy and to accelerate the conversion process. In order to select the best ideas for channeling new scientific developments into applied technological products for the marketplace, the bureaucracy was mobilized: task forces received assignments, blue ribbon panel members were chosen, conferences and meetings were planned, flow charts were erected, presidential statement drafts were circulated, and numerous other activities received copious attention. Its significance in the hierarchy of White House priorities was heralded by the fact that William M. Magruder, special consultant to the president for the NTO program, located his office adjacent to the Oval Office and reported directly to the president. Such access prompted several observers to compare Magruder's role in science and technology to Kissinger's role in foreign affairs.

This comparison appropriately reflects the link the administration saw between federal science policy and America's position in the world. Magruder described the NTO program in terms of "regaining America's technological lead" (Wade 1971b, 386), and David described the NTO program in terms of "the invigoration of the whole R&D enterprise" (Wade 1971a, 796). These prevalent views of the link between the nation's R&D enterprise and American power prompted the NTO program organizers to set about redesigning the country's vast technological infrastructure.

The NTO program began by reordering priorities, determining incentives, and selecting potential technologies for exploitation. In order to achieve these multiple goals, the program called for organizing two panels to assess potential technology projects "in terms of their relationship to urgent national problems, or significant economic opportunities."[19] These panels consisted of "1) a blue-ribbon 'Advisory Group on Technology' composed of outside-government people and 2) a low-key Domestic Council study along the same lines." Seventeen individuals were listed as "possible members" of the blue ribbon panel, including molecular biologists Joshua Lederberg and James D. Watson, congressman and science advocate Emilo Q. Daddario, and industrialists and Nixon advisers William O. Baker, Patrick Haggarty, and Simon Ramo. In selecting the panel's membership, Donald K. Rice, assistant director of OMB, along with Edward E. David, cautioned the NTO program organizers to avoid sparking any public controversy with its choices, considering the public's sensitivity about the militarization of science. They argued, "The members should be distinguished Americans. As a group they should represent a broad spectrum of viewpoints. A strong slant toward the 'military-industrial complex' should be avoided." Further instructions stated, "The Chairman probably should not be a person associated directly with the military-industrial complex."

Together, these two panels were viewed as an "inside/outside look at the substantive technological openings which could be exploited by the Administration."[20] In recognition that the U.S. traditionally excelled in "high technology products [as its] strength in foreign trade," both of these panels, along with six task forces, were organized to accomplish the program's far-reaching goals.[21] Peter G. Peterson, director of the newly created Council on International Economic Policy, headed the Long Range Planning Organization study, which concluded that "the federal organization of science, which includes NSF, AEC, NASA, and EPA, is not ideally organized for the 1970s, which we all visualize as being a highly commercially-competitive era."[22] As a result of this early assessment, five key objectives were set for the panels on technological initiatives:

1. Decrease unemployment among highly trained scientists and engineers
2. Increase productivity, particularly in the service industries
3. Aid our foreign trade balance
4. Provide ideas for leadership solving some of the nation's pressing social problems
5. Prepare the nation for the worldwide commercial competition of the 1970s

In order for the NTO program organizers to address each of these critically important short- and long-term issues, they recognized that the country would have to undergo a major transformation involving institutional and legal innovations to ensure that the United States would not relinquish its global leadership position. The scope of this agenda generated a deep-seated concern among senior policymakers who understood these grave stakes.

In one revealing example, Peterson prepared a sweeping appraisal of America's position in the world for Nixon called, "Projecting the Future Development of the U.S."[23] In it Peterson shared with the president his concerns about this historical crossroads:

Recently, I have been discussing with you my view that we should think through whether the rapidly changing economic, technological and social world we are living in doesn't require more systematic approaches to projecting the future choices for public policy. We are making these choices today, if only by inaction, but in some ways we are making the choices in the dark.

Peterson stressed that "we are living in a far more competitive world—competing with several countries who devote a great deal of energy to shaping their future." As a result of this growing global competition, Peterson argued, the U.S. government's "historic" reliance on the "market mechanism and the private sector" might no longer be sufficient to address the challenges of the 1970s. He shared with Nixon his concern over not being able to answer questions about America's future strengths:

I can't answer questions that I'm often asked ... in what fields and industries is America going to excel five or ten years from today? What is our country's worldwide competitive position likely to be in basic industries? Business experience tells us that projecting the future, often helps one anticipate problems and grasp new opportunities rather than reacting on a remedial basis.

Peterson's gloomy assessment shaped and inspired the viewpoints of the senior White House officials who were charged with executing the NTO program. The core group of administration officials involved in this effort included Peterson, George Shultz, Edward David, Peter Flanigan, and John Ehrlichman.[24] These officials worked closely to devise a strategic industrial policy for fulfilling the president's bold conversion agenda.

The capacity of the federal government to achieve these objectives preoccupied the program organizers. David, who was the first science adviser to come from industry rather than academia, characterized the inadequacies of present governmental mechanisms for executing the NTO program priorities:

The Federal Government presently lacks an adequate process to exploit technology to its full potential in meeting national objectives.... The critical failure—and, basically the raison d'etre of our present task force—is a lack of top down control. We are weak in overall planning, priority setting, and a Government wide management system. This is the traditional responsibility of the Executive Office of the President. Machinery is needed in the EOP which translates national objectives into strategies for technology development, and directs and assists Federal agencies in their support of technology within such strategies.[25]

Therefore senior administration officials viewed the concentration of more authority in the executive branch as an essential element for increasing the state's capacity and power to realize these national objectives.

One of the main themes that emerged during their numerous deliberations dealt with the idea of reprivatization. The program organizers believed fervently that this idea would assist them in thoroughly reforming government-business relations to advance the conversion process. They urged restructuring traditional relationships between business and government in order to promote reprivatization.[26] Reprivatization consisted of tax incentives; technology transfer between universities, government laboratories and industry; government procurement policies; liberalized antitrust laws; and relaxation of government-owned patent licenses. Importantly, these ideas were not simply about returning to an era of unregulated capitalism; rather, they were about creating a new type of entity, such as a hybrid, between the public and private sectors, in what Simon Ramo, president of TRW and consultant to the administration, called "the coming social-industrial complex."[27] In many respects, this idea encapsulated the program organizers' plans for replacing the military-university partnership with an industry-university partnership.

The scope and ambition of these efforts were extraordinary. The NTO organizers sought nothing less than to remake institutional partnerships between the military, industry, and university sectors while altering basic cultural assumptions about the role of science and technology in American society. Magruder insisted that to break past patterns, old structures needed to be torn down and outmoded relationships needed to end: "Now let's start it up again but let's do it with a program manager instead of just funding it any old way the way we did before. Let's do it in a controlled way" (Wade 1971b, 388). As the NTO program organizers brainstormed about ways to bolster the federal government's capacity to remake the nation's R&D enterprise, they strenuously argued for the need to separate the persistent association of science with militarism in Americans' minds. Therefore, their strategy for reordering domestic priorities and rebuilding new institutional partnerships involved explicitly linking technological leadership with peace and prosperity. Flanigan argued that by "choosing an appropriate area of social concern, and setting a specific goal," the NTO program organizers could more easily "mobilize our technological resources to get the job done."[28] In other words, reprivatization also served the purpose of moving the country away from believing in the force of the military-industrial complex to shape outcomes in American society.

Institutional Innovation I: Diversifying Federal Funding Sources for Science

A critical component of the conversion process centered on transforming the post–World War II federal science enterprise from one based on a pluralistic oversight structure to one that concentrated more authority in government, particularly the executive branch. Senior administration officials were convinced that this policy objective had to work hand in hand with diversifying federal funding sources for scientists who were continuing to object to the Vietnam War. As a result, DuBridge persuaded the president and his senior advisers that the National Science Foundation (NSF) should move to the foreground in providing the White House with the ability to execute its chosen policies. DuBridge hoped this move would reduce tensions among scientists who wanted a civilian agency to provide federal funding of university research.

In several respects, DuBridge's policy choice of concentrating authority within the NSF complemented the federal science agency's original mission. When Vannevar

Bush originally proposed creating the NSF in his landmark report, *Science: The Endless Frontier,* he had envisioned the new NSF as the primary agency for ensuring the continuation of America's scientific leadership after World War II. Despite Bush's lofty goals for the new agency in 1950, in the intervening years, many institutional developments vied for influence over federal science policy, leaving NSF to become just one of several federal science agencies. Yet in the early 1970s, the White House desperately wanted firmer political control over the nation's science policy machinery for executing the conversion process without undue societal interference. Nixon administration officials also believed firmer political control would help to regain Americans' support for science and technology by providing scientists with more funding choices than just the Department of Defense. DuBridge informed the president,

> In the past the pluralism of support by many agencies has been a healthy development, both for the agencies concerned and for the strength of American science. If a transition away from this pluralism is deemed desirable, we should plan it with great care through building up the National Science Foundation budget which Congress has never been enthusiastic about supporting.[29]

DuBridge's enthusiasm for vesting more authority in NSF led him to propose transferring upward of $100 million in funding from the Department of Defense to the NSF.[30] This funding transfer supported DuBridge's idea of creating "a newly strengthened NSF ... [with a] total purview of the nation's scientific enterprise."[31] DuBridge urged the president to go beyond budgetary increases for the federal science agency by also "bringing into the new NSF such things as ... basic chemical, biological, [and] medical research formerly supported by NIH." These bold ambitions complemented the administration's objectives for the conversion process.

Among these objectives, the administration hoped to quell protests among students and scientists regarding military research on university campuses. Even though DuBridge believed such protests were misplaced, he acknowledged that the status quo was unsustainable.

> Unfortunately, students and others have assumed that all defense supported research was aimed at specific military weapons rather than a general expansion of knowledge and have sometimes advocated the cessation of all research by DOD. More thoughtful people in and out of the universities, however, believe that this would be unfortunate both for DOD and for the strength of science in the country and damaging to the universities. Thus, many of us hope that such support of general university research which the universities themselves have asked for can be continued at a reasonable level. At the same time all of us would agree with you to have future expansion of university research supported by the civilian agencies, such as the National Science Foundation and the National Institutes of Health. This is desirable partly because there are individual investigators (actually a small minority) who would prefer to have their research supported by a civilian agency but find that such agencies have inadequate funds for the purpose. As NSF or NIH funds become more adequate these investigators will have an option as to the source of support they seek.[32]

DuBridge hoped these institutional changes would substantially broaden the appeal of science throughout the country by removing the taint of military funding because, as he put it, "Science, in short, needs a larger clientele—a much larger clientele" (DuBridge 1971, 11).

On January 26, 1973, a few days after his second inauguration, Nixon moved quickly to implement the institutional innovation first proposed by DuBridge for furthering the conversion decision. In a major proposal, Nixon called for streamlining the federal science establishment by concentrating the executive branch's science advisory capacity in the NSF and abolishing the post–World War II presidential science advisory mechanisms that had been built up over the previous two decades.[33] In echoing the sentiments first enunciated by DuBridge, Nixon argued that his reorganization plans simply restored NSF's original mission in providing oversight of the nation's entire R&D enterprise: "The National Science Foundation has broadened from its earlier concentration on basic research support to take on a significant role in applied research as well. It has matured in its ability to play a coordinating and evaluative role within the Government and between the public and private sectors." Subsequently Nixon informed Congress that on July 1 he would "transfer responsibilities to Dr. H. Guyford Stever," who had become director of NSF in April 1972.

On the heels of this announcement, most of the scientific community lambasted the plan. Nevertheless, several prominent scientists recognized the necessity of this historic change for overcoming the military dominance of basic research. For instance, Philip Handler, president of the National Academy of Sciences, told the *National Journal* that "one clear plus under the new arrangement is the mandate to NSF to undertake major policy studies, particularly with regard to allocation of federal resources. OST never had the staff or funds to do that" (Barfield 1973b, 462). Harvey Brooks, dean of engineering and applied sciences at Harvard University, noted,

> The American system, with its emphasis on pluralism, decentralization and competition among sectors for R&D funds, performed pretty well until the mid-1960s. However, we've moved into an era where resources for R and D are limited, thus necessitating more careful planning and coordination at or near the highest government decision-making level…. In addition, a new and more difficult task of interweaving science policy with national social, economic and political policies would seem to call for a unified, coherent strategy. (Barfield 1973a, 410)

DuBridge told the *New York Times*, "Times have changed radically." He added, "The National Science Foundation … is now capable of performing the role originally conceived for it as a focal agency of the Federal effort in science" (Sullivan 1973, 20). Indeed, *Science* pointed out, "there are some ironies in [the] rumored choice of [the] National Science Foundation as the lead agency in federal science," especially because "its proponents envisioned its developing into a kind of ministry of science" when it was founded in 1950 (Walsh 1973, 456). Therefore, this first institutional innovation centered on repositioning the NSF to provide scientists with alternative sources of federal funding while providing the White House with considerably more leverage over federal science policy.

Institutional Innovation II: Technology Transfer Between Public and Private Sectors

The second large-scale institutional innovation that the New Technology Opportunities program focused on dealt with expanding federal technology transfer from the public to the private sectors. The program organizers argued that this institutional change would advance the conversion process while jump-starting the economy. In particular, they advocated replacing the military-university partnership with an industry-university partnership to ensure the commercialization of molecular biology while simultaneously providing scientists with alternative funding sources.

Alan K. McAdams, senior staff economist to the president's Council of Economic Advisers, pointed out ways for the private sector "to capture" more of the federal R&D effort.[34] He suggested that the huge sums involved in the federal funding effort, which amounted to $15.4 billion in 1971, required more than simply tinkering on the margins since it would have "little net effect." McAdams wrote to Magruder about a number of conclusions he had drawn after assessing the nation's R&D infrastructure. He argued, "Improved connection[s] between the basic research of the university and private business appears desirable." He based this conclusion on a series of data that suggested "the university is the key institution performing basic research, expending $2.3 billion, or 55% of the total ... it is well connected to the Federal Government which provides 58% of these funds ... [however], it is not well connected to private firms which provide only 3% of its funds." Hence expanding technology transfer was seen as a prerequisite for the private sector to gain access to government-owned technology thereby getting "government-owned technology off the shelf and put [into] the marketplace."[35] The NTO program organizers and senior administration officials used the NSF along with a newly created Federal Laboratory Consortium for Technology Transfer to accomplish their ambitious goals.

In the immediate wake of the conversion process, Representative Daddario and Senator Edward E. Kennedy passed the Daddario-Kennedy Act of 1969, which amended the NSF charter, enabling it to fund applied research for the first time (Appel 2000, 5). Nixon administration officials welcomed this significant change within NSF, believing it would help to serve the broader conversion agenda. They also sought to expand significantly this newfound institutional capacity. James R. Schlesinger, acting deputy director of the Bureau of the Budget, vetted the selection of new members to the National Science Board. He told Flanigan, "We look to the Foundation as an agency which could do more to support research in areas of national concern, such as environmental research and the marine sciences. This is particularly true now that the Foundation has authority to support applied as well as basic research."[36] By 1971 the NSF allocated 12 percent of its overall budget to applied research activities (Barfield 1970, 1805). It accomplished this goal through a number of mechanisms, but it was greatly aided by the administration's creation of the NSF's Research Applied to National Needs (RANN) program in 1971. In light of its newly amended charter, this program funded industry and applied research directly. This seemingly radical departure from NSF's original mandate to fund only nonprofit basic research drew fierce criticism from its founder, Vannevar Bush, who wrote a scathing editorial in *Science* criticizing the White House for supposedly betraying the mission agency's core principles (Bush 1971). Nevertheless, by 1975, RANN had funded applied research upward of $80.8 million (Appel 2000, 239). According to historian Toby Appel, the NSF also "incorporated an entirely new element [in 1975], namely NSF's relation to the growth of new industrial biotechnology" (Appel 2000, 269). NSF's role in promoting commercial biotechnology accelerated throughout the decade, further solidifying the industry-university partnership begun in the wake of the conversion process.

For instance, President Jimmy Carter's administration launched several major reforms for the National Science Foundation as part of its sweeping domestic policy review (DPR) initiative. These reforms built upon and deepened industry-university partnerships, further elevating the NSF to the forefront in promoting industrial bio-technology. During the DPR, President Carter's senior advisers informed him of ways to strengthen NSF's role in promoting industry-university relations:

> The scientific and technological strength of American universities has not been harnessed effectively in promoting industrial technological advance. In order to achieve this end, in FY 1978 the NSF established a program for the support of high quality R&D projects that are proposed jointly by industry-university research teams with cost sharing. The program has successfully improved the linkage between university and industry R&D capabilities, but requires strengthening.[37]

Even though President Carter abolished the RANN program begun during the Nixon administration, he launched and supported new NSF programs with identical missions, extending NSF to work in conjunction with DOD, DOE, EPA, and NASA to "initiate such university-industry cooperative R&D programs." By the end of Carter's term, the NSF publicly announced its broadened mission to support engineering and applied science alongside its traditional focus on basic research. By placing a civilian agency at the forefront of biological R&D during the early phase of the conversion process, the Nixon administration positioned the NSF to guide the nation's scientific enterprise toward increased commercialization through strengthened industry-university partnerships. Throughout the 1970s, NSF laid the foundation for the commercialization of publicly funded research that the country witnessed firsthand throughout the 1980s and beyond.

In addition to expanding technology transfer between the public and private sectors through a reformed NSF, the Nixon administration created the Federal Laboratory Consortium for Technology Transfer (FLC) in 1971. This institution has come to play a major role in the commercialization of federally funded science and technology inventions. The FLC was initially developed and run "under the auspices of the Department of Defense to assist in transferring DOD technology to state and local governments and to the private sector" (Schacht 2005, 4).[38] According to the Congressional

Research Service, by the end of the 1970s, the FLC dramatically "expanded to include other federal departments in a voluntary organization of approximately 300 federal laboratories" (Schacht 2005, 4). Experience with both the NSF programs and the FLC contributed to congressional debates about the possibility of expanding the scope of technology transfer arrangements between the public and private sectors throughout the decade. In debates that led directly to the Stevenson-Wydler Act of 1980, Congress released a major report on technology transfer in 1977, noting the historical origins of "past attempts to develop a domestic technology transfer policy [began] with the New Technological Opportunities Program instituted in 1971 by the [Nixon] White House."[39] In fact, the report stressed that current congressional efforts on technology transfer legislation relied heavily on the past activities and recommendations of the NTO program, noting "many of the [current] recommendations are identical; all are related." Through an extensive, in-depth study of the NTO program activities and recommendations, the congressional report on technology transfer strove to "provide a total picture of how our present activities are responsive to the needs and priorities identified in the initial studies of the concept." Historians Dorothy Nelkin and Susan Wright have both observed that the Stevenson-Wydler Act dealt directly with and had a dramatic impact on accelerating the commercial exploitation of molecular biology (Nelkin 1987, 19; Wright 1994).

Legal Innovation I: Patent Law Reform for Reprivatizing Government Inventions

In conjunction with these two institutional innovations, the NTO program organizers launched substantial patent law reform to ensure the conversion process successfully transferred publicly funded R&D into the private sector. In the months leading up to the NTO deliberations, George P. Shultz, director of the Office of Management and Budget, suggested deploying patent law to fortify technology transfer arrangements between government laboratories, universities, and industry.[40] Shultz estimated the federal government owned "about 13,700 patents, increasing at a rate of about 1900 per year." Yet, he told Peterson, "a survey disclosed that [only] 10 percent of these reach the commercial stage." Shultz's concern over this low level of industrial utilization of government patents led him to suggest to Peterson, "Perhaps this area could be looked into as a special link in technical assistance for firms involved in the adjustment process." However, Shultz's concerns were not the only issue influencing the administration's policy deliberations. Rapid advances in molecular biology before and during the NTO program's work greatly impacted policymakers' views on the need to reform swiftly and thoroughly the nation's patent laws.

For instance, in 1971 the Patent and Trademark Office "first published guidelines on the deposit of microorganisms" (Office of Technology Assessment 1992, 397). These new guidelines were issued after Congress had debated substantial reforms to the nation's patent laws since 1967 in response to President Johnson's patent modernization reform legislation, which addressed ways for the patent system to expand its use of process patents due to their significance for molecular biology. Furthermore, the Office of Technology Assessment identifies the summer of 1971 as the beginning of "Phase I ... [when] the first awareness of risks to human health from experiments involving recombinant DNA (rDNA)" emerged (Office of Technology Assessment 1981, 315). All of these issues combined to influence President Nixon and the NTO program organizers in reforming the nation's patent laws.

In order to accelerate the reprivatization process, Nixon announced a major change in government patent policy on August 23, 1971.[41] From the steps of what Nixon called "the western White House" in San Clemente, California, Edward E. David told a hastily convened press conference that the government would now grant exclusive licenses to the private sector as an incentive to develop federally funded inventions made at the nation's laboratories and universities (Mintz 1971, A9). This historic decision was made after DuBridge "recommended that [Nixon] issue a revised Presidential Memorandum and Statement on Government Patent Policy" to implement a series of recommendations made by the Federal Council for Science and Technology between 1965 and 1970.[42]

Nevertheless, to some observers at the time, Nixon's sudden and unexpected announcement came as a surprise. The *Washington Post* characterized Nixon's policy change as startling: "There was no hint that such an announcement would be forthcoming, and no detailed explanation of what the new policy will mean or why it is being established" (*Washington Post* 1971, A17). However, another *Washington Post* article recognized its historical significance, pointing out the enduring controversy over the nation's patent laws since World War II:

> The new Nixon patent policy addresses itself to a question that has perplexed previous administrations and Congress for a quarter century: How should patent rights be allocated to inventions made with the estimated $175 billion the government has spent on research and development since the end of World War II, half of it in the last six years? (Mintz 1971)

Prior to this policy reform, patents on government-funded inventions had remained within the public domain, and exclusive licenses on government inventions were rarely granted to industry. In other words, the government retained exclusive title to its inventions.

On top of this policy change, the president submitted the Patent Modernization and Reform Act of 1973 to the Senate on September 27, 1972. The legislation built on President Johnson's 1967 patent reform bill as well as the recommendations of DuBridge and the NTO program organizers. The *New York Times* described Nixon's patent reform bill in the following dramatic terms: "President Nixon asked Congress today to enact major changes in the patent laws that would alter the basic procedures for granting patents and require publication of detailed information about patent applications before the patents are actually granted" (Shanahan 1972, 43). The White House fact sheet that accompanied release of the bill addressed the need for reform "in view of the technological and information explosion in recent years, which has resulted in the filing of approximately 115,000 new patent applications and the issuance of 70,000 new patents each year."[43] This remarkable pace of technological innovation required revisions to the nation's patent laws, since no major change had been completed since the Patent Act of 1836. In particular, the White House fact sheet addressed the need for immediate reform in light of the changing institutional composition of the nation's R&D enterprise to ensure the long-term vitality of the American economy:

> While the patent system has changed only slightly since the nineteenth century, the social and economic structure of our Nation has, of course, undergone profound change. The individual inventor, often working alone and unaided, still makes an important contribution, but the lead role in exploring new frontiers of technology is now played by organized research—sophisticated and highly capable teams funded by our Government, industry, and universities.

Accordingly, the fact sheet argued that this institutional change in creating teams of researchers and developers from the public and private sectors required a revised legal foundation to generate more validity in the patent system and to determine whether or not a change in the provisions for patent licensing needed to be made.

With Nixon's policy change, and the larger ambitions of the NTO's reprivatization plans, the administration reversed a long-established government practice, setting a new course for the country to exploit the biological sciences. The private sector's newfound access lifted the floodgates to the nation's R&D in a way that would fundamentally reform institutional partnerships between the public and private sectors by decade's end, while also altering the normative basis for that access. With these dramatic and far-reaching policy reforms in place, it now fell to subsequent administrations to protect the government's huge investments in science and technology and ensure America win the new science race in molecular biology.

Throughout the 1970s, the executive and legislative branches debated how the nation could reform its patent laws to ensure America's ability to win the new science race. While many pieces of implementing legislation were introduced, Nixon's patent reform bill continued winding its way through Congress. In conjunction with these congressional debates, the laws governing the patenting of life forms, such as microorganisms, were hotly contested after Ananda Chakrabarty, a General Electric (GE) engineer, was denied a patent from the PTO for an oil-eating microorganism in 1972. GE immediately appealed the decision, which was not definitely resolved until the Supreme Court overturned the PTO's original decision in 1980. In the meantime, several incremental legal decisions were made to grant patent rights to living organisms, such as the ruling by the U.S. Court of Customs and Patent Appeals in 1977 that certain microorganisms could be patented. In addition, and more importantly, the Carter administration became directly involved in staking out a strong position about this issue during its domestic policy review, which involved several subcommittees, including one on patent policy.

In December 1978 the White House received all DPR subcommittee reports. The *Report of the Subcommittee for Patent and Information Policy of the Government Domestic*

Review of Industrial Innovation, a very detailed and fairly long report, "identified four major goals to which attention must be addressed to enhance the innovation process through improvement of the present patent system."[44] These four major goals referred to three specific areas: commercialization of publicly funded inventions, internationalization of American patent law, and extension of patent rights to "new life forms." The goal of fostering commercialization of publicly funded inventions was thoroughly examined in the report, including recommendations for "march-in rights" and other policy mechanisms to protect the American taxpayer. These issues became central to the Bayh-Dole Act of 1980 (discussed below). However, I want to emphasize here that "Proposal X: Patent Rights to Be Available for New Technological Advance" explicitly urged the government to grant patents on microorganisms without delay. In fact, the proposal's authors strongly recommend that if the courts did not overturn the position of the PTO on the basis of Section 101 of the Patent Act of July 19, 1952, "it will be necessary to seek implementing legislation from Congress if non-plant life forms are to be patentable."

Six months after the Supreme Court ruled in favor of Chakrabarty and General Electric in 1980, allowing the issuance of patents on living things for the first time, Congress finally passed the Patent and Trademark Law Amendments Act (P.L. 96–517), commonly referred to as the Bayh-Dole Act of 1980 in honor of the legislation's sponsors. This major piece of legislation is usually discussed in an historical vacuum, suggesting it represented a clean break with the past; however, the evidence presented in this chapter shows clearly that it represented the culmination of over a decade's worth of effort by state actors who were determined to transition the country away from the institutional and legal standards of the immediate post–World War II era. In acknowledging this long gestation period before the 1980 changes took effect, Howard W. Bremer, president of the Society of University Patent Administrators, who was closely involved in patent law debates in the 1970s, argues:

> The passage of the Bayh-Dole Act was the reward for almost 20 years of effort by the non-profit sector to stimulate the transfer of technology through the vehicle of the patent system. It was the culmination of the many pieces of legislation introduced over many years that had sought to establish a uniform patent policy within the government. (Bremer 2001)

Importantly, Bremer points out that Nixon's patent law reforms in August 1971 were a key step that led to the eventual passage of Bayh-Dole. He also acknowledges the overlooked significance of the Bayh-Dole legislation, particularly as it pertains to the centralization of authority:

> It is also not universally recognized that the Bayh-Dole Act provided, for the very first time, statutory authority for the Government to apply for, obtain and maintain patents on inventions in both the United States and foreign countries and to license those inventions on a non-exclusive, partially exclusive or exclusive basis. Even where the government contractor (a university or other non-profit entity or a small business) chooses to retain title to an invention under the Bayh-Dole Act the government always receives

an irrevocable royalty-free license to practice such invention for governmental purpose. The government also reserved march-in rights for non-performance. In the face of such circumstances there is, in reality, a university-industry-government relationship.

Bremer's concluding observation is absolutely correct, insofar as the Bayh-Dole Act instituted a uniform patent policy by reserving certain rights for the government "to protect the public's interest" (Schacht 2009, 6). The bill states emphatically, "the government retains 'a nonexclusive, nontransferable, irrevocable, paid-up license to practice or have practiced for or on behalf of the United States any subject invention throughout the world.'" In other words, the American state protected and advanced its vital interests in federal science policy at home and abroad through the passage of this legislation.

Conclusion

This chapter has retrieved a lost episode in American political history in which President Richard M. Nixon harnessed the biological revolution by converting the nation's biological warfare program into the biological research program in November 1969. This momentous and unilateral decision arose during a key moment in the Cold War, providing senior policymakers with an unparalleled opportunity to remobilize the country under the auspices of détente with the Soviet Union rather than confrontation. This critical episode opens a window into the policy options and capacities of the U.S. government. Even though American citizens and many scholars perpetuate tales about the country's weak and powerless state in the domestic sphere, the birth of commercial biotechnology at this critical juncture demonstrates both state strength and state ingenuity.

The conversion process initiated by the Nixon administration and senior congressional lawmakers fundamentally altered the innovative climate within the country. At the highest levels of policymaking, government officials in the White House transformed the institutional and legal foundation to make the nation hospitable to commercializing molecular biology. This chapter has shown that the New Technology Opportunities program produced institutional and legal innovations that laid the basis for the well-known legislative and judicial decisions of 1980. While the Bayh-Dole and Stevenson-Wydler Acts of 1980 as well as the *Diamond v. Chakrabarty* Supreme Court decision that same year have widely been credited with jump-starting the biotechnology industry's rise to prominence, this chapter argued that these momentous policy and legal changes emerged after a decade of initiatives that built upon the reforms launched during the conversion process. In other words, 1980 represents the culmination of proactive institutional and legal reforms that sprang directly from the myriad federal science policy initiatives begun during the Nixon administration in the wake of the biological revolution.

This revisionist historical narrative contributes to the literature in two concrete ways. First, it resets the periodization clock for understanding when the prospects of molecular biology became apparent to policymakers, scientists, and business leaders. Rather than perpetuating the neoliberal myth that all market reforms began in the 1980s under the Reagan administration, the copious empirical evidence provided here demonstrates that the seemingly limitless prospects of molecular biology were widely acknowledged in the 1960s, contributing to Nixon's conversion decision and its subsequent aftermath. Second, it challenges the dominant assumption that the American way of innovation depends upon a decentralized environment where government involvement in the economy is minimal at best. Contrary to this assumption, senior policymakers actually increased the scope and breadth of state authority vis-à-vis the centralization of federal science policy during a period of neoliberalism's ascendancy. In fact, the geopolitical imperative of the Cold War science race shaped the perspectives of senior policymakers who were determined to navigate the conversion process, including the NTO program, through the treacherous waters of the antiwar movement. The dramatic institutional and legal innovations that emerged at this time should be viewed through the lens of the volatile antiwar climate where university scientists were increasingly reluctant to participate in classified research. One of the most consequential institutional innovations from this period stemmed from senior policymakers replacing the military-university partnership with an industry-university partnership to widen the federal funding options for university scientists. Senior policymakers fully recognized the imperative of bringing the nation's scientists back on board if the country hoped to win the Cold War science race.

The implications of recovering this lost episode in American political history demonstrate the need to revisit the national security lessons of World War II. The most important lesson is that technological superiority alters the balance of world power. The quest to attain technological superiority drives federal science policy and the mobilization of the nation's R&D enterprise. This lesson holds out both promise and peril for understanding the opportunities and constraints of innovation policy. On the one hand, the U.S. government's enduring commitment to this national goal offers seemingly endless ways to frame policy debates around the imperatives of economic and military might. For instance, proponents of alternative energy research have already begun to frame the need for additional federal resources in terms of national security as well as economics. On the other hand, the U.S. government's determination to achieve technological superiority at the expense of all else risks contributing to an ever-shrinking definition of what constitutes a public good. Recent calls for a new American innovation policy to meet the challenges of the twenty-first century should not obscure the military's hidden hand.

Notes

I would like to thank Fred Block, Matt Keller, Linda Weiss, Glenn Fong, Herman Schwatz, and Ronnie Lipschutz for their encouragement and support in strengthening the analytical foundations of this argument. Any remaining problems are entirely the author's responsibility.

1. For a few notable exceptions, see Friedberg 2000; Leslie 1994; Hooks 1990; Lasswell 1970; Sarewitz 2000.

2. A comprehensive overview of the literature on the knowledge-based economy is impossible here but it is well-known that virtually all accounts associate this macroeconomic transformation to forces other than the military even if they acknowledge the Defense Department's role in much earlier phases of economic change. For a good overview, see Harris 2001; Hughes 2005.

3. As Jonathan B. Tucker has noted, "Despite the importance of this step [Nixon's decision], the political and bureaucratic factors that led to it are poorly understood." Tucker provides an important contribution to understanding some of the factors behind the president's decision but doesn't speak at all about the biological revolution or the conversion process, see Tucker 2002; Guillemin 2005.

4. For a fuller discussion of these important topics, see Hurt 2009.

5. For a good overview of the headlines, hearings, and developments in the 1960s, see Science Policy Research Division, Congressional Research Service, Library of Congress, *Genetic Engineering: Evolution of a Technological Issue,* report to the Subcommittee on Science, Research, and Development of the Committee on Science and Astronautics, U.S. House of Representatives, Ninety-Second Congress, 2nd sess., Serial W, November 1972 (Washington, D.C.: U.S. Government Printing Office, 1972).

6. Memorandum: Michael Guhin to Dr. Kissinger through Robert M. Behr, "Top Secret" Subject: Review Group Meeting (October 23, 1969) on NSSM 59: U.S. Policy on CW and BW, October 22, 1969, declassified/released on April 12, 2002, by NARA on the recommendation of the NSC under provisions of E.O. 12958, National Security Council Institutional (H) Files, Meeting Files (1969–74), folder NSC Meeting 11/18/69 CBW (NSSM 59) [1 of 2], box H-025, *Nixon Materials.*

7. "Top Secret" Memorandum: DuBridge to Dr. Henry A. Kissinger, October 22, 1969, Declassified by Executive Order 12958 May 1, 2001, in Volume III: BIOWAR, "The Nixon Administration's Decision to End U.S. Biological Warfare Programs," National Security Archive Electronic Briefing Book no. 58, edited by Robert A. Wampler, October 25, 2001, www2.gwu.edu/~nsarchiv/NSAEBB/NSAEBB58. (Hereafter cited as Wampler.)

8. Even after Nixon's 1969 decision, a large portion of the research on defense capabilities remained classified. According to *Science* magazine, of the 1,085 personnel employed at Fort Detrick, 430 redeployed scientists would continue to "do defensive biological warfare research on a classified basis" (Goldhaber 1970, 454). See also Garthoff 2000; Wise 2000.

9. Memorandum: DuBridge to Nixon, Subject: "Agenda for Meeting December 11–11:45 AM," December 10, 1969, White House Central Files, Science Files, folder 12-6-68 to 12-30-70, Box 2 of 5, *Nixon Materials.*

10. Memorandum: Flanigan to President, Subject: "Meeting with Dr. DuBridge, March 16, 1970, "Memorandum D" "Secret" declassified by E.O. 12958, Sec. 3.6 on March 4, 1998, White House Special Files, White House Central Files, Confidential Files, Box 15, *Nixon Materials.*

11. Memorandum: Douglas L. Hallett to Ray Price, Subject: "Possible Presidential Speech on Present Attack on Science & Technology," March 25, 1971, White House Central Files, Subject Files Sciences, folder SC, Box 1, *Nixon Materials.*

12. Buchanan stressed, "In addition, it could give us new problems with that same Catholic community we are trying to win." See Memorandum: Patrick J. Buchanan to John Ehrlichman, March 2, 1971, White House Central Files, Special Materials Office Files, folder White House–BW/CW [1969–1970], Box 4, *Nixon Materials.*

13. Memorandum: David to Peter Flanigan, Subject: "Agenda for Meeting with the

President," February 22, 1971, White House Central Files, Subject Files Sciences, *Nixon Materials*.

14. "Exploratory Research and Problem Assessment (ERPA) Program on the Social and Economic Consequences of R&D," White House Central Files, Subject Files Science, Edward E. David files, folder McAdams [3.2] Al McAdams-Materials from His Sojourn Here, Box 110, *Nixon Materials*.

15. Memorandum: McCracken to The President, April 26, 1971, White House Special Files, Special Materials Office Files, President's Handwriting Files, *Nixon Materials*.

16. These names refer to George Shultz, Peter Flanigan, and John Ehrlichman, respectively.

17. Memorandum: John D. Ehrlichman, Assistant to the President for Domestic Affairs to Secretary of Defense, Secretary of Agriculture, Secretary of Interior et al., Subject: "Domestic Council Study-Evaluation of New Technology Opportunities," [no date], White House Central Files, Subject Files Science, folder EX SC Sciences 1/1/71-[1 of 2], Box 1 of 5, *Nixon Materials*.

18. For one such example, see Letter: William M. Magruder to Mr. Niedziela, December 14, 1971, White House Central Files, Subject Files Science, folder EX Science, Box 2, *Nixon Materials*.

19. Memorandum: Donald K. Rice, Assistant Director Office of Management and Budget, and Edward E. David, Jr., Director Office of Science and Technology to George Schultz, Peter Flanigan, Peter Peterson, John Whitaker, Subject: "New Technology," July 1971, White House Central File, Domestic Council FG 6–15, folder EX FG 6–15 Domestic Council [12 of 27, July 1971—September 1971] TABC, Box 2, *Nixon Materials*.

20. Memorandum: David to Ehrlichman, Subject: "Panels on Technological Initiatives," July 22, 1971, White House Central Files, Special Materials Office Files, Edward E. David, Jr., folder White House–Title Folder vol. V [1971], Box 1, *Nixon Materials*.

21. The Domestic Council oversaw six task forces: "1) Technology Opportunities; 2) R&D Incentives; 3) Anti-Trust and Patent Policies; 4) Standards Practices; 5) Restrictive Labor Practices; 6) International Technology Transfer." See Memorandum: Magruder to Ehrlichman, Subject: "Evaluation of New Technology Opportunities Program," September 7, 1971, White House Central Files, Subject Files Sciences, Edward E. David files, folder Task Forces, Box 110, *Nixon Materials*.

22. Memorandum: David to Ehrlichman, Subject: "Panels on Technological Initiatives," July 22, 1971, White House Central Files, Special Materials Office Files, Edward E. David files, folder, White House–Title Folder vol. V [1971], Box 1, *Nixon Materials*.

23. Memorandum: Peter G. Peterson to The President, Subject: "Projecting the Future Development of the U.S.," July 12, 1971, White House Central Files, Confidential Files, folder BE Business/Economics [1971–74], Box 2, *Nixon Materials*.

24. The *National Journal* also identifies these officials, except it mistakenly omits David. See Barfield 1972, 756–765.

25. The cited summary is entitled "Organizing for More Effective Technology Management" and is part of a larger package attached to Memorandum: David to Frank Carlucci, John Ehrlichman, Peter Flanigan, William Magruder, Peter Peterson, Donald Rice, and George Shultz, Subject: "Meeting of the Executive Group on Technological Initiatives," November 24, 1971, White House Central Files, Special Materials Office Files, Edward E. David files, folder Miscellaneous NTO–lag [1971] [1 of 2], Box 116, *Nixon Materials*.

26. Apparently the administration was impressed by a May 1971 *Wall Street Journal* article promoting the idea of reprivatization as well as a recent speech given on this idea by Peter

Drucker. As a result, "Ehrlichman set up a study group with a lead of Dr. Martin Anderson, representatives of OMB and the Domestic Council to study what government can do to mobilize the voluntary or profit motive in restoring private enterprise into action against social concerns." See Memorandum: Todd R. Hullin to Staff Secretary, RE: "P 1768, *Wall Street Journal* Article 5/27/71 Reprivatization," July 13, 1971, White House Central Files, Domestic Council FG 6–15, folder EX FG 6–15 Domestic Council [12 of 27, July 1971—September 1971] TABC, Box 2, *Nixon Materials*. For a cite to the above-mentioned quotes, see "Exhibit II, Report on National Growth Policy, Suggested Outline," in Memorandum: John R. Price to Committee on National Growth Policy, Subject: "Staff Recommendations for Future Tasks," July 27, 1971, White House Central Files, Domestic Council Files FG 6–15, folder EX FG 6–15 Domestic Council [12 of 27, July 1971-September 1971] Tab C, Box 2, *Nixon Materials*.

27. Simon Ramo described his expectations for America in 1990 as follows: "Our hybrid economy, part free enterprise and part governmentally controlled, will take on a new form constituting a virtual Social-Industrial Complex by 1990, this developing government-business teaming greatly influenced by resource and technology." See Ramo 1972, 314.

28. Memorandum: Flanigan to John Ehrlichman, George Shultz, Peter Peterson, November 23, 1971, White House Central Files, Subject Files Sciences, folder EX SC Sciences 1/1/71-[1 of 2], Box 67, *Nixon Materials*.

29. Memorandum: DuBridge to President, Subject: "Agenda for Meeting December 11–11:45 AM," December 10, 1969, White House Central Files, Subject Files Science, folder 12–6–68 to 12–30–70, Box 2 of 5, *Nixon Materials*.

30. Memorandum: Flanigan to the President's File, August 22, 1970, White House Central Files, FG 209 (PSAC), folder [EX] FG 209 President's Science Advisory Committee 1/1/70–12/31/70, Box 1 of 1, *Nixon Materials*.

31. Memorandum: Flanigan to President, Subject: "Meeting with Dr. DuBridge," March 14, 1970, Memorandum D, p. 2, Declassified by E.O. 12958, Sec. 3.6 March 4, 1998, White House Special Files, White House Central Files, Confidential Files, Confidential Files Box 15, *Nixon Materials*.

32. Memorandum: DuBridge to President, Subject: "Issues Discussed with National Science Board," May 28, 1970, White House Central Files, Subject Files FG 182, folder EX FG 182–1 NSF [1969–1970], Box 2 of 2, *Nixon Materials*.

33. President Nixon, "Message to the Congress Transmitting Reorganization Plan No. 1 of 1973: Restructuring the Executive Office of the President," January 26, 1973, Public Papers.

34. Memorandum: Alan McAdams, Task Force II to W. M. Magruder, Subject: "Another Look at Technology Initiatives and Incentives to Innovation," November 20, 1971, White House Central Files, Special Material Office Files, Edward E. David files, folder Miscellaneous NTO-lag [1971] [1 of 2], Box 116, *Nixon Materials*.

35. Letter: to William Magruder, November 29, 1971, White House Central Files, Edward E. David, Jr., folder [3.2] Al McAdams-Materials from his sojourn here, Box 110, *Nixon Materials*.

36. Memorandum: Schlesinger to Flanigan, Subject: "Selection of new members of the National Science Board," October 28, 1969, White House Central Files, FG 182, folder EX FG 182–1 NSF [1969–1970], Box 2 of 2, *Nixon Materials*.

37. Memorandum: Stu Eizenstat, Jim McIntyre, Frank Press to The President, Subject: The Domestic Policy Review of Industrial Innovation, October 22, 1979, White House Central Files, folder: Industrial Innovation 5/24/77–10/22/79, Box: 6, President Jimmy Carter Library, Atlanta, Georgia.

38. For a history of the FLC, which identifies 1971 as the date of origin and the DOD as

its originator, see "Technology Transfer Desk Reference," Prepared by the Federal Laboratory Consortium for Technology Transfer (April 2004): http://www.federallabs.org/ContentObjects/Publications/T2_Desk_Reference.pdf.

39. *Domestic Technology Transfer: Issues and Options,* prepared by the Subcommittee on Science, Research, and Technology of the Committee on Science and Technology, U.S. House of Representatives, Ninety-Fifth Congress, 2nd sess., Serial CCC, Volume I, November 1978 (Washington: U.S. Government Printing Office, 1978): 85.

40. Memorandum: Shultz to Peterson, Re: "Adjustment Assistance," March 2, 1971, White House Central Files, Subject Files BE 6, folder EX BE 6 P-I-C-T [3 of 8] November 1970–August 1971, Box 67, *Nixon Materials.*

41. President Nixon, "Memorandum About Government Patent Policy," August 23, 1971, in *Public Papers.*

42. Memorandum: George P. Shultz, Director of OMB to President, Subject: "Revision of Statement of Government Patent Policy," June 22, 1971, White House Special Files, Special Materials Office Files, John Dean files, folder Patent Policy, Box 53, *Nixon Materials.*

43. The White House, "Fact Sheet: Patent Reform," Office of the White House Press Secretary, September 27, 1973, White House Central Files, Deputy Assistant for Media Files, folder Patents, Box Vice Presidential Papers 154, *Nixon Materials.*

44. "Report of the Subcommittee for Patent and Information Policy of the Government Domestic Review of Industrial Innovation," December 14, 1978, White House Central Files, Oversize Attachment no. 7330, Carter Library.

CHAPTER 3

Political Structures and the Making of U.S. Biotechnology

Steven P. Vallas, Daniel Lee Kleinman, and Dina Biscotti

It's molecular politics, not molecular biology, and I think we have to consider both, because a lot of science is at stake.
Anonymous speaker at 1976 NIH conference, as quoted by Wright (1994)

Since the early 1970s, discoveries in molecular biology and biochemistry have fueled the establishment and growth of multibillion-dollar industries in medical and agricultural biotechnology. They have prompted entirely new approaches to pharmaceutical research, agricultural production, and biomedical interventions, leading to such developments as genetically modified food, tissue engineering, and genetic therapy. In addition, developments in biomedicine and biotechnology have spawned new forms of industrial and economic organization, including the rise of new start-up firms founded by academic scientists. Academic departments have developed intimate connections with the biotech firms in their regions, as complex networks have emerged that are of great interest to venture capitalists and multinational pharmaceutical corporations (Powell, Koput, and Smith-Doerr 1996). At the same time, university technology transfer offices have expanded dramatically since 1980 (Owen-Smith 2003), as part of the feverish effort to commercialize research in the life sciences. These developments have prompted a host of changes in the nature of science, as traditional career structures are rapidly transformed, and in local and state economic policy, as regional economic planning associations have sought to emulate the development successes of Boston, San Francisco, and San Diego (www.biospace.com/biotechhotbeds.aspx; Pollack 2002). In short, there seems little doubt that a historically new structure of knowledge production has emerged in the advanced capitalist societies, with the United States playing the leading role.

In this chapter, we examine an aspect of the biotechnology phenomenon that has not received the attention it deserves: the role of federal policy in fostering the birth and development of the industry itself. Where most previous accounts assume that the biotechnology revolution was spontaneously generated by the confluence of scientific discovery and profit-seeking incentives, we contend that political structures and federal policy have played an equally critical but as yet insufficiently acknowledged role (see Lazonick, March, and Tulum 2008). Put simply, we contend that the explosive growth of the biotechnology industry was in many senses orchestrated and shaped from above as an expression of federal initiatives. Our argument builds on the analysis of Block (2008), who contends that a stealth industrial policy emerged in the United States as an implicit response to the economic challenges of the late 1970s. Since neoliberal ideology blocked any explicit development of national industrial policy similar to that found in Japan, a decentralized patchwork of federal structures emerged that served as a de facto industrial policy pursued through other means.

We develop this contention on the strength of three major considerations. First, especially during the early to middle 1980s, the U.S. Congress enacted a broad and consistent array of measures aimed precisely at fostering the commercialization of biomedical research. Thus the growth of biotech has to a substantial extent been an outgrowth of federal efforts to maintain the competitive position of the U.S. economy in an era of global competition. Second, reflecting these efforts, the federal government has provided critically important funding for almost all of the leading blockbuster drugs sold by the U.S. biotechnology industry. Third, in establishing a set of industry-oriented governance mechanisms as the basis for scientific research, the federal government has in effect opened up a legally defined space in which biotech firms can pursue their research relatively free from public constraints. In making this argument, we intend to advance theoretical and conceptual understandings of an emerging knowledge regime that has implicitly governed economic policy during an era of rapid change.[1]

We begin by critically reviewing the dominant strands of thinking that have developed in recent social scientific accounts of the knowledge economy and biotechnology in particular, drawing attention to some notable absences, or silences, in these accounts. Next, we review the emergence of biotechnology, beginning with accounts of the most proximate influences shaping biotech—scientific discovery and the pursuit of economic profit—and then consider the ways in which the state, lacking an explicit and coordinated industrial policy nevertheless shaped the development of biotech. We introduce data that reveal the importance of federal funding for the development of blockbuster drugs and use these data to show the role of the federal government as a critical benefactor of the key raw material—scientific knowledge—on which biotech relies. Finally, we evaluate the character of the governance structures the U.S. state has established to support the furtherance of the industry. We intend this analysis as part of a necessarily larger effort to open up research on the social, cultural, and political forces that have shaped the knowledge economy, in effect advancing what some scholars have begun to call the new "political sociology of science" (Frickel and Moore 2006).

Molecules, Markets, and Mentalities: Institutionalist Accounts

The knowledge regime that emerged from the ashes of World War II, which has often been associated with Vannevar Bush's plan for the National Science Foundation, established a novel set of arrangements between academic science and the wider political economy (Kleinman 1995). At its most basic level, this contract provided important elements of autonomy for university scientists, who for the first time were able to get high levels of funding for basic research.[2] While applied science would remain the province of the corporate world, federal support for basic research was provided with the understanding (subsequently called the linear model of research) that fundamental scientific discoveries would eventually find practical applications downstream, in turn contributing to innovation and economic growth. The ability of Bush and his colleagues to win support for this approach was in no small part due to the successes shown by science during the wartime mobilization against Germany and Japan (Kevles 1987; Kleinman 1995). In fact, the establishment of support for basic science within the NSF and other mission agencies of the federal government like DOD, DOE, and DOA owed much to the political and ideological imperatives of the Cold War era with its emphasis on national security.

This postwar arrangement was variously interpreted by social scientists from Robert Merton to Michael Polanyi, with much debate over the norms that actually governed the scientific community and the tensions implicit within it.[3] Yet by the late 1970s, events had begun to develop that would overturn the postwar practices and the institutional ensemble on which they were based. The question, of course, is how these structural shifts developed, what forces prompted their emergence, and what their social and economic consequences have been for the nature of scientific work and the structure of knowledge production more generally.

Until now, observers have only obliquely attended to the importance of the federal government in the development of the biotech industry. The most prominent discussions of biotech growth have been advanced by a number of social scientists working in several overlapping fields, whose scholarship has typically drawn on theories of regional economic development, institutionalist accounts of organizational structures, and analysis of the rise of networks as a major form of economic organization.

Especially influential has been the work of such social scientists as Piore and Sabel (1984), Saxenian (1994), and Powell and his collaborators (Powell 1990; Powell, Koput, and Smith-Doerr, 1996; Owen-Smith and Powell 2001). Piore and Sabel's *The Second Industrial Divide* anticipated the demise of the Fordist mass production paradigm, arguing that centralized, vertically integrated firms were destined to give way to a new organizational logic called flexible specialization. Their argument was that regionally agglomerated clusters of smaller, flexibly organized firms will increasingly provide the functional equivalent of the large Fordist firm, yet with substantially greater dynamism and creative potential than the older arrangements allowed. So advantageous was this new technological paradigm that large firms have been compelled to emulate the example of the upstart networks, allying with them and spinning off whole divisions as a means of attaining higher levels of flexibility.

In a related vein, Saxenian's *Regional Advantage* applies a similar theoretical perspective to a comparative analysis of two important regional economies—Silicon Valley and Route 128 in Massachusetts. Examining the development of the information technology industry in these two regions, she finds sharp differences in the industrial systems they developed. Comparing each region's ability to cope with economic change and uncertainty, Saxenian contends that the newer, more flexible culture of innovation in Silicon Valley better equipped it to innovate and grow in the digital era than Boston, which had a more rigid, centralized style of operations.

Arguably the surge of economic growth shown by the biomedical industries corresponds very nicely to the theory of flexible specialization. Biotech firms, often embedded within networks, have emerged as an implicit alternative to the rigidity of large pharmaceutical firms. When these smaller firms collaborate with the Fordist structures, they extend the larger firms' innovative capacities beyond what Fordist structures alone could achieve. Indeed, so successful are these networks of small, flexible firms that they sometimes outperform their larger rivals.

Precisely this point has repeatedly emerged in the numerous empirical studies contributed by Walter Powell and his colleagues (see Powell and Owen-Smith 1998, 2002; and Powell et al. 2005). In their view (see also Kenney 1986b; Kenney and Florida 1993), the key characteristics of dedicated biotech firms (DBFs) are their reliance on the network form of economic organization, their spatially agglomerated clustering, and their delicate interweaving of the diverse participants' economic activity (e.g., through numerous alliances and partnerships between DBFs and big pharma).

Indeed, in Powell's view, the huge success of the biotech industry can largely be explained by its reliance on the network form of economic activity. Drawing on his earlier research on networks (1990), he contends that science-intensive industries like biotechnology can no longer rely on hierarchy as a model that can provide access to valuable scientific expertise. Given the uncertainty that surrounds the course of scientific discovery, firms cannot amass their own stores of scientific talent in-house but must instead seek to become embedded within the networks of research activity that have emerged around large research universities (Powell, Koput and Smith-Doerr 1996; Powell et al. 2005). Such networks incorporate not only DBFs and big pharmaceutical firms, but myriad other entities as well, including members of academic departments, university technology transfer offices, government laboratories and institutes, medical schools, and legal firms with expertise in intellectual property. The network ties that result take on a wide variety of forms, including partnerships and alliances, outsourcing of clinical trials to contract research organizations, licensing of intellectual property, and even direct corporate investment in academic programs.

Exploring the consequences of network embeddedness for subsequent firm survival and growth, Powell and his colleagues demonstrate that the nature and strength of network ties significantly predict the performance of biotech firms, and that network dynamics give rise over time to a complex ecology of scientific expertise. This emergent terrain increasingly defies the traditional institutional boundaries that characterized the earlier social organization of knowledge production, such as those between public and private, basic and applied, or academic and commercial research. This is why Powell and Owen-Smith conclude that "academic and commercial life scientists are now members of a single technological community," sharing kindred normative orientations, patterns of mobility, and prestige hierarchies (Powell and Owen-Smith 2002, 107).

It is true that Powell and his colleagues comment on the significance of legislative and political influences for the development of the knowledge economy from time to time. They do discuss the 1980 Bayh-Dole Act, which requires recipients of federal grants to consider patenting scientific discoveries made with federal research funding and provides powerful incentives for the commercial licensing of intellectual property. However, their work generally treats such federal legislation as holding only secondary importance (Colyvas and Powell 2006, 313) and gives much greater explanatory weight to organizational and institutional influences such as the shape of social networks, the capacity for commercialization on the part of particular regions and organizations, and organizational support for creative, interdisciplinary work.

This gap is especially apparent in Owen-Smith and colleagues' (2002) comparative analysis of the U.S. and Western European biomedical industries. In accounting for the differences between the regionally agglomerated network form in the United States and the more organizationally centralized structure in Europe, they assign little or no importance to political institutions, traditions, or strategies. According to them, it is not the state but the "social organization of innovative labor" that shapes the new knowledge regimes, despite the fact that their work reveals the National Institutes of Health (NIH) to be a core, central actor in their network models of the U.S. innovation system.

Equally noteworthy is a kindred series of empirical analyses by Lynne G. Zucker and her colleagues (Zucker, Darby, and Armstrong 2002; Zucker, Darby, and Brewer 1998). Their approach again uses a broadly institutionalist perspective, stressing the specific social ties and stocks of knowledge that develop within particular organizational and regional contexts. However their work also suggests that the commercialization of scientific knowledge depends on the informal practices through which tacit knowledge is shared and on the capacity of biotech firms to establish collaborative ties to prominent academic scientists. To measure the role played by these factors, Zucker and colleagues use citation data that capture the frequency with which commercial scientists collaborate with "star" academic scientists. Their findings indicate that the growth of biotech companies, their success in producing influential patents, and their ability to attract venture capital all depend on the knowledge stocks, network ties, and innovative capacities established among the scientists within particular geographic regions (Zucker, Darber, and Armstrong 2002; Zucker, Darby, and Armstrong 2002).

There are subtle differences between Zucker's research and that of Powell and his colleagues. Significantly, the former pays somewhat greater attention to the empirical significance of federal (especially NSF) funding made available to particular regional networks, over and above the influence of collaborative activities. But, like the work of Powell and his collaborators, here too the emphasis is on the social, organizational, and institutional ties that shape the capacity to innovate. At their core, both approaches employ ecological tropes to make sense of scientific innovation, and both construe knowledge production in largely organicist or evolutionary terms. Viewing innovation largely from below, these perspectives give short shrift to federal political influences and policy strategies. We wish to redress this analytical imbalance.

Revisiting the Emergence of Biotechnology: Governmental Impact

It is possible to trace the social and intellectual roots of the biotechnology industry as far back as the establishment of the National Cancer Institute in 1937, the bio-chemical research of Linus Pauling in the 1940s, and the discovery of the structure of DNA by Franklin, Watson, and Crick in the 1950s. But it was not until the early 1970s, amid a welter of significant breakthroughs, that the scientific foundations of molecular genetics began to emerge. Of critical importance was the research of the inventors of DNA cloning, Herbert Boyer and Stanley Cohen. In the 1970s, Boyer determined how to use restriction enzymes to cut DNA apart chemically at specific, known sites. Together, Cohen and Boyer were able to cut a plasmid—a small circular piece of bacterial DNA—and insert DNA from another organism into the plasmid. This technique, now termed recombinant DNA (rDNA), is the technical foundation for the biotechnology industry.

The excitement these developments generated stemmed in large part from the broadening realization that they embodied new possibilities for medical innovation, unlike those the pharmaceutical and chemical industries had relied on throughout the twentieth century (Henderson, Orsenigo, and Pisano 1999). Until then, big pharma had used large-scale screening methods to test slowly a wide range of compounds for desirable effects. By contrast, recombinant DNA techniques promised to give scientists far more control, allowing them to modify, augment, and delete genetic content to yield new molecular entities (NMEs) with potentially therapeutic effects.

State support of the emerging field was quickly reflected in federal funding priori-ties. Seminal studies conducted by Boyer and Cohen and by Paul Berg were among a small handful of molecular genetics projects conducted with NIH and NSF support in the early 1970s. By 1976, however, NIH support for this type of research had greatly expanded, funding 123 projects in this nascent field (Rabinow 1996). Mindful of the potential of rDNA for cancer research, NIH officials established a separate program for research into oncogenes, which when mutated or expressed at high levels can turn a normal cell into a tumor cell. This research enjoyed more than $100 million in funding by 1987. Established researchers began aligning their research proposals in this direction, and new investigators came to see molecular biological cancer research as "the research line of choice." Thus academic scientists, emerging biotechnology firms, and major pharmaceutical companies were encouraged to jump on this scientific bandwagon (Fujimura 1988).

Efforts to commercialize discoveries in molecular genetics proceeded slowly at first. Initial steps were taken by Berkeley Scientific Laboratories (BSL, itself partially funded by NIH and NSF grants), Cetus (which grew out of BSL), and eventually Genentech, founded in 1976 by Boyer and venture capitalist Robert Swanson (Vettel 2006, 192–193; Rohrbaugh 2005). In 1982 Genentech became the first biotechnology company to launch a commercial product, human insulin.[4] The company eventually provided the model that most dedicated biotech firms would pursue: first, create a start-up to capitalize on publicly funded discoveries made by academic scientists; second, locate venture capital or government funding to develop and test biomedical applications of the discovery; and finally, license the rights to a large pharmaceutical company for production, marketing, and distribution. Successful DBFs are those which have been able to hit on multiple drug applications and thereby enjoy several licensing streams.

Clearly, this model worked well for the biotechnology industry. An increasing proportion of the most successful blockbuster drugs are biotechnology products, as opposed to traditional pharmaceuticals. The largest biotech corporations, such as Amgen, have easily grown to rival pharmaceutical firms in their sales and market reach. Yet it would be erroneous to interpret the emergence of this model and the industry it sustains as merely the product of scientific knowledge and entrepreneurial activity. Such an interpretation has two pernicious effects. First, it encourages social science analysts to narrowly conform to the same economistic coordinates as those that often lead business analysts to celebrate of the "miracle" of biotech. Second, so narrow a view implicitly privileges the most proximate events involved in the emergence of biotech and fails to recognize the larger political forces that conjured biotech into being.

In the following section, we identify three analytically distinct reasons to conclude that state intervention has played a formative role in the emergence and growth of the biotechnology industry.

First, at the broadest level much of the institutional infrastructure that enabled biotech to thrive was brought into being through an array of federal legislation crafted during the 1980s. Prompted by concern about the competitive position of the United States within the global economy, these legislative measures explicitly aimed to use scientific knowledge to enhance that position. Second, our review of the available evidence on the current best-selling biotech drugs in the United States reveals that almost all of these drugs were discovered and/or tested with substantial federal support. Third, analysis of the institutions that have governed the emerging biotechnology industry indicates that these governance structures—especially intellectual property provisions and ethical controls—were designed to actively foster the ascent of U.S. biotechnology.

The Making of the Knowledge Economy: Bayh-Dole and Beyond

To the extent that the state's role in biotech has been acknowledged by analysts concerned with the knowledge economy, attention has been focused largely on the 1980 Bayh-Dole Act (formally, the Patent and Trademark Law Amendment Act). As noted, this legislation enables federal grantees (including individual scientists, universities, and corporations) to patent and license discoveries resulting from publicly funded research. As Jasanoff (2005, 235) observes, this marked a decisive shift in the previous knowledge regime, for it "changed the longstanding presumption that publicly funded work could not be privately owned and exploited."

The actual consequences of Bayh-Dole have been much debated, with some recent analysts casting doubt on its centrality in altering the intellectual property landscape

(Mowery et al. 2004; Henderson, Jaffe, and Trajtenberg 1998; Sampat, Mowery, and Ziedonis, n.d.; Berman 2008).[5] Bayh-Dole alone was not responsible for constructing the U.S. knowledge economy, but it embodied an attitude held by a state-led coalition of businesspeople, science policy advocates, and university leaders. These elites advocated the use of scientific knowledge to strengthen the competitive position of the United States in the global economy and aimed to piece together an ensemble of federal initiatives to realize this goal (Wright 1994; Slaughter and Rhoades 1996, 2004; Office of Technology Assessment 1984).

A useful window into the concerns of members of this coalition can be found in the Office of Technology Assessment (OTA) study, *Commercial Biotechnology: An International Analysis* (1984). This 600-page report contains an ambitious comparative analysis of the characteristics of the global biotechnology industry and reveals some of the thinking that shaped public policy during the 1980s. The study's authors viewed biotechnology as critical to the global position of the U.S. economy but saw the industry as threatened by rising competition from Japan and Western Europe. The report, therefore, called for enhanced public financing of R&D, policies to promote capital formation (such as tax credits), and stronger support for the training of scientists. A distinguishing feature of the U.S. biotech industry, the presence of small innovative biotech firms, was singled out as holding particular strategic value to the industry and worthy of dedicated public support. Of special concern to the report's authors was the need to reverse a worrisome trend in funding for the life sciences, which had declined in the preceding years.

That this report's outlook closely reflected federal policy at that time can be seen through a review of the legislative initiatives enacted by Congress during the 1980s. Table 3.1 summarizes seven major instances of federal legislation enacted during this decade (often with bipartisan support) that have bearing on the life sciences.[6] These initiatives established an infrastructure to encourage the commercialization of scientific research, or in the words of Henderson and Smith (2002), an "implied duty to commercialize." As mentioned above, the Bayh-Dole Act enabled universities, nonprofit organizations, and small businesses to gain proprietary rights to publicly funded research. The Stevenson-Wydler Technology Innovation Act, variously amended in the 1980s, moved aggressively to encourage the transfer of scientific discoveries made in university and government laboratories into private hands. It obliged federal agencies to create technology transfer offices (TTOs), which establish intellectual property rights and provide monetary incentives to scientists who make commercially relevant discoveries. TTOs also initiated a set of arrangements that eventually led to cooperative research and development agreements (or CRADAs), which enable commercial firms to use the resources of federal laboratories. Equally important was the Small Business Innovation Development Act, which draws funds from multiple mission agencies of the U.S. executive branch and expressly seeks to increase the share of federal R&D outlays flowing to small businesses. Small Business Innovation Research (SBIR) funding has been instrumental in the growth of countless biotech firms.

Finally, the Orphan Drug Act (ODA) has played an especially significant role in the development of the biotechnology industry. It not only provides expanded patent

Table 3.1 Legislation Fostering Entrepreneurial Activity Within Biomedical Research, 1980–1990

Year	Measure	Provisions	Consequences
1980	Bayh-Dole Act	Enabled universities and nonprofits to patent publicly funded discoveries	Encouraged university-industry relations Fostered "academic capitalism"
1980	Stevenson-Wydler Act	Established and funded technology transfer offices within federal departments Authorized CRADAs Instituted mechanisms for transferring technology from federal to commercial entities	Legitimated the commercialization of federal research Opened up commercial access to federal laboratories and personnel Established mechanisms for private licensing of intramural research
1982	Small Business Innovation Development Act	Established monetary incentives for the commercialization of federal research Established an interagency system of grants to fund research by small businesses	Incentivized entrepreneurial science, supported small firms
1983	Orphan Drug Act	Provided funding and tax credits for research on diseases affecting <200,000 patients Fast-tracked applications for FDA approval Provided exclusive rights to market orphan drugs	Provided certainty and exclusivity for markets involving small patient populations
1984	Trademark Clarification Act; Correlative Federal Regulations	Extended trademark protections to new forms of intellectual property (e.g., microchips) Issued regulations governing the licensing of federally owned discoveries	Strengthened intellectual property regime and attendant returns
1986	Federal Technology Transfer Act	Amended Stevenson-Wydler: defined technology transfer as the duty of federal agencies	Further emphasized the value of commercialization
1989	National Competitiveness Technology Transfer Act	Amended Stevenson-Wydler: extended technology transfer duties to contractor-operated laboratories	Extended the commercialization emphasis into contract research organizations

protection for discoveries that address "orphan" (genetic or rare) diseases but also gives labs and companies making these discoveries generous tax credits, dedicated funding for research, and a fast track path to FDA approval for drugs used in small patient populations. Indeed, the ODA promoted the development of biotech drugs that would not have seen the light of day without government support.

Interestingly, some of these orphan drugs have turned out to be blockbusters. Genzyme's most successful product, Cerezyme, is an orphan drug, the development of which benefited from the provisions of the ODA. The substance accounted for $839 million in revenues in 2004, $932 million in 2005, and $1,010 million in 2006 (Lazonick, March, and Tulum 2008, 30). As Lazonick and colleagues note, "For leading companies such as Genentech, Biogen, Idec, and Serono, orphan drugs are more than 90 percent of their product revenue" (Lazonick, March, and Tulum 2008, 31). When taken as a whole, the pattern of state intervention, including the seven pieces of legislation listed in Table 3.1, suggests that the knowledge economy did not spontaneously emerge from the bottom up but was prompted by a top-down *stealth industrial policy*: government and industry leaders simultaneously advocated government intervention to foster the development of the biotechnology industry and argued hypocritically that government should "let the free market work."

Federal Scientific Knowledge Policy and Production

The legislative measures depicted in Table 3.1 were part of a broader shift in U.S. industrial policy that dramatically expanded federal support for the life sciences. Although federal funding for the NIH had been relatively stagnant for the decade preceding 1985 (much as OTA lamented), the next fifteen years provided bountiful government support. While the NIH share of all federal R&D was about 12 percent in 1985, by 2000 that proportion had doubled. The NIH research budget accounted for nearly half of all nondefense R&D outlays in the United States, up from 30 percent in 1985 (Collins 2004, 86–87).

These numbers are, of course, aggregate figures, and they say little about the importance of federal funding in the development of successful biotechnology products. Perhaps the best way to explore the significance of federal research and funding support for the commercialization of biotechnology products is to trace the development of the leading blockbuster therapeutics in recent years.[7] This is a highly complex endeavor, not only because it is extremely difficult to link basic research to subsequent applications but also because the strategic significance of federal funding is poorly measured in simple dollar terms. With these caveats in mind, Table 3.2 presents data on the fifteen U.S.-developed biotechnology drugs classified as blockbusters by the industry, each having sales exceeding $1 billion in 2006. Excluded are four drugs with U.S. sales exceeding $1 billion in 2006 that were developed by foreign-based firms. Table 3.2 divides federal support for these fifteen U.S.-developed biotechnology blockbusters in terms of (1) significant federal support for drug discovery, development, and clinical trials; (2) significant federal support for clinical trials only; and (3) little or no federal support.[8]

Table 3.2 Federal Support for Leading Biotechnology Therapeutics (2006 sales exceeding $1 Billion)

Product	Company	2006 sales[a]	Indication	Role of Federal Support
Significant Federal Support for Drug Discovery, Development, and Clinical Trials:				
Epogen, Procrit, Eprex	Amgen, Kirin, J&J	$6.10	Anemia	NIH funding leads to patent at Columbia University
Enbrel	Amgen, Wyeth, Takeda	$4.40	Rheumatoid arthritis	NIH funding leads to patent at SW Texas Medical Center
Neupogen, Neulasta	Amgen, Kirin	$4.00	Neutropenia	NIH research for initial development (NIH licensed patent rights)
Rituxan/Mab Thera	Biogen, Idec, Genentech, Roche	$3.90	Non-Hodgkins Lymphoma	NIH (SBIR) funding, leading to IPO of Idec (now Biogen-Idec)
Remicade	J&J, Schering-Plough, Tanabe	$3.60	Crohn's disease,	NIH funding for research at NYU
Avonex	Biogen Idec	$1.70	MS, arthritis	NIH funding and market protection under Orphan Drug Act
Syagis	Medimmune	$1.10	RSV infection	NIH research, plus extensive SBIR funding
Cerezyme	Genzyme	$1.00	Gaucher's disease	NIH research, plus market protection under Orphan Drug Act
Significant Federal Support for Clinical Trials:				
Herceptin	Genentech, Roche	$3.10	Breast cancer	Corporate support (Revlon) for research; federal support for testing
Avastin	Genentech, Roche	$2.40	Cancer	Corporate support for development; significant federal support for clinical testing
Humira	Abbott	$2.00	Autoimmune diseases	Limited federal support for development; significant federal support for clinical testing
Humalog	Eli Lilly	$1.30	Diabetes	Limited federal support for development; extensive federal support for clinical testing
Betaseron/Betaferon	Bayer Schering	$1.20	Multiple sclerosis	Federal support for testing; market protection under Orphan Drug Act
Little or No Federal Support:				
Aranesp	Amgen	$4.10	Anemia	Modification of Epogen to gain patent approval
Erbitux	ImClone, Bristol-Myers, Merck, KGaA	$1.10	Cancer	No evidence of federal support found

a. *Source: Nature Biotechnology* 25 (2007), 380–382. Published online: 3 April 2007. Accessed June 2009.

The data reveal a number of important points. First, in thirteen of these fifteen cases of biotechnology blockbuster drugs, the record shows highly significant levels of federal support for initial drug discovery and preclinical development or for clinical trials to obtain drug safety and efficacy data. Only in the cases of Aranesp and Erbitux did federal support play little or no role in drug development. In most of the cases where substantial government support was found (eight out of thirteen), federal money directly funded discovery of the therapeutic. In five of these eight discovery cases, the federal government funded research conducted in academic labs and university medical centers and even sometimes in commercial firms. In the remaining three of these eight discovery cases (Cerezyme, Synagis, and Neulasta), the federal role was even more direct: the key discoveries were made by NIH scientists working in government labs. Proprietary rights to these federally funded discoveries were transferred to established pharmaceutical companies and entrepreneurial biotech firms, using a range of generous government-supported means of technology transfer.

Indeed, since the blockbuster drugs broken down in Table 3.2 have been instrumental in shaping the market position of the leading biotech firms, we would argue that the very landscape of the biotechnology industry bears the mark of federally supported research. Thus Biogen achieved its market position on the sales of Avonex, a therapeutic for multiple sclerosis (MS) that was underwritten by seventy-seven federal grants and protected by the Orphan Drug Act. The success of Idec (now merged with Biogen) was an outgrowth of generous federal funding (over $1 million in SBIR funding) that was used to develop Rituxan, a cancer drug that fueled the growth of both Idec and Genentech. And Amgen, currently the largest U.S. biotech firm, gained its leading position in two ways. First, it built on federally funded research that was conducted at the University of Chicago. Second, it shrewdly licensed Columbia University's Axel patents, on the strength of which the firm marketed the anemia drug Epogen and its successor drugs, which provided Amgen's revenue cornerstones (*Nature Biotechnology* 2007, 380).[9]

Perhaps most striking of all, however, is the case of the biotech company Genzyme, which we considered briefly in the previous section and describe here in detail because it epitomizes the tensions and contradictions embodied in the new knowledge regime. Founded by academic scientists at Tufts who worked at a research center that performed contract work for NIH, Genzyme was initially a small partnership of academics who supplied research materials to NIH in connection with ongoing federal research on Gaucher's disease, a debilitating and often fatal condition that prevents the body from breaking down fats in the bloodstream. As far back as 1965, NIH scientists had traced the etiology of Gaucher's to a particular enzymatic deficiency; by 1983 they had achieved success with the use of a placenta-derived enzyme as a therapeutic. The Tufts scientists, who had refined the NIH method for harvesting the enzyme from human placentas, established a for-profit partnership to capitalize on the NIH research. Using provisions of the Orphan Drug Act, they gained exclusive rights to the NIH-discovered enzyme, conducted clinical trials with federal funding, and received FDA approval for the drug in 1985. The resulting sales have positioned Genzyme to become the fifth largest biotech firm in the world. The company's success showed that the Orphan Drug Act could pave the way for wildly successful growth, even for firms targeting small-population diseases (OTA 1992; Brownlee 2004; Heuser 2009; Lazonick, March, and Tulum 2008).

Genzyme's success also had political repercussions. So extravagant was the company's pricing of Ceredase and Cerezyme, with annual per-patient costs that ranged upward of $350,000 or more, that news stories of the cost burden eventually prompted congressional committees to hold hearings on the public obligations of firms that commercialize federally funded research. The results are revealing. After thorough examination of the issue, the Office of Technology Assessment found that NIH had little information on the drugs it had helped bring into being. Furthermore, although NIH funding was critical for the development of forty-seven leading pharmaceutical and biotech drugs, the institute had retained licensing rights to only four of these drugs. Although federal law authorized NIH to exercise march-in rights (i.e., the ability to invoke federal privileges if access to drugs was not made available on reasonable terms), NIH had never exercised these rights and exerted no leverage over the private sector to ensure public access to drugs developed with taxpayer support. Congress sought to intervene (e.g., by potentially setting limits on lifetime profits of orphan drugs), but these efforts came to naught, owing to pressure from pharmaceutical firms.

Governing Biotech

Thus far we have argued that the growth of the biotechnology industry has been legislatively induced, and that federal policy in effect made the state a central producer of the scientific knowledge on which the industry relies. Beyond subsidizing product development and facilitating the production of scientific expertise, the federal government also constructed a robust regulatory infrastructure that establishes intellectual property rights and sets the sociolegal boundaries in which biomedical research can be performed. In this section, we briefly review the development of this regulatory infrastructure to show its significance for the growth of the biotechnology industry.

A crucial pivot in the construction of the intellectual property regime for the development of biotechnology was the U.S. Supreme Court's decision in *Diamond v. Chakrabarty*. In the early 1970s, General Electric microbiologist Ananda Chakrabarty sought patent protection for a microorganism he had genetically engineered to break down hydrocarbons in petroleum. Chakrabarty's goal was an oil spill eating "bug." The U.S. Patent and Trademark Office (USPTO) rejected his request for a patent on the basis that U.S. law did not extend property rights to living organisms. GE appealed the decision, and the U.S. Court of Appeals sided with the company. This decision was affirmed by the U.S. Supreme Court in 1980. The court ruled that the organism developed by Chakrabarty was a product of the scientist's creativity, imagination, and initiative and was not a product of nature, and it was therefore eligible for patent protection. This legal decision has proved foundational for biotechnology patents and crucial for the industry's development.

Beyond this landmark court decision, there is, of course, the often touted role of the Bayh-Dole Act, to which we have already alluded. While there is debate about how decisively Bayh-Dole altered preexisting trends, there is little doubt that the act greatly expanded industry's ability to capture intellectual property. Again, as we have noted, this law permits universities and small businesses to retain title to inventions developed as a result of federally funded research. If ad hoc efforts and the work of government managers in bureaucratic crevices pushed intellectual policy protection practices in this direction, the legislation is, nevertheless, worthy of attention since the prehistory of Bayh-Dole points to the role of state managers who worked not as part of a clear and well-developed industrial policy agenda but instead as bureaucratic agents who shared a similar normative orientation toward intellectual property management (Berman 2008).

A second aspect of the regulatory infrastructure in which biotech has come to operate concerns the federal protocols that have established the safety and ethical boundaries in which biomedical research could proceed (Jasanoff 2005; Wright 1994). In the mid-1970s, after years of internal government debate about the potential environmental, health, and military implications of advances in molecular biology, government officials solicited input from academic scientists to help formulate a governing framework to address public health, safety, and ethical concerns. Although the dominant historical narrative is that academic scientists initiated efforts to regulate recombinant DNA research, Shelley Hurt's chapter in this volume provides a detailed history which shows that government officials also provided the impetus for these efforts.

Paul Berg, a leading figure in molecular genetics, was invited to chair the National Academy of Sciences (NAS) Committee on Recombinant DNA and, in 1975, convened a historic conference at Asilomar in California at which participants drafted a set of strict guidelines. In the view of the scientists involved, rDNA research posed a distinctive set of concerns because it involves the creation of novel genetic combinations that conceivably might be unethical or dangerous. After soliciting input from scientists across the country, federal agency guidelines largely came to mirror the recommendations made at Asilomar. In 1976 the NIH created the Recombinant DNA Advisory Committee (RAC) that established, in a tentative manner, clear, consistent, and cautious boundaries concerning permissible lines of research.

By the late 1970s, however, pressures arose that moved federal regulation in a different direction. Although environmental groups and local municipalities raised concerns about the public safety implications of genetic engineering, U.S. scientists' anxieties came from a very different source. The sheer pace and momentum of scientific investigation around the world, coupled with growing awareness of the economic potential of molecular genetics, left U.S. scientists increasingly fearful that unduly restrictive guidelines would marginalize their position internationally. Sensing the latent power of rDNA research and aware of an intense lobbying effort by molecular scientists, their universities, and biotech corporations (Wright 1994, chap. 6), NIH's RAC began to limit the breadth of its guidelines. This prefigured an important political shift, indicating a "subtle change in the discursive practices established at the Asilomar conference" (Wright 1994, 275).

This erosion of the initial restrictions on rDNA research was evident in two respects. First, "the burden of proof was being shifted from scientists, to show that genetic engineering was safe, to the public, to show that it was dangerous" (Wright

1994, 275). Second, as the new approach unfolded, it attached less and less importance to the distinctive *process* that genetic engineering used to create its products, and increasingly viewed biotechnology using much the same criteria that were applied to any other industry's *product* (Jasanoff 2005, 45–52). Pivotal to this shift was the conclusion, eventually embraced, even by advocates of a strict regulatory regime, that the economic potential of the biotechnology industry was simply too great to impede (Wright 1994, 277). Again, concern for the competitive position of the United States in the global economy countermanded the Asilomar guidelines, blocked congressional action, and led the federal government to institute a governance structure that was as friendly as possible to the nascent biotechnology industry.

In sharp contrast to European policy, the U.S. federal government adopted a knowledge regime that limits the commercialization of biotechnology products only where there is positive evidence of likely harm (Kleinman and Kinchy 2003; Kleinman, Delborne, and Autry 2008). In so doing, the state has, in effect, constructed a broader and far more generous terrain on which U.S. biotechnology can operate than most of its European competitors enjoy. The value of the outcome to industry is nicely captured in a comment made by George B. Rathmann, former CEO of Amgen. When asked about the impact of federal guidelines for rDNA research, he said, "To my mind, you can attribute to them the big success of DNA [research] in the U.S., because [they] gave people the comfort level they needed."[10] That comfort, we would say, came not only from the certainty that an established policy provides in a nascent, highly complex field but also from the knowledge that biotechnology firms were operating in a regulatory environment that imposed few constraints on commercial development.

Conclusion

The biotechnology industry has attracted a growing body of social scientific scholarship focused on the distinctive form of social organization that characterizes the industry. Although valuable in shedding light on the character and function of the biotechnology industry, this work has paid scant attention to an important part of the equation: the numerous points at which the industry has depended on government interventions in the course of its development.

Seeking to redress this imbalance in the literature, we emphasize three factors that we believe provide empirical warrant for a political interpretation of the industry's formation. First, we suggest that the institutional infrastructure in which the industry has grown was conjured through a wave of legislation enacted in the 1980s, which actively conscripted the life sciences in the effort to enhance the competitive position of the U.S. economy. This wave of legislation, which included but was by no means limited to Bayh-Dole, created the legal and institutional apparatus needed to foster the private appropriation of publicly funded research. Especially in light of the massive shifts in federal R&D that were involved, it is difficult to avoid the conclusion that the knowledge economy was not born but made.

Second, on examining the discovery and development of the leading, blockbuster biotechnology drugs sold in the United States—drugs that have elevated the manufacturers into the front ranks of U.S. biotech firms—we find that federal support has played an indispensable role in the development of the most profitable drugs in the industry. It is important, of course, to acknowledge that industry conducts and aggressively funds its own internal R&D efforts and invests much in basic discovery and clinical development. Yet supplementing these purely private investments has been a ready supply of scientific knowledge that has been either funded or actually produced by federal agencies but then appropriated for private ends on the basis of the legal and administrative mechanisms adopted in the 1980s. Whether through such mechanisms as federally established partnerships between government labs and private industry (CRADAs), funding made available under Small Business Innovation Research grants, the various advantages provided under the Orphan Drug Act, or through other mechanisms, the federal government has established institutions and incentives that create and maintain "an implied duty to commercialize" (Henderson and Smith 2002).

A final point in our argument concerns the evolution of a federal structure for the governance of science. Partly owing to space limitations, we have excluded from our analysis any discussion of the FDA, which has undergone important structural changes that impinge on biotech since the early 1990s. Instead, we have focused on the processes through which an industry-oriented intellectual property and safety regime has emerged. From one point of view, it might be said that what is striking in this story is the withdrawal of state intervention from direct industry regulation. We argue instead that what is notable in the evolution of U.S. science governance mechanisms has been the use of political authority to create the broadest, most industry-friendly space in which molecular genetics can take place. Following *Chakrabarty,* patents came to be filed on living organisms. Now, in the post-Asilomar world of bioscience regulation, the burden of proof is on the public to justify any proposed limits on the conduct of biotechnology research. Moreover, ethical, environmental, and social equity concerns have been largely peripheralized.[11]

This argument has broached a number of additional points, which could only be touched on in the foregoing analysis. In our brief discussion of Ceredase and Cerezyme, the Genzyme-owned treatments for Gaucher's disease, we noted a key aspect of the existing knowledge regime that warrants much closer study than this chapter can provide: the role of the state as consumer or procurer of biotechnology products. It is obviously of vital concern to the biotechnology industry that there be constant or growing demand for its products, and at prices that will sustain generous profits. Yet the principle that has implicitly informed federal support for the life sciences generally, and has repeatedly been invoked by the industry on its own behalf, has been the assumption that virtually unlimited funding for health research necessarily redounds to the benefit of the public at large. The usual incantations invoked by industry in support of this assumption (concerning the hundreds of millions of dollars invested per successful drug, the long and uncertain lead time required before an FDA approved drug can be sold, etc.) are not so much false as misleading, especially when applied to drugs whose discovery and development have been heavily subsidized by the federal government. How do big drug company profits and consumer drug prices contribute to the public good? Some members of Congress have raised this concern and have insisted that legislation include clauses (march-in rights) that would allow the federal government to ensure federal grantees provide reasonable public access to their products. In practice, however, the industry's ideological ammunition has been so powerful that such clauses have almost never been invoked, and public health insurance programs such as Medicare and Medicaid have routinely paid what are in effect predatory prices for drugs that have been created at the taxpayers' expense. The effect is to subsidize industry twice: once by socializing the cost of a key raw material (scientific knowledge) and a second time by agreeing to pay what are in truth state-enforced monopoly prices that produce windfall profits—all in the name of economic competitiveness.[12] Here again, we see the implicit yet vital role played by governmental intervention, obscured by a powerful form of discursive alchemy that defines private ownership as uniquely positioned to address public needs.

Two additional points warrant discussion. Implied in our analysis is the strategic significance of small business, not only materially but also symbolically. Recall, for example, that in the early 1980s, federal reports began to acknowledge the distinctive nature of small DBFs as a resource in support of U.S. innovation. Likewise, congressional action toward the liberalization of intellectual property law hinged on the provision of special privileges for small businesses (at least until the legislation was passed). Finally, Congress made a determined effort (as expressed in the SBIR program) to increase the share of R&D outlays which fall to small capital. In the light of these facts, the question emerges as to whether federal policy has actively undergirded U.S. biotech's reliance on relational networks. Arguably, the symbiotic relation between biotech and big pharma did not arise and persist purely by virtue of its economic rationality; rather, political intervention has also played a vital role. This possibility warrants careful empirical research. If supported, then prevailing approaches toward network forms of economic activity will need to incorporate political logics more explicitly into their models.

Perhaps the most general question to be addressed in the current context, finally, is how it has been possible for the federal government to play so active a role in the emergence of the new knowledge regime even as the U.S. political culture has so fervently trumpeted the virtues of neoliberal policy. An important part of the answer, again, is the widely held assumption that funding for the life sciences involves the production of a generalized good that by its very nature serves the public interest. Clearly there is a compelling public interest in the development and provision of new drugs and other treatments that can provide relief from prevalent and pernicious diseases and disabilities. Yet there are multiple ways in which extravagant federal support for the life sciences can and often does diverge from the public interest in health. One concerns the arbitrarily narrow coordinates that NIH research funding so often adopts. These coordinates have implicitly ignored the need for research on the linkage between exposure to environmental toxins and the very diseases that biomedicine seeks to treat—research counter to the interests of many powerful U.S. industries. Another involves the willingness of federal administrators to provide lucrative funding for private firms with few obligations imposed on them in return. Here is a pernicious effect of the current knowledge regime that has rendered it difficult to articulate critical views without seeming to be antiscience or antibusiness. Only by acknowledging the inherently political nature of the current arrangements—especially those that apparently operate purely in accordance with an economic logic—can we begin to open up for discussion the often problematic results that stem from the private appropriation of publicly supported goods.

We raise one final observation in concluding. Neoliberally oriented presidential administrations, Congresses, and the judiciary have promoted industrial policy while denying the value of government intervention, but not all industrial policy is alike. Industrial policy decisions are not value-free, technocratic matters. To the contrary, whether ad hoc or systematically developed, these policies are premised on specific values and have broad social implications. Economic growth is not an adequate measure of the success of any policy. For example, public investment in regional economic clusters may tend to deepen social and economic inequality, as the knowledge economy supports ever-widening income disparities. So too the competitive race by states, counties, and municipalities to emulate the Silicon Valley model may well reproduce the futile patterns of urban renewal and reindustrialization. Additionally, public investment always involves selection. Deep investments in one area will inevitably mean slights to another. This all points to the need to bring into focus the myriad ways in which public resources have been used to leverage the production of wealth, knowledge, and conceptions of health and well-being. The benefits and costs of these policies must be scrutinized more carefully than has thus far been the case.

Beyond government research funding, regulatory orientations have broad impacts as well. Although we have focused largely on drug-related biotechnology, there is reason to believe that the minimalist regulation governing the development of agricultural biotechnology has advantaged corporate agriculture and hurt small-scale farming. In the area of intellectual property protection, legal scholars increasingly question the ever more restrictive forms of patenting that are sanctioned in the United States. They worry about these policies' long-term effects on innovation and their broader impacts on the accessibility of innovations. In this light, we believe that future research into industrial policies and the knowledge economy must devote serious attention to understanding how policies create winners and losers, and all of us must consider whether these are the outcomes we value.

Notes

The authors wish to express their appreciation to Fred Block, Matt Judge, Matt Keller, Penelope Kramer, Kelly Moore, and Andrew Schrank, whose critical commentary and counsel helped advance our argument considerably.

1. By "knowledge regime" we mean a set of institutional arrangements that govern the production and legitimation of knowledge within a given domain. We prefer this concept to

"national innovation system," so often used in studies of industrial policy, since the concept of knowledge regime is more sensitive to the role played by power and is not limited to scientific and technical innovation alone. Finally, we argue that knowledge regimes often foster myth or "misrecognition" about the functioning of economic institutions (Bourdieu 1984; Polanyi 2001 [1944]; Vallas and Kleinman 2008). We return to this point in our conclusion. On the knowledge economy, see Powell and Snellman 2004; Brint 2001.

2. Mirowski and Sent (2002) observe that prior to 1940, apart from research extension programs that were the legacy of the Morrill Act, few academic scientists had the resources to conduct laboratory research. During this period (which these authors refer to as marked by a "protoindustrial" regime), scientists doing research were customarily assumed to be employed within industry. On the development of the U.S. system of national innovation, see Mowery 2009a.

3. On the "republic of science," variously understood, see especially Merton 1973; Polanyi 1962; Mulkay 1979; and Hagstrom 1964.

4. The first Genentech recombinant DNA drug to hit the market was human insulin in 1982. It was licensed to the pharmaceutical giant Eli Lilly and Company.

5. The argument here is that although university patenting did increase roughly tenfold in the two decades following the Bayh-Dole Act, that increase had already begun as early as 1968, more than a decade before the act was passed. For discussion, see Berman 2008 and further below.

6. This is of course only a partial list; for the sake of parsimony, we have excluded measures deemed less consequential such as the 1986 Drug Export Amendments Act (which enabled U.S. firms to profit from the overseas sales of drugs that lacked FDA approval). For analyses that run parallel with ours, see Slaughter and Rhoades 1996, 2004; Block 2008.

7. For an early effort to connect biomedical markets to federal funding, see Mansfield 1991. His data deal with the 1975–1985 period, which largely predates the emergence of biotech. For a more recent effort that does connect biotech products to federal provision of R&D, see the investigative reporting conducted by the *Boston Globe* (December 1998). According to the latter study, forty-five of fifty top-selling drugs approved by the FDA between 1993 and 1998 received significant federal support.

8. Data were compiled using the following methods. We conducted Lexis-Nexis searches to construct a narrative of each drug in Table 3.2, including the names of their principal investigators. We then conducted more specialized searches, using databases such as the NIH Computer Retrieval of Information on Scientific Projects (CRISP), which provided information on the number and type of grants that led to each drug's development and testing. Data on the dollar amount allocated to each drug were not consistently available, but the data sufficed to support conclusions on the degree and type of governmental support involved in each case. Finally, we have sought to use the most conservative methods in categorizing each drug in Table 3.2. For example, in categorizing Humalog (an analog of insulin) as having received "limited federal support," we did so despite the massive federal investment made in the development of earlier forms of human insulin. Likewise, we classify the development of Aranesp as having "little or no federal support," even though this drug is directly akin to Epogen (which did receive substantial federal support). In these cases, we erred in the direction of underestimating the federal role.

9. Richard Axel's lucrative patents on cotransformation, a process that allows foreign DNA to be inserted into a host cell to produce certain proteins, were among the first to be granted on the products of federally funded research. When they were granted in 1983, some said it marked a turning point at which government made profit rather than knowledge the first priority of research.

10. Oral history conducted in 2003 by Sally Smith Hughes, Ph.D., Regional Oral History Office, The Bancroft Library, University of California, Berkeley, 2004. George B. Rathmann, Ph.D., was chairman, CEO, and president of Amgen, 1980–1988.

11. Indeed, the only significant constraint that has been imposed on molecular genetics—that involving embryonic stem cell research—has required a massive mobilization of institutional power on the part of the religious right.

12. To gain a sense of the scale of this issue, consider the case of Amgen's blockbuster anemia drug Epogen, which is routinely given to dialysis patients. Amgen receives roughly $2.9 billion in revenues from U.S. sales of this drug each year (Young 2009). Yet roughly two-thirds of this cost (approximately $2 billion in 2005) is supported by Medicare. Congressional hearings have been held on Amgen's pricing, and the automatic administration of high doses of Epogen for dialysis patients has been called into question, but Amgen's revenue stream persists. Interestingly, even government reports that question Amgen's practices seem unaware of the strategic role of the federal government in the initial development of Epogen.

CHAPTER 4

To Hide or Not to Hide?

The Advanced Technology Program and the Future of U.S. Civilian Technology Policy

Marian Negoita

In his 2008 article "Swimming Against the Current," Fred Block argued forcefully that a decentralized network of federal agencies working to spur technological innovation in the United States constituted a "hidden developmental state" because, though largely invisible to the public eye, it exercised a powerful positive influence on the economy. He found that the federal government has dramatically expanded its efforts to help private firms develop new technologies over the past few decades. However, policymakers have taken care to hide these efforts to avoid conflict with the reigning market fundamentalism, an extreme faith in unregulated capitalism that had come to dominate public debates during the last few decades.

The story of the Advanced Technology Program (ATP) told in this chapter confirms Block's theory that the United States has such a hidden developmental state. The ATP was created by the Department of Commerce to stimulate the early stages of development of advanced technology that otherwise would not get funding. Like other state agencies described in this book, the ATP effectively stimulated industrial competitiveness, had strong connections with industry and academia, and focused on innovation and learning.

However, unfortunately for its supporters, the ATP had one distinguishing characteristic: it never quite managed to remain hidden from political scrutiny. In fact, the ATP has been one of the most visible segments of the U.S. state apparatus devoted to technological innovation. Because of widespread political disagreement over its goals, strategies, and budget, the ATP may have received more public scrutiny than any similar state program. This unique distinction makes the ATP a case study in what happens when the hidden developmental state goes public.

In this chapter, I analyze the history of the ATP in order to describe the effects of a hostile political climate on developmental state building. My central claim is that as a result of the dominant neoliberal bias against government intervention, much of the energy institutions like the ATP could be using to increase efficiency and forge institutional connections is spent instead trying to deflect attacks and survive.

Although the agency may have excellent results—and the available data indicate that the ATP was successful—it falls short of what could have been achieved if it had not been under constant attack.

This chapter traces the ATP's history and impact on technology development. I begin with a description of the major phases in the program's history, examining the structure and operation of the program during each phase, tracing the relevant policy changes, and presenting the main relationships between the program and its political environment. Subsequently my approach becomes analytical. I describe the ATP's main effects on the development of new technologies and identify the major barriers to its effectiveness. In the last section, I develop some general thoughts on how to reform the U.S. developmental state.

ATP and Industrial Policy in the United States

Developmental states in developed countries are under constant pressure to "predict the future." The best path to follow is rarely clear, and development is a moving target because of the workings of global capitalism. When key economic sectors, such as auto manufacturing, become arenas of intense global competition, corporate profits tend to plunge, leading to disinvestment and threatening widespread economic crisis (Brenner 2006). The only way out of capitalist overproduction and stagnation is, to cite a classic statement on capitalism, "new consumers' goods … new methods of production or transportation … new markets … new forms of industrial organization" (Schumpeter 1947, 83). Not surprisingly, countries that develop such technological breakthroughs are poised to reap the most benefits from their innovation. Britain was the first to do this in the nineteenth century: the dazzling array of innovations coming out of their Industrial Revolution ensured uninterrupted domination in global markets for a hundred years (Hobsbawm 1999). More recently, the Japanese car manufacturers' revolutionary transition from mass production to a flexible production that allowed them to make smaller batches of a wider variety of products allowed Japan to become a global leader in car manufacturing and ended American dominance of the industry (Coriat 1997). The conclusion is clear: if leading countries want to keep dwelling among the economic elite, they have to foster innovation, and their governments have to get involved in the process.

From this perspective, it becomes easier to understand why the ATP emerged when it did. By the 1970s the United States was beginning to lose its competitive edge (Block 1977), and during the 1980s U.S. policymakers began to realize that the once uncontested American supremacy in global markets was waning. Even in areas long considered strongholds, American businesses were facing stiff competition from abroad and were no longer market leaders. This situation prompted policymakers to rethink the role of the state in generating innovation, leading to a change in the dominant industrial policy paradigm. The ATP was only one in a series of institutional efforts during the 1980s to reestablish the country's dominance in world markets (Block 2008).

For half a century, the dominant approach to industrial policy in the United States had rested on two principles. The first principle was that heavy investment in "basic" scientific research without any predetermined goal would lead to industrial innovations, which would then spread effortlessly to the private sector (Branscomb and Florida 1998). This was known as the pipeline model. The second principle of the dominant paradigm assumed that technology created for military purposes would cross the military/civilian boundary and add to the technological prowess of civilian industry. This two-pillar model reflected American supremacy in postwar world markets. It was also politically convenient because it avoided a public discussion of the role of government in generating technological innovation since Americans still generally agreed that the government should fund development of new weapons to fight the Cold War. However, in the 1980s, the perceived crisis in competitiveness led to the fall of the pipeline model. The problem, reasoned many U.S. politicians, was not that the U.S. research community was not being inventive enough; the trouble was that these inventions were not carried into successful commercial solutions fast enough. It was becoming apparent that the road from technological breakthroughs to commercial products was not as linear and effortless as the pipeline model had assumed: many years' worth of research and arduous efforts were needed to transform an idea into a product with market potential (Auerswald and Branscomb 2003). According to the new paradigm, the state would help speed the transition of technological innovations from laboratories to markets. The task of state agencies was to generate and administer links between government, university labs, and commercial enterprises to convert technological breakthroughs into commercially viable products. In the process, a developmental network state (DNS) was being created (Block 2008). It was a developmental state because the government was exercising some form of control over industry, and a network state because the links being forged were collaborative and decentralized rather than at arm's length and hierarchical.

At the same time, however, a major political and ideological shift was taking place. The same economic crisis that led to the rethinking of U.S. industrial policy was radically altering the overall political climate. In the 1980s free market ideas again came to dominate public discourses after an absence of four decades (Frieden 2006; Block 2007). The restoration of market fundamentalism, with its exaggerated belief in the capacity of free markets to bring about prosperity and freedom if government stayed out of the way, induced a fundamental tension in the revamping of U.S. technology policies. On the one hand, there was widespread agreement that, for the sake of U.S. competitiveness, the pipeline model had to be supplanted by a more interactive approach administered by the state. On the other hand, market fundamentalist discourse had a strong antistate bias. Since they think state interventions distort the signals that make free markets efficient allocative systems, market fundamentalists are against any kind of industrial policy.[1] Because this tension could not be resolved ideologically, policymakers took every precaution to make sure the new industrial policies remained hidden (Block 2008).

However, this was not always possible. The story of the ATP is instructive because it tells us what happens when developmental state agencies cannot be shielded from political visibility in a political economy dominated by market fundamentalism.

The Emergence and Early Years of the ATP

When the Advanced Technology Program was created in 1988, it was intended as a central component of the new paradigm in technology policy. More specifically, the ATP was charged with accelerating commercial development of early-stage technology—a focus that made it the civilian counterpart of the Defense Advanced Research Projects Agency (DARPA).[2]

Technology development is difficult and complex, especially in its early stages. When technologists attempt to turn a scientific insight into a new technology, many things can go wrong. Developers may discover that the new technologies require materials that have not yet been invented, or that the science they are using is faulty. Because innovative projects at this stage are closer to basic research than full-fledged commercialization, only a small fraction of them wind up as successful commercial developments. As a result, although it is perhaps the most important step in the cycle, private investors rarely fund early-stage technology development.[3] Few nonstate funding sources, such as venture capitalists, are willing to back aspiring innovators. Even so-called angel investors (wealthy individuals who act out of benevolence rather than an interest in profits) are typically less interested in early-stage technology development. In their well-known study, Philip Auerswald and Lewis Branscomb (2003) likened the situation of technological innovation to a "valley of death" that has to be crossed before successful commercialization can take place.[4]

The idea of a federal agency charged with boosting early-stage technology development was floating around government circles for much of the 1980s as a part of the larger shift in technology policy paradigm. Several members of Congress, together with members of the congressional Office of Technology Assessment (OTA), were aware of similar programs elsewhere in the developed world and wanted to emulate these policies (*The Economist* 1990; Hill 1998). One of the initial debates was whether this agency should be created anew or whether it should be placed under an existing federal agency (Hallacher 2005). Eventually key political actors—notably Senator Ernest Hollings (D-SC), arguably the strongest supporter of the ATP for almost its entire existence—concluded that the ATP should be in the Department of Commerce, under the relatively autonomous National Institute of Standards and Technology (NIST).

The choice of the NIST as the host of the ATP was an excellent one. Created in 1901 and known until 1988 as the National Bureau of Standards, it had a mission of promoting American competitiveness by providing nationwide technological and measurement standards. Standards agencies are vital for technology development since they introduce order into otherwise incoherent markets. Left to their own devices, individual firms would develop proprietary standards for the technology they issue. This would create a huge barrier to market transactions, since the resulting jumble of standards would erect unnecessary rifts between otherwise comparable market players.

One example should suffice. Because the U.S. rail network grew initially without any federal-level standardization, several regional operators emerged that developed their own standards for gauge size, time zones, and safety devices (Dobbin 1994). Because of different gauge sizes, trains could not operate on railways developed by other firms, thus drastically limiting the size of their potential market. In fact, before common standards were issued in the late nineteenth century, the U.S. railway industry was hardly an industry at all—more like a collection of regional markets.

During the last few decades, the explosion of high technology has made the role of the NIST even more crucial. Contemporary technological development requires complex communication protocols and expensive testing procedures. NIST provides the measurement infrastructure on which future technology is built (Tassey 2007). This particularity makes the NIST an important piece of the U.S. innovation system in its own right.[5]

The Omnibus Trade and Competitiveness Act officially instituted the ATP in 1988, but the program did not receive its first budgetary appropriation until 1990. During its first years—which coincided with the last years of the first Bush administration—the ATP budget appropriation remained fairly small, at less than $10 million, reflecting the experimental character of the program. The ATP was charged with funding high-risk, early technology projects that could enhance U.S. industrial competitiveness. In consonance with the objective of accelerated technology development, the ATP was conceived as an industry-driven program: for-profit firms were expected to lead the projects, either as single "proposers" or in joint-venture projects with other companies, universities, non-profit organizations, and federal laboratories as their partners (Chang 1998).[6] Moreover, consistent with the stated objective of intensifying links between companies, universities, and federal laboratories, ATP policy encouraged the formation of joint ventures by providing conditions that were more attractive to them. Thus single company recipients could receive a maximum of $2 million for up to three years, whereas joint ventures could receive unlimited funding (within the limits of ATP budget) for up to five years.

If commercialization and the forging of new partnerships were objectives clearly reflected in the program, other rules were aimed at deflecting potential criticisms of the program coming from market fundamentalists. Almost immediately after its inception, the ATP became a target of attacks from the right for allegedly promoting industrial policy and corporate welfare (Hallacher 2005).[7] Worried that the ATP might become an easy target for such criticisms, policymakers had included a series of supplementary rules. Against the possible accusation that the ATP constitutes industrial policy, it refrained from indicating special areas of interest. Instead, the goal was to fund generic technologies that would have effects across the board rather than for specific parts of the industrial structure (*The Economist* 1992). The idea was to distance the ATP from single-purpose government-funded projects such as SEMATECH, a multicompany consortium that received important sums of money from the government, which had been accused of being a pork barrel.

Another concern was to avoid accusations that the government was "picking winners and losers" in the marketplace, another favorite conservative allegation. In order to counter this charge, ATP policymakers wanted to ensure that the evaluation of project proposals would be unbiased. They introduced the principle of peer review, which they borrowed from the operating structure of the National Science Foundation and the National Institutes of Health (Hughes 2005).[8] The process began with the ATP announcing competition criteria. Depending on the number of applications received, one or more source evaluation boards (SEBs) were established to rank applications. The SEB then used independent reviews provided by outside technical and business experts to evaluate each proposal (Balutis and Lambis 2001). Whereas technical reviewers analyzed the proposals for technological innovation and feasibility, quality of R&D plan, and the proficiency of the technical staff assigned to the project, business reviewers judged the potential for broad-based economic benefits (Chang et al. 2002). During its first four years, due to its modest funding, the ATP announced only one general competition per year and convened only one SEB. During this period, reviews were conducted sequentially: all proposals were given technical reviews but only the semifinalists received business reviews (Balutis and Lambis 2001).

Finally, to guard against charges of supporting large companies that could afford to pay for their own R&D, ATP rules initially limited the participation of large companies. By capping the amount of financial assistance for single companies, the ATP wanted to avoid the monopolization of the program by large corporations (Chang 1998). In addition, Fortune 500 companies participating by themselves had to share at least 60 percent of the total project costs, whereas joint ventures were expected to contribute at least 50 percent (Balutis and Lambis 2001). In other words, larger companies were expected to contribute a larger share of total project costs.

During its first years, the ATP remained a small and largely insignificant program, adopted without much enthusiasm by the Republican administration and without much support from other political entities. By 1992, however, its fate was about to change, for the incoming Democratic administration had big plans for the ATP. The Clinton administration wanted nothing less than to transform the ATP into the nation's largest civilian technology assistance program. I describe the reasons for this process and its lineaments in the next section.

Delusions of Grandeur: The First Clinton Years

By the end of the President George H.W. Bush administration, ATP policymakers were growing impatient with the program's lack of progress. As public perceptions that U.S. competitiveness was faltering continued unabated, the insufficient support shown to the ATP was a reason for concern. The 1992 election, however, provided a window of opportunity. During the election campaign, ATP policymakers and a few business groups—the most active of which was the National Coalition for Advanced Manufacturing (NACFAM)—carried out assiduous efforts to create interest in technology policy in both the Bush Sr. and Clinton staffs (Hallacher 2005). Whereas these efforts were not particularly successful in the Bush camp, the Clinton campaign thoroughly embraced the idea of state-supported technology development.

Times were changing, as well. The biggest event of the decade for U.S. technology policy—and one that was about to reshift it radically—was the end of the Cold War.

Because the Soviet military threat practically vanished, the resulting cuts in military spending that seemed in order were threatening one of the two main pillars of U.S. technology policy—military-backed technological innovation. In a post–Cold War situation, the large sums devoted to research that had been channeled through the military no longer seemed politically justifiable. By the time Clinton took office, the defense sector was laying off thousands of employees (Hughes 2005). The time had come to rethink technology policy. And this was precisely what the Clinton administration attempted to do, at least during its first two years. Given reductions in military spending, the Clinton strategy was to move the focus from military to civilian parts of the government. His major move was to create the National Economic Council, a cabinet-level body that Clinton aimed to elevate to the same level of prominence as the National Security Council (Hughes 2005). In the process, the ATP benefited very significantly; indeed it became "the flagship of the Clinton-Gore civilian technology policy" (Hill 1998, 143).

The growth of the ATP under Clinton meant not only increasing budgetary appropriations but also significant transfers of expertise from other parts of the U.S. innovation system. From a relatively meager budget of $50 million in 1992, the ATP appropriation jumped to $340 million in 1995 (Wessner 2001, 42) and was assumed to reach $1 billion by the end of the decade. The second important move of the new administration was to appoint Arati Prabhakar, a former DARPA senior official, as the new NIST director. To the initiated, Prabhakar's appointment was very significant. During her seven-year tenure at DARPA—the famed U.S. military technology agency "responsible," among other things, for inventing the Internet—she had successfully managed a $300 million program of research in advanced electronics (Rensberger 1993). Before long, more assertive policies began to emanate from the new ATP leadership.

The new leadership's mature views on technology policy had little in common with neoliberal orthodoxy. Far from being afraid to "interfere" with markets, Prabhakar had a sophisticated understanding of the role that states play in markets.[9] To facilitate innovation, the ATP was tasked with formulating an integrated vision for change. In addition, the new DARPA-emulating approach led the ATP to consider risk an integral part of the process of technological innovation, reinforcing the idea that only a small fraction of ATP-funded projects could ever become viable, and that this was a tolerable price to pay for positive transformation (Schrage 1994).

Armed with greater funding and refreshed principles, the ATP spawned an entirely new array of policies. Consistent with the new objective that the state ought to create a vision for industrial transformation, the ATP introduced what it called "focused competitions." In addition to general competitions, which maintained a generic approach, focused program competitions were supposed to add depth to specific technology areas considered more important (Balutis and Lambis 2001). However, the government did not decide these areas unilaterally. Instead, firms were encouraged to send white papers outlining promising areas for technological development. Based on the number and the quality of these white papers, the ATP then built focused programs—each administered by its own source evaluation board (SEB)—around the topics that generated the most interest (Hill 1998). In 1994 and 1995, specific dollar amounts were assigned to each focused program, additional proof of serious support for the new policy.[10]

Overall, the ATP seemed well on the way to becoming a mature component of the U.S. national innovation system. Its growing financial capabilities and the influx of new ideas seemed to transform the ATP into an efficient civilian counterpart to the military program administered by DARPA. In spite of these positive developments, less than two years after the new orientation came into effect, the ATP would find itself increasingly cornered and marginalized. The election of the 104th Congress dominated by the Republican Party signaled the reversal of the technology policy championed by Clinton—a reversal from which the ATP would never fully recover.

Conservative Backlash (1994–2007)

There were two major causes of the ATP's decline after 1994. First, the dominance of Congress by the Republican Party brought a powerful counteroffensive to the policy initiated by the Clinton administration. Even though Clinton remained president until 2000, the fact that all budgetary appropriations had to be approved by Congress drastically limited the administration's ability to sustain its policies. With less money, fewer goals could be achieved. Second, during the sharp economic upturn that began in 1993 and continued throughout the 1990s, previous worries about U.S. competitiveness seemed to lose much of their urgency. The door was open for a backlash.

The instatement of the new Congress brought a counterattack against what conservatives called "corporate welfare" and "industrial policy," meaning government-funded programs aimed at technological innovation. Many such programs were targeted for extinction, and the ATP was among them.[11] In addition to conservative Republicans from Congress, policy intellectuals from conservative think tanks such as the American Enterprise Institute, the Cato Institute, and the Heritage Foundation rallied in opposition to ATP policy (Hill 1998; Hallacher 2005).[12] Administration support kept the ATP from being eliminated, but the increasingly hostile environment meant, first, that it had less money to spend on technology programs and, second, that much of its energy would be spent trying to protect the program at the expense of institution building and consolidation. Instead of learning to be better at what it did, the ATP was expending its energies learning to survive politically.

From an all-time high of $341 million in 1995—which Congress approved in 1994 after rescinding $90 million from the original request—ATP budgetary appropriations began to decrease noticeably. In 1996 the ATP budget was slashed by roughly one-third to $221 million, and it stabilized for the rest of the decade at just under $200 million (Wessner 2001). This was not a completely dire situation for the ATP, since this level of funding was similar to the 1994 level. However, compared to initial expectations that the program would eventually reach around $1 billion, this level of funding was a disappointment to ATP policymakers, and it was a sign that the Clinton policy would not be pursued in its entirety. After 1995, none of the focused programs sponsored by the ATP received a specific dollar amount, reflecting the uncertainty of future funding. Eventually, because of the failure of the budget to increase—and due to incessant criticism and scrutiny from some Congress members—the ATP suspended its focused program competitions, which the industry clearly preferred to the fuzzier "general competitions," and developed a hybrid model called open competition. In the new format, a single SEB was used in the selection process, but the board was divided into specific technology areas, so that proposals focusing on similar areas would be reviewed together. Although ATP policymakers claimed this was a step forward because it combined the strength of general and focused competitions (Balutis and Lambis 2001), it might equally be claimed to have been a step backward, because the technology areas being analyzed ceased to be the reflection of an articulated vision and became ad hoc selections. Thus from an active role, the ATP was reduced to a rather passive one.

In addition to scaling down its ambitious policy agenda, the ATP found itself on the defensive as it warded off increasingly sharp attacks in the political arena. Analysts unanimously agree that compared to its size and age, the ATP has been exposed to an extraordinary level of scrutiny (Hill 1998). In addition, the level of ATP scrutiny was higher than that of much larger government programs such as the Small Business Innovation Research (SBIR) program or the mission specific projects in the Departments of Defense and Energy (Wessner 2001). In the late 1990s the ATP had become so controversial that key legislators felt that if some political agreement could be reached on the ATP, a consensus on the approach to similar issues might be more easily achieved across a range of other government technology programs (Branscomb and Florida 1998).

After 2000 the ATP's situation became even shakier. The new Republican administration openly opposed federally funded technology programs, especially the ATP. The first budget advanced by the George W. Bush administration for the fiscal year 2002 proposed no funding for the ATP. In 2003 and 2004 both the White House and the House of Representatives opposed ATP funding, and only sustained support in the Senate managed to save the program (Hallacher 2005). Consequently the ATP survived, but its budgetary appropriation became progressively smaller. The final 2005 appropriation was $136 million, a 20 percent reduction compared to 2004 and the second-lowest appropriation for the ATP since its pilot years (Hallacher 2005). In addition, with the retirement of South Carolina senator Ernest Hollings in 2005, the ATP lost an extremely important supporter. It is probably no coincidence that less than two years after the senator retired, the ATP officially became history: after almost twenty years of tumultuous existence, the ATP was officially canceled in 2007 through the America Competes Act. Although a similar program, the Technology Innovation Program, replaced the ATP, the two programs seem sufficiently different to confirm that the ATP's story ended in 2007.[13]

The Developmental Effects of the ATP

Since the main focus of this chapter is the interplay between political ideologies and technology policy, I will not attempt a thorough evaluation of the ATP's accomplishments and drawbacks. However, in this section I intend to demonstrate that despite incessant attacks and insufficient funding, the ATP did contribute to key technological breakthroughs.

As noted above, the ATP was the most closely scrutinized program of technological innovation in the United States and perhaps the most scrutinized program of its kind in the world. The dozens of studies conducted to test its effectiveness present us with a wealth of information. Although these studies showed several key positive developments associated with the ATP, they are only partially helpful to the independent reviewer because they failed to address the key charges leveled against the ATP—most notably the accusation that the ATP provided "corporate welfare" and that it "picked winners and losers" (Tassey 2007). I will first review the official evaluation literature and then provide an independent analysis.

The Official Evaluation Literature

Between 1990 and 2006, the ATP held 44 competitions and evaluated 6,924 proposals for new technologies. The total value of the projects it funded was almost $4.4 billion, out of which the ATP paid a little less that half, $2.1 billion (AKOYA 2007, 4). The studies sponsored by the ATP indicated four types of positive effects: an increase in commercialization of high-risk technologies; increased collaboration among the ATP, the private sector, and universities; knowledge spillovers manifested through patenting; and social returns stemming from the technologies launched through the program.

The main mission of the ATP, of course, was to accelerate early-stage technology development. The ATP's own evaluation studies found that when it cosponsored a project, the firms' R&D cycle tended to become shorter, thus resulting in faster commercialization. A survey of the twenty-eight ATP awardees from 1991 indicated that participation in the program reduced the participants' research cycle time by 50 percent or three years (Laidlaw 1998, 35). This acceleration effect seemed to be confirmed by the comparison between winners and nonwinners of ATP projects. In a survey of applicants for ATP projects in 1998, the authors found that 62 percent of the nonwinners did not continue with the research they had proposed to the ATP. And although 37 percent of the nonawardees continued the project, they did so on a smaller scale than originally planned (Feldman and Kelley 2001, 203). In other words, ATP funding seemed to be awarded to exactly the kinds of projects it was intended to support: high risk/high reward projects that would otherwise have received little or no funding.

Second, evaluation studies showed that the ATP helped create a strong public-private network of businesses and government agencies pursuing technological innovation. An analysis of a sample of participants in ATP-sponsored projects indicated that 86 percent of respondents (including single company applicants and joint ventures) collaborated with others on projects; among these, 69 percent said that ATP participation brought about a high degree of collaboration (AKOYA 2007, 20). In addition, ATP awards sparked new opportunities for collaboration between firms instead of deepening already existing partnerships (Feldman and Kelley 2001).[14] Finally, most

ATP-funded projects were able to attract universities as partners, thus tapping into a rich reservoir of technical knowledge and creative potential. As of 2006, 55 percent of all ATP projects included universities as joint venture members or subcontractors (AKOYA 2007, 21).

Third, assessment efforts showed that ATP-funded projects generated significant knowledge spillovers. Since patent applications make new knowledge available to others and facilitate new and different applications of patented technology (Jaffe 1998), patents are a good indicator of knowledge spillovers. A study examining the years between 1988 and 1996 found that firms and organizations which participated in the ATP accounted for over 40 percent of all patents given to U.S. organizations by the U.S. Patent and Trademark Office (Darby et al. 2004, 146). One quarter of these firms' patents during this period are attributable to ATP participation (Darby et al. 2004, 157). Compared to their pre-ATP levels, program participants increased their patent production between 4 percent and 25 percent (Darby et al. 2004, 159). However, these estimates are conservative because the spillover effects increase with time. Overall, between 1990 and 2007, ATP awards resulted in more than 1,500 issued patents (Bartholomew, Bagchi, and Campbell 2007, 7).

Finally, although only a few studies focused on this topic, there were efforts to measure the overall social impact of the programs aided by the ATP. Social return on public investment programs such as the ATP is notoriously hard to measure in exact dollar amounts because it is very hard to detect all the areas where a certain program has an impact (Bingham 2001). In addition, social returns tend to accumulate over time, so measuring the effect too early will not reveal the entire contribution of the program. However, some evaluation attempts have been made. A study published in 2007 that analyzed fourteen projects (a minuscule proportion of the entire program) concluded that the returns to the American taxpayer from these projects had exceeded $1.2 billion. In addition, the projected total returns over the long run of these fourteen and an additional nine projects could be as high as $6.7 billion (AKOYA 2007, 4). An analysis of seven medical technology projects estimated they would generate returns of approximately $34 billion returns over a twenty-year period, with ATP funding expected to be responsible for about 31 percent of these returns (Bingham 2001, 221).

In sum, the official evaluation literature generated an extraordinary amount of data. Although convincing, these studies constituted only a weak defense against two important anti-ATP arguments—first, that the projects would have been funded anyway and, second, that the government was interfering with markets by picking winners and losers. However, serious inspection of these accusations reveals their strong ideological bias.[15]

The ATP's Substantive Contribution

The notion that all the ATP-funded projects would have obtained support from private sources if the ATP had not backed them is contradicted by research indicating that private investment in R&D, and especially early-stage technology R&D, is constantly less than optimal (Stiglitz and Wallsten 1999; Auerswald and Branscomb

2003). There are several reasons for this. First, because of the spillover effect, private investors know that they cannot appropriate all the returns from their investment, so they hesitate to invest their money in R&D projects (Stiglitz and Wallsten 1999). In the case of high-risk early technology projects, this reticence is compounded by negative risk evaluations—hence the "valley of death" effect documented in the literature (Auerswald and Branscomb 2003). Many companies require a proof of concept showing that a new technology works before they decide to invest in it (Tassey 2007). The existing ATP evaluation literature, however, failed to discuss these points because a large majority of the studies were narrowly crafted around quantitative and statistical indicators, thus potentially neglecting broader substantive and contextual contributions of the program. If we turn to actual case studies of ATP's programmatic efforts, the corporate welfare thesis is more difficult to sustain.

Market fundamentalists were especially critical of ATP funding for large companies because, the argument went, these companies could fund early-stage technology projects by themselves. But this argument is overly simplistic because it neglects the issue of international competitiveness. During the last few decades, several key U.S. industrial sectors have lost market share to foreign competitors with more supportive governments (Tassey 2007). In this situation, government support aimed at finding new technologies that would create a competitive advantage is especially relevant for large corporations whose decline might have a substantial impact on particular regional economies and on the U.S. economy as a whole.

ATP policymakers understood this when they launched programs specifically focused on innovations for the ailing U.S. auto manufacturing sector in the mid-1990s. For example, together with a consortium comprising Chrysler, Ford, and General Motors, the ATP cofinanced a project aimed at developing composite materials—blends of polymers and fiberglass—to create vehicles that were lighter, more corrosion resistant, and easier to assemble. As a result, GM offered an entirely composite-based truck box as an option for its 2001 Chevrolet Silverado. The project ultimately spawned an entire range of applications in the aviation industry. For example, Boeing is using structural composites to manufacture parts for the C-17 cargo plane used by the Air Force and has incorporated the technology into its latest passenger jet, the 787 Dreamliner (ATP 2004). Another notable project was the invention of flow-control machining, an automated finishing process for cast-metal parts that aimed to reduce friction in the engine's internal passageways. The process, invented by a relatively small company called Extrude Hone, was successfully applied to several Ford models. It improved the motor power and fuel consumption and earned several automotive awards. An improved version of this process was later applied to the engines of the space shuttle Atlantis before its 2002 takeoff (ATP 2006a).

Let us now turn to the second criticism: that the ATP interfered with markets by choosing winners and losers. This is a neoclassical argument in its purest form because it implies that markets are ideal devices for allocating resources and managing output, and any interference with them—government programs included—is likely to distort their efficiency. Outside a narrow segment of economists, however, this vision is almost universally dismissed as oversimplistic and anachronistic. Governments played an important role in creating infrastructural conditions for capitalist development by securing property rights, enforcing contracts, building communication and transport infrastructures, and maintaining peace (Polanyi 2001 [1944]). The state acquired even more roles—such as financing and planning industrial growth—in later sequences of development, beginning with Germany and Russia in the nineteenth century (Gerschenkron 1962) and continuing through the establishment of postwar Asian tigers after World War II (Wade 1990; Amsden 1992).[16] The notion that the U.S. economy does not need government intervention is at best a misinterpretation of available evidence and at worst purely ideological.

What is more, radical technological innovations—the kinds that the ATP aimed to develop—also do much more than correct market failures.[17] Government-sponsored technological innovations, in fact, can *create* entire markets out of nothing. In the United States, research sponsored by DARPA spawned the Internet (Block 2008), in the process creating a multibillion dollar market populated by the likes of Microsoft, Google, and Yahoo. Similarly, technological research sponsored by the National Institutes of Health arguably created the entire biotechnology industry (Tassey 2007).[18] Given its relatively small size and lifespan, the ATP was hardly in a position to compete with these accomplishments. It did, however, originate a number of key innovative technologies.

Perhaps the most visible breakthrough that originated within ATP-sponsored programs was research on small disk drives. In 1992 the ATP cofinanced a project with the National Storage Industry Consortium that led to the discovery of a new technology called giant magnetoresistance (GMR). Subsequent research by companies led to small hard disk drives that could hold 20 gigabytes of memory and more, thus paving the way for the multibillion markets in consumer products such as the iPod, Tivo, and Xbox (Tassey 2007). ATP-funded research also led to the invention of key developments in flat panels. For example, the partnership between Kopin Corporation and Philips led to a new projection-based technology for LCD panels that Philips used to create rear-projection LCoS (liquid crystal on silicon) television displays and Kopin developed into miniature screens for medical and military applications (ATP 2003). A last example of radically ATP-funded innovative technology is the research that led to the discovery of plant-based biodegradable plastics. The ATP cofinanced research on the project—undertaken by an alliance between Cargill and Dow Chemicals—for three years starting in 1995. By 1999, the project led to a polymer, subsequently called NatureWorks PLA, which used 30 to 50 percent less energy to make—even when considering the energy used to produce the corn—and was also compostable (ATP 2006b). By 2007 NatureWorks had become the largest U.S. commercial producer of bioplastics (Moran 2007). And although the ecological sustainability of corn is debatable, attempts were being made to adjust the technology to the use of other plant-based sources such as corn stalks and rice hulls. Given the impending ecological crises that seem to await us, bioplastics and other plant-based materials are likely to become one of the key technologies of the future.

ATP's Politically Induced Problems

After investigating the major effects of the ATP, in this section I focus on the areas of ATP operation that were impeded by ideological opposition. Arguably, the largest part of the ATP's problems stemmed from the hostile political environment in which it operated. By and large, the staunch opposition of market fundamentalists accomplished three major "victories": it ensured that the ATP remained small and underfunded; it blocked attempts to establish extensive connections with the business sector; and it affected the ATP's capacity to evaluate the commercial potential of project proposals.

Arguably, the biggest problems encountered by the ATP stemmed from the fact that it remained a small program. The Clinton policy, as we have seen, was to gradually transfer industrial policy from the military to civilian parts of the government. Accomplishing this, however, required that budgetary allotments for the latter would increase considerably. Because of conservative opposition, most civilian technology programs—such as the ATP and the SBIR—remained so small that extraordinary rates of growth were needed for the military/civilian balance to be significantly corrected (Branscomb and Florida 1998). As Arati Prabhakar rightly pointed out, even if the ATP's budget grew to $1 billion annually, that amount would still have constituted only 2 percent of the entire sum paid by the federal government for research and development (Sands 1993). Furthermore, because it was a program specifically aimed at correcting market failures, the ATP could not benefit from the strong support that more mission-specific government programs like SEMATECH generated. Its lack of financial muscle, combined with a diffuse clientele, made the ATP especially vulnerable to political attacks from the right.[19]

Second, market fundamentalists systematically sabotaged what little support the ATP did receive from business groups.[20] It is important to remember that the initiative to form the ATP came primarily from a small group in Congress with very little involvement by other constituencies (Hallacher 2005).[21] In order to be effective, the ATP had to build solid relationships with industry, since government embeddedness in business groups is a central component of any developmental state. However, because of the ATP's constant funding and explicit threats from conservative Republicans, industry largely refrained from cooperating with the ATP in an extensive way.

For a technology program that was supposed to be explicitly driven by industry, the uncertainty about the availability of funds from one year to the next was a major downside of the program (Wessner 2001). Most potential ATP collaborators were aware that in the United States, cooperative technology programs are always at risk of being suspended. Therefore, many companies approached such initiatives with either considerable suspicion or a heavy dose of opportunism.[22] Neither is conducive to long-term trust. When cuts in ATP funding started to threaten the future of many cooperative projects, many companies were disappointed. After 1994, these cuts sent a strong message to industry that the ATP and similar programs were unreliable partners (Scott 1995; Farley 1996).

What is more, sometimes company managers were explicitly discouraged from participating in the ATP. One of the main reasons for the lack of business support for the ATP was that industry did not want to alienate Republican majorities. Republican leaders in Congress, such as Representative Robert Walker (R-PA), personally contacted industry representatives in order to persuade them against supporting the ATP and similar programs (Hallacher 2005). This confirms the powerful alliance between the Republican Party and business communities begun in the 1970s. It also confirms recent findings which suggest that the power balance that initially favored business has shifted during the last two decades so that Republican politicians now effectively dominate business groups (Block 2007). The result was that, although industry wanted government support[23] and welcomed the idea of the ATP, it did not want to seem as though it was against the "free" market.[24] To summarize, uncertainty and political pressure, both of which were results of actions of market fundamentalists, made for a weak and inconstant relationship between the ATP and business communities.[25]

Finally, political pressure from neoliberals impeded ATP's activity because, in trying to avoid accusations of turning into a "pork barrel," the ATP adopted the peer review model of proposal evaluation. In turn, this model made it very difficult to evaluate the commercialization potential of projects. Given that industry representatives with good knowledge of markets were also likely to be competitors of the firms advancing projects, the resulting conflicts of interest prevented them from participating in SEBs (Evans 2002). As a result, the ATP had an extraordinary capacity to evaluate projects from a technological standpoint but only a weak ability to identify projects with commercial potential.

Conclusion: Where Do We Go from Here?

A noted analyst of the ATP once concluded, "One approaches the task of making recommendations to enhance ATP with some trepidation" (Hill 1998, 163). Fortunately for this writer, I do not have to worry about improving the ATP since it is now formally defunct. The point, however, is that U.S. technology policy did not die with the ATP. It behooves us, therefore, to analyze the ATP's experience to imagine institutional configurations conducive to a more successful approach to technology development in the United States.

In the introductory section I claimed that the root of the ATP's problem was its public visibility in a context dominated by the market fundamentalist ideology, and the available evidence confirms that claim. But should we assume that public visibility leads to failure and "invisibility" guarantees success? I would argue that this would be a simplistic interpretation of the ATP's fate, for two reasons.

First, relative invisibility does not guarantee that technology programs will be successful or have an impact. The ATP's successor, the Technology Innovation Program (TIP), is a case in point. During the last two years of the George W. Bush presidency, the official strategy toward early technology policy was to render it politically inconspicuous. The termination of the ATP was meant as a return to the pipeline model and an attempt to reshield civilian technology policy from partisan attacks. The "new" policy aimed to decouple technological innovation from commercialization prospects. Thus the stated goal of the TIP is not to accelerate technology development toward commercialization but to fund research in areas of "critical national need." Moreover, large companies are specifically excluded from leading joint ventures (but may participate as an unfunded partner). Eliminating commercialization prospects and the participation of large companies effectively rendered the TIP inconspicuous, but at the same time, the TIP budget shrunk to $65 million. With this minimal budget and limited programmatic focus, it is difficult to imagine that the program's imprint will be significant. Invisibility, quite clearly, is not always a guarantee of success.

Second and more importantly, we ought to sharply distinguish the fate of individual technology programs from the U.S. innovation system as a whole. While individual agencies may survive—indeed even thrive—if they are hidden, if many programs do this the aggregate result will weaken the national innovation system. Invisibility inhibits two major traits of successful developmental state building—institutional coordination and ideological coherence. What seems to be generally true across developmental states is that they are internally coordinated (Chibber 2002). What is more, civil servants share a sense of corporate coherence—an esprit de corps (Evans 1995). Whether they are more bureaucratic or more decentralized, developmental states are characterized by a sense of common vision that transcends their internal differences. When government agencies render themselves invisible, however, the quantity and quality of the relationships they are able to forge with other agencies decreases dramatically and the building of an esprit de corps is considerably harder.

From this perspective, the fact that presently the U.S. developmental state is comprised of an "alphabet soup" of state agencies that often operate in isolation from each other (Block 2008) is not a surprise. The cloak of secrecy surrounding many of these programs plays a major role in this. Correspondingly, going visible is usually conducive to institutional transfers and accelerated learning. The experience of the ATP provides solid evidence in this respect. As soon as the ATP became publicly visible, it started an accelerated process of learning and interagency linkage development. Of course, the effort was complicated because the agency was forced to learn both how to implement technology policy *and* how to navigate a divisive political environment. But the point is that transparency and openness promote institutional cohesiveness and learning.

Yet knowing that public visibility leads to successful technology policy is one thing; instituting visibility without running the risk of extinction is quite another. We should not forget that the fiercest attacks against the ATP began only after it had gained public visibility. How do we keep developmental state agencies in the spotlight without condemning them to continual politicization? Here I suggest a possible answer that starts from the notion that both political ideologies and developmental state building efforts vary over time. As we have seen, although there are times when politicians loathe the notion of state-supported innovation, there are other times when they are favorably inclined to build an integrated innovation policy. The trick is to initiate an array of decisive strategies during these policy windows (Kingdon 1995) in the hope that the resulting institutional structure will withstand future attacks.

To be successful, a reform strategy should unfold along two dimensions—communicational and institutional. At the communicational level, the strategy would involve a variety of civil servants, policymakers, and industry representatives carrying out conscious attempts to spread the ideas of the developmental state not only within the government, but also within civil society. This strategy, for example, would aim to inform the taxpayers about the enormous benefits brought by developmental agencies, to weaken accusations of wasting public money, to present a more accurate picture of their efforts, and to organize public debates where citizens can voice their opinions. Such a strategy requires that policies are grounded in reliable data about what "works," as well as mandating transparency in policy aims and decision making (see Block, Chapter 1). These steps would help to mitigate the possibility of political or economic capture, reduce the possibility that agencies will become overpoliticized, and simultaneously serve as mechanisms which enable review and social learning.

At the institutional level, the aim should be to create a federal network of agencies and programs by formally incorporating them into an overarching institutional umbrella coordinated by a central agency. This move would not reduce the risk that individual programs, such as the ATP, would succumb to political attacks, but it would greatly diminish the danger that the entire U.S. technology policy could be brought to a halt by the disappearance of key agencies. Indeed, a key lesson of ATP is that a focus or emphasis on a single or flagship civilian technology agency is fraught with peril, particularly in a contested political environment. Instead, a robust, encompassing, and coordinated strategy is more likely to sustain itself over time and across partisan shifts.

At the time of this writing, we are experiencing a policy window of the kind described above. The massive economic downturn that began in 2007 demonstrated once more that unregulated markets, financial or otherwise, are incapable of governing themselves and that the government's presence cannot be dispensed with. The election of Barack Obama in November 2008 is generating a new course in technology policy. In a manner reminiscent of the early Clinton years, the election of a Democratic government breathed new life into the U.S. developmental state. What is more, the new leadership seems keenly aware of the necessity for greater institutional coherence. In October 2009, the U.S. Commerce Secretary announced a plan to establish a new Office of Innovation and Entrepreneurship within the Department of Commerce. The new office would report directly to the commerce secretary and would help coordinate the federal government's efforts to help entrepreneurs turn their ideas into commercially viable products. This would include programs focused on education and training as well as facilitating access to capital. Because of its coordinating role, the new office could be exactly the kind of structural solution that would ensure a reasonable level of coherence over a broad array of government-sponsored programs, and at the same time prevent future market fundamentalist attacks from crippling state-funded innovation activities. However, only time will tell whether the new office will become a reality and, once instituted, how successful it will be.

Notes

1. In this context, the concept of industrial policy took on such negative connotations that its supporters consciously avoided using the term. Instead, many advocates of a more interventionist state have adopted the concept of technology policy, which sounds less threatening to conservatives (Palmer 1992).

2. For more information on DARPA, see Erica Fuchs's chapter in this volume.

3. In 1998, for example, less than 14 percent of funds spent nationally by various sources on research and development (R&D) flowed into early-stage technology development (Auerswald and Branscomb 2003, 232).

4. This argument can then be used to state that early-stage development is an "imperfect market." That early-stage technology is an imperfect market is not exactly a scientific breakthrough, as we know by now that "perfect" markets do not really exist. However, this argument had political usefulness, since it was one of the few available defenses against a market fundamentalist attack (if markets are imperfect, the state has to intervene).

5. In its quest for better measurement, the NIST has contributed to some of the most important technological breakthroughs of our time and has been a constant source of patents. For example, the NIST made a significant contribution to the emergence of the modern computer (Wessner 2001, citing Flamm 1988). NIST researchers created the protocols for data exchange without which the Internet and email would be unconceivable (Forsen 1995). Further, research conducted at NIST contributed to the technology that forms the basis of the global positioning system (Forsen 1995). But the main point is that the NIST had the technically competent staff needed to make sound assessments of ATP proposed projects and also the well-deserved reputation for integrity in judging complex technical issues (Hill 1998). In a report from 2002, the Commerce Secretary estimated that the ATP could evaluate technology to a degree unmatched in the federal government and private companies alike (Evans 2002).

6. Notably, even in joint ventures, at least two for-profit companies were expected to carry out substantial research and contribute to the cost share requirement (Chang et al. 2002).

7. The then White House chief of staff John Sununu, a declared enemy of the ATP, was quoted as saying, "We don't do industrial policy" (Fong 2000, 152).

8. According to anonymous congressional employees cited in Hallacher (2005), the program would have not withstood the opposition without adopting peer review.

9. In a *Washington Times* interview, after noting that the state accounted for 45 percent from the entire sum spent nationally on R&D, Prabhakar was quoted as saying, "The government is already playing such a major role in the market that it is silly to pretend it isn't. . . . The important thing now is to determine how to do it right, how to get the best use out of the government's efforts." This statement would not strike me as misplaced even in an authoritative scholarly analysis of the developmental state (Sands 1993).

10. There were also a few other additional improvements, the most notable of which was the Business Reporting System—a database aimed at tracking the progress of various projects funded by the ATP (Powell 1998).

11. In 1995 a proposal that the departments of Energy and Commerce (which housed the ATP) be dismantled was seriously debated in Congress and was only narrowly defeated.

12. See, for example, Moore (1997); Yager and Schmidt (1997).

13. In the new program, large companies are explicitly forbidden to participate. In addition, the entire commercialization agenda disappears; the program is not specifically aimed at preparing innovations to be commercialized but only strives to promote technological innovation.

14. Even studies conducted by entities not particularly sympathetic to the ATP, such as the

Government Accountability Office, had to admit that the program aided the formation of joint ventures and helped companies to attain their research milestones faster (GAO 1996).

15. In an influential study conducted by the U.S. Government Accountability Office (GAO) in 1996, all the winners and "near-winners" of ATP projects during its first four years of operation were interviewed. The study found that 63 percent of the applicants did not look for funding from private sources before applying for ATP grants (GAO 1996, 2). This seemed to reinforce the notion that ATP projects were "pork barrel spending."

16. For example, Robert Wade (1990) conceptualized the Taiwanese postwar development as an example of "governed markets," whereby the government exercised significant control over the pace and content of market transformations.

17. If that were true, state programs could always be attacked on the grounds that market failure is preferable to government failure.

18. For a detailed discussion on the emergence of the biotechnology industry, see Vallas et al. (Chapter 3) and Shelley Hurt (Chapter 2).

19. On the other hand, it is very likely that the failure to reverse the military/civil balance in R&D spending has protected the U.S. developmental state, keeping it "hidden" from the prying eyes of political opposition.

20. The only early supporter of the ATP outside the federal government was the American Electronics Association (Hallacher 2005).

21. At the time of its inception, one observer then involved in the proceedings remarked that it was hard to find witnesses from industry willing to testify on what the ATP's role could be (Hill 1999).

22. In a reportage published in 1995, when the ATP budget began its permanent decline, a senior associate with a consulting company was quoted as saying that "company managers knew there was no way the government would ever live up to these goals, but they went along because it was new money. Now, it looks like another case of the government calling 'wolf.' [Contractors] are disappointed, but they never really expected government support would be consistent. They expected the money to disappear" (Scott 1995).

23. An Ernst & Young survey of almost 500 U.S. manufacturing executives released in March 1993 found that 77 percent supported the necessity for a national industrial policy, either as government-developed technology to private firms or as tax breaks for research and development (Sands 1993).

24. For example, in 2001, the president of the Software and Information Industry Association stated that eliminating the ATP would be a mistake. However, he hastened to add that since the current administration wanted the government to be smaller, everyone would have to adjust and not depend on government support (Blustein 2001).

25. This does not mean that industry support did not exist. Over the years, besides the aforementioned American Electronics Association and National Association of Manufacturers, the ATP also received support from the Coalition for Technology Partnerships (a small group of companies led by IBM) and the Council on Competitiveness (Farley 1996; Hallacher 2005). However, the support received was clearly insufficient compared to the ATP's needs.

CHAPTER 5

Green Capitalists in a Purple State

Sandia National Laboratories and the Renewable Energy Industry in New Mexico

Andrew Schrank

Oil patch politics have frequently been portrayed as inimical to the growth of renewable energy in the United States (Lovins 1976; Pope 2000; Ayres 2001). Oil and gas interests defend the integrity of their asset-specific investments in land and physical capital by donating enormous sums of money to sympathetic parties, politicians, and political action committees. Oil patch politicians defend the interests of their private sector patrons by derailing the development of alternatives to fossil fuel. Oil industry analysts defend the reputation of the public and private officials they are supposed to cover by deriding the prospects for renewable energy (Gelbspan 2005). And the country's "inevitable" (Lovins 1976, 96) transition to a more sustainable energy future is thereby delayed—with potentially catastrophic consequences.

This chapter addresses a puzzling feature of energy politics in contemporary New Mexico. On the one hand, the state is firmly ensconced in the oil patch (Copeland 1999; Coleman 2001). New Mexico not only plays host to some of the largest oil and gas reserves in the United States (EIA 2005) but is governed and represented by politicians who are at least broadly sympathetic to fossil fuels, including Governor Bill Richardson (a former Energy Secretary); Senator Jeff Bingaman, the chairman of the Committee on Energy and Natural Resources; and until recently Pete Domenici, whom Bingaman replaced as committee chair in 2006. On the other hand, the state is home to a vibrant cluster of renewable energy enterprises—including start-ups, suppliers, and transplants—that are growing more vocal and influential by the day (Paskus 2005; Arend 2006; McCurry 2008; Grant 2008). Richardson and his allies have not only assumed a proactive position vis-à-vis environmental protection but have deployed tax incentives and mandates designed to transform their piece of the oil patch into the "Saudi Arabia of renewable energy" (Reese 2006, 33) by the middle of the twenty-first century. Oil and gas interests have responded to their perceived betrayal with barely disguised contempt (Sorvig 2008; Coleman 2008; *Santa Fe New Mexican* 2008). "The irony is that New Mexico has developed the highest country risk of any place I do business," asserts the president of the state's largest oil and gas company (Romero 2004, C1), drawing an unflattering comparison to Morocco and the Spanish Basque country in particular.

Who or what is responsible for New Mexico's unanticipated transformation? Why would savvy politicians like Richardson and Bingaman abandon their traditional oil and gas industry patrons for the unsubstantiated promises of unfamiliar entrepreneurs? And what are the broader implications of their efforts? While planners like Richard Florida underscore the growth of the "creative class" in and around Albuquerque (Florida 2002, 19; Andrews 2001), and thereby imply that the social bases of New Mexico politics have changed, their account suffers from "breathtaking circularity" (Peck 2005, 764)—for the growth of the creative class is as much a consequence as a cause of the state's ongoing political and economic transformation and is therefore in need of explanation rather than mere invocation. Why are "knowledge intensive industries" (Florida 2002, 18) and their stakeholders drawn to Albuquerque in large numbers? And what are the likely consequences of their arrival? I trace the growth, character, and consequences of the city's creative class not to local leadership but to federal science policy in general, and to the influence of Los Alamos and Sandia National Laboratories (SNL) in particular. By incubating ideas, innovation, and human resources and simultaneously encouraging their transfer to the private sector, I argue, the labs constitute a largely *exogenous* source of social and political change—one that stands above local politics and is therefore able to transform New Mexican society by stealth. "The federal labs," in the words of one local economist, "were superimposed on an agrarian economy" (Reinhold 1984, A16; Salazar 2005, 267).

I have divided this chapter into three principal sections. The first section introduces the debate over energy policy and pays careful attention to the political feedback loops that allegedly militate against the abandonment of fossil fuels for "softer" (Lovins 1976) energies like wind, solar, and geothermal in the United States. The second section traces the birth of the Albuquerque renewable energy cluster to the efforts of Sandia personnel and programs and adduces two distinct mechanisms by means of which they not only incubated ideas and human resources but simultaneously encouraged their transfer to the private sector: cooperative research and development agreements (CRADAs) and entrepreneurial separation. The third section concludes that the development of the Albuquerque renewable energy cluster has been facilitated by institutions that mitigate—rather than individuals who embrace—risk, self-interest, and competition and thereby calls the fundamental principles of the "market fundamentalist" (Block 2008) agenda into question.

Intellectual Context

Pundits and politicians are beginning to preach the virtues of renewable energy, and New Mexico is particularly well positioned to ride the wave. The state already plays host to "148 companies that install, manufacture and distribute solar energy products" (Matlock 2008a, A6), boasts a disproportionate share of the country's "green-collar jobs" (Grant 2008, 10), and anticipates massive green job growth in the years to come.[1]

Thus Bill Richardson has declared New Mexico "the clean energy state" (Matlock 2008a, A6).

The Land of Enchantment's commitment to clean energy is apparent on the demand side as well as the supply side. The state's utilities are currently obligated to purchase 6 percent of their power from renewable sources and to triple their commitment by the year 2020 (Matlock 2008b, A1). Albuquerque's Mesa del Sol is designed not only to employ and house tens of thousands of people in green buildings on state-owned land (Velasco 2005) but to attract renewable energy producers and equipment manufacturers who will meet their future needs (Chamberlain 2007; Robinson-Avila 2007; Webb 2008). And the Navajo reservation in the Four Corners region boasts hundreds of solar-powered homes and a desire to build many more (*New Mexico Business Journal* 2006).

New Mexico's commitment to a renewable future is puzzling, however, for fossil fuels are the state's largest and most lucrative industries, and their political representatives have traditionally been no less hostile to alternative energy than to taxation, regulation, and expropriation (*Santa Fe New Mexican* 2008; Sorvig 2008). In fact, the literature on energy policy is awash in path dependence and feedback loops, and no less an authority than Amory Lovins has therefore warned that a commitment to the "hard path" of nonrenewable resources will in all likelihood "make the attainment of a soft path prohibitively difficult, both by starving its components into garbled and incoherent fragments and by changing social structures and values in a way that makes the innovations of a soft path more painful to envisage and achieve" (1976, 96).

Nor is Lovins alone. Eban Goodstein agrees that energy policies are path dependent and adduces a number of "positive feedback mechanisms" (1995, 1030)—including sunk costs, scale economies, and consumer preferences—that militate against changing paths. Robert Ayres underscores the importance of clean energy entrepreneurs and worries that politicians from the oil patch will vote to derail their nascent efforts every time (2001; Farquhar 2008). Darren Goode and Christian Bourge document at least one recent episode in which "about two dozen oil patch Democrats" (2007, 5) broke ranks with their party's support for renewable energy mandates and tax credits and thereby validated his concerns.

Figure 5.1 offers a diagrammatic representation of the endogenous relationship between fossil fuel–friendly policy and fossil fuel producer power.

Of course, the converse is no less true: the development of renewable energy is undercut by a lack of political support. But fledgling renewable energy producers are unlikely to garner political support and are thus unlikely to mature in the first place.

Why, then, have New Mexican politicians embraced renewable energy with such vigor? Who are the state's "green capitalists"? (Grant 2008, 10) And where do they come from? While historians and social scientists have paid far more attention to the reproduction of endogenous feedback loops than to their transcendence and have thereby imbued the literature on path dependence with an unfortunate—and perhaps unnecessary (Martin and Sunley 2006, 402)—determinism, they are at long last beginning to discuss "'escape' routes from regional 'lock-in'" (Martin and Sunley 2006, 424) in a more or less systematic fashion. Thus Carolina Castaldi and Giovanni

Figure 5.1 The Fossil Fuel Policy Cycle

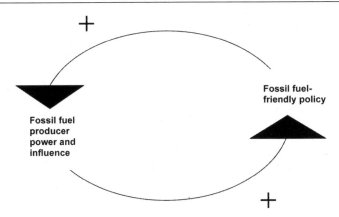

Dosi portray "invasions" of impacted regions by organizations or cultures "originally developed elsewhere" (2004, 24) as potentially powerful solvents. And Ron Martin and Peter Sunley incorporate their notion of invasion into a broader model of transplantation (2006, 422) that, in their words, "refers to the importation and diffusion of new organizational forms, radical new technologies, industries, firms or institutional arrangements, from outside."

Invasion and importation are by now broadly familiar to students of regional and national development (Cumings 1984; Westney 1987; Florida and Kenney 1991). Invasion is conceptually superior to importation, however, for the willingness to import new ideas and organizations is itself path dependent (or endogenous), and importation is no more likely than incubation in an otherwise hostile political economy. Consider, for example, the failed effort to import the iron and coal industry from the free soils of Pennsylvania to the slavocracy of Virginia in the antebellum era (Adams 2004). Invasion, by way of contrast, implies an imbalance of power and a lack of choice on the part of the receiving community and is therefore at least partly exogenous (Acemoglu et al. 2001).

Invasion is by no means the only alternative to path dependence and lock-in, however, for Sunley and Martin discuss a number of other "routes to regional de-locking" (2006, 424), including the diversification of "what were once core industries and technologies into related or derived industries and technologies" (2006, 423) that eventually expose new paths or pave new roads. Take, for example, oilfield service suppliers like Hughes Tool and Geophysical Services in early-twentieth-century Texas. The former gave birth to Hughes Aircraft in the 1930s (Chen and Sung 2001); the latter evolved into Texas Instruments in the 1950s (Rauch 2001). Divisions of both companies have recently been incorporated into defense giant Raytheon (Haber 1997).

Which mechanism is responsible for New Mexico's tentative steps on the road to a renewable future? Are Albuquerque's green capitalists the offspring of the oil patch or the shock troops of a literal or perhaps metaphorical alien invasion? Interviews with industry insiders and an admittedly incomplete review of their personal and corporate histories counsel for the latter interpretation. After all, New Mexican oil and gas interests have evinced little—if any—interest in renewable energy; on the contrary, they have decried efforts to develop alternatives to fossil fuels in their state (Coleman 2008; *Santa Fe New Mexican* 2008).[2]

Like much of the American sunbelt, however, New Mexico has been invaded by an "army of scientists" (Lamont 1965, 134) dedicated to the development and production of armaments, beginning with the architects of the Manhattan Project during World War II, accelerated by the arrival of a "reserve army of scientists" (Seidel 2001, 149) at Los Alamos and Sandia National Laboratories during the Cold War, reinforced by the growth of the state's research universities in the late twentieth century (Webb 2004; Vorenberg 2006), and disseminated to the private sector over time. By the early twenty-first century, therefore, New Mexico would play host to more Ph.D.-holding scientists and engineers on a per worker basis than any other state in the union (National Science Board 2008, 8–61).

The point is not that New Mexicans opposed these invaders but that they were for the most part oblivious to their arrival during the war and would have been all but powerless to stop it afterward. Herbert S. Marks, who would eventually become the general counsel to the Atomic Energy Commission, once remarked that the Manhattan Project "bore no relation to the industrial or social life of the country; it was a separate state, with its own airplanes and its own factories and its thousands of secrets" (Kelly 2006, 20). National security concerns dictated the absolute "separation of Los Alamos from the rest of the world" (Thorpe and Shapin 2000, 554; Salazar 2005, 267–268), and Sandia originated as a "small off-shoot of Los Alamos" (Furman 1990, 139) with a no less fanatical approach to security. "The scene inside the base resembled a penal colony," adds one historian (Furman 1990, 139). "Wooden guard towers stood like sentinels in strategic positions, and at night searchlights illuminated the fenced-in technical area."

Nor would New Mexicans have opposed being incorporated into the American "gunbelt" (Markusen et al. 1991) had they known it was happening. The Cold War not only legitimated the growth of the labs but ensured that the bulk of their efforts contributed to the development of hard energy resources with which New Mexicans were already comfortable. And the labs eventually transformed the Land of Enchantment "into a tax magnet, sweeping up $2 in federal spending for every $1 sent by its citizens to Washington" (Tatge 2006, 179).

The results have been nothing short of staggering. Figure 5.2 plots the logged density of Ph.D.-holding scientists against logged federal R&D obligations per civilian worker for all fifty states at the turn of the century. According to the National Science Board, the density of doctoral-level scientists speaks to the state's "ability to attract and retain highly skilled scientists and engineers" (NSB 2008, 8–60), and the relative weight of federal R&D is an indicator of "major federally funded R&D facilities in the state" (NSB 2008, 8–70).

The scatter plot therefore (1) confirms the unparalleled density of doctoral-level scientists and engineers in the New Mexico labor force; (2) underscores the state's

Figure 5.2. Highly Skilled Scientists = f (federal R&D spending)

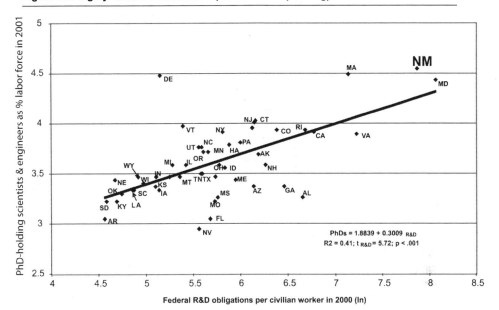

Note: Data from National Science Foundation 2008b (Tables 8-27 and 8-32). "PhD-holding scientists and engineers" is the natural log of the proportion of doctoral-level scientists in the civilian labor force in 2001 multiplied by 100 for ease of exposition; federal R&D obligations for 2000 are logged as well.

striking ability to attract federal research dollars; and (3) suggests that the former is in part a product of the latter, for the elasticity of Ph.D. holders with respect to federal R&D spending is .30 (p < .001). Cross-sectional data like these are at best suggestive (Lieberson 1985), however, and say nothing about renewable energy in particular.

The latter problem is particularly vexing, for the national laboratories that anchor the federal science mission in New Mexico trace their origins not to renewable but to nuclear energy research and development—that is, to the very hardest of the hard energies. Why, then, do I treat the growth of the Albuquerque renewable energy cluster as product of federal science policy? The answer demands a historical account of federal efforts to turn the labs into "tools of technology-driven industrial policy" (*The Economist* 1991, 80) in the aftermath of the Cold War.

New Mexico: The Saudi Arabia of Renewable Energy?

The Department of Energy assumed control of the laboratories established by the Atomic Energy Commission (AEC) in 1977. The labs were the brain trust of the American Cold War effort and perhaps the largest scientific research complex in the world. The largest of the labs—Lawrence Livermore in northern California, Los Alamos in northern New Mexico, and Sandia in Albuquerque—were government-owned, contractor-operated facilities that commanded multimillion dollar budgets, employed thousands of scientists and engineers, and were responsible for the bulk of the country's nuclear weapons research and development (R&D) in the Cold War era (General Accounting Office 2004, 2).

Nevertheless, Sandia differed from Los Alamos and Livermore in at least two important respects. First, Los Alamos and Livermore claimed to perform "basic research in the field of nuclear science" (Furman 1990, 331); Sandia developed nuclear ordnance (e.g., fuses, detonators, control systems, casings, etc.). Second, Los Alamos and Livermore were operated by the University of California; SNL was run on a nonprofit basis by AT&T. The second difference was in part a product of the first, however, for the UC regents felt that, unlike the basic research pursued at Los Alamos and Livermore, the "research and development of nuclear ordnance, as well as manufacturing (even though performed by outside contractors), was not a proper academic pursuit" (Furman 1990, 331), and thus asked the AEC to decouple Sandia from their contract in 1948.

The AEC immediately began to search for a less virtuous contractor who "could meet both the direct management needs of the Sandia operation and indirectly, because of close technical liaison, the needs of Los Alamos" (Furman 1990, 339). AT&T was all but uniquely qualified for the job, for Bell Telephone Labs (BTL)—the company's R&D division—had enormous experience with basic as well as applied research, and Western Electric—the company's manufacturing division—had unparalleled industrial capacity. President Truman therefore interceded on the AEC's behalf in 1949, and AT&T quickly agreed to perform "an exceptional service in the national interest" (Truman; quoted in Furman 1990, 342) by taking over Sandia for nothing more than the cost of expenses.

Sandia's goals and structure were obviously idiosyncratic in origin in the late 1940s; however, they would prove functional in consequence a half century later—when the labs were forced to reinvent themselves in the aftermath of the Cold War. First, the Sandians had a monopoly in their core area of competence (*The Economist* 1991). Only SNL worked on the detonation and control of fissile material. Second, Sandia had a diverse portfolio of ancillary activities (Johnson 1997; Brown 1998). The labs had developed expertise in microelectronics, photonics, high-speed computing, semiconductors, and a host of related activities with potentially lucrative commercial applications. Third, Sandia had an "AT&T-Bell Labs mentality" (Bray; quoted by Mintz 1992, F1; *The Economist* 1991) imported directly from Murray Hill, New Jersey. Albert Narath, who assumed SNL's presidency in 1989, was "the first to have worked his way up the ranks inside Sandia rather than coming in from Bell Labs—and he went away to Bell for a few years before moving into the top job" (*The Economist* 1991, 79).

Narath, a physical chemist with a Berkeley Ph.D., served SNL in a number of different capacities before assuming the presidency. For example, Morgan Sparks, who served as Sandia's president in the years following the first oil shock, had developed an acute interest in alternative fuel sources and had transferred Narath, a rising star in the weapons labs, to "solar, geothermal, and advanced energy research" (Johnson

1997, 171) in the 1970s. Narath acquitted himself admirably and ascended through the Sandia hierarchy: vice president with responsibility for energy projects in the late 1970s, executive vice president with responsibility for long-term research, advanced weapons design, and administration in the early 1980s; a five-year sabbatical at Bell Labs; and a return to the presidency of Sandia in 1989 (Johnson 1997).

Narath's former colleagues at AT&T would almost immediately abandon him, however, by withdrawing from an agreement that had grown increasingly burdensome in light of their own restructuring challenges (Johnson 1997, 337). Martin Marietta won the competition for control of the labs in 1993 and put their personnel "on notice" (Weisman 1996, 59) that the days of nonprofit management were coming to an end. Pressure to commercialize lab technologies had been mounting for well over a decade and would only intensify with the end of the Cold War. The amendments to the University and Small Business Patent Procedures (or Bayh-Dole) Act allowed the labs to retain the rights to intellectual property they had created with the help of federal funds (Rand 2003, 11–12). And the amendments to the Stevenson-Wydler Technology-Innovation Act not only allowed but compelled the labs to devote human resources and capital to technology transfer (Rand 2003, 11–12). Furthermore, President Bill Clinton and his congressional allies viewed technology transfer as a powerful rationale for continued lab funding in the aftermath of the Cold War (Belsie 1994; Weisman 1995a), and Narath agreed with their assessment. "We have to get out of this entitlement mentality" he argued (Weisman 1996, 59). "The government doesn't owe us constant employment levels."

Narath's new employers at Lockheed Martin (née Martin Marietta) were only too happy to oblige. They had premised their bid for SNL in part on their commitment to technology transfer and had not only developed a nonprofit business incubator known as Technology Ventures Corporation (TVC) to demonstrate their sincerity (Wall 1995) but had also hired six patent agents to beat the bushes for intellectual property that had been overlooked by their predecessors (*New Mexico Business Journal* 1994, 4). They had a number of other policy tools at their disposal, however, including the cooperative research and development agreements (CRADAs) sanctioned by the National Competitiveness Technology Transfer Act of 1989 (Simmons 2007, 2).

CRADAs spell out the terms of research partnerships between the labs and their private sector interlocutors. They specify "who pays for what, and how the results can be used. Some call for companies to foot the entire bill in return for proprietary rights to anything that is developed. But more typically, the labs chip in some cash, retain the rights to the resulting technology and give the corporations that contributed several years of free, exclusive use" (Deutsch 1997, 35).

By the mid-1990s Sandia would boast almost 300 CRADAs worth approximately $700 million with a typical public-private cost-sharing split of 35–65 (Spohn 1996). The labs were oversubscribed by a factor of eight and could therefore afford to pick and choose partnerships that would enhance their ability to pursue their core mission of weapons development (Weisman 1995b, 61). While new CRADAs had to have a connection to weapons work in theory, the connection could be exceptionally broad (Weisman 1995b, 61) in practice. Thus Sandia developed a concentrated solar power CRADA with Boeing in 2002 (Burroughs 2002), a fuel cell and photovoltaic CRADA with Sharp a few years later (Broehl 2005), and a CRADA with Stirling Energy Systems that would lead to "a new solar-to-grid system conversion efficiency record by achieving a 31.25 percent net efficiency rate" in 2008 (Burroughs 2008a; Woody 2007).

Sandia's private partners were for the most part foreign to Albuquerque (Brown 1998, 69), however, and the lab officials responsible for technology transfer believed that co-location and clustering were central to their long-term success. "While Sandia's goal for co-location of industrial partners is directly related to our desire to achieve our DOE mission responsibilities better and faster," they wrote, "co-location complements the goal of economic development organizations working to attract new high-tech businesses and industry to New Mexico in the hope of making Albuquerque the next 'Silicon Valley' or 'Route 128'" (Siemens 1997, 20). Therefore Sandia introduced a number of programs designed to incubate local talent by encouraging entrepreneurial separations to transfer technology (ESTT).

The ESTT program offered Sandians who wanted to bring their inventions to market leaves of absence of up to two years—with the possibility of extension—in which to do so. Narath's successor, Paul Robinson, provided the program's initial rationale in congressional testimony in 2001. "Entrepreneurial separations are notoriously risky," he noted, "and Sandia's entrepreneurial separation policy can permit a former employee to return if the venture fails" (Robinson 2001, 23). But ESTT also ensures that the scientists and engineers who developed and thus understand the products best are involved in their commercialization, "thereby increasing the likelihood of the start-up's success" (SNL 2005, 32). ESTT participants tend to draw on a host of other Sandia programs, including TVC's consulting and brokerage services to devise business plans, license technology, and develop connections to capital markets (Clark 2001, 5; Battelle Memorial Institute 2004, 15); the Small Business Assistance Program, which offers start-up capital, office space, and manufacturing extension services (Palmintera 2003, 49–50); and user facility agreements that provide continued access to lab materials and equipment (Clark 2001, 19).

ESTT is by now considered a model initiative among federal laboratories and technology centers. "Since the program was implemented in 1994," reports SNL, "126 entrepreneurs have left Sandia and have been involved in starting 40 companies and expanding 44 more. Of the 126 that have used the ESTT program," the report continues, "only 36 have returned to the Labs" (SNL 2005, 32).

Advent Solar is one of the best known ESTT spin-offs. The company was established by James Gee, an electrical engineer with more than two decades of Sandia experience who had developed and patented a laser-based approach to fabricating photovoltaic cells that both lowers production costs and improves light absorption. Gee took a leave of absence and founded Advent with the collaboration of Rusty Schmit, a solar industry veteran, in 2002. They received support from TVC, raised more than $100 million in venture capital, began selling their product in 2005, and moved into a $25 million design and production facility a mere two years later (SNL 2005; Tatge 2006; Schmit 2007).

But Gee is not the only Sandian to translate knowledge of photonics into solar success through entrepreneurial separation. Tom Brennan and Rob Bryan took a more circuitous path to an even more propitious outcome when they left Sandia to found Micro-Optical Devices (MODE) in the mid-1990s. Brennan and Bryan had been working with vertical cavity surface emitting lasers (VCSELs) for several years when they found themselves drawn to the siren song of the commercial path for the first time. Bryan left Sandia to found the Vixel Corporation in 1991, and Brennan accepted an assignment in the SNL technology transfer office, hoping to gain insight into the commercialization process a few years later (Clark 2001).

Brennan approached Bryan about the possibility of founding a new VCSEL company in 1995. Bryan signed on in 1996, and Brennan immediately took an entrepreneurial leave from Sandia to devote more time to their effort (Clark 2001, 17). They acquired office space and start-up capital with the support of TVC (Clark 2001, 19; Battelle Memorial Institute 2004, B-14). They began to develop products for the telecommunications and Internet markets (Robinson 2001). And they continued to search for second round funding, knowing full well that they couldn't get their products to market without more resources.

Emcore, a New Jersey–based fiber optics and photovoltaic company with preexisting ties to the labs, heard about their plight and decided to make Brennan and Bryan a purchase offer. MODE would diversify Emcore's holdings, and Emcore's deep pockets would allow MODE to move toward commercialization. Consequently MODE accepted the offer, and Emcore retained Bryan in an executive position at MODE.

Emcore's growing commitment to Albuquerque simultaneously convinced the New Jersey–based company to build a PV facility in the newly established Sandia Science and Technology Park (SSTP) and put Brennan and another former Sandian, Hong Hou, in charge of operations. The PV operation has been remarkably successful. The VCSEL unit continues to expand, and Emcore officials have decided to move their world headquarters to Albuquerque in 2006.

The publicly owned company now employs approximately 500 New Mexicans (Simmons 2007, 3), and Hong Hou has been appointed chief executive officer. Former Emcore vice president Brennan has returned to Sandia, where he hopes "to winnow out the best the lab has to offer in terms of commercial potential" in his new position as the lab's first "entrepreneur-in-residence" (Holtzman 2005; Burroughs 2008b).

The Sandia Science and Technology Park, where Emcore is located, is designed to turn the dream of co-location into a reality by drawing human, physical, and financial resources to a contiguous geographic space. The park's twenty-nine firms currently employ several thousand workers and pay an average salary of $70,000 per year (Bruns 2009). SSTP received the Outstanding Research Park of the Year award for 2008 from the Association of University Research Parks, an honor previously reserved for university-affiliated facilities (*Albuquerque Journal* 2008; Bruns 2009).

But SSTP is not the only source of clustering in the New Mexico solar patch. Advent's state-of-the-art facility is found in Mesa del Sol, a master-planned community on the south side of Albuquerque that has a CRADA with Sandia to develop smart grid technology (Fleck 2008b). It will soon be joined by a $100 million concentrated solar operation owned by Schott Solar of Germany with a potential workforce of 1,500 and a smaller concentrated solar facility owned by Arizona transplant SkyFuel (Rayburn 2006; Robinson-Avila 2007). Both companies cite proximity to Sandia Labs and their human resources as key factors in their location decisions (Rayburn 2006; Schott 2008; Quigley 2009). Suppliers are proliferating (Metcalf 2005), and other firms are waiting in line (Quigley 2009).

In short, Sandia Labs have fertilized the Albuquerque solar patch by developing human resources and technology that attract and fuel the growth of immigrant as well as breakaway firms. "New Mexico has the potential to become a Silicon Valley for solar," declare the industry's boosters (McCurry 2008). "The state can become a hotbed in terms of job generation, especially if government policy continues to support renewable energy in this country in the form of investment tax credits."[3]

Conclusion

Are New Mexico's hopes realistic? Does the state's economic future really lie in clean energy? And if so, what are the implications? While Albuquerque's green capitalists have confronted a number of challenges, including increasing competition, declining fossil fuel prices, and a credit crisis of historic proportions (Hartranft 2009b), they continue to grow in both number and sophistication (Boyd 2009; Hartranft 2009a; Quigley 2009), and their experiences run counter to three common social scientific tendencies—the fetishization of competition, the vilification of discretion, and the veneration of risk.

The fetishization of competition. Sandia Labs consistently outperform Los Alamos and Livermore on commercialization metrics (Spohn 1996; Weisman 1996; *Albuquerque Journal* 2002; Fleck 2008a), and a number of observers have ascribed the performance gap to the legacy of AT&T and Bell Labs (*The Economist* 1991). But the exact nature of the legacy remains unclear. What lessons or legacies did Sandia import from AT&T? And why do they matter? While the Sandians and their partisans tend to invoke Ma Bell's "businesslike culture" (Hartley 1999; SNL 1999; Hagengruber 2002) and underscore the fact that the UC labs "had an academic buffer between themselves and the federal government" that protected them "from the natural flows of the business cycle" (Weisman 1996, 59; Weisman 1995a), they arguably go too far by half, for Richard Lester and Michael Piore portray Bell Labs not as a businesslike organization but as "a sheltered enclave within AT&T that enjoyed the research ethos of an academic laboratory" (Lester and Piore 2004, 24).

Nor are they alone. Leland Johnson traces the original decision to place managers from BTL rather than Western Electric in charge of Sandia to AT&T's recognition of the need for "greater *organizational* emphasis on the development aspects of the job" (Johnson 1997, 46; my emphasis). Former Sandia executive Lee Bray asserts that "you'd be hard-pressed to tell the difference" between Bell Labs and the organization they created in New Mexico (Bray; quoted in Mintz 1992, F1; Connelly 1992). And

Al Narath admits that "private-sector companies in a competitive world are unable to support" the types of "long-range research activities" (Narath; quoted in Cordtz 1995) that made the labs famous. Of course, the implications are alarming, for Sandia's experience suggests that recent efforts to make the labs more "business-like and results-oriented" (Rezendes 1997, 5) may well have the unintended consequence of undermining their ability to nurture the kinds of "open-ended conversations among people from different professional and organizational backgrounds" (Lester and Piore 2004, 11) that have fostered innovation and product development in the past.[4]

The vilification of discretion. Do Sandia's achievements validate their industrial policy mission? While the Clinton administration viewed economic competitiveness as a viable rationale for continued lab funding in the aftermath of the Cold War and thus defended the DOE's "wild-eyed scientists" from congressional attack in the 1990s (Weisman 1995a, 54), their beneficiaries in the labs deride the possibility—let alone the actuality—of effective firm-level intervention. You'd have "to exercise the wisdom of Solomon" in order to do so, argued Narath's immediate predecessor in 1986 (Johnson 1997, 299). A decade later Narath denied that the labs were "picking winners and losers" (Narath; quoted in Cordtz 1995, 32). His denials ring hollow, however, for the oversubscribed labs were obviously making decisions about which CRADAs to accept, which leaves to approve, and which licenses to grant (on what terms) on a daily basis—and in so doing were in effect picking winners. The relevant question is therefore not whether the labs were actually picking winners but whether the social returns to their decisions outweighed the costs.

The answer is anything but obvious and isn't likely to be determined in an exploratory case study like this one, but the evidence I have adduced counsels against the uncritical acceptance of the naive "market fundamentalist" (Block 2008) notion that the "unfettered market," which is itself an ideological construct (see Block 2003), always and everywhere outperforms the embattled public sector. After all, the labs have arguably had at least three enormously positive consequences for the social and economic development of New Mexico. They have lured skilled workers and their families to a traditionally impoverished state (Lamont 1965; National Science Foundation 2008b) and thereby reallocated human and financial resources from better-off to less prosperous parts of the country. They have facilitated the creation of start-up firms and the relocation of transplants that have generated employment multipliers of their own (Spohn 1996; SNL 2005).[5] And they have bolstered the demand for high-quality state and local services like schools, health care facilities, and transportation and have thereby fostered the creation of the public goods on which the state's future prosperity will depend.

The veneration of risk. Efforts to make the labs more businesslike go hand in hand with the threefold perception that (1) most of their personnel are conservative bureaucrats "hunkered down in their old jobs, fearful that shrinking budgets will cripple or end their careers" (Broad 1992, A1); (2) the occasional entrepreneur is a dynamic risk taker who is "living on the edge" (Pugh 1997, 1); and (3) budget and program cuts will have the salutary effect of encouraging more entrepreneurial activity (Broad

1992). In other words, the diagnosis is risk aversion and the prescription is a cold bath of market forces.

The evidence from New Mexico, however, suggests that entrepreneurship is best cultivated not by augmenting risk but by mitigating it. Entrepreneurial ventures were almost unheard of prior to the development of the ESTT leave programs at Sandia (and Los Alamos; see e.g. Mott 2008) and have become not only more common but surprisingly successful since their adoption (Bruns 2009). Renewable energy development has responded in large measure to state and municipal mandates that guarantee the growth of the market (Matlock 2008b). The admittedly tentative prospects for the Albuquerque renewable energy cluster therefore derive not from the bold efforts of risk-taking entrepreneurs but from the cautious efforts of entrepreneurs who have been able to "minimize the need for risk, initiative, and 'entrepreneurship'" (Brenner 1972, 381) by exploiting their social and political capital, as is so often the case in a market society. While market fundamentalists would in all likelihood either reject such an interpretation out of hand or disdain Albuquerque's green capitalists as a somehow adulterated version of the original article, the weight of the historical evidence suggests that they are more rule than exception and that economic policy must therefore be designed with real human motivations and abilities—rather than simplified economic models—in mind.

Notes

1. For example, Albuquerque ranks forty-ninth among U.S. metropolitan areas in green job creation (Global Insight 2008, 2) and sixty-first among U.S. metro areas in population (U.S. Census Bureau 2000).

2. New Mexico energy politics have traditionally been dominated by the New Mexico Oil and Gas Association, which represents the interests of locally based producers, refiners, processors, and service providers, rather than by the international oil and gas companies. See Logan and Molotch 1987 on the disproportionate influence of local companies in local politics.

3. Nor are Sandia's renewable energy spin-offs limited to solar power firms. Randy Normann recently took leave from the labs to found Perma-Works, a start-up devoted in part to enhanced geothermal systems, with the support of ESTT and the TVC (Burroughs 2008b; *Sandia Lab News* 2008).

4. The differences between Sandia, Los Alamos, and Lawrence Livermore may pale next to the similarities, for Lester and Piore portray both corporate labs like BTL and research universities like the UC as "public spaces within which free-flowing conversations can occur" (2004, 119). All three labs were overseen by organizations imbued with a collaborative rather than a competitive ethos.

5. Green jobs do not necessarily demand higher education. "For instance, construction jobs related to retrofitting homes and commercial buildings to be more energy efficient are green because they lead to the reduction of greenhouse-gas emissions from those buildings," writes Marjorie Childress (2008). "The building trades are one of New Mexico's job sectors that will see green job expansion, and present a prominent path to higher wage jobs for many within New Mexico's lower-income population."

CHAPTER **6**

The CIA's Pioneering Role in Public Venture Capital Initiatives
Matthew R. Keller

While the U.S. government has played a strong role in stimulating technological innovation since World War II (Hooks 1990; Mowery and Rosenberg 1993; Hounshell
1996; Bingham 1998), its developmental apparatus has been significantly expanded over
the past three decades. The result is a decentralized structure of agencies, networks,
and cooperative mechanisms that support technological innovation and the transfer
of technologies from government research facilities to commercial markets—and vice
versa. Although much of the government's role as a developmental state has remained
hidden behind market fundamentalist political rhetoric, the lines dividing the "private"
and "public" roles in innovation dynamics have become increasingly blurred as networks
of technical specialists have become ever more critical to technological innovation
(Hargadon 2003; Lester and Piore 2004; Block and Keller, Chapter 8).

Perhaps the best demonstration of the convergence of the "market" and the "state," or
of the emergent developmental orientation of U.S. government agencies, is the proliferation of targeted public venture capital (VC) initiatives over the past decade. Inspired
by the success of Silicon Valley venture capitalists, these agencies are intended to foster
the development and adaptation of commercially viable technologies for government
agencies' needs. By taking equity investments in small technology firms and playing
a hands-on role in those firms' development, public venture capital programs provide
federal agencies a mechanism to tap into the networks of small and midsize technology
firms that have become increasingly central to innovation, particularly in fields like
information technology. Such programs also provide policymakers with analytic and
rhetorical ammunition to rebut the common argument that government technology
programs involve "corporate welfare." By working within networks of private sector
financing and private technology firms, public venture capital agencies offer the appearance, at least, of leveraging the resources of private investors and using market
mechanisms to promote the development of technologies in the public interest.

What is perhaps most surprising about federal agencies' adoption of public venture
capital strategies is that the primary point of origin for their recent proliferation has
been a historically secretive and insular agency—the CIA. But it was precisely the

CIA that established its own venture capital arm, In-Q-Tel, in 1999 as a means to foster the targeted development of commercial technologies and their integration into agency operations. Within its first few years of operation, the CIA's model had gained wide attention and praise within the federal government, and a host of defense, intelligence, and technologically oriented agencies quickly moved to explore or adopt venture capital initiatives of their own.

In this chapter, I examine the roots of the expansion of public venture capital agencies in the late 1990s and early 2000s, focusing on how a combination of shifts in federal defense and intelligence operations, the increasing commercial orientation of federal research programs, and the Silicon Valley technology boom of the 1990s converged to contribute to the rise of the CIA's In-Q-Tel experiment—and to the subsequent dispersion of the public VC model to other technology-oriented agencies. In documenting how a strategy for developing new technologies in commercial markets expanded across the acquisitions process of the defense and intelligence agencies, I also seek to show why these often secretive agencies have increasingly pushed their research and development processes into the public domain.

The chapter is divided into four parts. First, I briefly review the history of public venture capital initiatives at the state level and the introduction of several proto-venture capitalist programs within the federal government during the 1980s. Second, I trace the series of economic and political dynamics that generated a strategic realignment of government technology and innovation policies in the 1990s—particularly within the intelligence and defense agencies. Third, I trace the contours of the In-Q-Tel experiment, its reception, and its diffusion within the federal government. Fourth, I discuss key reasons why the venture capital model has had such widespread resonance. Roughly a decade after its adoption by a single agency with a $28 million budget, the model has spread to an array of programs spanning multiple agencies and involving hundreds of millions of dollars.

Public Venture Capital: From the States to the Federal Government

Public venture capital programs have an extended history in the United States—at the state level. Sociologists J. Craig Jenkins and Kevin Leicht (1996, 1998; also Jenkins, Leicht and Wendt 2006) traced the emergence of state venture capital programs to 1975, when the Massachusetts Community Development Finance Corporation was established by the Massachusetts state legislature as a quasi-public corporation dedicated to stimulating job growth and economic development. Fifteen years later, some seventeen states had adopted more than thirty venture capital initiatives aimed at stimulating local economic development.[1] Jenkins and Leicht found that the expansion of these programs was centrally tied to a decline in federal allocations to state governments, which in turn prompted states to adopt new strategies to attract entrepreneurial activity and stimulate economic expansion. In fact, cutbacks of federal outlays to the states for developmental and social programs were so pronounced in the

1980s, and state governments became so heavily involved in initiatives to stimulate development, that political scientist Peter Eisinger (1990) suggested that American states "did industrial policy" as much or more than the federal government.

At the federal level, the introduction of venture capital programs was far more gradual and halting. Some of the earliest federal initiatives which employed a quasi-VC approach were the grant and loan programs administrated under the auspices of the Small Business Administration. Prominent among these were the Small Business Innovation Research (SBIR) program, established in 1982 (which followed a pilot program begun under the Carter administration), and the Small Business Technology Transfer Program (STTR) in which federal agencies with large research budgets were required to set aside a small portion for the support of small firms. I call these programs "quasi-venture capital" in orientation because though they attempt to foster emergent technologies by bridging early-stage funding gaps and represent a more speculative, organizational "seeding" approach to stimulating technological innovation, they are in many ways a far cry from the private sector venture capital model. Under the SBIR program, for instance, the government does not gain proprietary rights to supported technologies or shares in supported firms; SBIR program staff provides minimal organizational support to grantee firms, and funding is limited in quantity and duration to two early phases of the development process (see Wessner 2008a). Nevertheless, as we shall see, the SBIR model provided an important step along the road toward the more fully realized venture capital models that would later emerge.

Yet even as late as 1997, when the Organization for Economic Cooperation and Development (OECD) issued a study comparing government venture capital initiatives, it could accurately argue that "even though there is a panoply of programs" like SBIR and SBA loan guarantees, the U.S. government's liberal, market-centric orientation to development had generated one of the most limited embraces of public venture capitalist programs among OECD member states. The report noted that:

> Particularly when account is taken of incentives at the state level, it can be argued that the US government minimises its involvement in that investment decision-making is left to the private sector. (OECD 1997)

Thus, though the report described U.S. support for private sector development through the "innovation" of allowing pension funds to invest in private venture capital funds, the establishment of Small Business Investment Companies (SBIC), which received tax advantages and favorable loan rates, and the government's provision of tax breaks to certain types of firms, these programmatic orientations were rightly treated as relatively minimal and indirect forays into public venture capital strategies.

And indeed, as of 1998, one of the few federal proto-venture capital initiatives that directly invested in small- and medium-size technology firms was under investigation for mismanagement and on its way to closure.[2] The USDA's Alternative Agricultural Research and Commercialization Corporation (AARCC), authorized by Congress in 1990 and initiated in 1992, had been established to "invest in companies that are commercializing ... products, processes, or technologies that use raw materials derived from agriculture, forestry, or animal by-products" (Armstrong 1999). After uncovering irregularities during a 1997 audit, the USDA Inspector General submitted a critical investigative report in late 1999, and the program's budget allocation was canceled for FY 2000.[3]

Yet the timing of the OECD report was less than fortuitous. Within two years of its publication, the first of what would later become a steady stream of venture capital–oriented initiatives emerged. The new wave of VC initiatives followed the example of what seemed to be an unlikely source: the Central Intelligence Agency, an agency neither regarded as a technology policy innovator nor as eager to embrace commercially available technologies. But it was precisely the CIA that established In-Q-Tel, Inc., in 1999 (initially named Peleus, Inc.) as its private, not-for-profit venture capital wing. Within five years of its initiation, the positive reception gained by the CIA model would herald a broad expansion of VC or quasi-VC models within other defense and technology-focused agencies, including the Department of Defense, the Army, the Navy, NASA, the National Technology Alliance, and additional agencies tied to the management of the Department of Energy laboratories. Several of these agencies initiated their own venture capital programs; some partnered with a private venture capital firm; others established new offices or directorates charged with exploring VC models and creating networks and collaborations between government scientists, venture capitalists, and small technology firms. In sum, over the past decade, the public venture capital model has become a legitimate and widespread policy option. Virtually every federal agency with a technology-focused mission has explored public venture capital as a means to stimulate technological innovation and/or commercialization of federal research. As Gilman Louie, the first CEO of In-Q-Tel put it in a 2005 interview, "There wasn't really a government venture fund until we kind of showed up. Is it unique now among government venture funds? The answer is no, because everybody followed us" (Cooper and Kanellos 2005).

From whence did this sudden momentum for the public venture capital model arise? Surprisingly, although private venture capital agencies are at heart profit-making ventures, the initial imperatives driving the adoption of the VC model among federal agencies had little to do with stimulating economic growth. Rather, the main impetus for the introduction and rapid diffusion of VC-style agencies over the past decade has been the desire of defense and intelligence agencies to tap innovations developed for the commercial marketplace. The VC model was utilized as a strategic bridge into the networks of small, innovative firms—like those at the heart of the Silicon Valley boom of the 1990s—working in rapidly changing technological fields. By employing strategies drawn from private sector venture capital firms, government agencies were able to access cutting edge technologies that were otherwise difficult to capture in traditional procurement processes.

Understanding why the often secretive intelligence and defense agencies were at the heart of the charge into venture capital strategies requires an exploration of three related political and economic trends of the late 1980s and 1990s: (1) shifts in the government's approach to fostering innovation and economic development; (2) the consequences of budget tightening and the realignment of defense and intelligence strategies after the fall of the Soviet Union; and (3) the juxtaposition of increasingly outdated technologies within the intelligence agencies alongside an explosion of relevant, commercially available technological innovations. In the 1990s these trends converged to generate substantial pressures for and openness to new strategies for financing the development and integration of new technologies.

The Political Context of Public Venture Capital Initiatives

The Great Commercialization

In the 1980s, and particularly under the Reagan administration, fears of burgeoning international competitiveness in the technological arena helped to generate a plethora of federal legislation and new program initiatives aimed at increasing American competitiveness (Block 2008; Wessner 2008a; Jaffe, Fogarty, and Banks 1998, 184). Many of these programs were concerned with expanding economic growth by facilitating the transformation of technologies developed in federal research facilities and programs into commercially viable products.

Many of these early initiatives emphasized dual-use technologies that had both civilian and military applications. Over time, an emphasis on boosting economic competitiveness came to predominate—a trend that was reinforced by the collapse of the Soviet Union in the early 1990s. The end of the Cold War forced the defense and intelligence establishment to grapple with cutbacks in defense outlays (and threats of even deeper cuts), and to reframe or restructure programs in response to calls for strategic reorientation. By the end of the Reagan era defense buildup in 1989, the defense budget had reached nearly $300 billion and the defense sector employed nearly 7 million people (Alic 2007, 50). In the closing years of George H.W. Bush's presidency and then during the Clinton years, however, military spending and employment began to decline. Military bases were closed and funds for Cold War weapons programs reduced, all while broad debates on transforming the military to fit a post–Cold War environment lurched through Washington. Indeed, in the early 1990s some congressional supporters of the Reagan era defense buildup acknowledged that defense budgets appeared to be entering a period of "free fall" (Markusen and Hill 1992). Secretary of defense Dick Cheney's budget proposals from 1991 to 1997 brought annual defense expenditures down to roughly $244 billion, while other contemporaneous analyses were suggesting that defense outlays could be slashed to $200 billion or substantially less by the turn of the century (Markusen and Hill 1992, 7–8). Though these deeper cuts never materialized, the roughly one-sixth reduction in military outlays and the widespread agreement that cuts were necessary reflected a rare moment of vulnerability for military spending programs.

The economic implications of these developments were political landmines. Given the impending spending cuts and troop reductions, policymakers quickly recognized the importance of creating jobs in other sectors of the economy to offset military layoffs. The concerns applied to both low- and high-wage workers, as reductions of Cold War weapons programs and R&D initiatives threatened government and private sector scientists and engineers as well as rank-and-file personnel. The scale of the human capital involved was starkly apparent in the planned closure of scores of military bases that followed three biannual rounds of commission reviews mandated by the Defense Base Closure and Realignment Act of 1990.[4]

The ripple effects of the planned downsizing were also substantial. Spending cuts were bound to have an impact on the chains of contractors, suppliers, and service providers oriented to military production. Many large defense-oriented firms were entirely or almost entirely dedicated to government contracts; those that had attempted forays into cost-efficient production for consumer markets had a dubious record of success (Markusen and Hill 1992). Since defense contractors typically located headquarters and manufacturing operations within the United States, the risks for the American economy and the American worker were substantial. Concerns that communities or even regional economies might collapse were expressed by economists and officials at all levels of government.

Responding to these new political circumstances, the Clinton administration placed renewed emphasis on using government R&D facilities as supports for job creation and economic growth. In the face of conservative calls for the Department of Energy to be abolished as a vestige of the Cold War, and in the wake of the 1994 Galvin Commission's recommendation that the DOE labs be "corporatized," Energy secretary Hazel O'Leary responded by marketing the labs as a potential resource for American corporations and, more broadly, as committed to generating economic growth. "Our mission now is economic security," she remarked in a 1995 presentation to corporate executives on the changing focus of the labs, "it's about creating jobs ... If we don't create jobs, then it's a failure" (quoted in Gaul and Stranahan 1995).

Changes in lab strategies were often dramatic. Faulted in the late 1980s for failing to adapt their culture to potential corporate partners (Charles 1988), by the mid-1990s the labs were being criticized for favoring the interests of large corporations in research and licensing agreements, often to the detriment of entrepreneurial lab scientists and local or regional development (Markusen and Oden 1996). With the department committing substantial funds to subsidize corporate partnerships, the number of CRADAs (cooperative research and development agreements) exploded, giving rise to charges that government labs were subsidizing corporate profits. In response to a series of critical internal and external assessments, CRADAs declined just as dramatically over a subsequent two-year period (Lawler 1996; Department of Energy 2007), as the labs began experimenting with more diversified strategies for supporting technology transfer and commercialization. Alongside CRADAs, these included an expanding set of WFO (Work for Others) agreements, cooperative ventures with universities, licensing partnerships, and offering entrepreneurial consultations and brokering services for lab personnel interested in initiating their own ventures.

But the key point is that during the 1980s and 1990s, fears of declining American economic competitiveness and the conversion away from a Cold War military orientation fostered an era of strategic experimentation and cultural transformation for many of the federal government's research arms. The often insular culture of government labs was eroded by pressures to commercialize; scientists who had once relied solely upon government research funds were pushed to find external support; a cornucopia of strategies for fostering the transfer of government research into commercial products were explored. Government technology programs were becoming far more experimental, and far more attuned to the private sector.[5]

The Silicon Valley Boom

Government technology policies and the intelligence agencies' approach to commercial markets were strongly influenced by a second key factor: the central role of small start-up firms during the Silicon Valley technology boom of the 1990s. The explosion of new internet and computer-based technologies developed by these firms had a twofold impact on government intelligence capacities and approaches to technological development. First, enormous flows of investment capital into the technology sector made it more difficult for government agencies to attract software engineers at precisely the moment when programming was becoming critical to cutting-edge military operations and intelligence-gathering techniques. The astronomical financial windfalls that beckoned entrepreneurs potentially dwarfed the salaries and nullified the benefits of employment stability available in government agencies. Potential profits from commercial markets (or from selling new technologies to large corporations) were more rapidly accessible and more lucrative than government contracts; the flexibility and short-term relations of commercial markets provided entrepreneurs the chance to quickly exit one interest to start another, rather than remain locked into a long-term contract as a government supplier.[6]

Second, and equally important, was the dispersed nature of the computer-related technology boom. Relatively open programming architectures and the ability to start a new firm with limited initial investments had the effect of broadly distributing innovative capacities across a wide number of small firms and individual entrepreneurs. Rather than dedicate their own workforces to generating innovations in a rapidly changing field, many large corporations simply waited for small firms to develop promising technologies and then bought them out—a fact well-known by entrepreneurs hoping to profit from quick, profitable sales of their ventures. For government agencies attempting to remain on the cutting edge of new technological developments, however, this dispersed innovative environment created distinct problems. Agencies that contracted with the large firms and suppliers favored by traditional procurement contracts were by definition receiving "second order" technologies that had been created by a small firm, purchased, licensed, or adapted by a larger firm, and then finally passed on to government agencies as the end user. There was little room in such processes for shaping innovations to fit specific agency needs; agencies rather adapted commercially available technologies to fit their own, individual requirements—even when the technologies might not have been designed for the precise purpose they ultimately served.

Moreover, in the rapidly changing milieu of the technology boom, using second order technologies meant that government agencies were not only behind the product development curve, but that the technologies had often become outdated by the time they passed through the agencies' rigorous review systems. The CIA, for instance, required no fewer than six formal boards with multiple levels of review to approve a new technology before it could be integrated into agency operations (Business Executives for National Security 2001, x). Any agency employee could presumably set up his or her own personal computer with more advanced tools than the ones that had made their way through the approval processes. Although the government had loosened restrictions on commercial off-the-shelf (COTS) purchases in the 1980s, similar problems pervaded the defense and intelligence industries as new information and communications technologies exploded in the late 1990s. As former defense secretary and then vice presidential candidate Dick Cheney put it in a 2000 interview:

> We do need to think about how we invest in new technology—how we take advantage of the revolution in information technology, for example—and feed that into the force and use it. Vast numbers of our vehicles in the US military don't have Global Positioning System units on them ... yet many recreational boats have them. We have not made that investment in enormously valuable pieces of equipment that are cheap, and take advantage of modern technology. (*PBS Frontline* 2000)

Further, since small- and medium-size private firms were outpacing the innovative capacity of key government agencies—at least in certain industries critical to intelligence work—it also meant that the government was suddenly running into cost and dependency issues. Rather than developing new systems, they were purchasing old ones and relying on external agencies or individual technologists to adapt and update them, often at significant cost. Independent agencies and those requiring secrecy now risked becoming either technologically outmoded or dependent on external corporate suppliers.

But how to tap into the boom was a conundrum. The fact that the software-based innovations increasingly relevant for intelligence gathering were rooted in relatively open programming languages and architectural systems had critical importance. Whereas only a select few firms had the capacity and know-how to design and build a new missile or a fighter jet prototype, the nature of computer programming enabled individual entrepreneurs and small firms a much greater potential for innovation. This added to the complexity of the government's problem in developing and integrating novel technologies. On one hand, small firms rarely had the capacity or resources to file the requisite paperwork and endure the often lengthy delays involved in government procurement processes. On the other hand, the instability and niche orientation of the small firms involved in the technology boom of the 1990s meant that government agencies could not be assured that new partners had long-term viability. A specific firm might be absorbed or go bankrupt overnight. Establishing relationships with the purveyors of novel technologies thus posed a security risk for intelligence agencies. The proprietary rights to a technology developed by a small firm might be sold to the highest bidder, who might or might not have an interest in developing the technologies along the lines useful to government. And the enormous amount of time spent screening and approving a new supplier might go to waste if the company disappeared or was acquired by another firm. Traditional procurement processes were constructed for a far different and far more stable environment.

Of course, even if procurement processes could be adapted to the new context,[7] another problem remained: unlike traditional weaponry programs which had few potential clients, the internet and personal computer boom fostered the growth of an industry far more attuned to the consumer market. Few buyers could afford F-14s or Patriot missiles, so their producers built them to government specifications. But with the personal computer becoming ubiquitous within the developed world, computer technologies were being designed for mass markets, and there was no guarantee that technologies seeking to capture market share could be modified to meet intelligence or defense agency needs. Government agencies needed new, flexible strategies to tap into and shape these consumer technologies.

Challenges to Intelligence Gathering: Limited Resources, Expanded Mandate, Outmoded Technologies

In parallel with these developments, the intelligence agencies were undergoing programmatic shifts of their own. In the early 1990s the CIA and other intelligence agencies were unable to escape funding cuts in the wake of the Soviet collapse. From 1990 to 1996 core intelligence allocations declined; from 1996 to 2000 they were basically flat, although in a few cases they were boosted by supplemental resources (as was the case in 1995, when the Clinton administration expanded the FBI budget and supplemented CIA resources following the bombing of a federal building in Oklahoma City and the sarin gas attacks in a Tokyo subway). In the midst of the cuts, some overseas intelligence offices were closed, and officer recruitment was curtailed.

In 1998 Congress and the administration initiated a longer-term rebuilding program for the intelligence apparatus. That process built upon ongoing debates concerning how to redesign the intelligence services to fit a post–Cold War world. The dissolution of the Soviet Union—the primary focus of intelligence operations for the previous half century—required a paradigmatic shift in intelligence tactics. Rather than focus on well-established Cold War adversaries primarily working with and through foreign states, the intelligence services had suddenly been left to grapple with often dispersed organizational networks operating outside the boundaries of the state system. Moreover, just as the agencies' resources were tightening, they were faced with an explosion of Internet and other communications technologies that could be used as a coordination tool by loosely linked and geographically distant groups. As one NSA official put it in testimony before the 9/11 Commission, the post–Cold War proliferation of communications technologies dramatically enhanced the "volume, variety, and velocity" of potentially relevant information that required monitoring and analysis (National Commission on Terrorist Attacks upon the United States 2004, 86).

As the 9/11 Commission further documented, the emerging situation required a dramatic change in the intelligence agencies' orientation to technology policy and data sharing. During the Cold War, the intelligence services had focused on preventing foreign agents from hacking into or compromising classified data, and thus they had typically set up carefully guarded and delinked agency-specific data repositories. In the CIA the bunker mentality was exacerbated by a decentralized organizational structure and the embarrassment of the Aldrich Ames scandal (Ames was arrested for selling information on American agents in 1994, despite the agency's nearly decade-long awareness of a leak).

But it was becoming increasingly clear that strategic shifts were necessary. President Bill Clinton captured the building momentum for transforming agency tactics in a 1995 speech to the CIA, when he remarked:

> I want to work with you to … meet the demands of a new era. Today our government is deluged with more and more information from more and more sources. What once was secret can now be available to anybody with cable TV or access to the Internet. It moves around the world at record speed.… That means we have to rethink what we collect and how we organize the intelligence community to collect it. (Clinton 1995)

By the mid- to late-1990s, a host of advisory commissions and panels, including bodies such as the Aspin-Brown Commission (which was "chartered by Congress … to conduct a comprehensive review of American intelligence" [Commission on the Roles and Capabilities of the United States Intelligence Community 1996]), were generating recommendations on precisely how to rethink the process, increasing the momentum for reform. Less than a year after George Tenet's official confirmation as director of the CIA in 1997, he launched a Strategic Direction initiative that opened the agency's technology policies for review (Yanuzzi 2000). The initiative provided a fortuitous opening for the convergence of the aforementioned dynamics: a broad exploration of strategies for commercialization among federal research agencies; strategic re-visioning within the intelligence agencies; and the awareness of a rapidly growing technology gap between government agencies and commercially available technologies. An early proposal that came to Tenet's attention originated from Dr. Ruth David, the CIA's director of science and technology, who had recently come to the CIA after a twenty-year career in the Sandia National Laboratory—a DOE lab well-known for fostering commercialization (Schrank, Chapter 5). David and her staff proposed a relatively novel strategy for upgrading agency technologies by tapping into the commercial technology boom: establishing a public sector venture capital agency.

The In-Q-Tel Innovation

David's initial proposal quickly gained steam. In the summer of 1998, a task force charged with fleshing out the proposal spent some four months in a series of consultations with Silicon Valley venture capitalists, technology firms, and others (for an overview, see Yanuzzi 2000; Laurent 2002; Molzahn 2003; Belko 2004). The task force generated a modified and expanded proposal for the creation of an independent venture capital agency designed to serve the programmatic interests of the CIA. By the end of the year Norman Augustine, a former CEO of Lockheed-Martin and longtime DOD supporter and collaborator, was asked to take the reins in establishing the initiative. Augustine's willingness to lead the project signaled its seriousness: his influence in the DOD and reputation for a keen understanding of the intersection between public and private sector agencies led some to dub him "Saint Augustine" (Hartung 1996).

In February 1999, roughly a year after the venture capital proposal began making the rounds, In-Q-Tel was formally established by Congress as a private, independent, and nonprofit corporation that received its funding entirely from the federal government's intelligence appropriations. The new agency's initial annual budget was $28 million; since then it has grown to more than $60 million.

In-Q-Tel's mandate was to act as a "hybrid of the private sector and the CIA/government technology procurement processes" (Business Executives for National Security 2001). As such it "operated less like a conventional venture capital (VC) fund and more like a corporate strategic venture fund" (Lerner et al. 2004, 1). That is, the agency invested in the development of commercial technologies that ultimately had market potential and could be applied or adapted to meet CIA imperatives.[8] Those agency imperatives were established through a then-novel, agencywide survey that was translated into a series of "problem sets," or general interest areas, which were to guide investment decisions. The agency's operating style has evolved over time, but it generally adopted a hybrid strategy that combined elements of a private venture capital agency and a government laboratory or procurement agency. Thus, on one hand the agency supported technological development through equity investments in small firms,[9] provided strategic consultation and organizational guidance for supported organizations, and engaged in development partnerships with other venture capitalists or large firms, much like a private venture firm. On the other hand, In-Q-Tel also operated like a government lab or procurement agency by contracting with companies to purchase licenses or develop technologies and in offering some partners the use of its prototype laboratories for testing and product development.

One of the more novel features of this hybrid model—from the point of view of government technology programs—was the agency's willingness to work within funding networks, rather than as a sole or majority funder, or a lead partner. Rather than design promising technologies in-house, the agency attempted to specify and support promising technological developments. Indeed, In-Q-Tel's founders hoped that the support of a CIA-affiliated agency would serve a "certifying role" for supported firms that would help to *attract* additional investors, thus leveraging private resources to help develop technologies for use within the government.

This orientation had several critical implications that enhanced the reception of the concept within the government. First, it served to disperse investment risk, or at least criticism of the agency's investment choices. Venture capital strategies are necessarily given leeway for investing in ultimately unprofitable technologies; only a certain percentage of investments are expected to "hit." But by enlisting networks of well-regarded private investment firms as partners, agencies further insulated their choices from criticism. Private venture capital firms had already developed an array of tools for assessing technologies and their organizational purveyors, as well as techniques for guiding supported technologies toward commercial markets. Of course, many firms supported by private venture capitalists never become profitable. But by utilizing the well-refined assessment tools employed by profit-dependent firms, the new agency effectively shielded itself from charges of "picking winners" in an isolated fashion, and thereby distorting innovation and market processes. Even when In-Q-Tel "missed" in one or a range of its assessments, the odds were that an array of savvy, profit-focused investors had made the same mistake.

Second, by working within investor networks, the public venture capital model offered policymakers an effective rebuttal to the charge that government funding of private firms was "corporate welfare." In leveraging private investments for the support of technologies that could be adapted to CIA needs, In-Q-Tel could argue that its strategy had a "multiplier effect" on government research allocations. Who is leveraging whom in a public-private investment combination can always be contested. But early evaluations of In-Q-Tel clearly promulgated the notion that it was the government which was multiplying its investment dollars, and not the other way around. As one 2001 external review by a panel of corporate leaders crowed, In-Q-Tel had "leveraged 2.15 dollars for every dollar spent on equity, internal R&D, and entrepreneurial funded development" (Business Executives for National Security 2001, xv).

The logic of each of these positions can, of course, be turned on its head: the argument about cooperative funding can be transformed into suggestions of government investments subsidizing profits; the use of private investment firms' tools as a means of decision making can be depicted as a hallmark of dependence and conformity to the investment whims of others. This made early investment successes—and well-publicized ones, at that—particularly important to In-Q-Tel's longer-term viability. Generally, most assessments suggested that In-Q-Tel did succeed in its early investment decisions. Perhaps the best known In-Q-Tel investment involved its 2003 investment in Keyhole, a firm eventually acquired by Google, which marketed the technology as Google Earth.

The Keyhole investment reflected a broader pattern in In-Q-Tel's early investments, which tended to favor computer-based technologies in areas drawn from the agency's problem sets.[10] An early investment in Las Vegas firm Systems Research and Development to develop software for identifying nonobvious relationships (which has also been used by gaming casinos) was followed by support to a number of other firms (e.g., Endeca, Intelliseek, and Attensity) that were developing technologies aimed at searching, extracting, and analyzing unstructured data, often across multiple language platforms. In 2003, support to Language Weaver further reinforced an emphasis on automatic language translation capacities. Later investment rounds emphasized visual and display technologies (including support of the Canadian firm IDELIX for its pliable display technology, which promised improved manipulation and convergence of multiple visual data streams, and the U.S. firm MotionDSP for video enhancement technologies), and data storage, management, and security. Other emphases have come in the areas of energy technologies and nanotechnologies, where support has ranged from relatively obscure to well-known firms like NanoSys, a Palo Alto firm that has collaborated with Intel, among others, in its development processes. In total, In-Q-Tel has invested in more than 100 firms and 10 research labs in the United States and Canada; eighty-nine portfolio companies were listed on its website (www .iqt.org) as of October 2009.

Embedding Autonomy, or Disembedding the CIA?

One of the key challenges in the creation of a hybrid public-private organization such as In-Q-Tel concerns how to effectively "embed autonomy" (Evans 1995): to maintain oversight of and integration into the agency's operations, yet to provide the degree of flexibility and autonomy necessary to create partnerships with external networks—and to avoid undue regulation by nontechnical bureaucratic staff or agency operatives. The founders of In-Q-Tel clearly took this issue seriously; their solution was the creation of the In-Q-Tel Interface Center (QIC).

The QIC is at heart an integrative link between the civilian venture analysts employed by In-Q-Tel and the agency. Staffed by CIA personnel, its job is to compile and then convey the CIA's technology needs to In-Q-Tel, to monitor In-Q-Tel's technology investments to ensure their compatibility with CIA imperatives, and to serve as a vehicle for transitioning technologies into agency operations. Thus it is the QIC that develops the agencywide problem sets, monitors the In-Q-Tel portfolio to ensure its compatibility with CIA needs, and takes primary responsibility for integrating the technologies that result from In-Q-Tel investments.

In practice, the QIC's early efforts to achieve an effective balance between oversight and autonomy were rocky, at best. An external review conducted in 2001 found that two years after its founding, CIA decision makers remained relatively unaware of In-Q-Tel activities and resistant to siphoning off agency funds for an unproven experiment. Others within the CIA resisted the idea of integrating technologies not developed in-house. The QIC, the evaluation continued, had focused too much on the monitoring side and not enough on creating an environment in which technologies could be smoothly transitioned into the agency (Business Executives for National Security 2001). These problems were, however, mainly organizational in scope, and hardly amounted to fatal flaws. The agency subsequently "implemented several initiatives to streamline and expedite technology insertion ... and aggressively market In-Q-Tel's capabilities within the agency" (Molzahn 2003). Although there are few publicly accessible reviews available to assess the efficacy of the QIC's operations, given the agency's claims to have "delivered more than 260 technology solutions to the Intelligence Community" since its inception, and the willingness of other intelligence agencies like the FBI and DIA to invest in In-Q-Tel, it would seem that many of these early concerns have been addressed.

Yet even if the QIC has been able to enhance its effectiveness as a bridge between the CIA and In-Q-Tel, the issue of striking the right balance between embeddedness and autonomy is critical in a broader sense. The creation of flexible, public-private hybrid organizations on the model of In-Q-Tel raises the question of whether such arrangements could be used to effectively *disembed* an agency from federal oversight and regulatory structures.[11] Indeed, in 2005, the Congressional Research Service issued a report that openly wondered whether the expansion of quasi-governmental agencies like In-Q-Tel should be "viewed as ... a symptom of a decline in our democratic system of governance or as a harbinger of a new, creative management era where the principles of market behavior are harnessed for the general well-being of the nation" (Moe and Kosar 2005). In the former interpretation, the merging of private and public domains under the auspices of a quasi-governmental organization risks the loss of hierarchical controls and bureaucratic checks and balances covering the use of public funds, and insofar as such agencies blur the legal lines between public and private entities, they are likely to expand the potential for conflicts of interest. These concerns are particularly cogent in the case of the CIA, which has a long history of attempts to evade federal oversight.[12]

Employing the latter interpretation, however, supporters claim these new approaches offer a flexible and responsive structure of public management, open the door for innovative partnerships, and provide an opportunity to introduce more performance-driven evaluative criteria in the use of public funds. In such views, a failure to adopt flexible organizational strategies attuned to the development of novel technologies ultimately threatens both national security and national economic interests.

These issues remain unresolved in general terms and in the case of particular organizational incarnations. But one can see the potential for conflicts even in In-Q-Tel's publicly listed practice areas, which include bio, chemical, and nanotechnologies. In fact the CIA is prohibited from developing biological or chemical weaponry under the provisions of various international agreements. While In-Q-Tel's investments in this area are aimed at so-called defensive technologies (e.g., the identification of trace or bulk materials and point-of-care medical technologies), it is nevertheless clear that the line between defensive and offensive purposes is exceedingly blurry (Leitenberg 2003). The use of a privately held entity to develop such technologies for a public sector agency similarly falls into an ambiguous legal space. Given the record of CIA attempts to evade regulatory controls, such ambiguities are troubling.

A number of additional early criticisms from both inside and outside the government similarly focused on the issue of the agency's ability to strike a balance between autonomy and oversight. In the press, a series of *New York Post* articles accused In-Q-Tel, among other things, of serving as a "pump and dump" agency that manipulated investments for personal profit. A 2005 article alleged that several In-Q-Tel employees were involved in an insider-trading scheme in which they had "staged an end-run around In-Q-Tel's not-for-profit legal status" to "benefit personally from the fund's investments" (Bryon 2005, 2006a). These critiques of the agency emphasized the capacity for misuse of a profit-oriented structure and cast a new light on supporters' claims that it would take just one 'big win" for the agency to pay for itself (Business Executives for National Security 2001, xvi). Such critiques were enhanced by In-Q-Tel's salary structure—the company's relatively generous base salaries (scaled to a sample of wage rates for comparable positions in both the public and private sectors) were supplemented by departmental and individual performance bonuses. The agency maintained that these compensation policies were needed to recruit quality employees to work for the agency—an ostensible necessity given that In-Q-Tel is staffed by analysts who do not have CIA security clearances.

But generally, In-Q-Tel has received positive or neutral publicity from the press. The agency received a flood of applications from technology firms following the publication of articles covering the agency's launch in the *New York Times* and *Washington Post* (Laurent 2002). And even the *New York Post* eventually acknowledged that "no one batted an eye" after the initial publication of their accusations (Bryon 2006b).

Programmatic reviews have largely emphasized the promise of the agency's flexibility and market orientation. The 2001 external evaluation, conducted by a group of private business leaders, "applaud[ed] the CIA and Congressional leadership for breaking with tradition and demonstrating the willingness to take a risk when attacking a technological challenge." It argued that the agency's early activities provided "noteworthy accomplishments and the start of a good track record" even by private sector standards, adding that given this positive early progress and the difficulties of evaluating venture capital initiatives in the short run, In-Q-Tel should be free from additional substantive review until its initial five-year mandate ended in 2004 (Business Executives for National Security 2001, vii–xvii).

By the time that five-year window had closed, the broader verdict on In-Q-Tel had largely been set in stone. As early as 2002, In-Q-Tel was singled out by the Senate Intelligence Committee for effectively promoting a "symbiotic relationship between the intelligence community and the private sector using innovative approaches." In-Q-Tel, the committee's report continued, "shows great promise," and was recommended as a model for stimulating technological innovation that should be explored by other federal agencies (see Senator Graham's statement, *Congressional Record* S11572). Given that In-Q-Tel had only been in existence for roughly three years at that point, and that it typically takes a round of venture firm investments four to six years before it can be evaluated, the recommendation seemed premature. But it revealed how the adoption of private sector investment techniques could successfully appeal across partisan lines in a security obsessed post-9/11 atmosphere. New strategies for integrating leading-edge commercial technologies into defense and intelligence operations were in demand; the public VC model clearly fit the bill.

The Great Dispersion

The positive reception of the In-Q-Tel experiment helped generate and accelerate a broader push for adapting, adopting, or exploring public venture capital strategies within federal agencies. The push was enhanced by the reaction to 9/11, when criticisms of the intelligence agencies' failures to definitively foresee the attacks mushroomed into a broad critique of technology policies and capacities. The 9/11 Commission's narrative provided ammunition to critics of the intelligence community's technical capacities and the lack of information sharing networks and fueled calls for more rapid integration of technologies for the capture and analysis of information, as well as the development and integration of networked technological systems that promoted information sharing among security agencies.

Other federal agencies, which had been monitoring the In-Q-Tel experiment and its reception, rapidly began to assemble their own VC initiatives. There were, however, many options for tapping into venture capital markets and models; directly employing In-Q-Tel was not possible in the agency's early years since In-Q-Tel's founders and oversight agencies initially ruled out expanding its mandate to serve other organizational clients.[13] Other agencies were thus left to find their own way forward, and they adopted different iterations of the much-praised model (see Table 6.1). In late 2001, the Department of Defense created DeVenCI (Defense Venture Capital Initiative) to foster networks between DOD agencies and small firms working on technologies of interest. DeVenCI did not, and does not, directly fund technology firms; rather, it communicates information on the department's technology needs and facilitates collaborative relations between the DOD, venture capitalists, and small technology firms working in those fields. A cascade of venture capital programs established by different branches of the DOD followed. With an initial congressional allocation of $25 million, in 2002 the Army established OnPoint Technologies, its own nonprofit "venture capital investment corporation" (Defense Appropriations Act of 2002, PL 107–117, Section 8150). Like In-Q-Tel, OnPoint was designed to develop "better collaborative ties with young, small, growth-oriented companies that take risks and push innovation" (Army Broad Agency Announcement DAAB07–02–R-B223). One main organizational difference was that rather than establish its own structure, the Army selected the management of OnPoint through a competitive bidding process (see Osama 2008).

The Navy's Research Advisory Committee (NRAC) created a Venture Capital Panel in 2002 to study the agency's linkages with venture capitalists and its support of emergent technologies. Its recommendations led to the 2003 addition of a venture initiative to the Commercial Technology Transition Office (CTTO) of the Office of Naval Research. Much like DeVenCI, the Navy's initiative was not authorized to fund technologies but rather to act as a deal broker between small firms and naval acquisitions programs (Office of the Under Secretary of Defense 2004, F8). The Navy panel has not given the initiative a permanent role but rather has been working on short-term mandates to expand links with venture capitalists and small technology firms. Other Navy programs are designed to bolster networks between the Navy, small firms, university researchers, and investors. VCs@Sea, a program designed to familiarize the venture capital community with the Navy's technology needs, emerged from these initial explorations, as did the Center for Commercialization of Advanced Technology (CCAT), a program funded by Congress through the Office of Naval Research, which works through collaborative networks to fast-track the development of new technologies relevant to defense and security programs.

Outside the DOD, a number of agencies also strengthened or expanded the venture capital aspects of their operations. In 2002 Rosettex Technology and Ventures Group, a private consortium which manages the National Technology Alliance (NTA)

Table 6.1 New Federal Venture Capital Initiatives After 1999[a]

Established/ Contracted	Agency	VC Initiative	Type[b]
1999	CIA	In-Q-Tel	Targeted
2001	Department of Defense	DeVenCI	Networking
2002	Army	OnPoint Technologies	Targeted
2002	National Technology Alliance	Rosettex Venture Fund	Targeted
2003	NSA	NSA Office of Corporate Development	Unclear[c]
2003	Battelle/DoE Labs	Battelle Ventures	Commercialization
		Innovation Valley Partners	
2003	Navy	VCs@Sea	Networking
		NRAC VC Panel	
2004–2005	FBI	Each agency contracted with In-Q-Tel	Targeted
	DIA		
	NGA		
2006	Red Planet Ventures (funding allocation eliminated, 2007)	NASA	Targeted

a. For a list of VC-style programs in federal and state governments prior to 1999, see Lerner 1999b.

b. A "targeted" initiative makes equity investments in small firms and/or technologies deemed relevant to agency imperatives. A "networking" initiative does not directly fund firms but rather establishes ties, shares information, and/or brokers deals between government agencies, small firms, and private venture capitalists. A "commercialization" initiative is primarily concerned with spinning out research conducted in government facilities into the commercial marketplace. This categorization is based on the Homeland Security Institute's (2005) classification.

c. The NSA's venture capital arm is mentioned in a 2004 DOD publication, "Defense Industrial Base Capabilities Study: Force Application" (see page F-13). However, as of this writing, I have uncovered no records of its strategy, activities, or budget.

(a government program established in 1987 to foster dual-use technologies and their integration into intelligence and defense programs) signed a $200 million, five-year contract to use the newly created Rosettex Venture Fund to stimulate innovative technologies (www.nga.mil/NGASiteContent/StaticFiles/OCR/nima0202.pdf). In 2003 Battelle, the large nonprofit organization that manages a number of the Department of Energy laboratories, established Battelle Ventures (www.battelleventures.com), a $220 million, independent, and nonprofit venture fund that invests in technologies related to "security, health and life sciences, and energy and environment." Battelle also maintains "a $35-million affiliate fund, Innovation Valley Partners (IVP) ... [that] proportionately invests alongside Battelle Ventures in all deals." In 2006 NASA partnered with a nonprofit venture capital fund, Red Planet Capital, to "gain access to new and innovative technologies through the venture capital community" (NASA Press Release, September 20, 2006). In sum, public sector venture capital strategies rapidly became broadly accepted tools for spurring mission-oriented technological innovation and/or to transform government research into commercial products.[14]

As noted in Table 6.1, not all venture capital agencies operate in the same manner. The venture funds affiliated with DOE laboratories are primarily focused on commercializing innovations spawned by DOE research scientists, not on integrating commercial technologies into lab operations. Unlike In-Q-Tel, OnPoint and Red Planet ventures were designed to be managed by external firms. Yet though these initiatives have different objectives, are relatively small in scale, and are often justified as experimental in nature, their rapid diffusion within a heavily bureaucratized environment signals a newfound openness to private sector strategies and networks, and an acknowledgement of the widespread belief that links with networks of small, private firms and private investors can help stimulate the development of technologies more rapidly and effectively than traditional procurement processes and internal R&D.

Public Venture Capital as a Means to Tap Networks of Innovative Small Firms

The federal government has long been aware of the innovative role of small businesses (Wessner 2008a). But post–Cold War budget reductions, paired with the Internet and computer technology boom of the 1990s and the increasingly short cycle of innovation that it involved, pressured key federal agencies to explore new strategies for engaging small, innovative firms working in fields critical to agency operations. In the wake of 9/11, integrating small, innovative firms into networks of agency suppliers and experts became a de facto mandate rather than an option to be considered.

But the question of why the public venture capital model diffused so quickly across the defense and intelligence agencies bears elaboration. Five key factors seem to have bolstered the resonance of the model. The first concerns the failure of traditional government procurement processes and arm's length contracting procedures to either build the technical capacities of personnel *within* agencies, or to effectively integrate technologies in rapidly changing fields. In many cases, those charged with procurement do not have the expertise to monitor the quality of cutting-edge technologies or expert contractors, and even when they do, there are often few incentives for career-oriented officers to blow the whistle on cost overruns or programs that no longer fit an agency's strategic needs (Alic 2007). But in the post-9/11 atmosphere, implementation delays or poorly working technological systems within the intelligence agencies suddenly became a matter of major political consequence. The public venture capital model adopted by the CIA offered, first, an opportunity to fast-track cutting-edge technologies into agency operations through the creation of interactive networks of financiers, small technology firms, and agency representatives.

There were other ways to speed technological acquisition. But a second critical advantage offered by the public venture capital model was the opportunity it provided to expand and strengthen the networks of experts at the disposal of federal agencies. Working in tandem with private sector venture capital firms and investors, public VC programs are able to coopt tools for assessing the viability of innovative firms and technologies that private agencies have honed through trial and error. Simultaneously, government agents are able to network with and learn from technical experts working in the small innovative firms that have typically fallen outside the ambit of procurement processes. In an innovation economy in which small firms play an increasingly central role (Hunt and Nakamura 2006; Block and Keller, Chapter 8), these networks play an instrumental role in keeping agencies abreast of emerging technologies.

Third, policymakers learned many of the limits of investing in small, commercially oriented firms along the lines of the other primary model available within the federal government: the Small Business Innovation Research program. On the one hand, critics have long charged that the program has given rise to "SBIR mills" that replicate the cozy personal and institutional relationships between large defense contractors and DOD agencies (Wessner 1999), although it is difficult to determine without detailed case analysis whether frequent SBIR award winners are "SBIR mills" or "SBIR champions" that consistently produce useable technologies.[15] But the existence of a small pool of serial SBIR awardees points to the more pertinent difficulty encountered by supporting commercially oriented firms at the start-up stage: the relative instability of small firms generates significant problems for agencies interested in particular technologies. If Microsoft or Google buys out a start-up that has developed a promising technology through an SBIR award, there is no guarantee that the corporate entity will have an interest in developing that technology along the same lines desired by a government agency. Moreover, a small firm developing a promising new technology may not have savvy marketing skills or the managerial expertise necessary to maintain long-term organizational viability. SBIR programs have long struggled with finding effective ways to support firms transitioning technologies into the marketplace. Over the past fifteen years, many SBIR offices have moved in the direction of the public venture capital model by increasing organizational supports to SBIR firms; by expanding programs aimed at brokering deals between prime contractors, venture capitalists, government agencies, · and awardees; and by experimenting with strategies to provide bridge funding during key points of the development process.[16]

Public venture capital programs essentially solve these problems. They allow a government agency to take a hands-on role with a supported firm—through membership in a small firm's board of directors, cooperative prototype testing, and ongoing organizational and technical collaboration. Establishing tighter direct links with the product developers allows the agency to shape early stage technological developments in ways that meet agency needs. Even if the firm is eventually acquired by a larger corporation, the relationship between the original innovators and the government agency is left intact. Those ongoing relationships offer the opportunity for further collaboration with the product developers to, for instance, adapt the technology for new or unforeseen purposes that were not required in the commercial version of the product. One limitation is that an In-Q-Tel cannot make an extensive investment in nearly as many firms as a program such as SBIR. But by leveraging external resources and targeting mission-oriented programs with clear application potential, it can play a key role in advancing desired technology streams.

In this respect, public venture capital programs also play a certifying role for private investors, as the selection of a company signals the potential opening of a new market for the technology. By no means does the purchasing power of the intelligence community guarantee profitability, but the ability to open a restricted market provides potential value added to private sector investors. If public venture capital agencies prove adept in integrating technologies across a variety of government agencies, this sort of certification likely will become increasingly important.

One can thus view the SBIR program as an important part of a social learning process. SBIR's limits, arrayed alongside the program's numerous positive evaluations, revealed many of the important dimensions that the new public venture capital programs have sought to address.

Fourth, and as mentioned, there are unquestionable strategic advantages in working with smaller and more flexible firms rather than with the traditionally large and bureaucratic government contractors. To some degree, agency investments can be "hedged" across a broader set of firms, lessening dependence on single suppliers. Decision makers are more insulated from the political fallout that may come with the almost inevitable delays and cost overruns that characterize large-scale procurement projects. Venture capital programs are acknowledged to involve risk; they allow a far easier exit from underperforming private firms or situations involving unforeseen technical or organizational problems; and they proceed on many different fronts, allowing failures to be downplayed so long as other investments flourish. Given the defense and intelligence agencies' need to be at the leading edge of computer-based technological developments, the public venture capital model allows these agencies to tap small-firm led innovation environments and to stay abreast of the short innovation cycles characteristic of commercial markets.

The fifth factor helps to explain the defense and intelligence-centered nature of the new public venture capital initiatives. Clearly, changing historical circumstances, political pressures, and the burst of commercial technologies of the 1990s are a part of the story. But another key element is the peculiar development of the U.S. government's innovation policy in the face of the market fundamentalist ideology that has dominated political discourse over the past several decades. While civilian agencies like the now defunct Advanced Technology Program in the Department of Commerce faced relentless political pressure and constant threats to its survival (Negoita, Chapter 4), innovative and *durable* developmental strategies and programs have tended to emerge under the protective guise of national security interests.

Indeed, national security has often served as the only justification immune from the charge that government action serves to distort market processes. The point is clearly made by the rapid demise of Red Planet Ventures, NASA's venture capital experiment. Though Red Planet was established after an extensive planning process, it lasted only three months before the Bush administration revoked its budget allocation in early 2007. OMB director Rob Portman singled out Red Planet in response to a question about the 140 government spending programs slated for concurrent elimination: "We don't think the government ought to be investing in venture capital" (www.whitehouse.gov/news/releases/2007/02/20070205–3.html). This statement was clearly contradicted by the expansion of In-Q-Tel and the founding of OnPoint under the Bush administration's watch. Yet neither of those funds—which were more closely intertwined with "national security" imperatives—was threatened.

Despite their relative immunity from criticism, one of the costs of these initiatives for defense and intelligence agencies is the loss of secrecy involved in shifting research investments into the public domain. But even on this score, the CIA has often been able to conceal its specific interests in a technology, even from the firm developing it. Indeed, the public disclosure of CIA interest in a particular technology has, at least in some cases, added intrigue. After all, if I can view virtually any location on earth—albeit with limited magnification powers—through satellite images on Google Earth, what might the CIA be able to do? So long as specific applications of a particular technology remain obscure, the public nature of the investments may well reinforce the reputation of the agency's technical capacities. That, again, can backfire in the event of a crisis, but it can also bolster short-term political capital and enhance a certification role within investment networks.

Conclusion

Relatively speaking, the new public venture funds established in the federal apparatus are small—working on budgets of hundreds of millions of dollars rather than the billions that are passed through traditional procurement channels and federally funded research and development centers (FFRDCs). Public venture capital strategies are unlikely to replace traditional procurement methods, nor should they. But the recent push toward venture capital–inspired models are substantial, transforming from a single agency's $28 million budget in 1999 to a multiagency cornucopia of VC initiatives that involves hundreds of millions of dollars. Less than a decade after In-Q-Tel's founding, these agencies have carved out an important niche within the defense, intelligence, and R&D establishments.

While none of the general features of the public VC model determines the success or failure of an agency in generating positive outcomes (that depends far more on the specific networks and actors involved in a given endeavor), the approach does provide a means for government agencies to tap, and create, innovation networks centered around the dynamic small firms that have proven difficult to support through traditional procurement processes. But the model has its limits. It is attuned to short-term, commercially oriented, and often incremental innovations developed for the market rather than to long-term, paradigm-shifting research. Its reliance on short-term relations with small firms offers many advantages over longer-term procurement relations with large contractors (e.g., avoiding single supplier dependence and rebuffing charges of political favoritism), but it is much less attuned to the creation of the tight networks of trust that may have some collaborative benefits in the design and production processes. And, unlike FFRDC's, the public VC model is not able to stimulate the development of new ideas conceived by government agents. At least in its current configurations, it is designed to access markets, not to create them. In other words, different strategies and mechanisms for promoting innovation are likely to foster different sorts of innovation "outcomes," and the public venture capital model is unsuited to many sorts of innovative environments and aims.

The rapid rise of this new strategy nevertheless reveals the breadth and the complexity of the U.S. government's developmental apparatus. Although planning outcomes is not possible in innovative processes—nor effective as an overarching mode of governing them—an examination of the components of this largely "hidden" developmental state, and its role in boosting economic productivity, might well serve to heighten the degree of coordination and information sharing, foster the determination of best practices, and allow more deliberate strategizing among the different innovation paradigms such that network failures including overlaps, mismatches between policies and desired outcomes, network "involution," and an overemphasis on a single model of innovation might reasonably be mitigated (Whitford and Schrank, Chapter 13).

It is also reasonable to wonder whether continued experimentation with the public VC model can escape its security-centric roots—in which the public interest is typically defined through a fiat of amorphous national security interests—and be deployed in support of technological developments in areas determined through a more deliberative, transparent, and public process. The question remains open. But as free market ideology continues to hemorrhage under the weight of the financial crisis, and as a growing cross-party consensus continues to congeal around the necessity of developing alternative energy technologies, it appears that a rare window could be opening in which innovative strategies for stimulating technological development are able to break free from their militaristic moorings. Indeed, during the 2008 presidential campaign, Barack Obama's energy platform included a plan to establish a $15 billion venture fund for clean energy technologies, while postelection programs in the Department of Energy and other agencies have continued to foster close ties with small technology firms and the venture capital community.[17] Understanding the organizational strengths and the dilemmas presented by public venture capital initiatives can help to ensure that such programs serve a reinvigorated and transparent conception of the public interest.

Notes

Special thanks to Fred Block, Shelley Hurt, and Sheri Kunovich for their insightful commentary on earlier versions of this chapter. I also benefited from comments received at the 2008 annual meeting of the Society for the Advancement of Socio-Economics. Any oversights are the responsibility of the author alone.

1. By 1997, Lerner (1999b, 287) reported that "at least" thirty states were involved in at least "43 state venture funds or SBIC programs."

2. Several Department of Energy labs established commercialization-oriented arms prior to 1999, but they were not administered by the federal government. For instance, Sandia National Laboratory's Technology Ventures Program was established in 1993 as a subsidiary of Martin Marietta Corporation. The Argonne-University of Chicago (ARCH) Development Corporation was established in 1986 to foster the commercialization of lab technologies, but neither was it administered by the government. Lerner (1999b) counted at least six such funds run by DOE contractors from 1985 to 1997. Lerner also notes that DARPA briefly operated an "experimental venture capital investment program" focused on small firms in the late 1980s. It made one grant.

3. The review ultimately "disclosed that AARCC provided federal assistance to program participants with little or no assurance that benefits would be derived ... [and] did not monitor the actions of investees who had received funding to protect the government's interest; as a result, the majority of its investments have been, or are in jeopardy of being, lost. These significant weaknesses stemmed, in part, from the absence of internal controls prescribed by management to safeguard assets and efficiently fulfill the legislated mission." *USDA IG Audit Report* no. 37099-1-FM.

4. The ubiquity of the rhetoric on cutbacks is evident in the commission's 1995 report, which noted, "The end of the Cold War, combined with the growing urgency to reduce the Federal budget deficit, compels the United States to reduce and realign its military forces" (Defense Base Closure and Realignment Commission 1995, ix).

5. Nor was this post–Cold War trend limited to technology programs or U.S. borders. The fall of the Soviet Union was followed by the creation of quasi-governmental enterprise funds designed to foster entrepreneurship in former communist nations. The Support for Eastern European Democracy Act of 1990 (SEED) (P.L. 101–179; 22 U.S. C. 5401) established two such funds and later amendments added nine more. These funds were "chartered as private nonprofit corporations ... but funded by government appropriations" (Moe and Kosar 1995, 25).

6. Ó Riain's (2004a) account of software developers shows how long-term relations with a single employer came to signify a *lack* of individual creativity and initiative during the boom.

7. The Department of Defense, for instance, initiated a "fast track" initiative in its SBIR program in the 1990s to speed the process of translating technologies developed by small firms into government procurement contracts or commercially oriented products. There are also grounds in some cases for seeking exceptions to the bureaucratically burdensome federal acquisition regulations. Those regulations have, however, been designed to foster a modicum of transparency in the use of public funds.

8. In-Q-Tel's 2000 charter specified that it was to "exploit and develop new and emerging information technologies and pursue R&D that produce innovative solution to the most difficult problems facing the CIA and Intelligence Community."

9. According to a 2005 *Washington Post* article, the agency had spent approximately 15 percent of its budget allocation on equity investments. Terence O'Hara, "In-Q-Tel, CIA's Venture Capital Arm, Invests in Secrets," *Washington Post*, August 15, 2005, D5.

10. Examples of early problem sets can be found in Business Executives for National Security 2001, Appendix B-1. The interest areas currently listed on the In-Q-Tel website include "Application Software and Analytics; Bio, Nano, and Chemical Technologies; Communications and Infrastructure; Digital Identity and Security; and Embedded Systems and Power."

11. Defense and intelligence agencies already have some leeway in evading certain federal acquisition regulations. FAR 6.302–6 notes that "full and open competition need not be provided for when the disclosure of the agency's needs would compromise the national security unless the agency is permitted to limit the number of sources from which it solicits bids or proposals." This exception was a key element in initially establishing the legality of In-Q-Tel. World Trade Organization agreements to which the U.S. government is signatory also contain exceptions for national security.

12. Among other things, the CIA was accused in the 1970s of setting up private shell corporations to develop prohibited technologies.

13. This policy changed. Originally, the founders of In-Q-Tel were concerned the agency could be weakened by overly diffuse priorities.

14. It is unclear how concerned agencies like the CIA or the Army are with economic development; generating mission-oriented technologies must be regarded as these funds' central purpose. Private sector profitability and the potential for generating funds for reinvestment are, however, powerful legitimating mechanisms.

15. For instance, the Small Business Administration's Tech-Net database reveals that Foster Miller received some 741 SBIR awards between 1983 and 2006, while at least 42 additional companies had received 100 or more awards during that period. In a recent series of evaluations of the SBIR program, the authors sharply dispute the characterization of these organizations as "SBIR mills" (Wessner 2008b).

16. Thus, for instance, the NIH SBIR program received a waiver to increase the size of its awards above the stipulated limits and to extend Phase II funding over multiple years. It has also offered financial support to grantees at the clinical trial phase to help ensure they survive delays associated with the drug approval process. Other SBIR programs have established commercialization assistance programs (CAPs) or experimented with expedited review processes and funding extensions to enhance support to awardees.

17. To be sure, part of the focus on and resonance of boosting U.S. energy R&D is tied to the framing of energy independence as a national security issue.

CHAPTER 7

DARPA Does Moore's Law

The Case of DARPA and Optoelectronic Interconnects

Erica Fuchs

In 2005, the computing industry set down a path many believed was destined for disaster. Facing the near-term physical and atomic limits of cramming over 592 million transistors onto a single microprocessor chip, AMD and Intel Corporation switched from increasing the number of transistors per microprocessor to adding more and more processors—cores—per chip. While in the short term this switch to a multicore paradigm avoided the physical limitations associated with the previous thirty-year trajectory, unprecedented technical land mines lay on the immediate horizon. Unfortunately the computing industry did not seem ready to tackle what was likely to be its greatest challenge in over thirty years. In the 1950s and 1960s, vertically integrated computing firms were home to research and development, but more recently large firms have outsourced their innovation needs to small and medium-size enterprises, universities, and government labs, which are more flexible and innovative. This disintegrated innovation model, however, created challenges, both in coordinating technology development incentives across the multitude of players and in supporting long-term research. In addition, with the primary source of demand in computing having moved from the military to the commercial sector, the long-term supporter of the computing industry—the defense industry—was struggling to maintain its power as well as its technological edge. And yet suddenly there in the fray, despite being proclaimed "dead" by the very computing academics with whom it had once founded the industry, was the computing industry's long-time supporter, the Defense Advanced Research Projects Agency (DARPA) funding a technology that could help save the day. This chapter tells the story of the crisis in Moore's Law, the dramatic change in both the computing industry and the military-industrial complex at the start of this crisis, and the controversial emergence of a new role for government in the form of the computing industry's savvy, beloved, and controversial supporter—DARPA.

Background: Computing and Moore's Law

In 1965, Gordon Moore, director of Fairchild Semiconductor's research and development laboratories, wrote an article foreshadowing the future of the semiconductor industry for the thirty-fifth anniversary issue of *Electronics* magazine. In setting the paradigm for the industry's future, Moore writes,

> The complexity for minimum component costs has increased at a rate of roughly a factor of two per year.... Certainly over the short term this rate can be expected to continue, if not to increase. Over the longer term, the rate of increase is a bit more uncertain, although there is no reason to believe it will not remain nearly constant for at least 10 years. That means by 1975, the number of components per integrated circuit for minimum cost will be 65,000. I believe that such a large circuit can be built on a single wafer.

Moore goes on to state, "Clearly, we will be able to build such component crammed equipment. Next, we ask under what circumstances we should do it" (Moore 1965). Since its original coining (Yang 2000), Moore's Law has come to mean much more than the yearly doubling of the number of components per square inch of integrated circuit real estate (and a corresponding decrease in cost per component) suggested in the 1965 paper. In his subsequent 1975 and 1990 papers, Moore adjusts the rate of Moore's Law from doubling the number of components every year, to doubling every two years. The International Technology Roadmap for Semiconductors first settled on doubling every eighteen months, later on every two years, and most recently on every three years. Common industry interpretations on what is doubling have included the doubling of processing power on a chip every eighteen months, the doubling of computing power every eighteen months, as well as the price of computing power falling by half every eighteen months. In other areas both within and outside the industry, Moore's Law has been extended to refer to exponential growth. Regardless of the myths surrounding and the specific definition of Moore's Law, an incredible amount of innovation has had to occur both up and down the supply chain, in hardware and software, for this regular advancement in microprocessors to persist. Further, this continual advance in microprocessor and industrywide performance has been a key to the revival and acceleration of productivity experienced since the 1990s by the U.S. and world economy, as well as to many qualitative economic gains (NRC 1999; Jorgenson et al. 2005; Jorgenson and Vu 2005).

While Moore's paradigm of regularly doubling the number of transistors per square inch of chip real estate and thereby doubling the performance and halving the cost per transistor has met extraordinary success over the past thirty years (see Figure 7.1), today Moore's Law is facing unprecedented challenges. Since Gordon Moore's 1965 paper, increased processing performance has traditionally been achieved at reduced cost by increasing the number of components—particularly transistors—per chip. As the number of transistors on a single chip has increased, however, so have the technical challenges. Particularly difficult has been managing power and heat dissipation problems associated with ever more densely packed transistors. These challenges, along

Figure 7.1 Processor Performance Improvement Between 1978 and 2006

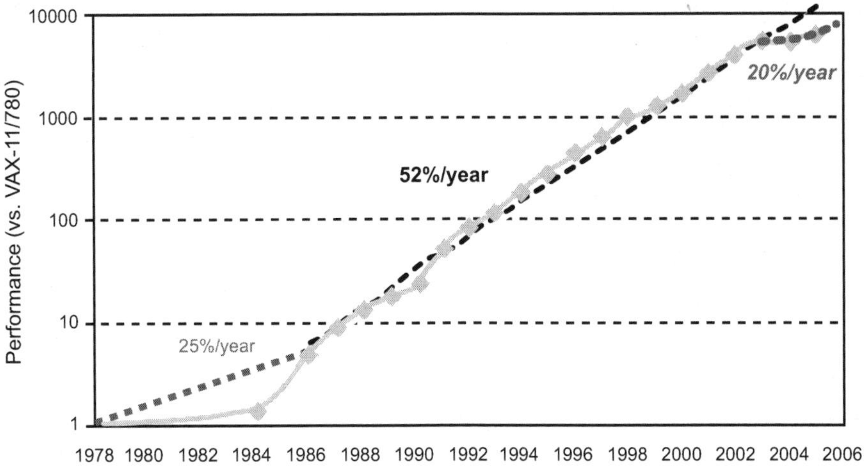

Source: Hennessy and Patterson, 2007, 3.

with problems in cross-talk between copper wires, have become known in the field as the interconnect bottleneck (Kimerling 2000). In the past this bottleneck has been overcome repeatedly, allowing the number of transistors per chip to increase. Recently, however, technical and industry experts have begun to see Moore's paradigm of putting more and more transistors onto the same wafer real estate as no longer viable. In 2001 the International Technology Roadmap for Semiconductors (ITRS)—the annual technology direction-setting document negotiated by the members of microprocessor supply chain—admitted having reached the fundamental limits of the traditional scaling mechanism that had driven Moore's Law:

> Traditional scaling, which has been the basis of the semiconductor industry for the last 30 years, is indeed beginning to show the fundamental limits of the materials constituting the building blocks of the planar CMOS processes. However, new materials can be introduced in the basic CMOS structure to replace and/or augment the existing ones to further extend the device scaling approach....
>
> Despite the use of these new materials it will be challenging to maintain the historical rates of improvement in electrical performance by relying exclusively on improvements in technology. Innovation in the techniques used in circuit and system design will be essential to maintain the historical trends in performance improvement. (ITRS 2001)

One such technique in circuit and system design is switching to a multicore trajectory.[1] Multicore microprocessors represent a radical change in both the architecture and the scaling mechanism of the microprocessor. In particular, rather than increasing performance and reducing cost by increasing the number of transistors squeezed onto constant-size wafer real estate that comprises the microprocessor, a multicore trajectory increases the number of microprocessors (renamed "cores") on a single microprocessor chip while keeping the transistors per microprocessor constant. Performance is then enhanced on this multicore microprocessor by distributing work tasks in parallel across these multiple cores.

Since the ITRS first hinted at a need to change the architecture of the microprocessor, industry leaders have slowly shifted onto this multicore path. IBM introduced POWER4, the first dual-core processor, in 2000. Five years later, AMD released its dual-core Opteron server/workstation processors (April 22, 2005) and its dual-core desktop processors, the Athlon 64 and X2 family (May 31, 2005). On January 5, 2006, Intel followed with its Core Duo. Later that year, Intel introduced its Xeon (March 14, 2006) for servers and workstations, and its Core 2 Duo and Core 2 Quad (July 27, 2006) for mobile and desktop systems. The conventional wisdom has since become to double the number of cores on a chip with each silicon generation (Asanovic et al. 2006).

In a recent interview with *ACM Queue,* John Hennessey and David Patterson, the writers of the classic textbook on microprocessor architecture, emphasize the significance of the current period in microprocessor evolution. Hennessey begins, "I think this is nothing less than a giant inflection point, if you look strictly from an architectural viewpoint—not a technology viewpoint. Gordon Bell has talked eloquently about defining computers in terms of what I might think of as technology-driven shifts. If you look at architecture-driven shifts, then this is probably only the fourth." To make his point, Hennessey identifies the three previous architectural shifts: the first generation electronic computers, the IBM 360 and the notion of an instruction set architecture, and the beginning of pipelining and instruction level parallelism. He continues, "Now we're into the explicit parallelism multiprocessor era, and this will dominate for the foreseeable future. I don't see any technology or architectural innovation on the horizon that might be competitive with this approach." Hennessey's coauthor and longtime collaborator, David Patterson, builds on Hennessey's comment, "Back in the '80s, when computer science was just learning about silicon and architects were able to understand chip-level implementation and the instruction set, I think the graduate students at Berkeley, Stanford, and elsewhere could genuinely build a microprocessor that was faster than what Intel could make, and that was amazing." Patterson continues, "Now, I think today this shift toward parallelism is being forced not by somebody with a great idea, but because we don't know how to build hardware the conventional way anymore." He concludes, "This is another brand-new opportunity for graduate students at Berkeley and Stanford and other schools to build a microprocessor that's genuinely better than what Intel can build. And once again, that is amazing" (Olukotun 2007).

As hinted at in David Patterson's statement, a suite of particularly difficult technical problems loom on the horizon along this new multicore trajectory. In the first few years, the switch by processor manufacturers to a multicore paradigm should not present significant technical problems. As the number of cores increases, however, fundamental problems arise in communicating and dispersing work tasks between the cores and in getting information on and off the chip. These challenges begin to become significant around sixteen to thirty-six cores (Asanovic et al. 2006). Further, while current industry technology trajectories may be viable through hundreds of cores, they are not scalable to thousands of cores (Asanovic et al. 2006). Although aspects of these problems have been seen before in embedded and high performance computing (Asanovic et al. 2006), the problems were not solved at that time, and the most effective solutions may or may not be the same for microprocessors.

Solutions from formerly fringe technical communities in both hardware and software will be critical in overcoming these challenges. These fringe technology groups are in hardware, optics, and in software, parallel programming. While both hardware and software solutions will be necessary, this chapter focuses on the challenges in hardware and consequently on optics. As the number of cores continues to double on this multicore paradigm, a bottleneck rapidly arises in the communication and dispersion of tasks. The challenge is achieving sufficient bandwidth at low enough power and without cross-talk in the communications (facilitated by what are called "interconnects") from core to core, core to memory, and core to accelerator. (See Figure 7.2.) Photonics researchers believe that switching from electronic to optoelectronic interconnects may be critical to overcoming this bottleneck (Kimerling 2004; Ram 2004; Shah 2005; Greene 2007; Shah 2007). These optoelectronic interconnects would use light, or photons, instead of electrons to send and receive information.

The technological advances of the information age—in computers, computer software, and digital transmission technologies—were originally based exclusively in electronics. In the past thirty years, a new science—photonics—has begun to play a role in the sending and receiving of information. With their higher information carrying capacity, photons have been critical to meeting consumer demand in telecommunications for increased bandwidth (Schabel 2005). Transatlantic telephone cable using optical fibers has created virtually lossless transmission, while innovations in land area networks and fiber to the home have brought ultra high-speed Internet, telephone, and television services to users (Fuchs and Kirchain 2010). In the military, optoelectronics has provided not only these network capabilities but also key sensor capabilities for the war fighter and other manned and unmanned military applications (Sternberg 1992). The bandwidth advantages of photons are also great for microprocessor applications. In addition, the higher power density (leading to lower power consumption) and ability to run multiple particle waves simultaneously (lack of cross-talk problems) make them particularly attractive for microprocessor technology, where heat issues and cross-talk between the existing copper interconnects are a growing problem (Kimerling 2000; Shah 2005; ITRS 2006; Shah 2007). The technical hurdles to bring the cost and size of optoelectronic interconnects into a range that would work for the microprocessor, as well as turn the optoelectronic interconnects' materials platform into one that could be integrated into the existing mainstream electronic semiconductor production process, are monumental.

Figure 7.2 Presentation by Intel to the Optoelectronic Community of Multicore Architecture and Associated Interconnect Challenges

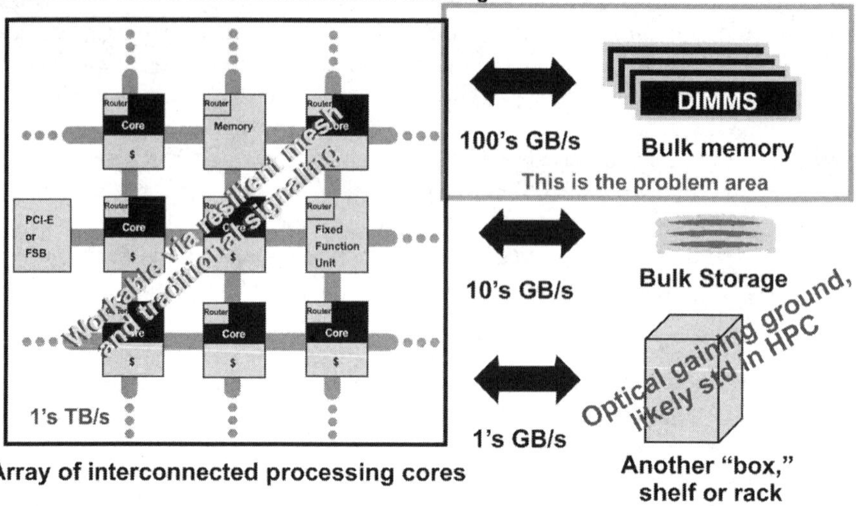

According to a presentation by an Intel representative in 2006, in the short to medium term the most pressing interconnect problem in microprocessors may be in getting information off the chip to memory.
Source: J. Bautista, Intel Corporation. Proceedings from Biannual MIT Microphotonics Conference, October 2006.

DARPA and Computing

The government and particularly the military have a long history of supporting computing and associated semiconductor research in the United States (Flamm 1988; Bresnahan and Greenstein 1999; NRC 1999). While the first large electronic calculating machines in the United States were developed in World War II, and the Air Force and Office of Naval Research (ONR) led computing research through the 1950s, computing research activities were led by DARPA soon after its founding (Flamm 1987).

The Advanced Research Projects Agency (ARPA) was founded under President Eisenhower in February 1958 as a direct consequence of the Soviet Sputnik launch in 1957 (NRC 1999). ARPA's first priority was to oversee space activities until NASA was up and running (Roland 2002). By 1960 all ARPA civilian programs were transferred to the National Aeronautics and Space Administration (NASA), and all of its military space programs were transferred to individual services. With space oversight behind it, ARPA focused on ballistic missile defense, nuclear test detection propellants, and materials (Roland 2002). In 1962, under the direction of ARPA's third director, Jack Ruina, J. C. Licklider created and became director of ARPA's Information Processing Techniques Office (IPTO). Licklider's vision of man-computer interaction, including shared computer resources and real-time machine response to input from operators, became one of the guiding conceptualizations for computing in the 1960s and 1970s (Roland 2002). During this period, Licklider also had the original vision for ARPA-NET (Roland 2002). Licklider's successors at DARPA played out his agenda (Roland 2002). In April 1969 BBN received the DARPA contract to develop ARPANET. Going forward through the 1970s, IPTO's budget accounted for most of DOD-supported basic research and roughly 40 to 50 percent of DOD's applied research in math and computer science (Flamm 1987). Then, between 1983 and 1993, DARPA spent an extra $1 billion on computer research. This effort, known as the Strategic Computing Initiative (SCI), was conceived in 1981 by IPTO director Robert Kahn. Kahn, who joined ARPA in 1972, had led the BBN team that laid out the conceptual design of the ARPANET. From the outset, Kahn envisioned SCI as an integrated plan to promote computer chip design and manufacturing, computer architecture, operating systems, networking, languages, and artificial intelligence software (Kahn 1983). He created a scheme consisting of a pyramid of related technologies, in which he believed progress would materialize as developments flowed up the pyramid. His goal was to develop each of the layers and then connect them. (See Figure 7.3.)

Kahn's SCI pyramid laid the groundwork for fundamental advances in strained silicon and gallium arsenide semiconductor materials technologies, processing foundries, computer-aided design tools, and very large scale integrated (VLSI) systems technologies that subsequently became critical parts of continuing Moore's Law in the mainstream commercial semiconductor industry. Kahn's focus within his pyramid on networks and signal processing simultaneously laid the groundwork in optoelectronic integrated circuit material and processing technologies that later would also become critical for computing.

While SCI officially ended in 1993, developments in optoelectronics continued through the 1990s. Consequently by the year 2000, when IBM was introducing the first dual-core processor, much was in place to begin to develop the first chip-to-chip and then the on-chip optical interconnect technology.

Figure 7.3 Kahn's Strategic Computing Program Pyramid (Kahn 1983)

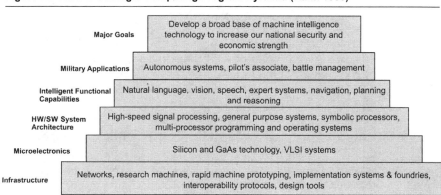

On January 20, 2001, however, George W. Bush took office as the forty-third president of the United States, and DARPA's focus on dual-use technologies came to an end. On June 18, 2001, Tony Tether was appointed as the new director to head DARPA. Having served for four years as the director of the DOD's National Intelligence Office (1978–1982), Tether came to the position of DARPA director under a directive from Secretary of Defense Donald Rumsfeld to make DARPA "an entrepreneurial hotbed that will give the U.S. military the tools it will need to maintain the nation's access to space and to protect satellites in orbit from attack" (*Rensselaer* 2002). Less than three months after Tether was appointed, the U.S. peacetime landscape also began to change. On September 11, 2001, two hijacked planes were flown into the World Trade Center in New York City, a third hijacked plane was flown into the Pentagon, and a fourth hijacked plane attempted an attack on Washington, D.C. In response, on October 7, 2001, the United States invaded Afghanistan, and on March 21, 2003, it began its invasion of Iraq (Fuchs 2010).

During his time at DARPA, Tether made significant changes to the agency's policies, which brought on an outcry from the computing community, especially in academia (JointStatement 2005; Lazowska and Patterson 2005; Markoff 2005). In his March 27, 2003, statement to the House of Representatives Tether highlighted DARPA's role in "bridging the gap" between fundamental discoveries and military use (Tether 2003). Although overall funding by DARPA remained constant, the proportion going to university researchers dropped by nearly half (Lazowska and Patterson 2005; Markoff 2005). Several other policy changes further acted to discourage university participation and signaled a shift from pushing the leading edge of research to "bridging the gap" between fundamental research and deployable technologies (JointStatement 2005; Lazowska and Patterson 2005). These changes included increased classification of research programs and increased restrictions on the participation of noncitizens (JointStatement 2005; Lazowska and Patterson 2005). In contrast to the flexibility and discretion of DARPA's broad area announcements for which it was famous, funds were tied to "go/no-go" reviews linked to specific deliverables and applied to research at twelve- to eighteen-month intervals (JointStatement 2005; Lazowska and Patterson 2005; Markoff 2005). Finally, many solicitations precluded universities and small start-ups from submission as prime contractors, instead requiring the formation of teams and forcing start-ups and universities to hook up with large established vendors (DefenseScienceBoard 2005; Fuchs 2010).

While Tether bore the public banner associated with these changes and indeed pushed DARPA farther than ever before, many changes in the organization and structure of the computing industry over the previous two decades had already begun to stimulate these changes.

The Changing Military-Industrial Complex in Computing

The computing industry funded by DARPA in the 1960s was radically different than the computing industry today. Two trends have been particularly remarkable. First, as the field of computing and the computing industry has matured, the cutting edge of technology has moved from niche markets dominated by defense contractors to high-volume markets dominated by mainstream consumers. Second, along with this shift in the locus of demand, the locus of innovation has also shifted from being centralized in a few large, established computing companies, to being spread across millions of suppliers in a vertically disintegrated supply chain. Together, these two changes have reshaped the military-industrial complex in computing.

In 1960, computer science was just starting to emerge as a field (NRC 1999). In that year, 1790 mainframes were sold (Wright 2008). These high-end mainframes were entirely purchased by defense contractors. By 1970 computer sales had more than doubled and included both mainframes and minicomputers (Wright 2008); however, the primary market for these computers remained the government. Then, in 1977, Apple introduced the first desktop computer, followed by IBM in 1981. By the mid-1980s, the computer market could be divided into three types of demand—business data processing in organizations (met with mainframes), business individual productivity applications (met with personal computers), and technical computing (met with minicomputers) (Bresnahan and Greenstein 1999). The rise of networked computing technologies led to a convergence of these markets. Networks of personal computers and workstations were able to compete with and eventually overcame many minicomputer and mainframe markets (Bresnahan and Greenstein 1999). By 1990, 20 million personal computers were sold globally, and innovation in commercial IT was outstripping that of the military.

Figure 7.4 Timeline of the Computer Industry Structure and Demand Sources

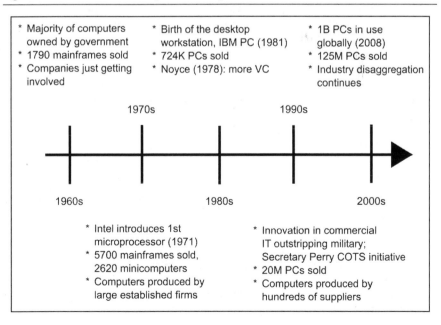

Realizing that the military was no longer the primary source of demand or the technical cutting edge in computing, in 1991 Defense Secretary William Perry announced the Department of Defense Strategic Acquisition Initiative (SAI). This initiative mandated that defense contractors first look at commercial off-the-shelf (COTS) products when developing new technology upgrades. In 1994 Perry extended his earlier mandate with what became his defining memorandum, "Specifications & Standards: A New Way of Doing Business," which became known as the COTS Initiative. It mandated the preference for commercial over customized products (Saunders 2004). Today, while defense contractors custom-build the front end of computing applications, they buy the back end from industry suppliers. This shift in purchasing patterns has created new challenges for the military for influencing the direction of corporate research.

As the locus of demand and the cutting edge of technology have shifted from the military to commercial applications, the structure of the computing industry and consequently the organization of its innovation activities have likewise shifted. In the 1950s and 1960s, computing research and development activity was primarily housed within corporate laboratories such as Bell Laboratories, GE Research, IBM Research, and Xerox Parc (Mowery 1999; NAS 2007). These large U.S. corporate laboratories performed much of the fundamental research that underlies the mainstream semiconductor technology used by the computing industry today (Macher et al. 2000). As late as 1980, IBM alone still conducted 50 percent of the R&D in the computing industry (NRC 1999). Beginning in the 1980s, however, a combination of competitive pressure, the perception of disappointing returns from investments in R&D, and the change in federal antitrust policy led many U.S. firms to externalize a portion of their R&D operations (Mowery 1999). Today, complex networks of firms and close collaborations between users and producers of hardware and software now play an important role in developing new products. Recent research has documented challenges in this new distributed environment in the coordination across firms in advancing technology platforms (Gawer and Cusumano 2002; Iansiti and Levien 2004), in aligning incentive structures across interdependent firms (Casadesus-Masanell and Yoffie 2005) and, in particular, in supporting long-term research. Although the leading U.S. merchant semiconductor firms, such as Intel, TI, Micron, and AMD, spend 10–15 percent of revenues on R&D, the bulk of these expenditures focus on new product development (Macher et al. 2000). Further, none of the new leading small firms in digital communications maintain internal semiconductor R&D, instead focusing their efforts on product definition, system design, and marketing of their end products (Macher et al. 2000). And yet it is precisely advances in semiconductor technology that they may now need to push forward Moore's Law.

DARPA and Optoelectronic Interconnects for Computing

For optoelectronics to meet the demands of computer interconnects—particularly communications between cores, core-to-memory and core-to-accelerator under the

Table 7.1 Shifting Innovation Ecosystem and Industry and Market Structures in Computing

	First Three Decades (1950–1980)	Recent Three Decades (1980–present)
Δ in Innovation Ecosystem	Corporate R&D labs (Macher 2000; Mowery 1999; NAS 2007)	Increased reliance on external sources of R&D (Mowery 1999)
	Firm-based innovation trajectories	Complex networks of firms, universities, government labs. Interdependency of innovation trajectories across products (NRC 1999; Mowery 1999; Powell and Grodal 2005)
Δ in Industry Structure	Few pioneering firms supplied computers	Hundreds of loosely linked suppliers (Bresnahan 2000)
	Primary demand government contractors	Primary demand (high volumes) commercial applications
Δ in Demand	Government contractors order customized products	Government contractors customize commercial products.

Source: Fuchs 2010.

new multicore paradigm—researchers believe it will be necessary to develop large-scale optoelectronic integrated circuits (Kimerling 2004; Ram 2004; Shah 2005, 2007). Such integrated circuits would consist of five critical components—a laser, modulator, waveguide, photo detector, and receiver. To bring all of these components together on a single chip, a sixth component—an isolator—would also likely need to be integrated. Currently, mainstream photonic semiconductor devices such as for telecommunications and mainstream electronic semiconductor devices such as for microprocessors are produced in different material systems. While photonic semiconductors are transitionally produced out of materials from row III and V of the periodic table, electronic semiconductors are traditionally produced in silicon (which is in row VI of the periodic table) and other materials in or matching row VI of the periodic table. Given these different material systems for photonic and electronic devices, three options exist for microprocessors going forward: all microprocessor functions could be attempted in optics, using III–V materials; microprocessor functions could shift toward being a combination of optics and electronics but be entirely in silicon and other row VI–compatible materials; or a way must be found to combine III–V and silicon material systems on a single substrate. Of these three options, given the existing Si-CMOS manufacturing infrastructure and the technical challenges associated with all-optical computing, the latter two options have been pursued most aggressively. To shift optoelectronic devices from a III–V material platform to Si-CMOS is far from elementary. Photonics have traditionally been produced in III–V materials because III–V materials are significantly better for the light emission ("lasing") necessary to send information. Lasing has only, as of 2005, been demonstrated in silicon (Rong

2005, 584), and the capability to achieve the lasing power necessary for a microprocessor may still be many decades off. If, on the other hand, lasing, modulating, and the other necessary optoelectronic circuit functions cannot all be achieved in silicon, it is unclear whether the material systems mismatch between III-V and silicon can be sufficiently overcome to feasibly (both from the perspective of technical performance and the perspective of processing cost) integrate components across the two material systems.

By 2005, when AMD released its first multicore microprocessor, the ITRS road map was suggesting optical interconnects may be needed in multicore microprocessors as early as 2012 (ITRS 2006). And yet it was looking less and less likely that the necessary technical advances in optoelectronic integration would come from the computing industry or the traditional source of innovation in optoelectronics—small and medium-size enterprise in the telecommunications industry, whose advances many firms in the computing industry had been hoping to leverage through technology alliances and acquisitions. In the 1980s and 1990s, as optoelectronics was revolutionizing telecommunications, the telecommunications component manufacturers' competitiveness depended on being fastest at bringing the latest innovation to market (Fuchs and Kirchain 2010). With the burst of the telecommunications bubble in late 2000, however, firm survival became a function of unit cost (Fuchs et al. 2006; Fuchs and Kirchain 2010). With costs threatening their survival and technological advance no longer paramount, the majority of firms in the industry moved manufacturing to East Asia and reduced or abandoned efforts in the latest optoelectronic integration technologies (Fuchs and Kirchain 2010). By 2005 the only firms left manufacturing in the United States and pursuing the integrated technologies were those with government funding or private venture capital backing (Infinera, Kotura, and Luxtera). Whether these firms would survive was unclear (Fuchs and Kirchain 2010).

A different player, however, was about to come into the fray. In 2005, with the majority of the telecommunications industry having moved manufacturing offshore and abandoned integrated technologies, DARPA program manager Jag Shah initiated two critical programs—Electronic-Photonic Integrated Circuits (EPIC) and Ultraperformance Nanophotonic Intrachip Communications (UNIC). Shah came to DARPA in 2001 after a career in optoelectronics at Bell Labs. By the time Shah joined DARPA, it had a long history in funding optics, including being credited with funding the creation of the laser (Bromberg 1991, 423). DARPA's optoelectronic integrated circuit program had begun under program manager John Neff in 1984 in response to the network and high-speed signal processing needs outlined under Kahn's 1983 Strategic Computing Initiative (SCI). Through the 1980s and 1990s, more than fifteen program managers were involved in putting together the technological pieces necessary to advance the performance of optoelectronic devices and eventually bring optoelectronic technology onto the Si-CMOS. Neff focused on the materials growth and characterization necessary for optoelectronic integrated circuits as well as the 3-D free-space architectures he believed would be necessary for optical computing. In 1989 Andy Yang funded the first program seeking to create hybrid integration of optoelectronic integrated circuits—in particular, the connection through bonding techniques of multiple optoelectronic lasers on a single chip. In 1993 Anis Husain, Robert Leheny, and Brian Hendrickson funded wave division multiplexing for fiber optic communications and optical signal processing technologies. In 1997 program managers Elias Towe and David Honey began funding the hybrid integration of lasers onto mainstream Si-CMOS semiconductor materials. Thus by the time Jag Shah joined as a program manager in 2001, much was in place to begin to develop the first chip-to-chip and then the on-chip interconnect technology.

The goal of Shah's EPIC program, which opened in February 2004, was to enable the integration of complex electronics and photonics circuits on a single silicon chip. In doing so, EPIC sought to eliminate the multiple materials platforms used at the time to accomplish high-performance photonic device functionality, and provide a seamless interface between photonics and electronics. Researchers were welcome to respond to the solicitation in one of three main areas: (1) The development and demonstration of a complete suite of high performance silicon photonic devices fabricated in a CMOS-compatible process within the extended communications band (i.e., a suite of devices relevant to applications in the converging tele- and data-communications space). (2) The fabrication and demonstration of integrated circuits that integrate a full set or subset of the necessary photonic devices with the complete set of necessary electronic devices required for a functional electronic-photonic chip. This integrated electronic-photonic chip should be especially relevant to defense applications and exceed performance typical of discrete devices. (3) The development of a novel photonic device not currently available in silicon, including but not limited to light emitters and lasers, wavelength converters and other nonlinear optical devices, and optical amplifiers (Shah 2004). The program was broken into two phases, the first phase being eighteen months, with a go/no-go milestone at sixteen months, and the second phase, thirty months, with go/no-go milestones at twelve months, twenty-four, and thirty. Applicants were encouraged to apply in teams that included an established Si-CMOS manufacturer. Award winners from the February solicitation that focused on the first two objectives—developing a complete suite of high performance silicon-photonic devices and then demonstrating an application specific electronic-photonic integrated circuit—included Luxtera, BAE Systems, and MIT/Lincoln Labs. Award winners from the February solicitation that focused on the development of novel devices in silicon included Caltech, UCLA, University of Michigan, Brown University, and the start-up company Translucent, a subsidiary of Silex Systems (Shah 2004, 2005).

Having learned from EPIC, Shah's UNIC program built on EPIC scientifically and in its structuring of teams to ensure desired outcomes. In the case of UNIC, Shah narrowed his focus specifically to the problems facing the microprocessor community. The goal of UNIC, the solicitation for which opened in late 2005, was to demonstrate low power, high bandwidth, low latency intrachip photonic communication networks designed to enable chip multiprocessors with hundreds or thousands of computer cores to realize extremely high computational efficiency. Shah wrote in the solicitation:

> Processor chips with multiple cores have arrived, and the trend is expected to continue to hundreds or thousands of cores on a chip. Electrical communication between these cores,

and from the multiprocessor chip to external memory and peripherals, is expected to have limited bandwidth due to power constraints. This will increase the imbalance between the computation performance (FLOPS) and the communication bandwidth (Bytes/s), leading to actual performance much lower than the theoretical peak performance of the multicore chip. The UNIC program challenges the community to demonstrate that low power, high bandwidth, low latency intrachip photonic communication, with seamless interface to the external world, will allow the actual performance to track expected increase in the theoretical peak performance of the chip multiprocessors while minimizing programming efforts. (Shah 2007)

Shah created the UNIC program to have two technical areas of interest that respondents to the proposal were required to address in a comprehensive manner. The first technical area built on Shah's previous EPIC solicitation, and required the development of flexible and scalable architectures for intrachip photonic communication and the photonic devices necessary to realize intrachip photonic architectures. The second technical area of interest required respondents to demonstrate functional intrachip communication links incorporating all critical photonic and electronic technologies working together at a performance level that validates the design. Here, the solicitation explicitly stated that the goal of this second technical area was "to establish the credibility of intrachip photonic communication and increase the likelihood that this technology would be accepted by the microprocessor community" (Shah 2007).

The research teams that won UNIC funding (Table 7.2) each brought together universities, start-ups, and established mainstream electronic semiconductor manufacturers. The UNIC program consisted of three phases. The first phase, which lasted nine months, required the "development, fabrication, and demonstration, of silicon nanophotonic devices." The second phase, which lasted two years, focused primarily on designing and validating photonic networks between the devices developed in Phase I, and "established the credibility of the technology within the microprocessor community." Program submissions were required to establish "interim milestones every six months," associated with "demonstrable, quantitative measures of performance." With the exception of MIT I, established companies like Hewlett Packard, IBM, and Sun Microsystems were placed in the position of prime contractors, while universities (MIT II, Stanford, UCLA) and start-ups (Luxtera, Kotura) were members of the contractor-led team. In each phase, teams were eliminated and the institutional members of the team shifted, with the final $44 million Phase III contract being awarded to only one team, led by Sun Microsystems, and whose members included two start-ups and two universities.

Conclusion

Technical advance in microprocessors, as predicted by Moore's Law, and the associated hardware and software that has been needed to meet these ever-faster microprocessors, fueled economic growth in the United States and globally throughout the 1990s. For

**Table 7.2 DARPA Microsystems Technology Office (MTO) Ultraperformance
Nanophotonic Intrachip Communications (UNIC) Program[1]**

	Phase I	*Phase II*	*Phase III*
Award Date	February 2006	November 2006	March 2008
Description	Super-seedling, validity demonstration		$44M
Timeline	9 months	2 years	5½ years
Primary Contractor Awardees	1. HP 2. IBM 3. Sun Microsystems 4. MIT I 5. ?	1. HP 2. IBM 3. Sun Microsystems 4. MIT I	1. Sun Microsystems
Additional Team Members	1. ? 2. Luxtera 3. Luxtera 4. BAE Systems 5. MIT II	1. Intel 2. Luxtera 3. Luxtera 4. BAE Systems	1. Luxtera, Kotura, Stanford, UCLA

1. Information in Table 7.2 is drawn from news reports, corporate and DARPA press releases, and archival records. These sources did not list all participants. The gaps in information are represented in the Table by question marks.
Source: Fuchs 2010.

this type of advance in microprocessors to continue, however, the computing industry must overcome some of its most difficult technical challenges in over thirty years. This need comes at a time when the computing industry seems, if anything, least fit to address such challenges. The established computing firms' large corporate R&D laboratories of the 1950s and 1960s are gone, replaced by a fragmented industry in which technological advance must be coordinated across thousands of suppliers, academia, and industry. At the same time, the commercial sector has replaced the defense industry as the primary source of demand and, consequently, some areas such as microprocessor processing as the leading technological edge. In the midst of these challenges, the defense industry's classic supporter of the computing industry—DARPA—has been heavily criticized for no longer providing the same support to the university computing community. And yet while DARPA's new focus since 2001 may not be providing the critical early-stage research support to universities, as demonstrated by the case of DARPA's funding of optoelectronic integrated circuits under program manager Jag Shah, DARPA may be playing a different and no less important role in the current climate.

Shah's EPIC and UNIC programs responded to the pressing microprocessor hardware needs of the computing industry for continuing Moore's Law. The structure of the programs—representative of the broader structure of programs under Tether at DARPA—was also timely. To advance optoelectronic integrated circuits for military microprocessing and sensing needs for networked warfare and the war fighter, DARPA needed to find a way to influence the direction of the commercial computing industry. At the same time, the computing industry, no longer conducting its own long-term research, needed a way to make sure that innovation activities in universities and start-ups across a multitude of high-performance photonic devices would both work together and be able to be produced in the existing, mainstream Si-CMOS capital equipment used for electronics.

To achieve this goal, Shah's program solicitations were written so as to ensure both that the variety of devices produced would work together and be able to be manufactured on the existing Si-CMOS fabrication equipment. To plausibly achieve these ends, university professors and start-ups needed to team up with established system manufacturers. This support from DARPA led established vendors to become more aware of university and start-up activities, and university professors and start-up technologists to become more aware of the challenges in integrating their designs into a mainstream high-volume silicon process. In addition, DARPA's support not only provided critical funding to the start-ups and university professors, but also acted as validation to other funding agencies and the established companies—both those that did and did not receive funding, that silicon photonics was a viable direction for future microprocessors.[2] Thus, while Tether's new direction for DARPA may have been understandably unpopular within the academic computing community, which lost both funding and power, it did manage to bring together teams of academics, start-ups, and established computing manufacturers to develop optoelectronic integrated circuits manufacturable on the mainstream Si-CMOS platform, as was critical both to the military and to the computing industry for continuing Moore's Law.

Notes

1. Engineers debate the benefits of a multicore architecture versus a 3-D architecture that mimics communication mechanisms typical in the human brain. Whereas the multicore architecture is currently being followed in industry, 3-D architectures do not yet have signs of industry adoption and are arguably not as developed.

2. Admittedly, by underscoring the viability of bringing photonic integrated circuits onto mainstream Si-CMOS, DARPA's program may have shifted the spotlight away from other technology alternatives, such as producing most of photonics in III-V materials systems and upgrading the existing III-V manufacturing infrastructure.

PART II
Scale, Significance, and Implications

While the case studies assembled in Part I sought to explore the texture of the decentralized approach to innovation policy that has emerged over the last four decades, they conveyed only part of the story. The chapters in Part II are intended to *evaluate* different strengths and weaknesses of the U.S. approach to technology policy. The goal is to provide a set of conceptual tools necessary for constructing an effective policy paradigm for spurring technological innovation.

Evaluating the impact of public-private partnerships has long posed substantial difficulties. Counting resources on the input side—dollar amounts of funding, the number or type of awards granted, and so on—measures the *commitment* to research and development, but not its effectiveness. Indeed, government resources may flow to projects that private firms would be willing to fund on their own, or they may support bloated budgets and cost overruns—as frequently documented in large-scale military procurement programs (Alic 2007). Similarly, mapping the complex networks of relations among public and private entities may well reveal the fundamental interactivity of innovation processes, but demonstrating the centrality of federal agencies to innovation networks does not, in itself, tangibly demonstrate that such relations are effective or, more precisely, that they are more effective than other possible relational configurations. Standard measures of outcomes—tabulating the number of patents per grant or awardee, the number of citations of scientific articles written with federal support, or measuring the revenues generated or broader economic impact of some innovation funded by the federal government—also have clear limitations. Patent regimes become more or less stringent; academic currents shift; federal support is typically only one piece of a complex series of elements that generate a particular innovation. And we cannot rewind the tape of history to show what would have happened in the absence of federal support or if an alternative policy regime had been in force.

The first four chapters in this section approach the question of evaluation from different angles, in effect triangulating different evaluative approaches. Block and Keller take a broad view of the U.S. innovation system, using a novel sample of award-winning technologies to show the fundamental transformation of the innovation environment over the last four decades. Their analysis of the *R&D 100* award winners reveals that cutting-edge technological innovations have increasingly arisen from networked forms of organizational collaboration in which small firms and public sector institutions play a central role. While the importance of networked relations to innovative discoveries has been definitively documented in the biotechnology and computer industries, Block and Keller's data suggest that such relations have come to characterize wide swaths of the U.S. innovation system, and that federal support—often from sources that have been neglected by researches such as the Small Business Innovation Research program and the Department of Energy Laboratories—has become a central pillar of the innovation economy.

Yet as Block and Keller suggest, the importance of the decentralized federal role in fostering these innovation networks neither implies that a deepening of federal involvement would provide a panacea, nor that the current structure of federal technology policy is without serious shortcomings. Pushed largely underground by market fundamentalist attacks on government involvement in the economy, the system has taken decentralization to a radical extreme. There is no central repository that collects data on the "alphabet soup" of agencies supporting research and development, and as Vallas, Kleinman, and Biscotti point out in Chapter 3, agencies themselves often have difficulty monitoring and evaluating the impact of their contributions. There is little coordination between agencies that share technology targets. There is little cross-system planning to ensure that the strategies pursued by individual agencies add up to a coherent *policy* that balances attention between short- and long-term horizons; between so-called radical and incremental innovation; between early and later stages of the research, development, testing and evaluation processes.

Indeed, one of the signal weaknesses of the U.S. government's approach to technology is in the area of deployment: the ability to push promising or socially beneficial technologies over critical barriers to their implementation. For technologies like broadband Internet and flat panel displays, key initial discoveries were made by U.S. scientists. However, other nations have assumed global leadership in these fields through the implementation of coordinated standards and policies that foster their adoption. Such policies can create a virtuous circle in which widespread adoption of a technology spurs the growth of cadres of specialized scientists and technicians who install, monitor, and evaluate the technology, generating both jobs and the potential for new clusters of innovative activity. While it is clear that governments can—and do—focus on what prove to be the wrong technologies, the U.S. decentralized approach generally blunts the risk of overinvestment in a single technology or technology trajectory. Yet its routine failure to foster the adoption of socially beneficial technologies at the deployment stage can push new innovation centers offshore while simultaneously placing U.S. consumers and firms at a global disadvantage. One recent survey found, for example, that the United States now ranks fifteenth in a composite measure of broadband integration, speed, and price, despite the fact that broadband technologies were initially developed in the United States (ITIF 2008).

Chris Knight's chapter hones in on this issue through a careful analysis of photovoltaics. He shows that while key discoveries in the field were made by U.S.-based scientists, the hyper-decentralized structure of U.S. innovation policies left few viable options for scaling up solar technologies to compete with cheap but dirty carbon-based fuels. In the absence of federal leadership, states were left to create their own policies, which in turn created an uneven patchwork of standards and incentives (or disincentives) for solar manufacturers, effectively leaving them in the lurch. Instead, it has been foreign governments that have capitalized on the development of alternative energy technologies by setting national standards, building public support for implementation, and setting clear incentives and defined mandates for deployment. While the race to develop, manufacture, and deploy solar and other alternative energy technologies is not lost, the United States clearly risks falling farther behind its global competitors.

Knight's cautionary tale of U.S. implementation failures pushes us to consider the U.S. case in comparative context. What can we learn from other nations that have effectively fostered economic growth on the strength of decentralized policy networks? How are key U.S. competitors structuring their approaches to innovation? Are decentralized developmental policies politically sustainable in a divisive political environment?

Chapters by Ó Riain and by Appelbaum et al. weigh in on these questions by providing a comparative perspective on the developmental network state (DNS). Ó Riain's analysis of the Irish DNS after twenty years reveals key strengths and weaknesses in this model. As Ó Riain shows, the success of the flexible, networked state structure that gave rise to the "Celtic tiger" was inadequately understood. Instead of building on the strengths of a system that had flexibly harnessed resources into the networks of expertise in which Ireland had a comparative advantage, politicians instead began to dismantle key pillars of the Irish DNS through lowered taxes, decreased restrictions on foreign investment, and the consolidation of science and technology-focused agencies. In short, rather than strengthen the state's hitherto effective support of technologists in the wake of its economic success, Ireland instead turned toward a "market managerial-ist" approach that merged neoliberal assumptions with the bureaucratic centralization of science policy. The result was a period of illusory growth, during which foreign investments flooded not into expanded technological development but rather into real estate and other speculative investments. Once the real estate bubble burst, revenue shortfalls and the balance of trade deficit plunged the state into fiscal crisis. Ó Riain's analysis shows the political fragility of the Irish DNS and documents the ongoing risks of recentralization to the flexible networks that had been at the core of Irish high-tech growth. While Ó Riain holds out hope for a revival of Ireland's DNS, it is also possible that pressures for further tax cuts and spending reductions will erode the state's capacity to recover.

The chapter by Appelbaum and colleagues takes a different tack in analyzing the nanotechnology sector in China. Whereas the Celtic tiger was built on developing a comparative advantage in high-tech industry, Chinese growth over the past several decades has been built on a manufacturing base. Yet Chinese officials have been increasingly concerned with leveraging the skills and resources developed through their rapid economic gains to make a "great leap forward" in high technology. Perhaps surprisingly, Appelbaum's analysis of Chinese policy shows that the centralized Chinese government has actually adopted a more decentralized path than might be expected. While the Communist Party retains a strong hand in directing technology policy, the Chinese approach has nevertheless attempted to foster technological leapfrogging through the creation of regional innovation clusters that bring together a university-based core with business incubators designed to spin off new technologies. While funding from the central government plays a critical role in the development of these centers, regional and local authorities also play a role in funding technological development. In sum, although the Chinese investment in nanotechnology continues to be dwarfed by the scale of U.S. R&D spending, the Chinese government seems to grasp the necessity of decentralization in its attempts to build innovation networks.

The final three chapters provide a collective capstone by engaging three critical issues that emerge from the careful case studies and comparative analyses found in the volume. In Chapter 12, John Alic reminds us that a national innovation system is built from the ground up and involves much more than supporting high technology. Innovation is by definition unpredictable, it emerges from unexpected sources, and it depends on both formal and informal learning, codified technical knowledge, and tacit knowledge. His analysis suggests that innovation typically bubbles up from below, and that as Schumpeter predicted, the creative destruction of innovations often serves to disrupt established interests and practices rather than support them. On the one hand, embracing the uncertainty inherent in innovation dynamics thus requires an ability to craft innovation policies and agencies that are able to resist the pull of dominant firms and well-established institutions and "experts." On the other hand, Alic's analysis suggests the importance of creating educational policies and professional training programs that integrate theoretical insights with experiential learning—practices that have been steadily deemphasized in the American system.

In Chapter 13, Josh Whitford and Andrew Schrank provide the critical theoretical underpinnings for a new policy paradigm consistent with what successful U.S. innovation policies actually aim to achieve. Drawing on the insights of Dani Rodrik and Fred Block, Whitford and Schrank convincingly argue that as industrial innovation dynamics increasingly shift toward decentralized networks and multidimensional teams, a critical aspect of effective innovation policy is the ability to correct "network failures"—to bridge concerns about the competency and trustworthiness of potential partners in innovation networks. Indeed, they suggest that overcoming potential collaborators' fears of either "getting screwed" or having a partner who "screws up" is precisely what successful U.S. agencies like DARPA have managed to accomplish in fostering the types of collaborations that have led to key breakthroughs. Network failures are not, of course, at the root of all industrial or technical failures, just as networked organizations are not the ideal organizing principle for the production and procurement of all goods and services. But the increasing salience of network relations to technological development suggests that the paradigmatic organizing principles of many of the old industrial policy debates—centering on how to correct "market failures" or "bureaucratic failures"—lead to a distorted, ineffective vision of the state's proper role in the economy. By adding a theoretically grounded notion of network failure to the toolkit of policymakers and scholars, Whitford and Schrank push forward ideas for a new policy paradigm that escapes the tired, overly ideological character of the "big government" versus "small government" debates.

Finally, in Chapter 14, Christopher Newfield tackles an issue of critical importance to technology policy in democratic polities: how can government programs meaningfully foster public participation in the policy process? Using the case of a National Nanotechnology Initiative project, Newfield shows that the notion of transparency in federally mandated public reports often consists of the production of overly technical and opaque reports that obscure rather than reveal what these programs actually do—and which fail to illuminate their contribution to the public good. Newfield's description of these reports evokes the "staleness of imagery" and "lack of precision" that George Orwell once derided in *Politics and the English Language*. Unfortunately, such writing remains a routine characteristic of contemporary scientific and social scientific discourse. Yet the abstract and technical nature of such reporting also serves as a sort of political shield—a means to avoid scrutiny and preserve investigatorial authority and autonomy within a divisive political climate (where debates continue to rage about the value of teaching evolution, much less the public funding of R&D). It may also be a defensive response to a scientific and industrial ethos marked by intensive concern about preserving proprietary information. But Newfield's central point—echoing the accounts of Whitford and Schrank and of Alic—is that the history of innovation shows that new breakthroughs almost always come from *engagement* with the public. In the absence of effective translations of the aims and potential applications of publicly funded research, it is difficult to achieve the benefits that such engagement can bring. Moreover, it is difficult to envision sustained public support for continued research. As Newfield argues, without mechanisms to ensure an effective, participatory, and balanced partnership between government, universities, private corporations, and the public, no nation can hope to maintain a flourishing innovation system.

CHAPTER 8

Where Do Innovations Come From?

Transformations in the U.S. Economy, 1970–2006
Fred Block and Matthew R. Keller

In the 1970s, there was a lively debate on both sides of the Atlantic about deep discontinuities in the development of advanced market societies. Much of this debate centered on the idea of postindustrial society—emphasizing a shift from goods to services and the rise of science-based production. A wide range of scholars argued that U.S. society, in particular, required significant institutional changes to take advantage of these new productive possibilities (Bell 1973; Brick 2006; Touraine 1971). Parallel arguments for discontinuity were made by theorists of fifty- to sixty-year economic long waves (Mandel 1980) and by contributors to regulation theory, who also argued that capitalist societies required new regulatory structures (Aglietta 1979).[1] These arguments continued into the next decade, as reflected in the wide interest generated by Piore and Sabel's argument in the *Second Industrial Divide* (1984) for a fundamental shift in the organization of production.

However, in the 1990s and 2000s, this call for government and business to adapt to the postindustrial world largely receded from view.[2] With the renewed ascendancy of free market economic ideas in the political arena, academic analysts of market societies focused their attention on the strengths and weaknesses of the different varieties of capitalism, comparing the Japanese model, the German model, and the Anglo-American model (Crouch and Streeck 1997; Hollingsworth and Boyer 1997). Because much of the resulting literature focused on the differences in various countries' economic structures, work on developmental changes in the U.S. economy was deemphasized. To be sure, some scholars had been arguing that the unchecked growth of global financial activity was creating dangerous instabilities (Arrighi 2007; Block 1996), but it was rare for analysts to link financialization to underlying structural weaknesses in national economies. For this reason, it is safe to say that the eruption in 2008–2009 of the worst global economic crisis since the 1930s took much of the scholarly community by surprise.

This chapter is an attempt to reconnect to the earlier debates about how and whether the U.S. economic structure would be transformed in the postindustrial age. We argue that although free market ideas were hegemonic from 1980 to 2006, the transformative

154

trends that Daniel Bell and others identified in the 1970s wer
time. Most specifically, scientific advances became increasin
production, and this produced significant changes in the org;
the ways government interacts with business firms.

Some of these trends have been documented in recent s
Etzkowitz 2003; Slaughter and Rhoades 2002; Tassey 2007
key findings have only been known to academic specialists. ᴛ…ᵢₛ ᴄᴴᵃᵖᵗer adds new
evidence from a unique data set—the winners of *R&D Magazine*'s annual awards
competition for innovative products between 1971 and 2006. This sample of key
innovations in the U.S. economy dramatizes some of the economic shifts that have
occurred over thirty-five years. Since the production of innovations is a major marker
of postindustrial change, this data set provides a useful window into larger processes
of economic restructuring.

Reviewing the Literature

In *The Coming of Post-Industrial Society,* Daniel Bell provided a systematic elaboration
of postindustrial theory. In his analysis, this change is driven by business and government's systematic harnessing of science and technology to expand and update the
production of goods and services continually. For Bell, the rise of the computer industry
in the 1950s and 1960s with its armies of skilled technologists was a paradigmatic case
of this broader process of transformation. Bell anticipated that as business became
increasingly dependent on scientists, engineers, and technicians, both government's
role and the organization of business itself would need to change significantly.

Bell also anticipated that scientists and engineers would increasingly transform both
products and processes across the full range of industries in much the same way that
nineteenth-century inventors had seen their industrial technologies diffused across
all sectors of the economy. In the postindustrial era, Bell said, craft knowledge and
traditional production techniques would give way to sophisticated science-based approaches that enhanced efficiency and created a cornucopia of new goods and services.
"This new fusion of science with innovation, and the possibility of systematic and
organized technological growth, is one of the underpinnings of the post-industrial
society" (Bell 1973, 197).

Bell foresaw a similar transformation in the corporation as scientists, engineers, and
other members of a new intelligentsia gained importance. "If the dominant figures of
the past hundred years have been the entrepreneur, the businessman, and the industrial executive," he argued, "the 'new men' are the scientists, the mathematicians, the
economists, and the engineers of the new intellectual technology" (344).

His argument pointed both to the growing role that technical experts would play in
top management positions and to shifts toward less hierarchical forms of organization.
While Bell did not address the issue explicitly, this argument paralleled those of Burns
and Stalker (1961) and Bennis and Slater (1968), who held that the growing centrality
of technological expertise would push organizations to be less authoritarian and less

hical, moving from steeper to flatter organizations with greater emphasis on rdination by multidisciplinary teams.

Bell was even bolder in arguing that postindustrial change would transform the relationship between business and government. On the one side, government's influence and power would be enhanced by its central role in financing scientific and technological research. On the other, Bell argued that, given the importance of basic research, corporations would have to move beyond narrow profit-maximizing strategies if they were to take full advantage of the new technological possibilities. Hence in 1973 he foresaw a new balance of power between business and government:

> It seems clear to me that, today, we in America are moving away from a society based on a private-enterprise market system toward one in which the most important economic decisions will be made at the political level, in terms of consciously defined "goals" and "priorities." (Bell 1973, 297–298)

Although few theorists now refer to Bell's framework (contra Block 1990; Brick 2006), several scholars have followed up on these arguments. In the last two decades a growing number of researchers have focused on national systems of innovation. They are tracking how different societies organize the complex task of turning scientific research into innovative products and processes (Collins 2004; Lundvall 1992; Nelson 1993). This literature rests on the idea that a nation's capacity for innovation determines its ability to gain advantage in the world economy.

Many of these studies of innovation systems focus on the links between the public and private sector. They look particularly at public funding of research and higher education, the growth of the scientific and technical labor force, the systems for establishing and protecting intellectual property rights for innovators, and ways to speed the movement of ideas from the research lab to the market. The strength of this literature is that it looks simultaneously at the roles of government and business and raises important questions about the interaction between the two. However, though it raises an important issue, this work has not yet identified the significant differences in the ways various nations organize their innovation systems, or looked at what causes these differences.

A second relevant body of work analyzes the shift of business firms, particularly in the United States, toward more collaborative, networked forms of organization. This shift represents the reversal of a pattern of corporate development that started in the last years of the nineteenth century. Back then, successful U.S. firms aspired to a high level of vertical integration, which meant controlling many different stages of the production process under one corporate roof (Fligstein 1990). Ford Motors, for example, integrated all stages of production, including the making of the steel at one location. Some of these firms attained high levels of self-sufficiency, often financing their growth with retained profits and drawing much of their technology from their own research laboratories. However, over the last half century, the dominant business model has, with gathering speed, shifted away from vertical integration (Castells 1996; Powell 2001).

Many firms have farmed out key parts of the production process to supplier firms. Nike has outsourced the production of its athletic shoes to factories across Asia, and

Detroit automakers have increasingly relied on subcontractors to produce many key parts of their automobiles (Whitford 2005). The pattern also extends to research and development as many firms rely less on their own laboratories and more on complex webs of collaboration with other firms, universities, and government laboratories (Hounshell 1996; Mowery 2009a; Powell 2001).

Much of the literature on networked firms implies that they will provide more fluidity than vertically integrated firms. New firms will continue to spin off from existing firms and university and government laboratories. Moreover, some of these newcomers will be able to exploit their initial role as subcontractors to establish superiority in important new technologies, just as Microsoft gained strategic control over the operating system for IBM's personal computers. Large established firms are at risk of precipitous decline if they fail to remain at the frontier of innovation.

This observation brings us to the first of the three research questions addressed in this chapter: over the last four decades, has there been a decline in the largest firms' role in developing innovative new technologies, or have they continued to serve as the central nodes of innovation networks?

The second question relates to the rise of a networked industrial structure, which is particularly obvious in biotechnology and the computer industry (Powell et al. 2005; Saxenian 1994). In both industries, small and large firms are involved in elaborate collaborative networks, and it is widely recognized that innovation grows out of processes of cooperation between organizations. But so far research has not made clear whether this pattern of interorganizational collaboration is characteristic of the entire economy or is confined to the most technologically dynamic sectors. As a result, our second research question is whether or not the shift toward interorganizational collaboration in the innovation process is unique to the technology sector or has it been a general trend across the entire economy.

The third question addresses funding. A final body of literature has documented the emergence of a triple helix of intertwined efforts by government, universities, and corporations to produce more rapid innovation. Extending Bell's analysis, this body of work shows how tightly university-based science efforts are now linked to industry, but it also shows that government agencies are playing an increasingly central role in funding, managing, and facilitating the process of technological development (Block 2008; Etzkowitz 2003; Geiger and Sa 2008; Kenney 1986a). For example, the Human Genome Project was organized by NIH and the Department of Energy, and the Strategic Computing Initiative by DARPA. In both cases government officials played a central role in setting technological goals and providing the funding to facilitate joint efforts by university-based researchers and business (Kevles 1992; McCray 2009; Roland 2002).

These targeted government programs have been combined with a highly decentralized system for encouraging innovation. Starting in the 1980s, new incentives were created for publicly funded researchers at universities and government laboratories to pursue commercial applications of their discoveries. Such efforts have been supported by funding programs, such as the Small Business Innovation Research (SBIR) program through which government agencies set aside a small percentage of their R&D budgets for projects proposed by small firms, many of which are newly created spin-offs from university or federal laboratories (Wessner 2008a). Other programs have been created to encourage joint ventures between researchers in university and federal laboratories and business firms (Block 2008; Geiger and Sa 2008). This provides us with our third research question: has there been a marked increase in the public sector's role in funding and facilitating innovation efforts?

Exploring each of these questions requires finding some way to measure innovative activities. However, the measurement of innovation has been a long-standing problem for social scientists. It is not adequate to count the dollars spent on research and development or the number of scientists and technologists at work, since these are simply inputs to the innovation process. Many studies have used patent statistics as a proxy, but these are unreliable because of variations in the quality of patents and in the criteria that are used to approve patent applications (Sciberras 1986; Taylor 2004).

In this chapter, we use a data set of award-winning innovations to illuminate structural shifts in the U.S. economy that have occurred over the past four decades. Our aim is to show that the developmental discontinuities predicted by postindustrial theory have in fact happened, but they have not been accompanied by the kind of political reconfigurations that Bell and others anticipated.

Introducing the Data

For more than forty years, *R&D Magazine* has annually recognized 100 innovations that are incorporated into actual commercial products. These awards are comparable to the Oscars for the motion picture industry; they carry considerable prestige within the community of research and development professionals. Organizations nominate their own innovations, and a changing jury that includes representatives from business, government, and universities collaborates with the magazine's editors to decide upon the final awards. (The nomination and selection procedures are described on the magazine's website at www.rdmag.com/Awards/RD-100-Awards/R-D-100-Awards.) The awards go to commercial products that were introduced into the marketplace during the previous year. The entry forms require evidence of the availability of the product and its price. Because 100 innovations can be recognized, juries are able to recognize the full range of innovative products instead of focusing solely on dynamic sectors like electronics or biotechnology.

We coded all of the winning innovations for three randomly chosen years in each of the last four decades to identify the types of organizations that were responsible for nurturing the award winners. (Full data are provided in Appendix A, page 300.) Since 1971, somewhere between five and thirteen of the awards each year went to foreign firms that had no U.S. partners.[3] We excluded those cases and focused our analysis on the roughly ninety award winners each year that involved U.S.-based firms.

While the awards recognize innovations in a wide range of different industries, there are some biases in the process. The awards are tilted toward product innovations rather than process innovations—those that are designed to raise the efficiency of the production process for goods and services. Some process innovations, such as a new type of machine tool or a more advanced computer program for managing inventories, are recognized, but many important process innovations are not considered because they involve complex combinations of new equipment and new organizational practices. Many military innovations are also excluded, since cutting-edge weapons are usually shrouded in secrecy and unavailable for purchase. Since the great bulk of federal R&D dollars are still directed toward weapons systems, many government-funded innovations lie outside of this competition.

Furthermore, the awards are structured to recognize just the tip of the proverbial iceberg—the last steps in the innovation process. The many earlier steps are submerged and out of sight. This bias means that the awards understate the role of university-based research, since detailed case studies suggest that many key innovations can be traced back to scientific breakthroughs in university laboratories (Roessner et al. 1997).

What other biases might enter the awards process? Questionable decisions and politics will always be a factor as jury members seek to reward friends and deny recognition to enemies. But for our purposes, it is not necessary that these awards recognize *the very best* innovations of any particular year. All that is necessary is that the awardees represent a reasonable cross-section of innovative products and that there is not a consistent bias that favors awardees of a particular type.

Another potential source of bias in competitions is the unequal resources different organizations have to prepare their nomination materials. Big architectural firms, for example, can hire the best photographers and devote considerable resources to a nomination while the hard-pressed solo practitioner might throw the application form together in a few hours (Larson 1993, 1994). There is probably a similar bias in these awards, with larger organizations having more expertise at putting together persuasive nomination packets.

However, there are reasons to think that the magnitude of this bias would be limited. For one thing, the universe of applicants is limited to organizations that have actually developed a commercial product, and since winning the award is a powerful form of advertising, even the tiniest firms have strong incentives to devote resources to an effective application. For another, the quality of "coolness" that engineers and technologists admire in a product is substantially easier to convey in words than the more abstract, aesthetic qualities that architectural or film juries might be rewarding. Finally, over the years there are many one-time winners, which reinforces the impression that it is the quality of the product and not the quality of the nomination packet that wins awards.

There are, however, two distinct biases in the awards that are important for interpreting our results. First, it is very rare for the *R&D 100* awards to recognize new pharmaceutical products. While there are many awards for medical devices and equipment, there seems to be a deliberate decision to avoid medications of all kinds. Our assumption is that this reflects an abundance of caution by the magazine, which does not want the bad publicity or legal liability of recognizing a product that might later be found to have negative side effects.

A second exclusion is more surprising. Few awards over the past twenty years have gone to products—either hardware or software—developed by the largest computer firms. Apple did not win an award for the iPod, Microsoft has received only one R&D award since it began, and firms such as Intel, Sun Microsystems, and Cisco have each won only once. Many of the products of this industry represent incremental improvements such as new versions of software packages or slightly improved notebook computers, and it is logical that the jurors ignore these. But it also seems likely that even when they produce a more dramatic innovation, jurors hold them to higher standards than those used for other organizations.

While these two exclusions indicate the need for caution in interpreting our results, they are analytically fortuitous. Since the data largely leave out big firms in the two industries—biotechnology and computing—that are generally seen as paradigmatic examples of science-based production, strong network ties among firms, and substantial governmental involvement in the innovation process, the awards data allows us to take a broader view of the innovation economy. We can see the degree to which the same trends affecting sectors that have not been as strongly associated with science-based production.

Coding

It would be ideal to code both the type of organization and the funding sources for every innovation awarded in the twelve competitions that we analyze. But while the type of organization can be established with a reasonable amount of research, uncovering the funding sources for almost 1,200 different innovations is an almost impossible task. The primary difficulty is that tracking flows of federal support to businesses is laborious and complicated.[4] In our data, we coded the organizational auspices as completely as possible for the roughly 1,200 innovations. Our approach to establishing the funding sources of the recognized innovations represents a compromise. We performed a detailed analysis of federal funding to award-winning firms and innovations for the years 1975 and 2006 to provide a snapshot of the contrast across time.

In organizational terms, the data revealed seven distinct loci from which the award-winning innovations originated:

Private
1. Fortune 500 firms operating alone.
2. Other firms operating on their own; this is a residual category that includes small and medium-size firms.
3. Collaborations among two or more private firms with no listed public sector or nonprofit partner. Industrial consortia are included in this category.[5]

Public or Mixed
4. Supported spin-offs. These are recently established (less than 10 years from founding) firms started by technologists at universities or government labs who have been supported by federal research funds.
5. Government laboratories—working by themselves or in collaboration. Most of these innovations come from the federal laboratories run by the Department of Energy, but some come from NIH, military laboratories, and labs run by

other agencies. If a university is a partner in one of these collaborations with a laboratory, it will be reported here and not under university.

6. Universities—working by themselves or in collaboration with entities other than federal labs.
7. Other public sector and nonprofit agencies—working by themselves or in collaboration with private firms.

Analyzing the Data

The R&D awards data provide powerful evidence on all three research questions. We start with the second question—whether the shift towards collaboration has become a general trend. Analysts of the networked firm have argued that innovation increasingly results from collaborations between two or more organizations (Hargadon 2003; Lester and Piore 2004). The connections between knowledge embodied in one organization and the knowledge embodied in other organizations are critical for the innovation process. The sparks generated when these different approaches are combined facilitate the discovery of effective new approaches (Hargadon 2003). Our data provide support for this claim. Figure 8.1 shows a dramatic rise in the number of domestic award-winning innovations that involve interorganizational collaborations. On average, sixty-seven innovations were attributed to a single private sector firm operating alone in the 1970s, but that has dropped to an average of only twenty-seven in the current decade.

Figure 8.1 R&D 100 Awards to Inter-Organizational Collaborations

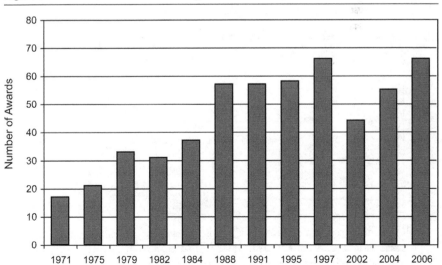

In part this shift reflects the growing importance of public sector agencies as award winners, since we code all public agencies as engaging in collaboration since they invariably employ private partners to market their innovative products. But even among the dwindling number of private sector winners, the frequency of formal collaborations rose from 7.8 percent in the 1970s to 17.5 percent in the current decade.

An equally striking finding addresses the first research question—the role of large corporations in the innovation process. Figure 8.2 shows the dramatic decline in both solo and collaborative winners from the Fortune 500 firms. While these firms were the largest single winner of awards in the 1970s, by the current decade, solo winners from the Fortune 500 could be counted on the fingers of one hand. Even with collaborators, they averaged only ten awards per year.

To be sure, this is the place where the almost total exclusion of large computer industry firms and pharmaceutical firms impacts the data. Data on U.S. patent applications shows that firms such as IBM, Microsoft, Intel, and Sun rank among the most prolific U.S. firms in the number of patents received (U.S. Patent and Trademark Office: www.uspto.gov/web/offices/ac/ido/oeip/taf/reports.htm). They also represent important exceptions to the tendency for big firms to reduce their outlays for R&D over the past twenty years. So the fact that their R&D effort is only rarely recognized in the *R&D 100* means that Figure 8.2 overstates the declining innovative capacity of Fortune 500 firms. But even if the large computer industry firms were collectively receiving ten of these awards per year, Figure 8.2 would still show a significant downward trend.

The situation with pharmaceutical firms is more complicated. While the established large firms such as Merck and Pfizer and the most successful of the biotech firms such as Genentech and Amgen continue to fund significant research efforts, the number of innovative drugs they bring to the market in recent years has been quite limited. The

Figure 8.2 R&D 100 Award Winners from the Fortune 500

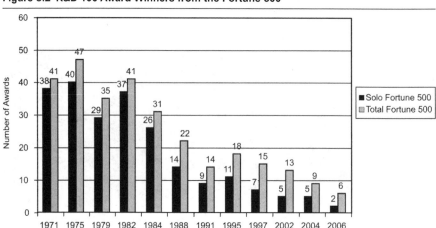

drug industry has its own awards for innovation published by *Prescrire International.*[6] Their highest award, the Golden Pill, recognizes new drugs that represent a major breakthrough. But between 1997 and 2006, only two drugs received this recognition, and there were only twelve others that received second place recognition as a clear advance over existing therapies. This suggests that if the *R&D 100* competition had recognized prescription drugs, the results in Figure 8.2 would not have changed much at all.

The real significance of Figure 8.2 is the decline in awards won by general purpose manufacturing firms such as General Electric, General Motors, and 3M. Firms like these dominated the awards in the 1970s, but they only rarely won in recent years. This decline parallels the trend in their patenting activity, strongly suggesting diminished innovative efforts. Figure 8.3 shows a dramatic decline in the percentage of U.S. corporate patents won by nine of these manufacturing firms that have been in continuous existence and are outside the computer industry.

These declines can be traced to the priorities of corporate executives faced with continuing pressure over the last several decades to improve the quarterly financial results of their firms. Many firms have cut back R&D efforts or shifted funds toward product development. After all, research is expensive and its contribution to the bottom line is likely to come long after the current CEO's tenure in office. At the same time, the financial orientation of top executives means that they see new technologies as simply another asset that can be acquired rather than produced internally. They are confident that when the time comes, they can either license the technologies they need or buy up the firms that are producing innovations (Estrin 2009; Tassey 2007).

Figure 8.3 Percent of Total U.S. Corporate Patents Received by GE, Kodak, AT&T, DuPont, GM, Dow Chemical, 3M, United Technologies, and Ford, 1971–2006

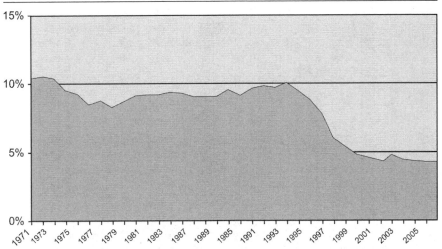

Source: U.S. Patent and Trademark Office data available at: www.uspto.gov/web/offices/ac/ido/oeip/taf/h_at.htm.

The magnitude of this shift is indicated by employment trends among scientists and engineers working for private firms. According to data collected by the NSF, in 1971, 7.6 percent of R&D scientists and engineers working for industry, or 28,200 individuals, were employed by firms with fewer than 1,000 employees. By 2004, this had risen to 32 percent, while the actual number of people had grown to 365,000. NSF data also indicate that Ph.D. scientists and engineers have become even more concentrated in small firms; in 2003, 24 percent of those working for industry were employed at firms with fewer than ten employees and more than half were at firms with fewer than 500 employees.[7] It is, of course, impossible to know how much of this shift reflected push factors that led technologists to leave large firms and how much was the attraction of working in smaller firms. Either way, the trend in the awards away from big firms follows the trend of the technologists who create the innovations.

As the role of large corporations declined, there has been a corresponding gain in awards for public and mixed entities. This provides answers to the third research question—whether the public sector is playing an expanded role in the innovation system. As Figure 8.4 shows, the majority of awards are now won by federal laboratories, universities, or the firms that we have categorized as supported spin-offs. In the last two decades, federal laboratories have become the dominant organizational locus for winning these awards. They now have about the same weight in the overall awards as the Fortune 500 firms did in the 1970s, averaging about thirty-five awards per year.[8] This is a surprising finding because many observers hold the federal laboratories in low esteem and doubt their capacity to contribute to innovation. Most of the winning innovations originate in the Department of Energy laboratories that were created to develop atomic weapons in the early years of the Cold War. The sinister image of Ph.D. physicists and chemists working assiduously to develop ever more destructive weaponry has certainly colored the public image of these facilities.[9]

After the federal laboratories, the next most important public or mixed entities are the supported spin-offs. These entities—on their own—averaged close to eight awards per year in the current decade, and they also win some additional awards in partnership with government laboratories or universities. Moreover, as we will see later, firms that began as supported spin-offs but have been in existence for more than ten years are coded as "other firms"—part of the private category—and their weight in the awards has also increased over time.

The typical pattern of a supported spin-off is that a professor or a scientist at a university or federal laboratory makes an important discovery and consults with university or lab officials as to how best to protect the resulting intellectual property. In many cases, the organization encourages the innovator to start his or her own firm to develop and ultimately market the new product. The more entrepreneurial universities and laboratories function almost as venture capitalists by helping the individual find investors and experienced managers who could guide the firm (Geiger and Sa 2008).

The final category in Figure 8.4 encompasses awards won by universities and other public sector agencies and nonprofit firms. Surprisingly, the direct weight of universities among award winners is relatively modest. There are several reasons for this. First, some innovations that originate in university laboratories show up in the supported spin-offs category because the researcher started his or her own firm.

Figure 8.4 Awards to Federal Labs, Supported Spinoffs, and Other Public Entities

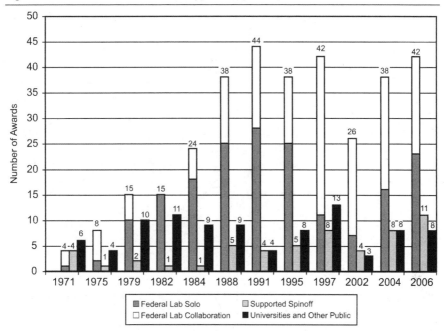

Second, university-based researchers are increasingly part of collaborations with federal laboratories and our coding system attributes those innovations to the labs. In 2006, for example, universities received two awards in partnership with other firms and seven in partnership with federal laboratories. In short, even though the importance of scientific discoveries at universities has become ever more central to the innovation process, most of the transition into commercial products is mediated through spin-offs and the activities at federal laboratories.[10]

Yet a focus on organizational auspices alone does not capture the full extent of U.S. government financing of the innovation process. Figure 8.5 shows the role of one of the most important—but little known—federal programs: the Small Business Innovation Research (SBIR) program. Firms that have won SBIR awards represent a large share of winners in the current decade. SBIR is a set aside program that requires that federal agencies with large research budgets devote 2.5 percent of their R&D budgets to support firms with 500 employees or less. It also provided initial funding for many of the supported spin-offs. The program awards up to $100,000 in no-strings support for projects in Phase I and up to $750,000 for Phase II projects that have shown significant progress in meeting the initial objectives.[11] In 2004, the SBIR program gave out more than $2 billion for some 6,300 separate research projects. As the figure shows, current and past SBIR award winners have come to constitute roughly 25 percent of domestic winners each year.

In Figure 8.6, we try to provide a more comprehensive measure of the role of federal financing over time by looking in greater detail at funding for award winners in 1975

Figure 8.5 Awards to SBIR-Funded Firms

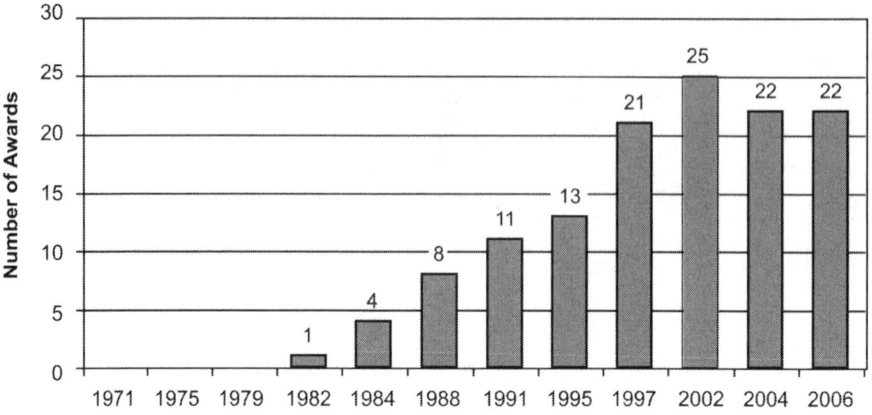

Note: The single firm listed in 1982, Radiation Monitoring Devices, received funding from the SBIR precursor program, a pilot project operated under the auspices of NSF.

and 2006. The bottom part of each graph shows the various public sector winners that rely heavily on federal funding. As indicated earlier, this shows a dramatic rise from fourteen to sixty-one of the awardees. The top part of the graph shows the number of "other" and Fortune 500 firms that received at least 1 percent of their revenues from the federal government.[12] This 1 percent screen picks up both large defense contractors and firms that have received substantial federal grants to support their R&D efforts. In 1975, twenty-three awards were won by private firms that received at least 1 percent of their revenues from federal support. Prominent among these was General Electric, which in that year was responsible for nine award-winning innovations.[13]

In 2006, we found that of five private collaborations, the federal government directly funded three. Of the twenty "other firms" that won awards, thirteen had federal support above the 1 percent threshold, and we were able to link the federal money directly to the specific innovation that received the award. Hence sixteen of these "private" innovations count as federally funded. The overall result in Figure 8.6 is that the number of federally funded innovations rises from thirty-seven in 1975 to seventy-seven in 2006.

In 2006 only eleven of the domestic award winners were *not* beneficiaries of federal funding. Two of these eleven—Brion Tech and MMR Technologies—were recent spin-offs from Stanford University, but they had not received federal funding after their launch. In short, Figure 8.6 probably understates the magnitude of the expansion in federal funding for innovations between 1975 and 2006. After all, in 1975, we count innovations as federally funded even if support was not going to the specific unit of the firm that was working on a particular innovation. For 2006, however, a demonstration of federal support required showing that the federal funds were going to the same unit that was responsible for the particular technology that won the award.

Figure 8.6 Federal Involvement with Award Winning Innovations, 1975 and 2006

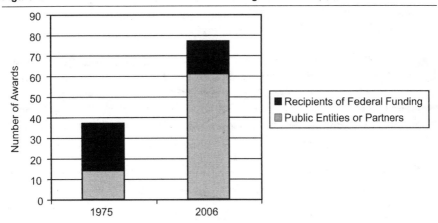

Even in the period that Fortune 500 corporations dominated the innovation process, they drew heavily on federal funding support. If one is looking for a golden age in which the private sector did most of the innovating on its own without federal help, one has to go back to the era before World War II (Hounshell 1996). Nevertheless, over the last forty years, the awards indicate a dramatic increase in the federal government's centrality to the innovation economy. In the earlier period, U.S. industrial and technology policies were almost entirely monopolized by the military and space programs (Alic 2007; Hooks 1990). More recently, a wide range of nondefense agencies have been involved in supporting private sector research and development initiatives. Key agencies now include Commerce, Energy, NIH, Agriculture, NSF, and Homeland Security.

Discussion

Our data set provides evidence of three interrelated changes in the U.S. economy over the past generation. These are the declining centrality of the largest corporations to the innovation process in the United States, the growing importance of small start-up firms and interorganizational collaboration in the innovation process, and the expanded role of public sector institutions as both participants in and funders of the innovation process.

The last of these shifts is the most surprising, since this change coincided with the period in which market fundamentalist ideas dominated public policy debates. But it is important to recognize how different the U.S. federal role is from other countries' models of centrally planned technological change. In Chalmers Johnson's (1982) classic account of the Japanese model of industrial policy, he shows how government officials, working at the Ministry of Trade and Industry, operated as both coordinators and financiers for the conquest by Japanese firms of new markets. The key was that the government officials were implementing a shared plan that linked investments in particular technologies with specific business strategies to win in particular markets—both domestically and internationally.

In the U.S. case there is no unified plan, and different government agencies often compete with each other to support new technologies. This approach is more like Mao's "let a hundred flowers bloom": the United States has created a decentralized network of publicly funded laboratories whose technologists have strong incentives to work with private firms and find ways to turn their discoveries into commercial products. Moreover, an alphabet soup of different programs gives government agencies opportunities to help fund some of these more compelling technological possibilities.

Alongside this "if you build it, they will come" approach, there are also targeted government programs designed to accelerate progress across specific technological barriers. These programs are also implemented in a decentralized fashion by small agencies. The model developed by DARPA of setting technological goals and working closely with researchers to accelerate breakthroughs has now diffused across the federal system (Block 2008).

Because these programs contradict the market fundamentalist ideology that celebrates private enterprise and denigrates the public sector, they have remained largely unknown to the public. Journalists rarely write about government technology initiatives; for example, the *New York Times* has mentioned the SBIR program in its news coverage fewer than ten times over the last twenty-seven years. To be sure, Congress periodically debates the design and funding for these programs, but reports on these discussions are rarely covered in the *Wall Street Journal* or other general, widely circulated business publications. Since the programs are largely unknown, they simply do not figure in public policy debates (Block 2008).

Ironically, the parameters of these little-known state programs fit the model of a developmental network state (DNS) outlined in Seán Ó Riain's (2004a) study of the Irish government's efforts to encourage high-tech growth in that nation (see also Breznitz 2007). Just as in Ireland, government efforts are highly decentralized, rely on strengthening technological networks that cut across the public-private divide, and require public sector officials to play a multiplicity of roles in supporting entrepreneurial efforts.

Recently, Schrank and Whitford (2009a; Chapter 13 of this volume) have helpfully depicted these government programs as efforts to compensate for failures that are endemic to networked forms of economic organization. In contrast to market failures, network failures occur when economic actors are unable to find appropriate network partners who are both competent and trustworthy. The programs of a developmental network state (DNS) help stitch together networks and work to improve and validate the competence of potential network partners. Furthermore, the federal laboratories, industry-university research centers sponsored by the NSF, and informal meetings sponsored by agencies such as DARPA create "collaborative public spaces" (Lester and Piore 2004) where network participants share key ideas.

However, the DNS also addresses a classic market failure—the difficulty of funding new technologies in the early stages of development. While private sector venture capital has gained wide attention, the reality is that most VC investments do not go to newcomers or early-stage research; rather, they go to companies that already have developed a commercial product (Branscomb and Auerswald 2002; Gompers and Lerner 2004).[14] Government agencies have moved into this gap, and they self-consciously use a venture capital model in which they may fund twenty separate initiatives, assuming that only a fraction will achieve significant breakthroughs, but these breakthroughs will more than cover the costs of the failures.

The SBIR program fits this model. Many government agencies were initially resentful of SBIR because it kept them from spending a portion of their R&D dollars on their high priority efforts (Wessner 2008a). However, many of the agencies have come to see SBIR as a valuable mechanism that works better than collaborating with large established firms to get the innovations they need. But since SBIR support for firms is generally limited to about three years for any particular project, a number of government agencies have now set up their own venture capital operations. The CIA's venture capital arm, In-Q-Tel, maintains its own website and lists ninety recent start-up firms in which it has invested. Congress provided a $28 million initial fund, and just as with private sector venture capital, the idea is that agency funds will be replenished and expanded as In-Q-Tel sells its stake in firms that become successful. The Department of the Army has followed the CIA model while the Department of Energy has partnered with Battelle—the large nonprofit organization that manages several DOE labs. Battelle has now created its own not-for-profit venture capital arm with an emphasis on supporting start-up firms that originated in DOE's laboratories (Keller, Chapter 6).

It is too early to tell whether this experiment in public sector venture capital will be expanded. But the fact that such initiatives flourished even during the free market–oriented administration of George W. Bush reinforces the point that the United States has changed fundamentally over the past three decades in the direction of smaller technology firms, more complex interorganizational collaborations, and a greater public sector role.

The most critical point is that these postindustrial changes occurred "behind the back" of both social actors and social scientists; they were not accompanied by any postindustrial awareness or any publicly visible renegotiation of the relationship between state and economy. On the contrary, they coincided with the resurgence of the free market ideas that had been marginalized through the 1940s, 1950s, and 1960s (Block 2007). Moreover, under the reign of free market liberalism, the U.S. economy experienced three decades of spectacular growth of the financial sector (Krippner 2005)—a development that had not been anticipated by postindustrial theorists and that also diverted attention and resources from the structural changes documented here.

Conclusion

There is a direct connection between the story elaborated here and the global economic crisis of 2008–2009. Despite its considerable accomplishments, the emergent U.S.

innovation economy of small and medium-size firms working with public institutions has been chronically underfinanced throughout its history. One reason that government agencies such as the CIA have launched their own venture capital operations is that the flow of private sector venture capital to these smaller technology firms has been woefully insufficient, particularly in the early stages of technology development. The literature describes these firms as struggling to cross "the valley of death"—the funding gap during the years it takes to transform technological breakthroughs into commercial products (Branscomb and Auerswald 2002). Even when venture capital is offered, the terms can be unattractive; inventors are asked to cede control over a start-up's intellectual property and decision-making rights in return for an initial investment (Lerner 1999a; Wessner 2008a). Aside from government programs, there is no systematic mechanism available to direct private capital to these firms in their early stages.

At the same time, the federal government's spending in support of research and development has fallen from nearly 2 percent of GDP in the mid-1960s to about 0.7 percent in recent years (American Association for the Advancement of Science 2008 at www.aaas.org/spp/rd/usg07.pdf; Tassey 2007). Programs designed to accelerate the commercialization of new technologies have been forced into a destructive zero-sum battle with programs designed to support fundamental research, and scientists in different fields have been pitted against each other to win funding. In fact, over a thirty-year period of chronic tax cutting, the federal government's total civilian investment spending—on research, on education, and on infrastructure—has fallen from 2.7 percent of GDP to 1.8 percent. Moreover, public universities have also been hit hard by declining support at the state level (Newfield 2008).

In short, all parts of this new innovation system have suffered from insufficient financing—in spite of the massive amounts of money foreign countries have lent the United States to cover its chronic trade deficit (Bernanke 2005). In addition, large nonfinancial corporations in the United States, such as the Fortune 500, have also been net purchasers of financial assets, adding to the pool of savings in search of profitable investment outlets. Many analysts believe that this growing pool of surplus saving was responsible both for the stock market bubble of the 1990s and the disastrous housing bubble of the 2000s, and it was the bursting of the U.S. housing bubble that triggered the global economic downturn.

If capital markets had been structured more effectively, some of that pool of excess saving could have been channeled into financing the U.S. innovation economy in a sustainable fashion, and that might also have worked to strengthen the U.S. balance of trade.[15] One can only speculate as to whether the existence of more productive outlets for capital investment might have attenuated the housing bubble. However, looking forward, there is an urgent need for structural reforms that expand government funding of research, development, and higher education, as well as dramatically increasing the availability of consistent, long-term, patient financing for the thousands of small and medium-size technology firms that increasingly form the productive core of the U.S. economy. Such reforms might also reduce the U.S. economy's vulnerability to destructive financial bubbles.

Notes

This chapter was supported with funding from the Ford Foundation. A different version was published as a report by the Information Technology and Innovation Foundation in Washington, D.C. Rob Atkinson, ITIF president, and a number of anonymous reviewers made helpful criticisms of that draft. Jason Logan, John Kincaid, and Chris Knight provided valuable research assistance, and we are grateful for comments received in several different settings where we presented the findings, including the Power and Inequality Workshop at UC Davis and the American Sociological Association meetings, August 2008. We are particularly grateful to the reviewers and editors of *Socio-Economic Review* for their constructive suggestions. This version is reprinted with permission and with some additional editing from *Socio-Economic Review* 7 (July 2009): 459–483.

1. The social structures of accumulation approach was similar, but it began slightly later with the publication of Gordon, Edwards, and Reich 1982.

2. Some work in these different intellectual traditions continues (Block 1990; Boyer and Saillard 2002; Kotz, McDonough, and Reich 1994; Wallerstein 2004), but this scholarship of discontinuity has received little attention beyond expert communities. There were also some exceptions to the general trend; Manuel Castells (1996) continued an active dialogue with earlier work on postindustrialism.

3. The only exceptions occur when a foreign firm owns a large, established U.S. business, such as when Chrysler was owned by Daimler Benz. In such cases, we code the firm as a Fortune 500 firm.

4. This discussion neglects in-kind government support, which is an increasingly important factor in technology policy. For instance, in 2006, the Department of Energy, which runs many of the large government laboratories, reported that there had been 2,416 active arrangements where DOE labs did work for others with some partial compensation and 3,474 user agreements where firms were allowed to use laboratory equipment. Unfortunately, the DOE does not publish the names of the firms that benefit from this assistance.

5. We list any innovation as public as long as there is a collaborator that is public or a supported spin-off. We avoid double counting by listing collaborative winners under just one of these categories. If a government laboratory is a participant in a collaboration, the innovation is attributed to the laboratory regardless of other participants. If no government lab is involved but there is a university, then the innovation is attributed to the university. If there is another public or nonprofit participant, the innovation is attributed to that participant. If there are multiple private participants, then it is coded in category 3—private collaboration. Table 8.1 in the appendix provides sufficient detail to show that this particular coding scheme does not bias our results.

6. We are grateful to Donald Light for bringing these awards to our attention.

7. "Number of full-time-equivalent (FTE) R&D scientists and engineers in R&D-performing companies, by industry and by size of company" is available at: www.nsf.gov/statistics/iris/search_hist.cfm?indx=24 and www.nsf.gov/statistics/nsf07314/pdf/tab41.pdf. These figures should be taken as approximations due to changes in NSF's procedures for collecting and estimating this data over time. Data on Ph.D. employees are provided in figure 3.18 in National Science Foundation 2008a at www.nsf.gov/statistics/seind08/figures.htm.

8. In the cases that we have coded as solo, the innovation award went solely to a federal lab or a university. This presumably indicates that the partner enlisted to commercialize the product had no ownership of the intellectual property involved in the innovation.

9. Even in the scholarly literature, it is rare to find recognition of the innovation productivity

of the labs. For an overview of the labs, see Crow and Bozeman 1998. One of the rare sources that recognizes the increased commercial productivity of the labs is Jaffe and Lerner 2001.

10. Even if we recode collaborations that involve both a federal lab and a university as "university," the number of award-winning innovations involving federal labs still substantially outweighs those involving universities.

11. The NIH has applied for and received a waiver that enables it to exceed these caps.

12. The logic of using a 1 percent of revenue screen is that it is common among large firms to devote only 3 to 4 percent of revenues to R&D expenditures. Hence federal awards or contracts of that magnitude could help fund a significant increase in R&D effort.

13. Five additional awards went to Fortune 500 companies that had contracts to manage government laboratories in 1975—two each for Union Carbide and DuPont and one for Monsanto.

14. Price Waterhouse Coopers provides a database that shows trends in private venture capital financing both in terms of dollars and number of deals (www.pwcmoneytree.com/MTPublic/ns/index.jsp). In 2005, for example, private venture capital financed 1,061 firms at start-up or at early stages with a total of $4.7 billion. Since the data cover the entire U.S. economy, these are quite small numbers.

15. The Internet bubble of the 1990s channeled vast amounts of capital to high-tech firms in search of quick, speculative profits. The key is to create patient flows of capital to smaller technology firms.

CHAPTER **9**

Failure to Deploy
Solar Photovoltaic Policy in the United States
Chris P. Knight

Since solar photovoltaic (PV) energy systems were first used in terrestrial applications in the 1970s, the American public has been fascinated with them (Perlin 1999). Solar PV systems are among a select group of energy technologies that generate electricity with no direct carbon emissions and have practically inexhaustible power supplies. PV systems have the additional benefits of generating electricity silently, having a long life, and needing little maintenance (DOE 2006; see Appendix at the end of this chapter for an introduction to solar photovoltaic electricity systems). In an era of high energy prices and concern over carbon-induced global climate change, PV systems have an important role to play in our future (Metz et al. 2007).

Yet despite these attractive features, and after billions of dollars in public and private research and development expenditures on PV technologies and a hundredfold decrease in system costs over half a century, solar PV accounts for only a fraction of 1 percent of U.S. electricity supply. The relatively high cost of solar PV systems is somewhat to blame for this, as is the low cost of electricity generated by American fossil fuel–fired power plants. But other countries with fewer financial resources than the United States, such as Germany and Spain, have overcome similar barriers in order to secure the benefits of photovoltaic energy systems for their citizens. The most crucial difference is that these countries have formulated consistent and well-funded deployment policies in order to increase the market share of PV systems.

There is a substantial literature that helps make sense of the policy patterns depicted in this chapter. For some, our story of the federal government's aggressive leadership role in solar photovoltaic R&D carried out since the beginning of the Cold War will be a surprise. This chapter attempts to expose in more detail the role of the hidden developmental state in the American economy, described by Fred Block (2008). In contrast to the centralized activities of the East Asian states in administering the industrial policies of the "tiger" economies, the U.S. developmental state's role is better characterized as "networked" (Ó Riain 2004a). An illustrative case study within this paradigm is Glenn Fong's (2001) examination of U.S. government programs in the creation of the personal computer. Our story also intertwines with the research approach that emphasizes the regional impacts of the developmental state's networked elements, demonstrated by Andrew Schrank's chapter on Sandia National Laboratories (Chapter 5) and most famously by AnnaLee Saxenian's (1994) work on Silicon Valley.

While accepting the fundamental premise of this scholarship—that interactive networks of public and private actors have played an important role in technology development and diffusion—in the case of photovoltaic energy systems we question the extent to which these networks have delivered on their promise. If we view the solar electricity supply chain as a network of people and institutions connecting the laboratory to the rooftop of a solar household, it can be argued that the gap between America's substantial R&D activities and the actual deployment and market diffusion of PV technology constitutes a "network failure," in Josh Whitford and Andrew Schrank's terminology (Chapter 13). As for many high-tech breakthroughs, PV supply chain network failures may be responsible for disappointing public impacts (Mandel 2009).

The longer-term dynamics that contribute to the network failure in the solar photovoltaic supply chain—as well as to the network failures in the environmental technology supply chain more generally—have been analyzed by a number of authors. First, what we term the "failure to deploy" is actually a uniquely American paradigm of deployment, emphasizing technology customization and diverse applications over efficiency and scale (Shum and Watanabe 2007). Japan and Germany may have more PV systems installed, but the United States has a greater variety of systems, and variety may generate more utility for U.S. consumers. Also, different cross-national levels of institutionalization of the environmental or green movement have generated more political will for enacting deployment policies in Germany than in other countries (Schreurs 2002). In one of the most compelling lines of renewable energy technology and policy research, Gregory Unruh (2000) has shown that the current hegemony of the fossil fuel energy system is being maintained largely by a mutually reinforcing relationship between technologies and institutions. One corollary is that under a "locked-in" energy regime, politicians may choose to generate funds for R&D rather than actually deploy energy systems that displace fossil fuel generation and thus create political repercussions.

In the following pages, we seek to build on these theoretical foundations by analyzing the specific policies that have hampered the deployment of PV systems. Whatever the historical developments and dynamics behind them, specific levels of funding and specific policy designs have influenced the solar photovoltaic electricity supply chain. Analyzing these policy trends can show more clearly why they have produced the outcomes they have in the solar PV market, an understanding that is crucial to policy reform. For data, we rely heavily on reports from international organizations and NGOs, including the International Energy Agency's Photovoltaic Power Systems (IEA-PVPS) program, the Interstate Renewable Energy Council (IREC), and Network for New Energy Choices (NNEC), all of which specialize in renewable energy policy analysis.[1]

This chapter consists of two sections. The first tells the story of extensive U.S. public sector involvement in R&D in photovoltaic energy systems since the 1950s. Functional crystalline silicon solar cells were first demonstrated in Bell Labs in 1954, and most of the radical technological innovations in PV over the next two decades came from federal investment in solar cells for use in satellites. After the second energy crisis in

1979–1980, the federal government drastically increased energy research and development funding. Also, beginning in the mid 1970s, U.S. policy innovations such as public-private partnerships created U.S. leadership in thin-film, nonsilicon, and high efficiency solar PV technologies. To this day, the United States is still a global leader in these technologies.

The second section of this chapter describes and analyzes U.S. solar photovoltaic deployment policies. We begin with a series of figures showing which countries and U.S. states have installed the most photovoltaic systems and which have gained the most PV industrial activity. In almost all cases, leading countries in these categories are those with the most rigorous deployment policies. Despite the larger U.S. land area and the intense solar radiation the United States receives (more than other wealthy countries), U.S. deployment policies are comparatively weak, heterogeneous, and inconsistent. The United States operates according to a trickle-down PV deployment paradigm: most of the responsibilities are left to the lowest levels of governance. Particularly troublesome are the permitting and interconnection practices of municipalities and electric utilities, which are a central reason why installed PV systems are more expensive in the United States than they are in Japan or Germany. The most successful international PV deployment policies involve feed-in tariff mechanisms which legally require all utilities to buy back solar electricity at higher than market rates, typically over a period of twenty years, thus helping owners to recoup the price of their PV systems. Feed-in tariff policies were responsible for increasing the total amount of solar PV in Spain, Portugal, Korea, and Italy by several hundred percent in 2008 (IEA 2009c). Without such mechanisms, it will be left to exceptional utility managers, like S. David Freeman of the Sacramento Municipal Utility District, to cost-effectively deploy solar PV systems.

U.S. PV Research and Development

Research and development (R&D) is crucial to increasing the efficiency by which solar cells convert sunlight into electricity, as well as reducing the cost of manufacturing solar PV modules.[2] Scholarship by Gregory Nemet (2006) has found that improved cell efficiency is second only to increased production plant size as an important factor in explaining PV price decline from 1980 to 2001, responsible for 30 percent of the price change during this time. High levels of R&D expenditures are associated with high levels of innovation in photovoltaic technologies as shown through patenting activity (Kammen and Nemet 2005). Federal policies supporting R&D include funding for more researchers and new laboratories, innovation grants like the Small Business Innovation Research (SBIR) program, and public venture capital funds.

International Patterns of R&D

Measured in terms of funding, diversity, or commercial impact, the U.S. federal government has the best photovoltaic research and development program in the world. Over the last several decades, federal R&D programs have supported research in semiconductor materials other than silicon, such as Cadmium Telluride, Copper Indium Gallium Selenide (CIGS), and organic semiconductors, as well as experimentation with high-efficiency multiple layer (multijunction) solar cells. Federal R&D programs have also helped develop thin-film solar modules—which are cheaper and more efficient to manufacture. U.S. solar PV firms such as Arizona's First Solar, San Jose's Nanosolar, and Boston's Konarka are now working to commercialize advanced solar modules based on these technologies. In fact, of the roughly 100 active U.S. solar PV cell and module manufacturers, 73 are start-ups working on advanced technologies (IEA 2009c).

Starting in the mid 1970s, the U.S. government was far and away the global PV research and development leader. In fact, until the mid 1980s, U.S. R&D expenditures were often double those of runners-up Japan and Germany, despite the antisolar sentiment of the Regan administration. Starting after a lull in the early 1990s, Japan and the United States both ratcheted up their PV R&D expenditures. In 2005 and 2006, U.S. and Japanese PV budgets were several times that of Germany—around $150 million U.S. dollars compared to Germany's $50 million (IEA 2008).

Figure 9.1 shows the historical trends among select industrialized countries in government support for photovoltaic research and development. Although the U.S. PV R&D budget may be low when viewed in light of pressing environmental and economic imperatives, it is competitive with that of other leading industrialized nations.

The Beginnings of PV R&D Policy

Figure 9.1 presents just the latest evidence of a longer-term trend of U.S. dominance in PV research and development. Silicon solar photovoltaic cells were first demonstrated

Figure 9.1 Trends In Government Support for PV R&D Among Selected Countries Through 2008 (IEA 2009a)

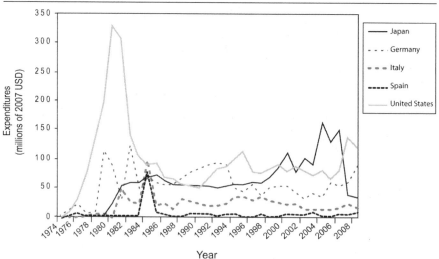

at Bell Labs in 1954, at around the same time as the transistor. Although PV energy systems were recognized as an exciting technology, they were overshadowed by other energy sources during the postwar era. Unlike transistors, which had no real competition, photovoltaic cells had to compete for market share and federal funding against "locked-in" energy sources with much larger constituencies: nuclear energy, imagined to be "too cheap to meter," and oil, priced at several dollars a barrel. Decades of continued research and development were necessary before the promise of PV systems would be better understood and acted upon (Perlin 1999).

During the 1950s, 1960s, and early to mid 1970s, public investments in PV cells provided crucial early markets for a technology that was too expensive for private consumer use. In 1956, shortly after being demonstrated for the first time, a one watt solar cell cost $300. At such a price, PV electricity was hundreds of times more expensive than a 1950s household would be accustomed to paying its local utility. The only location where solar cells were cost-effective was outer space, and in the late 1950s, the U.S. government contracted with Hoffman Electronics to provide solar cells for use in its nascent space exploration program (Perlin 1999). During the 1960s, support from the National Aeronautics and Space Association (NASA) and the formation of a federally sponsored communications satellite corporation known as COMSAT helped further improve PV technology for space use (Taylor et al. 2007; Berger 1997).

In the 1970s, with initial support from the National Science Foundation's Research Applied to National Needs (RANN) program, photovoltaics began to be produced for terrestrial applications (Taylor et al. 2007). In 1972 the RANN program funded research at the University of Delaware's Institute for Energy Conversion (IEC), the world's first dedicated solar photovoltaic research and development center (DOE 2002). One of the most successful early PV firms was Solarex, whose founders were ex-COMSAT scientists (Berger 1997). By the 1970s, Solarex and other firms were producing PV systems used to power a diverse group of off-grid terrestrial applications: lights for oil rig platforms, Coast Guard buoys, highway call phones, remote telecommunication transmitters, and residential systems for remote houses. From 1956 to 1973, the price of solar PV cells declined from $286 to $20 per watt of capacity, driven by innovation induced by these early applications (Perlin 1999).

R&D Policy Innovations

The United States was also the first country to make use of cost-shared public-private partnership (PPP) arrangements in its photovoltaic R&D program. Public-private partnerships—one example of a broader suite of measures the United States undertook in the 1980s to enhance commercialization of national lab innovations and improve national competitiveness in high technology—involve jointly managed R&D projects where the government and private firms each pay a share of the expenses (Margolis 2002; Ruttan 2001). With PPPs, private firms benefit from an easier time commercializing inventions, while the federal government benefits from conducting research with a larger impact while spending less.

The first U.S. solar PPP was the Navy Jet Propulsion Laboratory's flat-plate solar array project, which in the late 1970s helped develop amorphous silicon solar modules, a technology that has since won substantial market share. During the 1980s and 1990s, the amount of money the federal government and private industry invested in public-private partnership projects continued to rise (Margolis 2002). Prominent efforts during the 1990s attempted to demonstrate that large PV installations could take the place of fossil fuel power plants. These included the Photovoltaics for Utility Scale Applications (PVUSA) and the Technology Experience to Accelerate Markets in Utility Photovoltaics (TEAM-UP) programs. More recently, the Solar America Initiative (SAI), launched in 2006, promoted research and development partnerships with many PV firms around the country in a bid to make electricity from solar PV systems competitive with conventional electricity by 2015 (Strahs and Tombari 2006).

Using private sector funds to supplement the Department of Energy's renewable energy budget gives DOE programs more influence than they might otherwise have. Partly as a result of these partnerships, metrics of innovation like the number of DOE-related energy patents remained remarkably strong during the 1990s, in spite of the decline in government spending on energy R&D at this time. While the number of patents "assigned" to the DOE for renewable energy or fossil energy innovations declined, the number of patents "assigned or related" to the DOE for such innovations increased. The "related" patents appear to reflect the result of public-private partnerships (Margolis 2002, 49–51, 57).

R&D Policy Achievements

Although the United States has not sustained late 1970s levels of PV R&D expenditures, it has still spent much more cumulatively than other industrialized nations, building up a substantial base of researchers and laboratories. The United States spent $3.3 billion on PV R&D from 1974 through 2008, while Japan spent $2.1 billion and Germany spent $1.9 billion over this period (IEA 2009a). The results of this sizable U.S. investment include world renowned research institutions such as National Renewable Energy Laboratory (NREL) and the University of Delaware's Institute for Energy Conversion (IEC). Founded during the first year of the Jimmy Carter administration, for the last three decades NREL has worked on R&D specializing in advanced thin-film solar PV cells, solar PV manufacturing process improvements, and record-breaking high performance PV systems. The University of Delaware's IEC has also survived over three decades, generating multiple world record efficiencies in photovoltaic cells during that time. Even the institutions that ultimately did not survive—such as the regional solar energy centers (RSECs) that were created along with NREL in 1977 but did not make it through the Reagan years—added to a national network of experts who have been advancing PV technology (Taylor et al. 2007). Year after year, this network has produced record efficiency gains in PV cells. The examples in Table 9.1 are just a few of these records (DOE 2002; IEA 2009b; NREL 2008).

Table 9.1 Selected PV Efficiency Milestones Achieved in the United States

1954	Bell Labs produces the first silicon PV cell, featuring 4% efficiency
1957	Hoffman Electronics creates PV cells featuring 8% efficiency
1960	Hoffman Electronics achieves 14% efficient PV cells
1976	RCA Corp. develops the first amorphous silicon thin-film solar cell
1980	The University of Delaware creates a thin-film cell with over 10% efficiency
1992	The University of South Florida develops a 15.9% efficient thin-film cell
1994	NREL produces the first solar cell to exceed 30% efficiency
1999	NREL works with a private firm to produce a 32.3% efficient solar cell
1999	NREL develops a record 18.8% efficient thin-film solar cell
2007	The University of Delaware develops a solar cell with 42.8% efficiency
2008	NREL develops a record 19.9% efficient thin-film solar cell
2008	Two of the Four Editors Choice awards at *R&D* magazine are awarded to PV technologies resulting from partnerships between NREL and private firms

Solar PV Deployment

While research and development activities are important for the improvement of a technology, it is ultimately deployment that results in social gains (Alic et al. 2003). In the case of solar PV modules, deployment results in systems that are installed and generating carbon-free electricity for use by households, business, or industry. Deployment also reduces the cost of PV modules. Ryan Wiser and colleagues (2009) find that "markets with large PV deployment programs often tend to have lower average installed costs for residential PV" (2). Gregory Nemet (2006) finds that the increased scale of manufacturing necessary for broad deployment was responsible for 43 percent of the price decline in PV systems from 1980 to 2001. Furthermore, the installation and interconnection of PV systems necessary for deployment generates a significant number of jobs for skilled laborers (Kammen et al. 2004). Policies that support deployment include subsidies, mandates, and tax breaks, among others.

International Patterns of Deployment

The U.S. commitment to discovering advanced PV technologies is not matched by a similar commitment to deploying photovoltaics for broad public use. The United States has a relatively low installed capacity of PV systems, a weak PV manufacturing base, and a high cost of installed solar PV systems. As we argue shortly, these outcomes are attributable to U.S. deployment policies that are comparatively poorly funded, inconsistent, and heterogeneous.

While U.S. labs were setting PV efficiency records with novel semiconductor materials and manufacturing techniques, the United States was falling farther behind in the number of PV units installed. One powerful example of this comes from Robert Margolis (2002, 89), who describes a public-private partnership between U.S. solar firms and the DOE that led to significant improvement in amorphous silicon thin-film PV cells. The private sector partners—Cronar, Solarex, and Energy Conversion

Devices—had experience in industrial operations and wished to scale up production and capitalize on their innovations. However, once the basic technology was developed, a lack of federal commitment to deployment led Japanese firms to dominate the amorphous silicon industry.

As seen in Figure 9.2, the United States has installed considerably less PV capacity than Japan, Germany, and Spain in recent years. In 2008, aggressive deployment programs resulted in Spain and Germany installing 2700 and 1500 megawatts, respectively (the y-axis in Figure 9.2 is truncated at 2000 megawatts). In contrast, the total PV capacity installed in the United States through the end of 2008 was 1160 MW. Thus Spain and Germany were able to install much more solar PV capacity in one year then the United States—a larger and wealthier country—has been able to install in thirty years. Furthermore, when viewed relative to population, the U.S. position falls even farther, as Figure 9.3 shows. From 2007 to 2008, the U.S. rank in watts of solar photovoltaic systems installed relative to population fell from eighth place to tenth.

However, the figures above do not show the variation of PV installations among states. In reality, a few states account for the vast majority of photovoltaic installations. California is responsible for the lion's share of U.S. installations, accounting for 62 percent of grid-connected U.S. solar PV capacity installed in 2008. Looking at cumulative installations in Figure 9.4, the differences are even more stark. Cumulatively as of 2008, 528 megawatts of grid-connected solar PV systems had been installed in California, compared to just 70 megawatts in runner-up New Jersey, followed by Colorado with 36 megawatts and Nevada with 34. Bringing population into the picture, in forty-four states the cumulative solar PV capacity per capita is lower than the national average. The remaining six states pull the average up.

The data also show that, for the most part, the industrial development benefits of the solar photovoltaic industry go to countries that have enacted strong deployment

Figure 9.2 Annual PV Installations In Selected Countries Through 2008 (IEA 2009c)

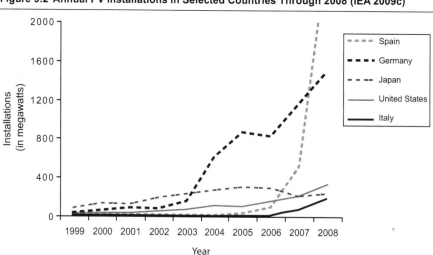

Figure 9.3 Cumulative PV Installations Per Capita Among Selected Countries Through 2008 (IEA 2009c)

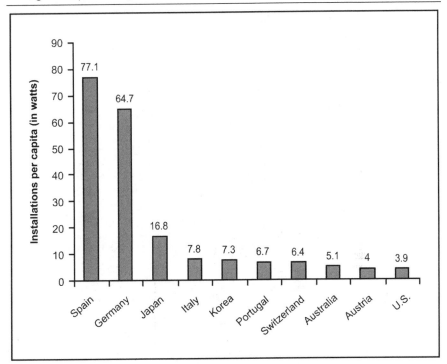

policies. Among IEA-PVPS countries, the production of solar PV modules is concentrated in Germany, Japan, and Spain, all of which have used robust deployment measures to install large numbers of solar electricity systems. Starting in 1999, a few years after it implemented its highly successful rebate program, Japan became the global leader in PV module production (IEA 2000). Likewise, in 2007, starting a few years after it enacted a generous feed-in tariff, Germany became the global leader in module production (IEA 2008). Figure 9.5 below shows PV module production by leading IEA-PVPS country in 2008.

China and Taiwan are notable exceptions to the rule that strong PV deployment policies are needed in order to gain significant domestic PV manufacturing operations. In recent years, these countries have emerged to compete with Germany for global leadership in PV cell and module manufacturing, even though China had an installed base of less than 200 megawatts of solar PV systems through 2008. Reports suggest that China manufactured well over 1000 megawatts of solar modules in 2008, with Taiwan not far behind (IEA 2009c).

Figure 9.5 also shows that the strongest U.S. industrial position in PV is in the production of thin-film solar modules, where it was a close second to Germany with total production of 267 megawatts in 2008 (IEA 2009c). U.S. strength in this area comes at a fortuitous time. Thin-film production expanded from 6 percent of

**Figure 9.4 Cumulative PV Installations Among U.S. States Through 2008
(Sherwood 2009)**

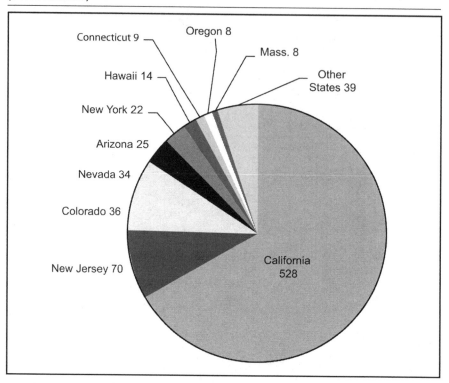

IEA-PVPS module production in 2005 to 22 percent in 2008, and is forecast to make up over one-third of the global market in 2009 (IEA 2008; IEA 2009c; Osborne 2009). Many observers believe that thin-films are the future of the solar PV industry; however, in the past thin-films have had difficulty overcoming the market share of crystalline silicon technology (Levratto and Lestringant 1999).

The United States is also lagging internationally when it comes to the cost of solar PV systems. The most recent, precise data comparing international PV costs comes from Ryan Wiser and colleagues (2009), who report that 2007 residential solar PV installed costs were $5.90 per watt in Japan, $6.60 in Germany, and $7.90 per watt in the United States (Wiser et al. 2009, 14). A number of other reports suggest that the total installed costs of solar PV system in the United States are between 10 and 40 percent higher than in the leading countries.[3] Because market conditions are always changing, it is difficult to determine the international distribution of installed costs of solar PV systems with any precision, but the variety of sources documenting these price differences suggest that they are accurate. Ten to forty percent may not sound like much, but it can add $2,000 to $8,000 to the price of a residential PV system that would cost $20,000 in Japan or Germany.

Figure 9.5 PV Module Production by Type Among Selected Countries in 2007 (IEA 2009c, 23)

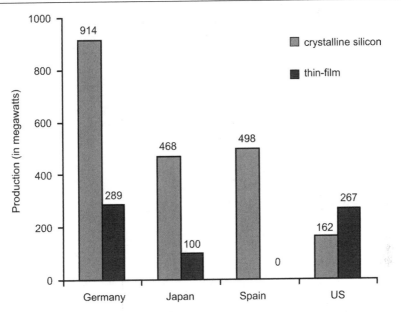

Deployment Policies

In the United States, a lack of strong federal policies supporting PV deployment has encouraged states, municipalities, and electric utilities to formulate their own measures affecting the ease of installation and use of PV systems. Various policy measures in place in the United States in 2008 that directly affected solar photovoltaic electricity systems included tax credits, PV-specific green electricity pricing schemes, renewable portfolio standards (RPS) that require utilities to produce a certain share of energy with alternative energy including a specific "carve-out" to encourage PV use, investment funds designed to finance PV systems, net metering rules that require utilities to purchase electricity from PV systems, sustainable building requirements, and miscellaneous commercial bank and utility programs. All in all, the IEA reports thirteen different policies in the United States in 2008 that supported PV systems, compared to nine policies in the next most diversified country (IEA 2009c). Furthermore, an additional layer of complexity is created by the policies of municipalities and electric utilities. Taking these variations into account pushes the number of distinct regional PV deployment policies into the hundreds.[4] However, variety is no substitute for quality, and the United States is sorely lacking in this respect.

U.S. solar deployment policy is formulated according to a trickle-down paradigm, where policymaking authority is handed off to lower and lower forms of government, apparently with little regard for the consequences for the cost or installed quantity of solar PV systems. States have assumed some responsibility for deployment, implementing measures such as renewable portfolio standards and net metering polices. However, only some states have chosen to implement these policies, and among those that have, the quality of the specific measures varies widely (NNEC 2008). This has left significant discretion for local policymakers in municipal governments and the electric utility industry to implement what measures they see fit. The overall low quality of municipal and utility regulations has played a big role in making solar electricity more expensive in the United States than it is in other countries (Solartech 2007). Furthermore, the varying policies enacted through the federal and state governments, municipalities, and utilities have eroded business confidence and impeded economies of scale in the production of PV components destined for U.S. markets (Navigant 2006).

In contrast to the U.S. trickle-down paradigm of PV deployment, countries such as Germany and Spain have implemented well-planned, consistent deployment policies at the federal level. Federal-level feed-in tariff mechanisms have proven especially successful at drastically increasing the quantity of solar PV electricity in a number of countries. A feed-in tariff mechanism does not guarantee booming PV installations, but no country without one has exceeded an annual installation rate of 300 megawatts of solar PV, such as Germany and Spain have achieved for consecutive years. Of the nine countries with more PV installed per capita than the United States, seven have national feed-in tariff policies (IEA 2009c). Still, however, only very small-scale or watered-down feed-in tariffs have appeared in the United States.[5]

Coverage of best practices in PV deployment policies should also include the notable success of the Sacramento Municipal Utility District (SMUD). SMUD has used policy measures incorporating the same principles of volume and consistency that are embodied in feed-in tariff regulations in order to cheaply deploy solar photovoltaic systems in large quantities. Our analysis suggests that absent widespread replication of the exceptional leadership that guided SMUD's PV deployment policies, national regulations such as feed-in tariffs will be needed which mandate that utilities become active agents of PV deployment. We begin by analyzing U.S. PV policy measures that are primarily at the federal and state levels—including tax credit and rebate subsidies, renewable portfolio standards, and net metering legislation—and continue by covering measures that are mostly controlled at the local and utility levels, such as building regulations and grid interconnection requirements.

Subsidies. As noted in the first section of this chapter, R&D programs are the best way to improve the efficiency by which solar cells convert sunlight into electricity. On the other hand, the best way to increase the scale of solar PV production is to increase demand for photovoltaic modules through the use of subsidies. Subsidies grow the market for solar electricity through lowering the prices of PV systems, which in turn leads consumers to buy more solar panels and firms to expand and improve their operations. Subsidies can be in the form of up-front compensation to consumers, such as with investment tax credits and rebates, or payments made over a number of years to consumers as they produce electricity with the technology, such as with feed-in tariffs or production tax credits. In either case, subsidies reduce the net to consumer cost of PV systems, drawing more participants to the market. The price of PV systems then declines more quickly as production plant size grows more rapidly, allowing the subsidy to be decreased over time until consumers are buying PV systems without subsidies (Duke 2002).

In the United States, federal and state subsidies are the primary drivers of solar PV installations. Typically, neither state nor federal subsidies are enough by themselves to drive solar PV deployment, but together they are effective. "The combination of federal and state incentives created (solar PV) markets" (Sherwood 2009, 8). Periodically over the last three decades, the U.S. federal government has offered a tax credit for between 10 percent and 30 percent of the value of selected solar photovoltaic installations. In addition to the federal government's tax credits, in 2009 twenty U.S. states—led in scale of commitment by New Jersey and California—have PV subsidy programs for at least some of their residents and businesses (DSIRE 2009). The combined amount of federal and state subsidies has been increasing in recent years in response to climate change and higher energy prices. U.S. federal and state governments spent about $180 million on PV deployment subsidies in each of 2004 and 2005, $443 million in 2006, $452 million in 2007, and $505 million in 2008. In 2008, around 60 percent of the U.S. subsidy total came from the California state government's California Solar Initiative, which has a budget of $3.2 billion to be spent from 2007 through 2016.

In contrast, the IEA suggests that the level of subsidization provided by German feed-in tariffs for PV in 2006 was roughly equal to the total subsidies from all other IEA PVPS countries in that year, about $1 billion, while Spain spent about $1.4 billion on PV payments in 2008 (Larson 2009). The IEA reports that total solar PV feed-in tariff payments among its member countries was over $7 billion in 2008 (IEA 2009c). In most cases, these generous annual payments will be maintained over two decades to fund the energy produced over the lifetime of a renewable energy system. Yet because of their long time frame and large funding base, feed-in tariff policies have a relatively minor financial impact on citizens. Financed through all customers in a utility district, the German feed-in tariff has added only about $2 dollars to the monthly bills of German electricity customers (Farrell 2008). The same twenty-year time span that generates financial certainty for investors allows subsidies to have a gentle impact on consumer pocketbooks.

The federal and state subsidies commonly used in the United States have a number of shortcomings. Just as with the RPS and net metering policies described below, significant variation exists in rebates among states and utilities, creating uncertainty in the market. In 2007, the total subsidy for residential PV systems provided by federal, state, and utility incentives varied from $2.50 per watt of solar PV power in Maryland to $5.70 per watt of PV power in Pennsylvania (Wiser et al. 2009, 27). The greatest issue with U.S. federal subsidies is inconsistent implementation. Since they were introduced in the 1978 Energy Tax Act, PV investment tax credits have been shifted three times in the 1980s, once in 1992, once in 2005, and again in 2008 (Taylor et al. 2007). Unlike the declining subsidies that have been used in Germany, Japan, and Spain, which are intended to match the subsidy level to the decreasing cost of PV systems over time, shifts in U.S. tax credits have occurred unexpectedly due to fickle politicians. U.S. tax credit inconsistency has created boom-and-bust cycles in investment and has lowered industry confidence (Sawin 2004). If it can be maintained through upcoming political shifts, the recent eight-year extension of a 30 percent federal tax credit for consumer and business investment in PV systems will be a welcome change to this inconsistency (Sherwood 2009).

It might seem that Spain, Germany, and the rest of the countries with feed-in tariffs are making arbitrarily, maybe even irrationally large investments driven mainly by green movement political action, but by and large their expenditures have been rationally planned and executed, more so than in the United States. The rates of payment in feed-in tariff policies are set according to the cost of generating electricity from each different eligible technology, not according to market rates. Thus the investor who builds a PV system under a feed-in tariff policy will be paid enough per kilowatt-hour of solar electricity generated to make a reasonable profit, even if the general market price of electricity is substantially lower (this is in contrast to the market rates of the neo-feed-in tariff policies enacted in California, described in note 5). Feed-in tariff payments decline year after year for new installations in order to account for, and to encourage, technological progress in renewable energy systems. Technological progress is also more likely to be sustained through feed-in tariff policies because they are managed and funded through electric utilities. Thus feed-in tariffs are budget-neutral for governments and less susceptible to irrational manipulation by politicians (Kravetz 2009).

The United States is more susceptible to an accusation of making arbitrary or irrational subsidy payments. First, the existing federal 30 percent investment tax credit is not enough by itself to make solar PV electricity economically competitive with conventional forms of electricity generation. As a result, cash-strapped states are required to provide their own subsidies, and PV systems in many of the states that have subsidies are still not cost-effective. Despite this, the United States continues to pay out hundreds of millions of dollars per year in subsidies that result in solar panels being put mostly on the homes of the wealthy; they generate insufficient market volume to encourage cost declines in PV system components. It is true that feed-in tariff subsidy levels can sometimes lead to rapid PV deployment, such as in Spain in 2008. While the rates of payment for solar PV in Spain's 2008 feed-in tariff policy were not set at an optimal level, the quantity of PV installed demonstrated the feasibility of truly large-scale solar deployment. Furthermore, solar PV electricity in Spain still accounts for only a small percentage of the country's electricity supply. The United States would do well to learn from Spain's example of setting subsidy levels high enough to make solar PV electricity systems attractive investment opportunities.

Renewable Portfolio Standards. To date, thirty-three states and the District of Columbia have passed RPS laws (EPA 2009). California, with the most ambitious policy, is requiring that by the year 2020, 33 percent of its electricity be generated by a group of eligible renewable energy technologies, including wind, solar PV, hydroelectric, geothermal, and several others. In general, renewable portfolio standards do not guarantee the installation of solar PV power. Because solar PV is relatively expensive compared to well-developed technologies like wind and hydroelectric, these cheaper options may substitute for it. To deal with this, some states have created "carve-outs" for solar PV in their RPS programs that require solar electricity to make up a certain percentage of the total renewable energy (EPA 2009).

However, the fact that many U.S. states have formally implemented renewable portfolio standards belies the significant differences in policies from state to state. The amount of renewable electricity that RPS policies are designed to integrate varies widely, from a low of 4 percent to a high of 30 percent of total electricity load (EPA 2009). Some states have RPS goals that are legally nonbinding, with no punishment for utilities that fail to achieve them (Wiser and Barbose 2008). Only eleven of the thirty-four RPS policies contain solar PV carve-outs, and they account for only a small fraction of the total renewable energy required, often less then 1 percent (EPA 2009).

Renewable portfolio standards also suffer from potentially serious problems with their design. For one, there is a large gap between RPS requirements for clean energy and the financing tools provided to meet those requirements. Thus, while RPS policies mandate that utilities generate a certain amount of clean electricity, they do not supply the rates of return necessary to attract financing for projects that build clean electricity generation systems. Second, RPS policies have encouraged utilities to build the cheapest renewable energy facilities possible, often with too little regard for how their energy will be delivered to the grid.

Feed-in tariffs, however, can complement RPS policies and solve some of these issues. Feed-in tariffs deal with the financing gap with guaranteed contract terms and a stable investment environment, which in turn increases investor interest in renewable energy projects. Feed-in tariffs deal with the second issue by taking some planning responsibility away from utilities and giving it to renewable energy investors, who have a clear interest in building clean electricity generation systems that can be sited quickly and that have access to transmission lines (Cory et al. 2009).

Net metering. Because of its importance in determining the cost-effectiveness of solar PV power, many consider net metering to be one of the most critical policies affecting the solar photovoltaic market. If a solar PV system actually generates more electricity than a household needs, net metering policies require the local electric utility to bank the value of that excess generation for the household's future use. While net metering policies encourage the use of a distributed electricity generation system, they are especially beneficial for solar because PV electricity generated during sunny months can be used to pay bills during the winter when there is less sunshine. This makes the economic payback period of solar PV systems shorter than it would otherwise be. Forty U.S. states plus the District of Columbia have enacted some form of mandatory net metering regulations, while three other states have voluntary policies. However, the same diversity that exists in renewable portfolio standards is also present in net metering. New Jersey is a national model, with no limit in the number of households that can participate. Georgia, on the other hand, limits net-metered electricity to one-fifth of 1 percent of total electricity load, and grants the value of excess electricity *to the electric utility* at the end of every year. The Network for New Energy Choices, a U.S.-based nongovernmental organization, recently graded net metering regulations among U.S. states. Over half earned a C or below (NNEC 2008).

Municipal and utility regulations. The absence of strong federal-level, and in many cases state-level, solar PV deployment polices has left a vacuum for local and regional actors to implement their own measures. Municipalities affect the deployment of solar PV systems primarily through their control of local construction activities, in particular the permitting and inspection practices that solar electricity systems must undergo. Electric utilities also play a large role in solar PV deployment through their policies affecting the interconnection of distributed generation systems such as solar PV. Inefficiencies in the permitting, inspection, and interconnection regulations controlled by these actors have contributed to a waiting time of between twenty-nine and fifty weeks before a solar PV system is actually installed and in use, and they are a key reason why solar PV systems are more expensive in the United States than other countries (Solartech 2007). Heterogeneous U.S. policies regulating the connection of solar PV systems with the electricity grid (known as interconnection requirements) contrast sharply with the federal-level streamlined interconnection regulations that are usually included as part of feed-in tariff policy packages (Larson 2009).

Municipal and utility policies affecting grid interconnection play an especially important role in determining the nonmodule costs of solar PV power, which, due to declining module costs, have come to make up a significant share of total system costs. PV nonmodule costs consist primarily of the balance of system (BOS) components necessary for the installation of the system, as well as labor and permitting expenses. (See Appendix A, p. 194, for a description of the basic components of a solar PV electricity system.) Because module costs have fallen to around $5 per watt, nonmodule costs, at $3 to $4 per watt, have gained salience. In fact, the majority of recent cost declines in PV systems in Japan and California have come from nonmodule cost improvements. In Japan's New Sunshine residential subsidy program, module prices declined by a factor of 2 from 1993 to 2001, but installation costs fell by a factor of 5, and BOS costs fell by a factor of 8 (Duke 2002, 115). A similar trend, though not as dramatic, has been observed in California (Wiser et al. 2006; Wiser et al. 2009). While module costs are determined on international PV markets, nonmodule costs are largely determined by local factors. Given the control local PV deployment policies have over such costs, Ryan Wiser and colleagues (2006) argue that these policies should focus on reducing BOS and installation costs rather than module costs. Unfortunately, local policymakers in the United States have done poorly at this task.

Permitting and inspection policies. With their jurisdiction over the safety and appearance of rooftop solar PV systems, municipal building departments have an important role in determining the cost of solar PV systems. The role of municipalities starts with processing the building permit for a PV system, which may take anywhere from one day to eight weeks and cost several hundred dollars (Solartech 2007, 24). After the building permit is obtained and installation is complete, municipal building inspectors must visit the site to determine if a PV system is in compliance with state, local, and federal construction and electric codes. Large time windows for municipal inspectors to "drop by" add to the cost of PV systems by requiring skilled installers to wait for the inspector to arrive (Solartech 2007, 18). Municipalities also have a reputation for not following the best practice technology standards formulated by national trade groups. Municipal regulations often require the electrical grounding of inverter systems, although this is not practiced in Japan or Europe and is also not required by the U.S. National Electric Code (Navigant 2006). Municipal building inspectors sometimes reference outdated versions of the National Electric Code, not accounting for recent changes that have improved regulations for PV installations (Solartech 2007).

Interconnection requirements. Interconnection requirements are the technical rules and procedures that utilities enforce regulating customer-sited electricity generation systems such as solar PV. Households that wish to install a grid-connected solar PV system must apply for an interconnection permit from their electric utility. The application process typically takes two to three weeks and costs several hundred dollars on top of building permit fees (Solartech 2007, 24). The utility approves the permit and physically interconnects the customer's PV system only if it meets the utility's requirements.

In the United States, heterogeneous interconnection requirements prevent efficient mass production of PV components, while poorly formulated requirements are a direct barrier to quick, cost-effective installation of PV systems. Because most of the 3,100 electric utilities in the United States have their own interconnection requirements, PV electricity systems often need to be custom engineered for small markets, which makes them more expensive (Willey and Hester 2001, 24). The lack of economies of scale is a particular problem for the electricity inverters used in PV systems (discussed below), which are subject to widely varying regulations in different U.S. markets (Navigant 2006). The Network for New Energy Choices has found that over half of U.S. states are failing with their interconnection requirements, earning a grade of D or lower (NNEC 2008).

The barriers that interconnection requirements present for the solar PV industry are nothing new. During the 1990s, the TEAM-UP public-private partnership between the U.S. Department of Energy and electric utilities brought attention to the excessive interconnection requirements hampering the grid integration of PV systems (Willey and Hester 2001, 23–25). The U.S. Federal Energy Regulatory Commission has formulated best practice guidelines for interconnection of PV systems, including guidelines for interconnection application fees, but utilities can ignore them if they wish (NNEC 2008). States can pass legislation streamlining the interconnection process, but relatively few have chosen to do so.

The story of electricity inverters—which make up the majority of the cost of the BOS components necessary to run a PV system—is an excellent case study showing the negative effects that poorly formulated utility interconnection regulations can have on a technology. The first problem is that outdated utility regulations do not allow the most economical inverter technologies to be used. For instance, "transformerless" inverters are cheaper, more efficient, and lighter than traditional electricity inverters and are already used in Japan and Germany. However, even though they are used internationally and sanctioned by the U.S. National Electrical Code, U.S. electric utilities commonly do not approve them (Navigant 2006).

Worsening the situation, many states and utilities require manual disconnects on the electricity flowing out of PV electricity inverters. Manual disconnects are used to cut off the power from the grid-tied PV system by hand, a response to one of the perceived dangers of distributed power generation called "islanding." This can occur when a power line goes down and needs to be repaired, but individual electricity generation systems are still feeding power into the grid, creating a serious safety hazard for line crews. However, modern inverters are designed to shut off automatically in unsafe circumstances and thus prevent islanding (Navigant 2006). This feature combined with quadruple redundancy in other safety measures renders the external disconnect unnecessary: "If a utility worker is following proper protocol, none of the levels of safety measures preceding an external disconnect switch will ever be used, much less the switch itself" (NNEC 2008, 30). Yet through 2008, twenty-five U.S. states still required manual disconnects on some PV systems, while others leave the choice of whether to require manual disconnects to utilities (NNEC 2008). This extra safety requirement is one of the primary reasons that the installation costs for a solar PV system in the United States are twice as high as in Germany (Navigant 2006, 66).

The role of electric utilities. Electric utilities are some of the most important actors affecting PV deployment; however, they are often not committed to solar energy systems (Margolis and Zuboy 2006). In general, the electric utility industry does not go out of its way to promote renewable energy systems, and the restructuring activities carried out during the 1990s have not changed this fact (Heiman and Solomon 2004).[6] Electric utility expenditures on research and development give a telling picture of the industry's commitment to progress and innovation. While information technology and pharmaceutical companies typically invest between 10 and 20 percent of revenues on research and development, in 1995 the private energy sector invested about 0.5 percent of revenues on R&D (Kammen and Margolis 1999). With such low levels of research, innovation has stagnated. The typical twenty-first-century electric utility is half as energy efficient as the typical nineteenth-century utility was. Recycled energy expert Tom Casten asks, "What other business throws away two-thirds of its input?" (Casten and Schewe 2009, 28).

The restructuring policies of the 1990s that were meant in part to increase consumer choices, including for green power, actually resulted in less diverse energy sources. Under the influence of restructuring policies, between 1993 and 1995 advanced generation R&D expenditures from investor-owned utilities in California dropped 85 percent, and their contributions to the Electric Power Research Institute—the electricity utility sector's R&D consortium—dropped 50 percent. Restructuring also led PG&E to quit its leadership role in the TEAM-UP public-private partnership (Taylor et al. 2007, 18, 36).

One striking contrast between the commercial energy sectors of Europe and the United States are the differing levels of autonomy that electric utilities have to promote or deter the deployment of renewable energy systems. As was shown above, U.S. electric utilities often have substantial autonomy to formulate regulations affecting the speed and cost of connecting solar PV systems to the grid. With the feed-in tariffs common in European countries, this is not the case. Feed-in tariffs are typically implemented at the national level and require all utilities within a country to efficiently interconnect and make above-market rates of payment to renewable energy investors (Larson 2009). U.S. experience has shown that without comprehensive regulatory measures like feed-in tariffs that ensure utility commitment to the deployment of renewable energy systems, it takes exceptionally idealistic leadership and a strategic policy vision to achieve effective PV deployment. The Sacramento Municipal Utility District (SMUD) is a good example of an isolated success driven by exceptional leadership. In the following paragraphs we describe how SMUD made use of feed-in tariff-like principles in order to successfully deploy PV on a local level.

The special case of SMUD. The Sacramento Municipal Utility District is the sixth largest municipally owned utility in the United States, providing electricity to 1.4 million people in the greater Sacramento area of northern California. During the 1990s, SMUD became famous for its PV Pioneers rooftop photovoltaic installation program, which at the time resulted in the largest orders for PV modules the world had known. SMUD calls its approach to deploying PV systems "sustained orderly development and commercialization" (SODC), which features large volume purchases made consistently over time in order to cause price declines and generate a large installed capacity. "SMUD's commitment to sustained purchasing has resulted in long-term contracts with PV manufacturers that have helped reduce the cost of the grid-connected systems to SMUD and its customers" (Mortensen 2001, 3). By 2001, the 10 MW of grid-connected PV power installed within SMUD's boundaries constituted over half of all grid-connected PV in the United States. The commitment to large volume orders also lured solar PV modules and inverter manufacturers to the Sacramento area (Osborn 2001).

Instead of going with the market majority and contracting for crystalline silicon PV modules, SMUD specifically chose to work with a firm that specialized in low-cost amorphous silicon thin-film PV technology, even though such systems made up a small share of the market at the time. In 1999, SMUD spent $3.75 per watt of capacity for PV systems complete with thin-film modules and BOS components. Installation expenses added only 75 cents per watt of capacity to the system price, for a total cost of $4.50 per watt of PV capacity, which is roughly half what was paid in U.S. markets in 2007 (Aitken et al. 2000; Wiser et al. 2009). Analysis from the National Renewable Energy Laboratory found that in the late 1990s SMUD was installing PV systems for 40 percent less than they were being installed elsewhere in the United States (Mortensen 2001, 3).

SMUD's approach to PV deployment has changed somewhat since its PV Pioneers program, but it still deploys solar PV systems more effectively than almost any other U.S. utility. After PV Pioneers, SMUD started working with homebuilders to coordinate the construction of new home communities featuring houses with solar panels integrated into their roofs, known as "roof-integrated" PV systems. Roof-integrated solar PV systems are the cheapest way to harness solar PV electricity, and have been used in Japan's economical PV deployment program (Duke 2002, 123; Shum and Watanabe 2007). In 2007, SMUD entered ten deals to build some of the largest solar home developments in the United States, for a total of 4,153 new energy-efficient solar homes. If construction goes as scheduled, by 2009 solar homes will comprise 30 percent of the new home market in Sacramento County (Wasserman 2008).

SMUD's case highlights a trade-off in solar PV deployment. The experiences of SMUD on the one hand, and Germany and Spain on the other, suggest that either exceptional local leadership or comprehensive national policies are needed to make electric utilities into active agents of PV deployment. SMUD received leadership from the "green cowboy," lawyer and engineer S. David Freeman who was general manager of SMUD from 1990 to 1994. Freeman's life was steeped in civil rights and progressive activism, and he had served as director of the Tennessee Valley Authority in the late 1970s, steering it away from heavy reliance on nuclear energy. Having achieved breakthrough results for SMUD, Freeman moved on to the Los Angeles Department of Water and Power to initiate a similar decentralized PV program (Perlin 1999).

In the absence of more leaders with such experience and vision, national-level policies will be needed to spread best practices in PV deployment among municipalities and the 3,100 utilities that operate in the United States. A host of best practices in permitting and interconnection standards are already known, none of them particularly costly or difficult to implement. The city of San Jose is reducing its installation permitting fees because it has determined that it can sell more permits at a lower price to generate the same amount of revenue (Jern 2008). Similarly, the northern California utility, Pacific Gas and Electric, has recently reformed its interconnection practices for most residential applications, no longer requiring the use of manual inverter disconnects (Solartech 2007). If they were carried out at a higher level of government, these types of reforms would go far to improve the U.S. solar PV market. Combining national standardization of interconnection, permitting, and inspection practices with the consistent subsidies of a federal feed-in tariff policy could drastically decrease the cost and increase the quantity of solar PV electricity systems in the United States.

Conclusion

Over the last half century, the United States has leveraged significant investments to build up a considerable domestic base of technical expertise in solar photovoltaic energy systems. As a result of these investments, the U.S. solar PV R&D apparatus is the envy of the world. The prominence of U.S. laboratories and firms in the history of radical advances in PV technology speaks for itself. However, the U.S. commitment to research and development has not been matched by a commitment to putting solar PV systems into public use. When compared internationally, U.S. policies that facilitate the installation and interconnection of solar electricity systems are weakly funded, poorly organized, and overly subject to short-term political pressures.

Given the heavy concentration of PV installations in certain states, as well as the wide variety of policies from state to state—not to mention utility to utility—it would be difficult to argue that the United States has a coherent national deployment policy. The subsidies it offers for the installation of solar PV systems are at a low level overall and are unevenly distributed among states. The southwestern United States has excellent levels of solar radiation, and even the Southeast has solar radiation levels 60 percent better than Germany's, yet states in these regions have few policies supporting deployment (SEIA 2009). California has a comparatively well-planned PV deployment program, but the severe fiscal crisis it entered in 2009 casts doubt on the ability of any state to adequately subsidize renewable energy systems. In general, the balkanized U.S. PV deployment regulations have created confusion in the market, impeded economies of scale, and slowed the diffusion of best practices. One recent report on international policies supporting solar PV ranks the United States fifth, behind Germany, France, Greece, and Italy (Kravetz 2009).

Leading international PV deployment programs have been more rationally organized and consistent than the U.S. efforts. In the majority of countries with more solar PV capacity per capita than the United States, feed-in tariffs have been implemented. Such policies compel utilities to streamline interconnection requirements and pay out generous, above-market rates—typically for two decades—for the electricity generated by PV and other renewable electricity sources. This package of regulations turns electric utilities into active agents of PV deployment, replicating on a national scale the successes of local electric utilities such as the Sacramento Municipal Utility District. These policies have paid off impressively in Germany and Spain, with each installing a greater quantity of solar electricity systems in 2008 than the United States has over the last thirty years.

If the United States wants to secure the economic and environmental benefits that come from the deployment of PV systems, it will need to adopt the principles of the feed-in tariff. It needs to make the payment of subsidies consistent both over time and between regions of the country, as well as scale best practice regulations affecting BOS and labor costs to a higher level of governance. There is some reason for hope. Policies embedded in federal economic stimulus legislation, combined with a new U.S. president with more favorable views of renewable energy, suggest that the U.S. position as a laggard in PV deployment may change. As it passed the U.S. House of Representatives in June 2009, H.R. 2454—the Waxman-Markey climate bill—contains vital elements of deployment policy, including a federal renewable portfolio standard (RPS). If the United States is able to augment its burgeoning renewable energy deployment policies with measures to generate more demand for advanced solar PV thin-films, it could secure the environmental benefits of solar electricity while growing the next-generation PV industrial base at home.

Appendix: The Components of a Solar PV Electricity System

The two major subsystems of a photovoltaic energy system are the module and the balance of system (BOS) components. The module, also referred to as a solar panel, is nothing more than a group of interconnected solar cells, encased and framed. The solar cell is the basic building block of a solar electricity system and is composed of semiconductor materials such as silicon, cadmium telluride, or cadmium indium gallium selenide (CIGS). Semiconductor materials are useful in generating electricity because photons of light are able to knock their electrons out of orbit and form a direct electrical current. In production, groups of solar cells are put together onto a backing to form a module, while modules can be grouped together to form an array. The modules or arrays are able to combine the electrical output of the many solar cells they comprise.

PV balance of system (BOS) components are the hardware necessary to make use of the electricity produced by the modules. The most important component is the DC/AC electricity inverter, which transforms the direct current (DC) electricity produced by the module into an alternating current (AC) form compatible with household appliances and the commercial electric grid. Other balance of system components include wiring, fuses, and circuit breakers. Additionally, off-grid or stand-alone PV systems—PV systems not backed up by commercial electricity that are often found in rural areas—usually need batteries to store the energy produced by the modules. While module costs are reasonably standardized across domestic and international markets, balance of system costs are highly affected by the particularities of local interconnection and permitting regulations.

Notes

1. The International Energy Agency's Photovoltaic Power Systems (IEA-PVPS) R&D program is accessible on the web at www.iea-pvps.org. Data on solar PV are shared on a voluntary basis by IEA member countries. Unfortunately, even though they may have significant PV industrial activity, nonparticipating countries such as China are rarely represented in the data sets. China's status in PV module manufacturing is briefly discussed above.

2. We characterize the solar electricity supply chain as consisting of research, development, and deployment (RD&D) components, which is a useful framework for presenting the arguments in this chapter. Economist Joseph Schumpeter viewed the technology pipeline as consisting of invention, innovation, and diffusion, while many commentators since then have come up with their own categories (Alic et al. 2003).

3. According to a solar industry executive, the installed cost of a residential solar PV system in 2005 was $6.50 to $9.00 per watt in the United States versus $5.00 to $6.00 per watt in Germany (Navigant 2006, 66). Janet Sawin reports that a solar PV system cost $5.50 per watt of capacity in Japan in 2003 (Sawin 2004, 33). Another study finds that installed costs are $6.00 per watt in Japan versus $9.00 in California (Solartech 2007). Using records from the state of California, Ryan Wiser and collaborators find that the average installed cost of PV systems

in 2005 was about $8.50 per watt (Wiser et al. 2006). The IEA suggests a narrower range of prices in 2008 with small, grid-connected systems in the United States varying from $7.00 to $9.00 per watt compared to $6.90 per watt in Japan and $5.70 to $6.60 per watt in Germany. With larger, grid-connected systems, however, the United States is farther behind at $6.50 per watt versus $5.20 per watt in Japan and $5.40 per watt in Germany (IEA 2009c).

4. For a more detailed glimpse into the complex web of federal, state, local, and utility programs and regulations affecting solar PV and other renewable energy systems, see the Database of State Incentives for Renewables and Efficiency, accessible on the web at www .DSIREUSA.org.

5. There is some feed-in tariff political activity in the United States, but so far it has been minor. Gainesville, Florida, is the only U.S. city to enact a European-style feed-in tariff. The state of Vermont has passed a feed-in tariff, but the rates of payment will not be set until 2010, and above-market rates face political obstacles (Larson 2009). The state of California and SMUD have both passed feed-in tariffs, but neither feature payment rates high enough to promote significant solar PV deployment (Gipe 2009). A number of other states have introduced feed-in tariff bills into their legislature. Representative Jay Inslee has introduced feed-in tariff legislation into the U.S. House of Representatives, but the bill has yet to be seriously considered.

6. Federal and state electric utility industry restructuring policies implemented during the 1990s supported the legal separation of the generation, transmission, and distribution functions of vertically integrated utilities to strengthen retail and wholesale competition. Policies also supported the creation of regional transmission organizations to better govern restructured markets. Utility restructuring is sometimes referred to as "deregulation," but it is more accurately described as "re-regulation."

CHAPTER **10**

From Developmental Network State to Market Managerialism in Ireland
Seán Ó Riain

The Developmental Network State Under Threat

In 2009, in the midst of heated debates about banking crises and public debt, Irish policymakers turned their attention to promoting research and innovation. In the process, they faced once more the vexed question of what governmental strategies and structures would best foster innovation and industrial development.

The model of success was not an Irish technology firm, or even an international technology investor like Intel—it was the Finnish technology giant, Nokia. Government leaders hoped to create an "Irish Nokia" that could drive economic renewal. The Nokia model was used to justify a series of initiatives to promote research and innovation in hopes that publicly funded research would spawn successful new products and companies to sell them. At the announcement of an "innovation alliance" between the two largest Dublin universities, UCD and Trinity, the Taoiseach (prime minister) referred explicitly to the goal of creating an Irish Nokia through such initiatives. Even as they espoused liberal understandings of economic growth, government leaders clearly saw state bodies playing a strongly directive role in shaping technology and innovation.

Opponents said such talk placed too much emphasis on research and government as drivers of growth. They said there was far too much emphasis on science-led innovation in Irish industrial policy and that exposing firms more fully to the demands of consumers, suppliers, and other actors closer to the market could drive growth more effectively. They also claimed the Nokia imagery covered a grab for control by the government, particularly centralized institutions promoting science and innovation policy (Jordan 2009; O'Leary 2009). The market was to provide the impetus for growth, not planned state interventions.

But the debate was not simply ideological or theoretical. What drove this debate was not just the 2009 economic crisis rooted in construction bubbles and financialization, but a concern that, after significant progress in the 1990s, Ireland's industrial development had stalled. This was all the more surprising because Ireland's economy had grown so fast in the 1990s it became known as the Celtic tiger. By the late 1990s, the country seemed poised to build upon the industrial upgrading of the previous decade, and after 1999 the government made major investments in research and science to develop that potential.

But by 2009 indigenous high-tech growth among Irish-owned firms had stagnated, spin-offs from research funding had been relatively minimal, and the driver of economic growth had shifted from high-tech exports to domestic demand and construction (with disastrous consequences once the real estate–driven financial crisis hit). The question remained, what happened to Ireland's high-tech growth?

In this chapter, I explore this puzzle. I argue that Ireland's supposedly liberal, free market model of development actually contained significant and necessary elements of government coordination. To understand the ebb and flow of high-tech industries in Ireland, we need to understand the variety of forms of coordination undertaken by state agencies and how these coordination efforts succeeded and failed at different times and under different conditions.

The industrial upgrading of the 1990s was facilitated in crucial ways by state agencies. However, the form of coordination that dominated in technology and innovation was based on networks of state agencies providing a diverse range of financial and organizational supports to firms across a range of technology sectors. While central agencies remained important, this broader network of structures, strategies, and supports together formed a developmental network state within the broader Irish political economy (Ó Riain 2004a). Crucially, such institutions force us to rethink the identification of statism with centralization and to recognize the various forms that state coordination can take. However, despite the emergence of new firms and industries, research spending remained weak, and science and technology policy remained marginal in Irish economic development policy through the 1990s, always in the shadow of high-profile successful efforts to attract foreign firms like Microsoft, Intel, and Google.

Science and research was brought to the center of the policy agenda in the late 1990s, with cabinet-level attention to the need for investment leading to major increases in the levels of research funding. However, the coordination of innovation policy and supports also changed. As science and technology policy became more politically important, the government's economic planning system was centralized. The government placed greater emphasis on big science, concentrating research efforts on biotech and ICT and centralizing the government's control of research. At the same time, core funding to universities was cut from a low base and even greater emphasis placed on research centers becoming self-sustaining through external funding. Central control and market pressures combined to form a policy regime of market managerialism that increasingly sidelined the strategies and structures developed in the 1990s. Yet even as research activity grew rapidly, many of the expected industrial development benefits of market managerialism surprisingly failed to materialize.

In this chapter we will also examine the conditions that prompted this shift to market managerialism—in government institutions, Irish politics, and economic commentary. The emergence of the agencies of the DNS in ways that allowed it to remain hidden within the dominant institutions of the industrial policy regime and the dominant market and enterprise discourse both allowed the DNS to develop largely unchallenged in the 1990s but also rendered it vulnerable once the policy area and the relevant agencies became visible to the national political system at the end of the decade.

This chapter concludes with a look at the difficulties of institutionalizing a networked form of state organization. In contrast to economists who say Ireland's innovation policy is a seamlessly integrated element of a neoliberal economic system, and to critical scholars who see the new forms of state intervention in innovation policy as part of a "competition state" that is symbiotic with the moves toward greater marketization (Cerny 2005), I argue that the liberal market context tends to undermine the public investments and public spaces that have been crucial to the success of those innovation policies pursued by the DNS. The best way to institutionalize the successful structures and strategies of the DNS is to expand the protections around public spaces and to enhance public investment.

The Irish Innovation Puzzle

More and more is being written about the emergence of innovative funding programs that are forms of developmental network statism. While some analyses offer vital insights into how such interventions work, this chapter explores how they become embedded in national political economies and the conditions that determine whether they are institutionalized or marginalized. Ireland presents an interesting case. Its economy has seen the emergence of new institutions promoting innovation policy over time, first the government agencies designed to facilitate the search for foreign investment that began in the 1960s, then a network of state agencies promoting an indigenous innovation capacity in the 1990s, and finally a better funded science and innovation policy in the 2000s.

However, there is a puzzle here too. Ireland's economy boomed from the mid-1990s until 2007. But this overall growth masked significant economic changes. In the 1990s growth was driven by exports, largely from the high-tech sector. While foreign firms dominated, there were surprising signs of life in indigenous Irish industry. After 2001, however, homegrown consumer demand for technological products and, increasingly, the boom in real estate and construction drove economic growth. For most of the decade, the faltering export and high-tech performance was papered over by the booming construction and consumer economy. But when the financial crisis of 2008 hit Ireland, this failure was exposed as a crucial weakness that would slow economic recovery.

Tables 10.1 and 10.2 provide employment figures for firms assisted by industrial development agencies in the 1990s and the 2000s. Because both tables stretch across 2001, the high-water year for many technological sectors, they understate the most dramatic twists and turns of the export economy. In the 1990s, as Table 10.1 shows, employment growth was spread across the high-tech sector with spectacular growth in computer manufacturing, chemicals, medical devices, software, and financial services. Foreign-owned firms dominated employment, but for the first time in Ireland's economic history, Irish-owned firms significantly increased employment in export-oriented technology sectors. While the rise in financial services employment may have ultimately proved a mixed blessing, the growth in the software industry was a spectacular success. The signs of coming challenges were also present in the continuing decline in sectors such as textiles and clothing, but they were masked by the rise in high-tech manufacturing.

In the 2000s, however, computer manufacturing and associated supply industries like metals and plastics joined other industrial sectors in their decline. Table 10.2 shows an overall decline in export performance, with even the ICT and chemicals sectors—well funded thanks to the new science policy—faring worse than in the 1990s because of the bursting of the dot-com bubble in 2001. By the late 2000s, these sectors had recovered, coming through the economic crisis with fairly stable levels of employment by late 2009.

Judged by its own criteria of employment creation and industry development, Irish innovation policy in the 2000s had seen very limited success in the face of admittedly difficult conditions.

Coordinated Innovation in Liberal Capitalism

It would be tempting to conclude that the presence of state funding actually damaged industrial development as the funding surge for research was associated with the era of relatively weak performance. However, the evidence suggests that state grants have had positive effects on exports and employment (Kennedy et al. 1991; Ó Riain 2004a; Girma et al. 2008). We need to look elsewhere for the answer to the puzzle of why Ireland's innovation push failed to build on the industrial foundations laid in the 1990s. In particular, we need to examine the forms of coordination that sought to link science and innovation policy to the creation and marketing of new products.

The recent literature on the varieties of capitalism identified two main forms of organization of capitalist economies—coordinated market economies where government played a central guiding role and which had generated growth in Germany, Japan, and other European and Asian economies; and liberal market economies where free market mechanisms played a more central role in organizing labor, the workplace, capital, and university-industry relations (Hall and Soskice 2001). But if Hall and Soskice recognized that there were more players on the capitalist stage than the liberal market economies, they gave all the good lines to the Anglo-American capitalisms (Crouch 2005). They specifically identified the innovation economy of high technology as well suited to the institutions of liberal capitalism, where flexible credit and labor markets could quickly allocate resources to new areas of innovation. On the other hand, the incremental learning of high-quality manufacturing industries has been best suited to the institutions of coordinated capitalism because the protections and cooperative relationships within those economies encourage workers and firms to identify ways of improving processes and products without the fear of being hurt by such improvements,

Table 10.1 Employment Change in Selected Sectors, Ireland 1994–2003

| | Foreign | | | |
	Employment in 1994	Employment in 2003	Total Employment Change	Percentage Employment Change
Industrial, including:	95,330	104,687	9,357	9.82
Chemicals	13,848	19,981	6,133	44.29
Medical and precision equipment	8,917	16,798	7,881	88.38
Office machinery and computers	7,435	15,591	8,156	109.70
Electrical machinery and equipment	7,218	6,586	−632	−8.76
Electronic equipment	5,680	3,921	−1,759	−30.97
Other International Services (Computer Software)	9,231	35,386	26,155	283.34
International Financial Services	1,597	8,263	6,666	417.41

Source: Forfás Employment Surveys (agency assisted exporting firms only)

such as automation that in liberal economies might lead to layoffs (Hall and Soskice 2001; Casper, Lehrer, and Soskice 1999).

Ireland is usually placed firmly within the liberal market camp—partly because of its relatively weak public spending, social and employment protection, and highly globalized economy, and partly due to its deep economic connections to both British and American capitalism. Because Ireland sought to duplicate America's success, its search for an "offshore Silicon Valley" meant that the Anglo-American models were

Table 10.2 Employment Change in Selected Sectors, Ireland 1999–2008

| | Foreign | | | |
	Employment in 1999	Employment in 2008	Total Employment Change	Percentage Employment Change
Industrial, including:	111,133	94,090	−17,043	−15.34
Chemicals	18,241	21,285	3,044	16.69
Medical Devices (Foreign and Irish, predominanty foreign firms)	11,687	19,587	7,900	67.60
Computer, electronic, and optical products	28,645	19,994	−8,651	−30.20
Electrical equipment	6,297	3,719	−2,578	−40.94
Electronic equipment	5,680	3,921	−1,759	−30.97
Publishing, Broadcasting, and Telecomms	298	277	−21	−7.05
Computer Programming	16,054	17,233	1,179	7.34
Computer Consultancy	9,837	13,477	3,640	37.00
Computer Facilities Management	6,004	8,095	2,091	34.83
Other ICT Services	860	2,465	1,605	186.63
Financial Services	5,139	15,372	10,233	199.12
Business Services	604	859	255	42.22

Source: Forfás Employment Surveys (agency assisted exporting firms only)

	Irish		
Employment in 1994	*Employment in 2003*	*Total Employment Change*	*Percentage Employment Change*
106,252	116,209	9,957	9.37
3,117	3,812	635	19.99
1,237	2,933	1,696	137.11
681	1,551	870	127.75
2,945	2,678	−267	−9.07
1,883	2,208	325	17.26
5,395	35,386	26,155	283.34
1,597	2,410	1,857	335.80

prominent in debates on innovation and industrial upgrading. Indeed, in the debate between different models of capitalism around the world, liberal capitalists said high-tech growth and Silicon Valley–style work organization proved the strength of the Anglo-American liberal model of capitalism. But the varieties of capitalism literature overstated the distinction between liberal capitalism and the coordinated planning in a developmental state. Most crucially for our purposes of understanding developments in the increasingly liberal Irish political economy, it ignored the variety of nonmarket

	Irish		
Employment in 1999	*Employment in 2008*	*Total Employment Change*	*Percentage Employment Change*
116,488	103,075	−13,413	−11.51
3,563	3,480	−83	−2.33
4,941	5,569	628	12.71
4,017	2,788	−1,229	−30.59
1,883	2,208	325	17.26
3,987	4,214	227	5.69
0	140		
8,342	13,652	5,310	63.65
0	0		
998	1,409	411	41.18
1,638	4,552	2,914	177.90
4,155	8,597	4,442	106.91

mechanisms of coordination at work in the liberal economies (Block 2008). Some of this coordination is carried out by private actors who nonetheless coordinate economic activity through relationships that go well beyond simple exchange relationships. As Crouch (2005) notes, Silicon Valley's venture capitalists are heavily involved in building the organizational capacities of the firms in which they invest, with little sign of any arm's-length market relationships. Public agencies too play coordinating roles in liberal economies, as we shall see, although these coordinating actions often remain hidden behind the liberal veil.

Nonetheless, it is also clear that the imagery of a classic developmental state planning for "Irish Nokias" does not fit Ireland's experience in recent decades. Our existing theories of developmental statism, developed largely for the East Asian tigers, offer only a limited guide to recent international experiments in state-run innovation policies. In contrast to the more "centralized developmental bureaucratic states" (Ó Riain 2004a) that steered East Asian industrial progress, innovation in the most dynamic regions today is often underpinned by networks of decentralized institutions. Also, the target of those institutions has increasingly been the construction of communities of innovative firms and institutions rather than the promotion of the kind of leading individual firms that dominated technology policy in the past.

For example, the Nordic economies have been resurgent in recent years based on innovation across a wide range of industries (high tech in Finland, medium tech in Denmark, for example). These countries' public and private investments in human capital and research are among the best in the world, but their investments are supported by two more factors: (1) a networked system of governance that has produced a diverse set of agencies and forums for policy formulation and implementation that allow for experimentation and learning and (2) a welfare state system and active labor market policy where extensive supports for child care, training, balancing work and family, and more, support high rates of labor force participation and utilization of human capital (Kristensen 2009; Huber and Stephens 2001).

Even Nokia itself does not bear out Ireland's vision of the Nokia story. With a long history in manufacturing Nokia unexpectedly became a leader in the science-intensive sector of telecommunications. That transition was strongly bolstered by Finland's diverse and extensive network of supports for innovation—including government funding for basic academic research and applied research leading to the invention and marketing of technological innovations as well as government-supported telecom standards. However, Nokia did not emerge from a policy of supporting national champions and commercializing big ideas. The innovation system from which Nokia emerged was characterized by diverse supports for research and enterprise, a wide range of smaller firms, and administrative and regional decentralization. This innovation system was located within a broader infrastructure of strong welfare state and public investments. Rather than a radical break with Finland's industrial past, Nokia represented an intertwining of its own industrial past with an emerging innovation system that promoted decentralized networks of innovation. These networks included small firms, research centers, industrial development agencies, government ministries, and more (Saxenian and Sabel 2009).

Furthermore, although it was hidden from public view, the growth of a developmental network state has also played a key role in high-tech dominance in the United States (Block 2008; Block and Keller 2009; Jenkins, Leicht and Jaynes 2008). The model also applies in the emergent high-tech regions that are most closely linked to the United States and, particularly, Silicon Valley. In Israel and Taiwan, this took different forms as Israel built on an existing scientific community to grow and diffuse the research system, and Taiwan built on its infrastructure of public science and networks of transnational entrepreneurs (Breznitz 2007; Saxenian 2006). In all of these places measures included R&D support; networks of supports for developing management, marketing, and exporting; cofunding programs to stimulate early-stage venture capital; building closer ties with migrants and technical communities; building government-funded science parks; and sponsoring industrial associations. Although Breznitz (2007) finds significant differences between them, his account of innovation in Israel, Taiwan, and Ireland also notes similarities in state strategies to promote development within a networked innovation economy.

Therefore, there are clear signs that new forms of state innovation policy that operate largely through decentralized networks of supports are emerging in both social democratic coordinated economies and liberal market economies. It is possible to characterize much of this support as "developmental network statism" in which networks of public agencies provide diverse supports to firms and seek to build the social and associational worlds of production and innovation in emerging industries. In these DNS programs, industrial development is guided primarily through "making winners" by supporting research and development of innovative new technologies by university labs and small new firms and by developing their organizational capacities, rather than "picking winners" by subsidizing the country's largest corporations (Ó Riain 2004a).

Looking at Ireland, we can see the evolution of developmental network state institutions within a national political economy and examine which conditions allow those institutions to support sustainable prosperity—and which don't.

From DNS to Market Managerialism

It matters which form of economic coordination a country adopts. To understand the shifting performance of Irish high-tech manufacturing and services, we need therefore to investigate not simply the flow of funds into research, innovation, and enterprise but the evolution of the government's innovation policies and institutions over time.

Foreign investment and the IDA way. As economies around the world have sought to emulate Silicon Valley, many have pursued foreign investment as a source of both investment and know-how. In this respect, Ireland has been remarkably successful. Ireland secured an estimated 40 percent of U.S. foreign direct investment (FDI) in electronics in Europe from 1980 to 2000. Firms were attracted by Ireland's corporate tax rates, which varied between zero and 12.5 percent, its supply of young (and increasingly skilled) labor, a supportive state, and, increasingly, improved technological and innovation capacities (Gunnigle and McGuire 2001; Ó Riain 2004a). In the process, Ireland came to have one of the highest proportions of foreign capital stock in the Organization for Economic Cooperation and Development (OECD) and to be among the most open trading economies in the world.

The policy of attracting FDI is a state project as much as it is a response to free market conditions. A large corporation's decision to locate in a given country is less dependent on free market conditions than on the conditions put in place by hierarchical state agencies. It is best seen as a system of competitive bargaining between corporations and states than a market transaction in the conventional sense. In Ireland, the government's Industrial Development Authority (IDA) took on the role of "hunter and gatherer" of FDI and became unusually powerful within the national state system. Working closely with its foreign client companies, it provided a one-stop shop for meeting their tax and regulation needs within the country, often promoting new policy measures based on their conversations with managing directors of foreign firms (an increasing proportion of whom were Irish-born). Thus the IDA combined planned targeting of key technology sectors with ongoing briefings from local managers of foreign firms.

Foreign investment undoubtedly was central to economic growth in the 1990s, and many facets of the foreign-owned sector were upgraded: the workforce was professionalized, R&D grew in foreign firms, and linkages to local firms and suppliers were enhanced (Ó Riain 2004b). However, continuing weaknesses in links between foreign and domestic firms, the low level of technical sophistication at many transnational corporation (TNC) operations, and the existing innovation system's lack of ability to capitalize on TNC resources hampered efforts to create a stronger industrial base. Using the foreign investment strategy, Ireland wasn't able to escape the limitations of its weak national system of innovation (Mjoset 1992; Ó Riain 2004a). Nonetheless, the attraction of FDI remains the dominant policy approach to the present day.

Developmental network statism. Could Ireland go beyond this? During the 1990s, it seemed to. Beneath the veneer of a flowering of Irish entrepreneurialism was a great deal of state coordination. A government agency called Enterprise Ireland was founded in 1994 (initially called Forbairt but renamed in 1998) to support Irish firms and meet the development challenges of growing an indigenous industrial capability. It had been preceded by many similar agencies. Their efforts are best explored through a brief account of Ireland's software industry, the star of indigenous development in the late 1990s. The software industry's success was largely due to the country's industrial and innovation policy system and the impact of that system on relatively marginalized elements of high-tech industry. In the 1980s and particularly in the 1990s, a series of entrepreneurs emerged and started small software companies. Some came from the multinationals, some from the universities, and many had international experience. These entrepreneurs formed a technical community somewhat separate from the foreign-owned high-tech sector and often were involved in lines of business that were quite different from the computer services companies of the 1970s and 1980s. Where many of the earlier companies had designed systems for large local firms, the new generation of companies were developing products for global technology markets.

Although some of these firms, including Iona Technologies and CBT/Riverdeep received financing from private sources, their link to the state agencies was crucial, with statistical analysis revealing a positive net effect of grant aid on employment, exports, and ability to produce software products that promised increased revenue streams (Ó Riain 2004a). More important than the funds involved is the form these supports took. (See Breznitz 2007 for a similar argument regarding Israeli and Taiwanese state programs.) Grant aid was small but was a way for firms to access a network of supports that included R&D networking, management development, training, mentoring networks, and more. Ireland's support network was similar to those in the Scandinavian countries and the high-tech regions of Israel and Taiwan—though on a much smaller scale—in that it supported enterprise and innovation and delivered funding to networks of firms in relatively flexible ways.

In fact, as Enterprise Ireland and similar government agencies learned from their client companies what the technology industry needed, they often responded by expanding their network of supports or by promoting new sources of labor, capital, and technology within the industry. It was the state that drove the new supply of technical labor in the late 1970s and early 1980s, not demand from students. Although the improvement in venture capital financing in the 1990s was partly driven by private business angel investors (Breznitz 2007), the state played a leading role in enticing new funds and investors into this market, especially at crucial moments such as before the Celtic tiger boom had made Ireland an attractive market and right after the dot-com bubble burst in 2001. Irish investment in research followed a similar logic: having heard from companies (especially foreign-owned high-tech companies) that they depended on high-quality research and a labor force with advanced qualifications, Ireland's IDA and other agencies set out to develop such a labor force.

State agencies sponsored the activities of industry associations and technology centers. The state played a critical role in the creation of a network of industry and trade associations, universities, innovation and technology centers, and other forums and groups that provide an associational infrastructure for information sharing, cooperation, and innovation. While bodies such as the Software Manufacturers Association, Software Localization Interest Group, and the Programs in Advanced Technologies (PATs) (which created centers of small-scale applied research within the higher education system) were outside the state or semiautonomous from it, in most cases they had been founded through state initiatives and underwritten by state guarantees and funding.

The state played a critical role in creating the social support systems within the technology industry. Enterprise Ireland's Enterprise Development Program was Ireland's major program for developing high potential firms, and it involved senior industry figures in mentoring and networking. These ties were forged through the state program. A more general state mentoring program in industry also proved successful, most significantly by arranging for veteran business executives to advise companies during the early stages of their development and to help them plan their strategies and activities (Ó Riain 2004a).

Furthermore, the new policies were pursued through a network of agencies. As a result of IDA's ongoing discussions with their client multinational companies, the agency often changed policies and strategies to meet a company's specific needs. Enterprise Ireland adopted a similar model of working closely with client companies, although the challenges of indigenous development proved more diverse and difficult.

Nonetheless, in the 1990s, policies supporting foreign and indigenous firms worked in parallel to drive development in a range of sectors. While the links between the development of foreign and indigenous sectors were often indirect (Ó Riain 2004b), the networked state institutions allowed two loosely integrated policy regimes, focused on foreign and indigenous firms, to evolve side by side.

Market managerialism. In the late 1990s, Ireland's enterprise and innovation policy shifted from focusing on enterprise development and small increases in R&D support to placing science, technology, and research firmly at the center of industrial policy. The state's science budget (including higher education spending) as a whole grew from €1.12 billion in 1999 to €2.65 billion in 2008 (an increase of 59 percent, accounting for inflation). More immediately relevant, gross government spending on research and development grew from €232 million in 1999 to €1029 million in 2008 (in today's currency).

The major initiative of the late 1990s was the establishment in 1999 of Science Foundation Ireland (SFI), with historically unprecedented funding for research. Between 2001 and 2006 SFI made awards totaling €468 million (SFI 2007). SFI's goal was to promote research in information and communications technology (ICT) and biotech, typically by attracting international scientists into the university system. The existing networks of researchers, businesses, and state agencies developed in the 1990s to promote smaller-scale innovations were generally closed (e.g., the Programs in Advanced Technologies, the National Software Directorate) or marginalized as the SFI came to dominate the world of science and research.

Along with their science departments, universities were strengthened in the late 1990s, as funding and hiring picked up again after many years of neglect. In 1998 the Program for Research in Third Level [Higher Education] Institutions (PRTLI) began. PRTLI put some €605 million into third level research infrastructure from 2000 to 2006, largely though the funding of a series of research institutes within universities and institutes of technology around the country (HEA 2006). Almost 50 percent of that funding went into biotech and biomedicine research. Two research councils were set up to provide funding for research sabbaticals and research projects—one for the humanities and social sciences in 2000, and one for the sciences in 2001. In 2008 their budgets were €12.5 and €26.3 million respectively. Together, the research councils received less funding than a number of agencies dedicated to research in specific sectors like the Health Research Board (€49.2 million), Sustainable Energy Ireland (€40 million), and an agency that focused on agricultural research called Teagasc (€66.4 million, supplemented by €17 million for the Marine Institute). All were significantly smaller than SFI's annual funding budget in 2008 of €174 million (Forfás 2008).

In the initial years of these new institutions and funding initiatives, these funds came with relatively few strings attached. PRTLI funding was awarded to institutes that were seen to serve the purposes of national development but also filled important needs within the academic landscape and across the range of disciplines. The institutes had a great deal of discretion in how the funds were used within the funding period, subject to general consistency with the mission of the institutes, reporting requirements, and satisfactory outputs in terms of research activity and publications. In many respects, these new institutes became the focus of the associational life of research and innovation, as many of the earlier generation of innovation centers became less important and programs like the PATs were discontinued.

This surge of funding was much needed as the networks of supports and agencies in the 1990s, while innovative, survived on relatively small budgets and direct research funding was at an exceptionally low level by international standards. However, the new funding was tied up with an organizational model that ultimately undermined some of its goals. Market-inspired demands for self-sustaining research centers were combined with an increasingly managerial emphasis on schemes and programs which demanded that researchers and universities respond directly to centrally defined policy goals and targets. Markets and managerialism combined to weaken the networked system of supports that had developed in the 1990s.

Marketization pressures always existed within the innovation system. In the 1990s, funding programs like Programs in Advanced Technologies directed grants to innovation centers that would create marketable products and become self-funding. However, there has been a consistent tension between the demand that funded laboratories and innovation centers become self-financing, and the demand that these centers use government money for the public good—by doing basic research regardless of its marketability and by providing a public space for scientific networking.

Perhaps the primary reason for the collapse of the National Software Centre in the 1980s was the conflicts generated by the demands put on it to undertake a mission of upgrading the industry, while at the same time requiring it to be commercially viable. Caught between devolving into a development services organization and competing with the major firms in the industry, the center lost industry funding and was ultimately closed (Ó Riain 2004a). The PAT centers also suffered under pressures to be self-funding. As a director in one of the innovation promoting institutions told me, "Our promotional role ended when the money ran out.... We made the same mistake with the PATs. If people want missionary work then they have to pay for it." Ultimately the PAT program ended, with a division between those centers that were able to fund themselves and the others that were wound down.

This question of sustainability of funding and commercialization of research became even more central to policy in the 2000s. PRTLI schemes increasingly demanded that institutions include in their applications plans to become self-funding. Sources of external funding and internal matching funds were to be specified. Meanwhile, SFI programs came under increasing pressure to generate commercial spin-offs and were increasingly subject to external criticism for the low number of start-up firms.

In tandem with these pressures toward the marketization of research, the innovation system also became more closely controlled by central organizations. When new funding streams started to emerge again in late 2005, the terms of the funding applications had shifted significantly. New funding mechanisms were introduced that linked increases in funding directly to universities competing with each other to serve government goals. For example, a portion of the university block grant was cut and moved to a Strategic Innovation Fund (SIF), where universities competed for funding based on proposals to undertake reforms to increase access for disadvantaged students, develop innovative teaching techniques, improve oversight, and other goals. The scheme was designed not to fund ongoing programs but to push universities to undertake new activities out of existing funding. At the same time, core funding of universities remained stable or even decreased, even as general education spending increased (see Table 10.3). But while the goals of the fund were worthy, the new competition for funding and new funding criteria combined with at best stable core state funding of universities to weaken the autonomy of universities and to direct research (as the policy explicitly intended) toward public policy priorities defined by government. Furthermore, the competition between departments and institutions to beat each other to lucrative, marketable innovations corrodes their ability to function as centers for the kinds of networking and idea sharing that are crucial to innovation (Lester and Piore 2004).

Meanwhile, even though commercialization was relatively weak, in terms of governance, universities became at times narrowly connected to industry. One example (from 2006) is particularly telling. The president of University College Dublin (UCD), one of the largest universities in Ireland, was a one time director of the Conway Institute, a leading center for biomedical research. Four of the seven vice presidents were also ex-Conway Institute employees. Elan, the leading Irish pharmaceutical firm, moved its headquarters to UCD to be closer to the Conway Institute. Meanwhile the chairman of the governing authority was on the board of directors of both Elan and United Drug, the leading Irish drug sales firm. The autonomy of universities was threatened both by increasingly close ties to industry and the heavy dependence for funding on an increasingly controlling state.

Table 10.3 Ireland: Real Non-Capital Public Expenditure on Education, 1997–2006

	€ per pupil/student at 2005 prices			€m at 2005 prices
Level				
Year	*First*	*Second*	*Third*	*Real non-capital public expenditure*
1997	3,401	5,254	11,239	4,820
1998	3,586	5,359	9,892	4,803
1999	3,714	5,449	10,136	4,914
2000	3,998	5,725	9,852	5,120
2001	4,140	6,269	10,242	5,403
2002	4,559	6,709	10,313	5,784
2003	4,978	7,199	10,130	6,162
2004	5,262	7,143	9,656	6,241
2005	5,303	7,347	9,901	6,364
2006	5,580	7,805	10,505	6,774

Source: CSO (2007, Table 5.1)

Ultimately, despite calls for innovation, the autonomy of researchers, research institute leaders, and university administrators was severely curtailed by both the need to be self-funding and the demands to conform to state programs. The problem was not the presence of oversight in and of itself; after all, improved structures of accountability had been an important part of the DNS (Ó Riain 2004a). However, the central government agencies displayed little interest in dialogue with, or learning from, the researchers and university administrators. Planning at the center dominated learning and dialogue as the driving forces in policy development.

Furthermore, the spaces where researchers and innovators could interact and share ideas—the crucial public spaces where conversations could take place (Lester and Piore 2004)—were weakened. The spaces where science and industry could interact that had developed by the end of the 1990s were eroded as the institutions that supported them—such as the PATs—were closed or marginalized. New spaces that emerged through SFI schemes heavily favored foreign firms that had the research capacity to absorb the kinds of research being done through SFI.

Even among researchers, new divides were introduced that weakened the diffusion of research capacity. The routing of research funding through stand-alone institutes like HRB and Teagasc and SFI researchers created a divide between the university research and teaching communities and the better funded researchers in these institutes. This extended in some cases to science departments where, for example, biology researchers working on biotechnology (supported by SFI) coexisted uneasily with staff working in other areas of biology. Other disciplines, such as chemistry, were marginalized in the new mix of sectoral policies.

The development of the DNS at the end of the 1990s required extensive new funding to secure and develop the foundations that had been laid. However, when that funding came, it was accompanied by organizational structures that strengthened market and state control. Ultimately, however, these structures weakened innovation itself, marginalizing local and systemwide dialogue and learning and weakening the crucial public spaces where researchers could interact with each other across the disciplines and institutions within the research world and even across the industry-academia divide.

DNS: Out of, and Back to, the Margins

The institutions that emerged as central to indigenous innovation in the 1990s— Enterprise Ireland, the universities, EU research programs, and a variety of associations and centers—continued into the 2000s. However, where these agencies had started in the 1990s to threaten the dominance of the FDI model and of the IDA as an agency, the FDI model was transposed to science and research policy, and the network of institutions that had supported innovation in the 1990s was once again marginalized. Far from building on those institutions, in most cases innovation policy now simply ignored them—or in cases such as the PATs, closed them down. Why was the developmental network state of the 1990s so easily marginalized, particularly given the weakness of compelling evidence that the new institutions were generating spectacular industrial development?

The answer lies partly in the origins of the developmental network state institutions. Competing with other institutionalized policy regimes within the state, the institutions of the DNS emerged largely as what Block (2008) has called a hidden developmental state. The institutions, policies, and programs of the DNS may have constituted a distinct policy regime, but it was a regime that was reluctant to proclaim its distinctiveness.

The reasons for this lie in the conditions under which the DNS emerged. Critical to its emergence was the carving out of a new institutional space for the regime. The IDA had been hegemonic within the development apparatus of the state, strongly legitimated by its success in attracting FDI. However, the economic collapse of the 1980s shook that legitimacy, dislodging the IDA and FDI as sole bearer of the project of national economic development. In addition, there had always been elements within the Irish state that had concerned themselves with indigenous development. These officials had played a role in a series of reviews of industrial policy in the 1980s and 1990s that promoted concepts allowing for greater emphasis on indigenous industry and state-supported industrial development, including active industrial policies (Telesis Report 1982), clusters of firms that competed and cooperated with each other (Culliton Report 1991), national systems of innovation (Mjoset 1992) and networks (NESC 1996).

These changes allowed space for institutional development as a series of other state bodies came into play that concerned themselves primarily with the science, technology, and innovation agenda and were oriented toward indigenous industry—although until the late 1980s their success in raising R&D spending levels and promoting innovation had been limited (O'Malley 1980, 62–63). These included the National Science Council, founded in the late 1960s and its successor the National Board for Science and Technology (NBST) founded in 1977. In the mid-1980s science and technology policies were reorganized significantly with a new Office of Science and Technology being formed under a minister of state (junior cabinet minister) in the Department of Industry and Commerce. The NBST was merged with the Institute for Industrial Research and Standards in 1987 to form Eolas, a new science and technology agency. An ex-employee of the NBST, still working within the development agencies, argues that "there was a kind of 'skunk works' [a project working beneath the radar] within the civil service to find ways of putting Science and Technology on the agenda. The National Science Council was the big breakthrough .... The next trick pulled by those civil servants was a Review of the Science Council.... The OECD will do reviews, to a very standard formula, if invited by the government. You'll find a whole series of those reports by the OECD on different countries. That led to the NBST. The early years of NBST were very exciting we were advocating involvement in international programs, in university-industry cooperation."

Around the same time various agencies were consolidated into one agency to deal with active labor market policy (FÁS) and into another to deal with export marketing (An Bord Tráchtála). In 1994 Forbairt, an agency focused solely on indigenous industry, was created incorporating most of the staff and functions of Eolas and the Irish Industry section of the IDA. In 1998 An Bord Tráchtála was merged into Forbairt, under protest from some local firms that feared a loss of marketing assistance. Finally these various agencies were folded into Enterprise Ireland, which consolidated them under one institutional roof. An increasingly sustainable and autonomous institutional space became available in which the indigenous development and national system of innovation agendas could be pursued.

These agencies turned repeatedly to external sources of support, drawing particularly on international agencies and global values of progress through science and technology (Boli and Thomas 1997) to legitimate innovation policy. The National Science Council was founded as the outcome of a joint OECD-Irish government review of science and Irish economic development, undertaken in 1963 as part of Lemass's push for industrial modernization; responsibility for indigenous industry still lay within the Department of Industry and Commerce (OECD 1963). An OECD review of national science policy in 1974 explicitly supported the National Science Council's recommendations for its successor's structure and even named the new entity, the soon-to-be-formed NBST (OECD 1974). A further review in 1978 was critical of the overemphasis on foreign investment (OECD 1978). Being able to draw on institutionalized international agencies was a powerful legitimation tool for this emerging skunk works within the civil service.

These science and technology agencies also turned regularly to Europe for funding and support. As one official put it, "Ireland did well in Europe; we had a good effect there. It was one of the few niches left to us in Irish policy, no one else looking at international issues, at the funding of research—that was our big contribution. European money kept research in universities alive." Peterson and Sharp (1998) document the many ways in which EU science, technology, and innovation policy has been bound up with improving the EU science and technology base and labor force in the interest of competitiveness but also with the goals of promoting collaboration across member states and promoting economic and social cohesion. The Irish indigenous innovation coalition was able to take advantage of not only the increasingly institutionalized world polity institutions dealing with science and technology but with a very elaborate set of specific programs operating within the European Union.

The new state institutions relied heavily on EU funds for their activities. Many of the programs undertaken in the science and technology arena were funded in large part by European structural funds, funds that were designated for Ireland as part of an effort to develop the peripheral regions of the EU in the face of the upcoming single European market in 1992. Many observers have commented on the impact of the influx of this capital from the EU, attributing Ireland's growth to these funds. However, what was significant about the European structural funds was that they were the means by which a variety of new, sometimes experimental measures could be taken without having to fight the rest of Ireland's state agencies for funding. The new development regime could grow alongside the old and did not have to challenge the old development model directly for funds and priority, except in rare cases. Furthermore, the EU funds came with significant requirements in terms of performance and outcome evaluation and accounting. While sometimes creating administrative nightmares, this also helped to foster a climate where regular evaluation of policies became the norm and where patronage and cronyism was mitigated. Therefore it was not only the financial impact of the EU funds that was crucial, but the institutional space it facilitated for new initiatives. In this case, international funds were used to promote an indigenous development agenda.

However, political support for this agenda was relatively weak. The state, through its heavy investment in education, had meanwhile created a new class basis for an indigenous technology promotion and business expansion agenda. In educating a technical labor force, the Irish state created a group of employees and potential entrepreneurs who were not part of the existing roads to accumulating wealth—agriculture, property, low technology, domestically traded products, and the established professions such as medicine and law. In many cases these employees set themselves consciously against the established way of getting ahead in Irish society. They were also critical of the opportunities available within the transnational corporations, as even high-profile companies like Digital often offered more manufacturing than research or engineering jobs. In many cases they chose emigration over the less challenging jobs available in the production-oriented transnational companies (Wickham 1989). This, then, was a ready constituency for a development project aimed at developing a technologically sophisticated, indigenous industry.

Such entrepreneurs have strong cultural and social legitimacy and have been—and typically continue to be—very supportive of agencies such as Enterprise Ireland (see, e.g., Horn 2009). However, these institutions' ability to shape politics and policy has been relatively weak. Their collective power is much less than that of the large foreign high-tech firms or of the large domestic firms in food and services. The representative organizations for business—the Irish Business and Employers Confederation and the Irish Small and Medium Enterprises Association—tend to focus on costs and wages rather than on developmental programs, despite their close cooperation with agencies like Enterprise Ireland in many other respects.

Economic discourse about innovation, which had been built on a legacy of planning within government departments and the IDA, shifted to a discourse of enterprise and the promotion of enterprise. But instead of taking a neoliberal form, this discourse took a peculiarly statist form. State agencies intervened very intensely in the "cultural production of enterprise" (Carr 1998) and ironically were unwilling to rely on the entrepreneurial spirit to produce concrete enterprising activities. Often, even those same development officials were at a loss to explain their own model of organization and action. As one agency official put it, "Ireland is a funny economy. We have a fairly statist economy. I'm amazed sometimes, you'd think we were communists the way we go on! The state has a strong but healthy hold on things. Quite a lot of central thinking goes on. There is a close relationship between the state and business. It might be out of sync, but it is almost Russian or Chinese in its way of doing things. The closest would be the French, the way they manage things, but without the French bureaucracy." Clearly the officials of the Irish state agencies do not have the vocabulary to describe their own rationalities and practices, often filling the void with talk of "enterprise" and "markets." This veneer of free market jargon was probably vital to allowing this regime to emerge, as it legitimated the actions of these agencies within the overall liberal economic policy regime. However, it meant that the officials in these agencies never formulated a clear public narrative to explain their successes in supporting indigenous industrial upgrading and innovation.

Despite its clever expansion of the institutional space available to it, the DNS emerged under cover of enterprise talk and with the support of a weak political coalition. In this sense, while the institutions of the DNS became more prominent in policy and politics, the underlying logic of the activities of the DNS—its developmental activities, its network structure, and its public character—were rarely made explicit or legitimate, even by the actors within its own institutions. This rendered the regime vulnerable in changed circumstances.

When science came firmly onto the agenda in the late 1990s, it did so in a changed institutional and political environment. Innovation policy was one of the drivers that was to generate the growth that would make this model sustainable. Based on foresight, projections of future technological trajectories, and ongoing consultations with foreign investors regarding what they'd need to maintain their locations in Ireland, the major planks of the new science policy were put in place in the late 1990s with significant new funding and new institutions approved by government and the parliament.

This policy emerged in an environment of ever stronger political and cultural support of free market narratives of economic development. Science policy was brought to the center of government policy by the new coalition government of populist center-right Fianna Fáil (FF) and its junior partner, the economically liberal Progressive Democrats (PD). While the PDs placed significant ideological emphasis on free market rhetoric and policies, FF's populism meant its ideological stance was less explicit. Nonetheless, a set of policies were undertaken in the late 1990s and early 2000s that cemented a more liberal free market turn in the economy, with falling income tax rates, capital gains taxes cut in half, tax incentives for property development and construction, weak regulation of the banking and financial sectors, and more.

Market talk had homogenized the various development options available to government under the same rubric of markets, enterprise, and competition. In the process, developmentalism was marginalized. For example, while the reduction of capital gains tax had been mooted by the PDs with a general appeal to improving access to risk capital, in practice the increased flow of capital into the economy went overwhelmingly into property and finance, rather than production and innovation (Ó Riain 2009). Equally, the recognition of the distinctive role of the indigenous development agencies was combined with an airbrushing out of the developmental public character of its activities. For example, Prime Minister Bertie Ahern spoke of the developmental state in a 2003 speech to the Irish Management Institute. However, his summary remarks clearly fudged the tension between developmentalism and market managerialism: "This is a state that supports business. It is the kind of state that I want to lead."

Finally, the institutional balance of power shifted. Given the continuing importance of the FDI regime and the close ties between the IDA and government, the IDA was always better placed than the indigenous development agencies to make more of a government focus on research. Being able to report on the growing concerns of foreign firms that Ireland develop its postgraduate researcher labor force and research base gave the IDA significant clout in these policy debates. Furthermore, the science and innovation policy field was led by Forfás, an agency founded in 1994 to provide strategic planning and oversight to the other industrial development agencies. Forfás's interest in science and technology placed it at the heart of the new policy regime; most of Forfás's early leaders had come through the IDA rather than the indigenous development or science agencies. The science and technology foresight exercises conducted in the late 1990s placed the new agencies at the heart of the science policy field and marginalized the existing weaker agencies. The resistance to networking the new science institutions with existing research structures was clear in initial discussions that broached the creation of SFI as two research institutes in biotech and ICT, located outside the universities. In early policy reports, the question of the location and form of these research centers was pointedly left open. However, the universities managed to fight a rearguard action that, at the last minute, linked SFI to the university sector.

Ultimately then, market managerialism was able to supplant developmental network statism as the dominant overall approach in innovation. This was because of a shifting institutional landscape that allowed the foreign investment development regime to place itself once more at the heart of industrial policy, marginalizing the DNS institutions, largely ignoring the existing institutional supports for innovation, and transposing the logic of FDI into science policy—in the process once more downplaying the potential of indigenous industry. This institutional shift was supported by the much stronger coalition surrounding the new model, with key multinationals backing the SFI proposal and universities attracted by the promise of funds previously unimagined. Finally, the ability to cast DNS activities in the language of enterprise and markets, crucial to emergence of the DNS in the 1990s, left it without a narrative to contest either the market mechanisms that undermined developmentalism or the centralizing tendencies that weakened network governance. The hidden developmental state of the 1990s had failed to develop a political or discursive framework that could support its institutional position. Once that position was outflanked by the market managerialism that ultimately accompanied the emergence of science policy, for the first time on the national governmental stage there was only one likely winner.

Publics and Networks: Institutionalizing the Fragile Network State

Is the DNS doomed, then, to emerge from the shadows only to be driven back once the dominant forces of market fundamentalism and centralized big science deem it necessary? The history of Irish innovation policy is a story of the fragility of networks. Networks are susceptible to several pressures. They may be subsumed into a hierarchy that is driven by organizational dominance and the unbalancing of interorganizational relationships (e.g., in the Irish case through the centralization of authority regarding science policy). However, networks are also susceptible to marketization, driven by the devolution of relationships in the face of self-interest (e.g., the competition between universities and firms in the context of the search for sustainable funding). Can these pressures be resisted?

The history of the DNS in Ireland suggests that it's the public aspect of network institutions that makes them critical to an economy. That's because public network institutions serve three key functions: they provide public space for dialogue, conversation, and mutual learning; their public funding plays a central role in securing the reproduction of key investments and protecting public spaces; and the public accountability of network institutions helps prevent hierarchical or market dominance. This triangle of public roles can underpin network institutions by protecting the spaces in which networks flourish, while making them externally accountable so that they do not devolve into clientelism and/or corruption.

Public spaces were central to the DNS in Ireland, as evidenced in the series of associational, networking, mentoring, and institution building initiatives undertaken from the 1990s. Lester and Piore (2004) argue that innovation depends not just on networks but on public spaces where conversations can take place that are interpretative in nature and allow for collaborative exploration and learning. The DNS, as noted above, contributed not only to investment in the critical factors of production for innovation industries and to the enhanced organizational capabilities of firms but also to the broader social worlds of production in which firms were embedded, most successfully in the software industry. The key agencies themselves become part of this social world, such that state intervention is probably not a useful way to conceptualize the role of state agencies whose effectiveness is based on network centrality within the industries they seek to develop. The market managerialist regime has placed less emphasis on support of such institutions. Nonetheless, the major investments in science have helped to create and strengthen scientific communities within the universities. SFI's main beneficial effect in the long term may be less in terms of direct spin-offs and more in terms of the funding of a science community. However, its effects in this regard are weakened by its institutional disconnect from the university departments around the SFI researchers, the lack of established organic connection between the (often newly arrived) research professors and the local scientific community, and the limited networking of these new centers of innovation with researchers and firms in the private sector.

These quasi-public spaces in education and industry were underpinned by public funding. Public funds were critical in the formation of new networks and associations but were ultimately threatened by pressure to be self-funding. The initial stages of the expansion of science and research funding suggested that a strong, publicly funded innovation structure might be combined with a networked set of institutions in both industry and the universities. However, this possibility was derailed by twin, apparently contradictory pressures. On the one hand, pressure to be self-funding increased, and new institutional initiatives were designed based on the assumption of declining future public support (with the exception of sectors that were eligible for SFI funding, where SFI funding usually counted as "external funding"' despite simply coming from another public source). On the other, the universities' dependence on state funding made them vulnerable to pressures from the state and reductions in autonomy. While this formal autonomy was legally safeguarded by the Universities Act of 1997, the practical workings of funding generated increased oversight and demands from central government agencies. The more that public funds were used to drive through strategic innovations, the more that public funding came into tension with the construction and flourishing of the public spaces that had depended in part on public funds.

The presence of mechanisms for making networks accountable to the broader public is crucial to prevent them from operating as structures of patronage or becoming involuted. The monitoring processes that occur across organizational boundaries are critical elements in the coordination of such networked organizational structures (Sabel 1994). An important mechanism in this monitoring is the increased use of formal standards, benchmarks, and measures of outcomes that act as metrics against which organizational performance is measured. Ideally, benchmarks—and organizations' performance relative to them—provide information and stimulate learning about local processes and best practices (Lester and Piore 2004). Structures of external evaluation and accountability have been critical to the development of the DNS in Ireland (Ó Riain 2004a). However, benchmarks on their own do not necessarily deliver a more open or deliberative form of governance. In different contexts benchmarks are just as compatible with hierarchical, disciplinary social relations where dominant organizations use benchmarks to discipline and rationalize subordinate organizations; or indeed with the marketization of organizations' environments where benchmarks (e.g., quality certifications) become elements in consumer decisions.

In higher education we can find evidence of benchmarks prompting deliberation, as universities around the country discuss how best to improve their standing on a variety of research, teaching, and other metrics. There are also examples of metrics (e.g., newspaper league tables) that become part of the "market for education." However, the dominant use of benchmarks and metrics has been disciplinary, as a wide variety of measures of higher education performance are introduced in the context of arguments to rationalize and transform higher education organizations. Metrics linked to university rankings, research funding, organizational change programs, quality reviews, and other initiatives have proliferated. However, it is the valorization of these metrics, independent of interpretation or judgment, that has been particularly damaging to the organic development of network structures. Although the fetishization of metrics may suit hierarchical control mechanisms, it closes off the interactions and conversations that are crucial to network relations and structures.

Where network state institutions have been supported by public spaces and funding and made publicly, or at least externally, accountable, they have been effective and have persisted. The erosion of the DNS was driven by the weakening of this always tenuous public support through an emphasis on marketization and "sustainable financing" but also by increased state support that took the form of hierarchical discipline rather than public supports for diverse research activity and public spaces. As policymakers seek again in 2010 to find a new role for universities and public agencies in supporting innovation, they face organizational dilemmas and opportunities once again, not only of markets and hierarchies but also of networks and publics.

CHAPTER 11

China's (Not So Hidden) Developmental State

Becoming a Leading Nanotechnology Innovator in the Twenty-First Century

Richard P. Appelbaum, Rachel Parker, Cong Cao, and Gary Gereffi

The Push for High-Tech Global Leadership

One way to gain perspective on U.S. government innovation policy is through comparing it with the efforts of other nations. While some nations were strongly influenced by Washington's antigovernment ideology and abandoned any active pursuit of industrial policy, China has done the opposite. Its theoreticians studied U.S. innovation policies carefully and have sought to imitate them. One of the clearest instances of this occurs in the field of nanotechnology. The U.S. government launched a major research and development (R&D) initiative in this area in 1999. China created its own national steering committee on nanotechnology in 2001, and by 2006 nanotechnology was one of the major priorities in basic science in the *Medium- to Long-Term Plan for the Development of Science and Technology* (MLP)—the guiding document for China's strategy of leapfrog development.

China is hardly alone in prioritizing nanotechnology: Germany, Japan, and some forty other countries are betting that nanotechnology, among other high-tech areas, will provide the key to a $2.6 trillion market by 2014—sufficient to confer global economic leadership on the country that attains first-mover advantage through innovation (Holman et al. 2007, iii). An estimated $11.8 billion was invested globally in nanotechnology R&D and commercialization in 2006—$5.8 billion from governments, $5.3 billion from corporations, and $700 million from venture capital (Holman et al. 2007, 11–12). Private investment slightly outstripped public investment for the first time in that year. Governments worldwide have clearly been drivers of nanotechnology during its early stages, and private venture capital remains limited.

In terms of government spending, the United States remains the world leader, with $1.53 billion allocated for 2009, roughly a quarter of the combined amount spent by governments globally on nanotechnology. U.S. government spending is coordinated through the National Nanotechnology Initiative (NNI), "a multi-agency U.S. government program aimed at accelerating the discovery, development, and deployment of nanometer-scale science, engineering, and technology" (US NNI 2008e). Initiated during the last year of the Clinton administration, the NNI has invested some $7.2 billion since it began funding programs and projects in 2001 (AZoNano 2008). Today it encompasses twenty-six federal agencies with nanotechnology-related programs.

The U.S. efforts in this area are explicitly linked to the goal of competitiveness: to make the United States a world leader in this emerging technology. The NNI identifies four overarching goals on its website (US NNI 2008b):

- Advance a world-class nanotechnology R&D program
- Foster the transfer of new technologies into products for commercial and public benefit
- Develop and sustain educational resources, a skilled workforce, and the supporting infrastructure and tools to advance nanotechnology
- Support responsible development of nanotechnology

In its early years, the NNI largely focused on funding basic R&D, but there has been a strong effort to support commercialization through three separate channels that are evident in other technology initiatives (Block and Keller, Chapter 8). First, strong incentives exist to encourage funded researchers at universities and federal labs to create new firms to exploit their technological discoveries. Second, a portion of nanotechnology dollars go to support these start-up firms through the Small Business Innovation Research (SBIR) and Small Business Technology Transfer programs. Between 2004 and 2007, federal government SBIR/STTR programs provided $294 million in support of nanotechnology-related projects, 22 percent coming from the NSF (US NNI 2009, 12).[1] Third, there is a strong emphasis on getting industry participants to collaborate with university and federal lab technologists. The program has funded more than sixty multidisciplinary research and education centers across the United States, primarily at universities but also at several of the national laboratories and some government agency facilities (US NNI 2008c) that are supposed to draw in industry participants.[2] These facilities built with nanotechnology dollars have aggressively marketed their services to industry so that firms can be spared the prohibitive costs of building their own laboratories. Yet notwithstanding the success of these programs, U.S. federal government support for nanotechnology remains heavily weighted toward the research end of the spectrum. A recent report prepared for the U.S. Department of Commerce Office of Technology Assessment, entitled *Barriers to Nanotechnology Commercialization,* identified a host of such barriers, concluding that "the most significant barriers to growth generally include funding which favors research over development and commercialization of nano products (McNeil et al. 2007, 10–11).[3]

In comparison with the United States, China, as a society that has recently transitioned from state-owned to privately owned enterprises, lacks the long history of small technology start-ups and does not yet have much of a private sector venture capital system. As we will see, China has sought to use a division of labor across different levels of government as a way to solve this problem. Whereas the central government provides much of the R&D funding, local and provincial governments have taken on the role of nurturing start-up firms to build new clusters of nano-based industries.

Data Sources

The following analysis is based on an examination of Chinese government publications (in Chinese and English), as well as field interviews conducted during five weeks of research carried out during the summers of 2006 and 2007. To date we have conducted fifty-nine interviews: thirty-eight in China (Beijing, Tianjin, Shanghai, Hangzhou, Suzhou, and Dalian), six in Hong Kong, eight in Taiwan, and seven in the United States. One of the authors (Cong Cao) has done extensive previous research on China's high-tech policy.[4] The breakdown of our interviews, by type of organization, is summarized in Table 11.1:

Table 11.1 Organizational Setting of Interviews

Type of organization	Number of Interviews
Governmental	10
Quasi-governmental (semi-private)	3
Government-funded Incubator	5
University, including labs	19
Companies	17
Other	5
Total	59

China's Emphasis on Government Support for Indigenous Innovation

During the past twenty years China has invested heavily in science and technology (S&T), using reforms in the S&T management system, including higher education, to boost the emergence of a national innovation system that could generate indigenous innovation (*zizhu chuangxin* in Chinese) in areas including biology, information technology, and nanotechnology. Beginning with the Third National Conference on Science and Technology in 1995, when the "decision on accelerating scientific and technological progress" was announced (U.S. 1996), "indigenous innovation" has been heralded as a major source of China's future economic development.[5] Science, technology, and education were identified as the tools that will create national prosperity. In October 2000, Chinese Communist Party secretary and Chinese president Jiang Zemin pointed out in his report in the fifth plenary session of the fifteenth party Central Committee: "We should concentrate our efforts to make breakthroughs on such fields as genome science, information science, nano-science, life science and geosciences" (NIBC 2006, 14). By the time the eleventh five-year plan (2006–2010) was unveiled in 2005, innovation had become the centerpiece of China's economic strategy, and the goal was to harness China's human capital to promote indigenous innovation through S&T in order to address the country's social, environmental, global competitive, and national security challenges.

The Chinese strategy can be termed "technological leapfrogging"—taking an industrialization shortcut. The term was coined in 1985 by Luc Soete with specific reference to the international diffusion of technology and the industrial development of economic growth associated with the microelectronics industry. Soete (1985) highlights the significant advantages that can be felt by "late industrializers" in terms of catching up to global technological leaders, citing Japan as the most apt example (at the time). More recently, it has been linked to countries such as China, which has explicitly jettisoned the traditional notion of sequential or "catch-up" industrialization typically advocated for developing nations dating back half a century or more (Rostow 1971).

China, in particular, is racing toward high-tech development, while continuing to exploit the advantage of paying comparatively low wages in labor-intensive industries (Friedman 2006). What makes China unique, however, is its attempt to build a single development strategy based on three national advantages: its low-cost advantage in export-oriented industrialization; its large domestic market for advanced manufactures that will become more profitable as China substitutes homegrown products for those it now imports, via import substitution industrialization; and its burgeoning talent pool of scientists and engineers associated with the R&D process in high-tech development, which happens to have cost advantage over developed countries.

Two powerful forces, globalization and the rapid advance of information technologies, have made China's distinctive approach to technological leapfrogging possible. These forces have compressed both space and time, reducing the impact of distance between people, products, and information to the point where China is able to upgrade and strengthen many areas of its economy simultaneously: labor-intensive exports (e.g., nondurable consumer goods), increased domestic manufacture and consumption of high-tech products like cars and electronics; infrastructure development (e.g., highways, ports, logistics, and communications), and government promotion of knowledge-based industries (e.g., biotechnology and nanotechnology).

The choice of this development strategy—to leap ahead in so many areas at once— can only be explained by China's expansive vision of its role as an emerging global power and its domestic politics oriented toward rapid economic growth and so-called market socialism. Whether China can successfully sustain this strategy is an open question, but it will require a complex and evolving set of policies and institutions to concurrently manage everything from exchange rates and industrial incentives to education, migration, labor market, and S&T policies. Nanotechnology development policy in China illustrates both the potential and the difficulties of this leapfrogging strategy, which ultimately seeks to help its economy bypass the traditional step-by-step movement up the value chain.

Some China watchers say technological leapfrogging—driven by initiatives that originate in the central government—is doomed to fail. Efforts to create an "innovative society" via leapfrogging are seen as hampered by a lack of private sector resources in China, as well as by bureaucratic rivalries among key state agencies (Suttmeier, Cao, and Simon 2006b). Innovation requires market-driven incentives, while China's investment- and export-driven growth is said to have been at the expense of consumption, and hence a drag on the economy (Lardy 2006). Furthermore, as a strategy for growth, "indigenous innovation" is viewed as suffering from "techno-nationalism," which is largely at odds with the foreign direct investment–oriented development model China has thus far used effectively to bring in new technologies (Serger and Breidne 2007).

We question the dismissal of China's innovation potential on the grounds that it is based on an exclusively Beijing-led model of development. We see in the Chinese model an emphasis on more modular, loosely coupled approach to innovation in terms of John Hagel III and John Seely Brown's perspective of creation nets, open innovation, and process networks (Brown and Hagel 2005; Hagel and Brown 2006). Such approaches favor open over closed systems, recognizing that a balance needs to be struck between open "pull" and closed "push." Similarly, Lynn and Salzman (2007a, b) argue that real innovation shifts are occurring in places like China, but to understand them we need to look at the role of cumulative and incremental innovations, the dynamics of collaborative advantage, and the role of local technology entrepreneurs.

China's Developmental State: Science and Technology Policy

Technological leapfrogging requires state investment in areas where business firms are unable or unwilling to invest (e.g., nanotechnology) that will take years to become commercially viable. Let us start with a brief description of China's science and technology policymaking framework to better understand how nanotechnology has evolved into one of the "leapfrogging" priorities. The National People's Congress (NPC), China's highest organ of the state power and legislature, through its Standing Committee and the Committee on Science, Technology, Education, and Health, has the authority to enact and amend S&T related laws, which are typically drafted by government agencies. The NPC also monitors the implementation of such laws and approves state budget on S&T. The various ministries in China's cabinet, such as the Ministry of Science and Technology (MOST), Education (MOE), Agriculture (MOA), Health (MOH), Industry and Information Technology (MIIT), Environmental Protection (MOEP), the National Development and Reform Commission (NDRC), the now-defunct Commission of Science, Technology, and Industry for National Defense (COSTIND), then allocate resources to programs related to their respective ministerial missions.

The Chinese Academy of Sciences (CAS), an entity with multiple functions in research, high-tech industrialization, technology transfer, and training, plays a significant role in S&T policymaking through its honorific members. So also does the Chinese Academy of Engineering (CAE), an advisory institution providing services for decision-making of the nation's key issues in engineering and technological sciences (Cao 2004). The national Natural Science Foundation of China (NSFC) mainly supports basic research and mission-oriented research projects through a competitive peer review process. Finally, the Ministry of Finance (MOF) has become increasingly important in scrutinizing budgets put forward by ministries and monitoring the usage of the funds. During the policymaking process, members of the Chinese People's Political Consultative Conference (CPPCC), an advisory body, also voice their opinions; this body includes many who are not members of the Chinese Communist Party (CCP). So do leading scientists. For example, in May 2000, a group of experts jointly proposed to the CCP Central Committee and the State Council that "our country should accelerate the industrialization of the nanotechnology and occupy this world-wide frontier area as soon as possible," which was quickly taken up as a priority research area by members of the CCP Central Committee (NIBC 2006).

Pressure for developing a national nanotechnology policy began in these science-based agencies. Initiated in 1982, *gongguan* is a national S&T program administered by the State Science and Technology Commission and its successor, MOST, to tackle critical and generic technologies pertaining to industrial technology and social development. MOST, the State Planning Commission (the predecessor of NDRC), MOE, NSFC, and CAS jointly analyzed the strength, weakness, opportunities, and threats in the development of nanotechnology in China (Figure 11.1). The outcome of the exercise was to establish a national steering committee on nanotechnology in 2001 that coordinates the efforts in nanotech research and industrialization and determines the priority areas for support. The committee formulated the Outline for the National Nanoscience and Technology Development (2001–2010) as a road map for the future of nanotechnology in China. Under the guidance and coordination of

Figure 11.1 The Framework of Nanotechnology Research in China

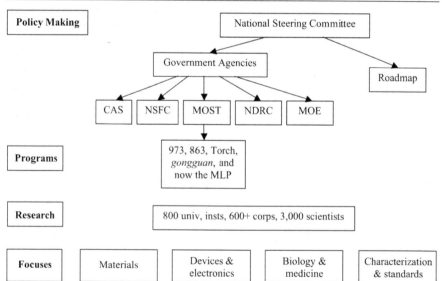

the national steering committee, chaired by the minister of science and technology (although its chief scientist, Bai Chunli, is from CAS), various nanotechnology-related programs have been supported and implemented at MOST, MOE, CAS, and NSFC; in the meantime, NDRC has provided funds for infrastructure building and research at private companies.

Ultimately, the CCP has final say in S&T policy formulation, as it does in virtually all matters in China. Although the CCP Central Committee does not set S&T policy directly, it does maintain a significant level of influence through the state "leading group" mechanism. A Leading Group usually is set up within the State Council to tackle issues involved with large-scale planning involving more than one government agency to mobilize resources and coordinate efforts. Its chairperson is likely to be a vice premier or higher-level figure who also belongs to the CCP Central Committee Politburo or its Standing Committee—China's de facto governing body. Given the importance attached to "strengthening the nation through science, technology, and education" (*kejiao xingguo*), China's S&T policy has became a national development strategy since the mid-1990s, and the State Leading Group for Science, Technology, and Education has been led by the premier. A vice premier or a state councilor runs the day-to-day operations of the Leading Group, which is also composed of the chiefs of the leading science, education, and economic agencies from MOST, NDRC, MOE, MOA, MOH, MIIT, MOEP, COSTIND, and MOF; the presidents of CAS and CAE; and a deputy secretary-general from the State Council. Many of the bureaucrats working at this level are scientists or engineers by training.

The State Leading Group for Science, Technology, and Education is responsible for studying and reviewing the nation's strategy and key policies, discussing and reviewing major tasks and programs related to these three areas, and coordinating important issues related to science education involving agencies under the State Council and regions. The Leading Group appears to be highly influential in setting the nation's science, technology, and education policy. It meets several times a year, usually prior to major national policy announcements or conferences, to discuss critical issues the nation faces in science and education, and to approve important initiatives and programs. The Leading Group also has invited high-ranking scientists to update its members and the State Council on "hot" science, technology, and education related topics, including nanotechnology.

The Leading Group led the drafting of the *Medium- to Long-Term Plan for the Development of Science and Technology* (MLP), the document that calls for China to become an "innovation-oriented society" by 2020 and a world leader in science and technology by 2050. Soon after Wen Jiabao assumed the premiership at the tenth National People's Congress in March 2003, he convened a Leading Group meeting on May 30 to accelerate the drafting of the MLP. Premier Wen also chaired the Leading Group of the MLP and presided over a series of meetings to review the issues in 2004 and 2005. The CCP Central Committee Politburo approved the MLP in late June 2005. In February 2006, the State Council formally issued the MLP, presumably after intensive negotiations between governmental agencies, especially on large-scale science and engineering programs, each of which may require some billion RMB. In

May 2006, Premier Wen convened another Leading Group meeting to discuss how to implement the MLP, after which the State Council issued a series of detailed measures to be carried out by various government agencies.

A central theme of the MLP is that China can afford to invest previously un-imagined sums of money in developing science and technology that might produce long-range breakthroughs that could significantly change the scientific landscape and bring about major economic benefit. However, given its limited financial and human resources, it is impossible for China to launch an effort on all fronts; instead, the MLP concluded China should "do what it needs and attempt nothing where it does not" (*you suo wei, you suo bu wei*).[6] China arguably has little choice but to be se-lective in supporting research endeavors that will concentrate and best utilize scarce resources. The challenge is how to make the right choices that not only embrace a globally competitive strategy of S&T development but also leverage China's existing advantages to realize its potential.

While MOST has the mandate to manage China's S&T initiatives, it is not the only government ministry that plays a significant role in making and implementing China's S&T policy. According to some estimates, MOST controls only about 15 percent of R&D expenditures appropriated by the Chinese government, which means other government agencies are as important as—if not more important than—MOST in planning, budgeting, and organizing S&T and R&D activities.

The strategy of limiting the resources funneled through MOST might well be a way to manage the risks of a highly centralized strategy. If the Chinese government chooses to prioritize the wrong area, the choice would be highly detrimental. For example, Japan made that mistake when the government over-invested in the fifth generation computer program in the 1980s. In other words, if the areas most critical to the basic scientific breakthrough are not the four—protein science, quantum research, nanotechnology, and development and reproductive biology—chosen for the bulk of government funding, not only would China be wasting enormous amounts of resources—both financial and human—and missing a new scientific revolution, the nation would also be trapped at its current level of S&T development for a prolonged period.

In fact, some Chinese scientists—especially those working overseas, who presum-ably had a better understanding of how science is "supposed to work"—were critical of MOST's approach of picking champions. Unhappy with the way that MOST organized the State High-Tech Research and Development Program (also known as the 863 Program)[7] and the State Key Basic Research and Development Program (also known as the 973 Program), whose achievements were viewed by some as in-commensurate with the amount of investment, skeptical scientists proposed limiting MOST's power or even dissolving MOST and replacing it with an Office of Science and Technology under the premier that would be responsible for formulating China's S&T policy only.[8] They also campaigned to divert MOST's funding power to mission-oriented government agencies and to increase funding to NSFC, which has been doing relatively well in administering resources for basic research in China. As it turns out, the opinions of overseas scientists and engineers were not taken seriously in the final deliberation (Cao, Suttmeier, and Simon 2006).[9]

Nevertheless, the fact that MOST controls only about 15 percent of R&D funds means that it has to persuade other agencies to endorse its priorities. The ongoing conversation among officials at different agencies provides a kind of check on the risks that MOST might be wasting its resources on a technological dead end.

China's Approach: A Hybrid Model

As a state-centered economy, China is trying to drive nanotechnology development from the top through large government investments. As early as 2001, addressing an international forum on nanomaterials, President Jiang Zemin stated explicitly that "the development of nanotechnology and new materials should be regarded as an important task of the development and innovation in S&T. The development and application of nanomaterials and nanotechnology is of strategic significance to the development of high technology and national economy in China" (NIBC 2006).

However, it is a mistake to see the Chinese model as exclusively top-down. China's approach is a hybrid model blending different government agencies, market forces (Xu 2006), and input from large and growing scientific and professional communities. In nanotechnology, this includes the physicists and chemists who have long worked in such areas as carbon nanotubes and nanopowders, the applied scientists and engineers who are transforming nanomaterials into commercial products, and an emerging group of entrepreneurs and venture capitalists who are concerned about bringing new nano-enabled products to the market.[10]

To be sure, each group has its own agenda. But the complex ties among these different communities of scientists, engineers, and businesspeople provide critical feedback that guides government policymakers. Moreover, the pressure for coordination among different levels of government (central, provincial, and local) and different government agencies ensures that promising technological directions are validated by multiple actors. These governmental actors have different agendas and incentive structures, and as a result nanotechnology projects are subject to conflicting and sometimes contradictory performance criteria. There is a division of labor in what and how they fund projects (e.g., people, equipment, cheap land, tax reductions). They also tend to have very different time horizons and attitudes toward financial risk. As one moves from central to provincial to local levels of government funding, the time horizon for return on investment becomes shorter, and there is a tendency to move from intangible (basic research) to tangible (commercial products) results. At the local level especially, government officials expect a quick turnaround in terms of technological development and market applications (Cheng 2007).

While the biggest individual grants come from MOST, NSFC provides many smaller grants (roughly equivalent to $30,000–$45,000 over three years), which are administered using objective and universal criteria. CAS also supports nanotechnology initiatives, but it has a more diversified funding philosophy than MOST. So even within the central government's support for R&D in China, there is a mixture of strategies that combines MOST's directed approach with CAS's bottom-up efforts.[11] Provincial governments also play a significant role, both in provinces containing the major cities (such as Beijing and Shanghai) and also in provinces such as Zhejiang, which neighbors Shanghai, that hope to promote their regional universities as major players by setting up collaborative university science centers. (Zhejiang, for example, has partnered with UCLA to set up the Zhejiang-California International Nanosystems Institute, although with mixed results.) Finally, local governments also play a key role, particularly in major cities (e.g., the Shanghai Nanotechnology Promotion Center and the Suzhou Industrial Park). Both provincial and local governments can also partner with foreign investors, as with the China-Singapore Suzhou Industrial Park Development Corporation.

The areas chosen for the largest public investments in technology and engineering, alongside basic science, mentioned above, are those that address the most pressing challenges facing China in agriculture, the environment, population, health, and national defense. Within nanotechnology, China plans to focus on those nanomaterials and nanodevices that promise the most immediate payoff in addressing such immediate problems as air and water purification, materials with great tensile strength that can be used in a variety of industrial applications, as well as targeted drug delivery. China is already a world leader in the production of carbon nanotubes, for example (Fan 2007). According to Liu Zhongfan, professor of physical chemistry at Peking University, "China is far better now than it was ten years ago—more people are working here and more [and better] instrumentation is appearing in China … policymakers are beginning to understand that nanodevices are actually the most important part of nanotechnology, not synthesis or incorporation" (Liu 2006).

The support of China's political leadership for nanotechnology has been bolstered with a push from leading scientists both inside and outside of China. CAS executive vice president Bai Chunli, a pioneer and champion of nanotechnology research in China, has been an alternate member of the CCP Central Committee, whose lecture to the Politburo and the State Council in 2000 was deemed influential.[12] Yet China did not realize how valuable nanotechnology could be to both science and the economy until much later than other, more technologically advanced countries. When they finally did, the fact that countries such as the United States had formulated national nanotechnology initiatives made it easier for Chinese scientists to make their case to the scientific and political leadership. Xie Sishen, who now heads up the National Center for Nanoscience and Technology in Beijing, explained to us in an interview that well-respected foreign scientists suggested to Jiang Zemin, Hu Jintao, and others that nanotechnology was worth paying attention to. In meetings with Chinese officials, "governments around the world and delegations from other countries, especially those from advanced countries, frequently mentioned nanotechnology," Xie Sishen said. Their "exchanges and collaborations" on the subject "provided information continuously, which made the Government realize its importance from pure basic research to application to impacts on economy and society" (Xie 2007a).

The connection of Chinese scientists to the international nanotechnology community, and especially to Chinese-origin nanoscientists and engineers overseas, has helped China move toward the frontier of international nanotechnology research. Chinese nanotechnology researchers have thus far achieved some impressive results, especially in nanomaterials. Furthermore, returnees and exchanges with overseas Chinese scholars have brought new ideas into the laboratory, along with increased participation by Chinese scientists and engineers in international exchanges, widespread international collaborations, and attendance at high-level symposiums (Xie 2007a).

The Chinese effort relies on a variety of different programs. The 973 Program of MOST is dedicated to fundamental research, the 863 Program (also of MOST) funds applied research, while the Industrialization Support Plan (also of MOST) supports projects in the initial stages of industrialization.

CAS positions itself in the national nanotech landscape by conducting cutting-edge research and turning out capable students to join the effort. NSFC awards grants to the best projects and researchers with the potential to achieve a breakthrough at the frontier of international research, as judged by peer review. As of summer 2007, there were some 670 ongoing projects with "nano" in the title, totaling RMB800 million (roughly $115 million), accounting for 8 percent of the NSFC total budget (Li 2007). Most of these were relatively small grants (RMB300,000, approximately $43,000) for three years of project funding, in such areas as nanomechanics, novel nanostructures, quantum dots, carbon nanotubes, and novel cancer and gene therapies.

For actual industrialization projects, usually the central and local Commission of Development and Reform provides funding. However, usually the commission only provides 15 percent of the total funding needed to set up the company—85 percent has to be raised by the potential company before it has even been formed. Sometimes these funds are provided by provincial or local levels of government. But this division is not rigorously observed; leading nanotechnology scientists and institutions are likely to receive funding from many available sources, which then outsource or subcontract the projects.

In the first two years of the MLP implementation, twenty-two institutions have been selected to lead twenty-nine projects (Table 11.2). Of those, twelve are CAS institutes, including the Chinese University of Science and Technology and the National Center for Nano Science and Technology (NCNST), which are also CAS affiliates; the rest are key (*zhongdian*) universities, with the CAS Institute of Chemistry, Beijing University, the CAS Institute of Physics, NCNST, and Tsinghua University having more than one project. Beijing, Shanghai, Jiangsu, and Anhui stand out as the leading centers of nanotechnology, and well-known nanotech scientists, such as Jiang Lei at the CAS Institute of Chemistry, Peng Lianmao and Liu Zhongfan at Beijing University, Li Yadong at Tsinghua University, Yang Hui at the CAS Suzhou Institute of Nano-Tech and Nano-Bionics, among others, are among the chief scientists leading the efforts. The projects are in the categories of nanomaterials, devices and electronics, biology and medicine, and characterization and structure.

While it remains to be seen whether the projects selected will contribute to China's ability to leapfrog in nanotechnology, it is not clear that the resource allocation is sufficient to accomplish the program's ambitious goals. The first two-year fund of RMB262 million ($38 million) has been allocated for the twenty-nine projects, which presumably are composed of researchers from more than one institution. Even when one adjusts for China's different costs structure, the funding intensity for each project—less than RMB5 million per year on average ($721,000)—is not generous. Also of concern is how scientists working on different projects collaborate with each other to generate

Table 11.2 Nanotechnology Projects under the MLP (2006–2007)

Leading Institution	Location	Number of projects	Funding (RMB million)
Dongnan University	Jiangsu	1	4.9
Chinese University of Science and Technology	Anhui	1	4.8
CAS Shanghai Institute of Applied Physics	Shanghai	1	11.2
CAS Shanghai Institute of Microsystems and Information Technology	Shanghai	1	14.0
CAS Institute of Chemistry	Beijing	3	35.5
CAS Institute of Semiconductor	Beijing	1	4.6
CAS Hefei Institute of Physical Science	Anhui	1	13.6
CAS Institute of Physics	Beijing	2	13.3
CAS Technical Institute of Physics and Chemistry	Beijing	1	5.0
CAS Institute of Theoretical Physics	Beijing	1	9.0
CAS Institute of Metal Research	Liaoning	1	5.8
Sun Yat-sen University	Guangdong	1	11.7
Beijing University	Beijing	3	31.3
Beijing University of Aeronautics and Astronautics	Beijing	1	9.3
Nanjing University	Jiangsu	1	8.7
Nankai University	Tianjin	1	4.8
Sichuan University	Sichuan	1	10.8
National Center for Nano Science and Technology	Beijing	2	16.2
Fudan University	Shanghai	1	11.2
Wuhan University	Hubei	1	5.5
Tsinghua University	Beijing	2	17.3
CAS Suzhou Institute of Nano-Tech and Nano-Bionics	Jiangsu	1	13.6
Total		29	261.8

synergy and what benchmarks will be used to evaluate the first two-year performance and determine continuous funding. It would be useful to know how these projects have been selected and whether scientists were on equal footing in the process. Although under the MLP, the projects are supposed to be oriented to basic research, some deal with applied nanotechnology. There are further questions about how they are related to other MOST-administered programs related to nanotechnology, especially the 863 Program and the Torch Program, which are focused on high-tech industrialization, and presumably led in some cases by the same chief scientists.[13]

Private Capital: A Limited Resource

In our focus on the developmental state in China, we have not directly addressed the role of private capital, in part because it has not been a large one. Because the bulk of nanotechnology's global commercial promise lies in the future, commercialization prospects remain limited. Nonetheless, we can offer some preliminary thoughts on the role of market investments, based on our research to date. These include centralized investments by large vertically integrated multinationals, various forms of network-based international collaborations, and small-scale start-ups that focus on commercial products.

Multinationals. A great deal of attention has been given to the more than 1,000 R&D centers that have been established by foreign-invested enterprises, including some multinationals, in China during the past decade. In many cases, these R&D centers seem much closer to the *D* of development (e.g., localization and debugging of products) than the *R* of research. However, the Microsoft Research Asia, formerly Microsoft Research China, in Beijing has been touted as "the Bell Labs of China" for its pioneering research activities (Buderi and Huang 2006), and IBM, General Electric, Siemens, and other top multinationals are also implementing innovative projects in China. Lynn and Salzman (2007a) make the case that significant innovation is taking place in emerging economies, but often this is in the form of process innovations rather than functional products.

International collaborations. There are many forms of international collaboration, including formal institutional partnerships between universities and corporations; university study abroad programs, particularly postgraduate degrees earned by Chinese in the United States, Japan, and Europe; exploiting ethnic ties, most notably by recruiting overseas Chinese scientists and engineers to return to China; and development of informal personal ties, as when American professors or business leaders mentor their former graduate students after they return to China. Universities are an important component of China's nanotechnology initiative because it is first and foremost a science-based program.[14]

Entrepreneurial initiatives, such as small firm start-up. In business terms, the "valley of death" refers to the transitional period between basic R&D for a new technology (technology creation)—typically supported by public funding and commercialization—and when a marketable product attracts private sector support. In China, the valley is long and deep. State-run firms—which still account for an estimated 43 percent of GDP, despite China's commitment to privatization—tend to be bureaucratic and conservative, shunning potentially risky investments in favor of short-term, more predictable returns.[15] The emerging private sector, including many small and medium enterprises (SMEs), remains small, undercapitalized, and generally risk-averse. This poses a challenge for the Chinese government's heightened emphasis on leapfrogging development through nanotechnology, whose major payback remains ten or more years in the future. The amount of money allocated from Beijing for nanotechnology is not large by international standards (Xie 2007b), although it is difficult to accurately estimate total public spending for nanotechnology in China, given the wide range of funding sources and the difficulty of defining what qualifies as nanotechnology. Consequently estimates vary widely, ranging from as little as $230 million for the five-year period 2000–2004 (Bai 2005, 63), to $160 million in 2005 alone (Bai and Wang 2007, 75), to $250 million in that same year (Holman et al. 2007, 25). Although even the highest figures are still considerably less than the United States is publicly investing (as noted previously, $1.5 billion in 2008), China's government spending on nanotechnology may not be far off when adjusted for differences in labor and infrastructure costs (nanotechwire.com 2005).

Throughout our interviews, the most pervasive theme to emerge was the importance of government funding and support for nanotechnology throughout the value chain, not only for basic research but well into commercialization. Esther Levy, editor of the journal *Advanced Materials*, who has reviewed numerous submissions to her journal by Chinese scientists, saw the question of government funding as key: "The Chinese are very hard working. As long as the government keeps funding them, they will progress. The question is, will the government funding be patient long enough"? (Levy 2006) As one interviewee commented, "There is a saying in China that those who do research on atomic bombs (*yuanzi dan*) don't make as much as those who sell tea eggs (*chaye dan*)" (Xu 2006). He noted that this situation has to change, since economic returns (rather than pure patriotism) will be required if China is to achieve its high-tech aspirations. Another informant—an academician with the Chinese Academy of Engineering and chairman of China's Desalination and Water Reuse Society—explained the challenges of developing seawater filtration that employs nanotechnology, a NSFC-funded project that has yielded promising results in the laboratory:[16]

> However, it is a little hard to estimate the timeframe for industrializing the new process. China Water Tech is currently working on optimizing the process. And speed for it to move to industrialization will depend on government funding and industrial interest. Government funding is usually not at all enough to industrialize a technological process, industrial involvement is crucial. However, larger scale demonstration of this process needs to be done (likely via government funding) before industry would become interested. (Gao 2006)

At the local level, various forms of incubation play a key role. For the Beijing region, the Nanotechnology Industrialization Base of China Entrepreneurship Investment Co. (NIBC)—located 100 kilometers from Beijing in the Tianjin Economic and Technological Development Area—serves this role. NIBC was established by MOST in December 2000, in conjunction with CAS, universities, and private enterprises. Its distinguishing feature is that it is essentially "a government organization run by market forces," reflecting the belief that

> pure state ownership does not work well for technology innovation or management.... What the NIBC does is to take results from universities and institutes, and help scientists to commercialize the results. It takes a systematic approach that goes to the end of the commercialization pipeline.[17]

NIBC is the vehicle for incubating new companies, acquiring existing companies, and preparing initial public offerings. In 2005, the Chinese National Academy of Nanoscience and Engineering (CNANE) was established under the same administration as NIBC with a primary focus on R&D rather than commercialization. It is unclear to us how large a role these institutions actually play; during our visit in 2006, the principal operation we observed was the manufacturing of non-nano pharmaceuticals, as a form of income generation for the facility.

Shanghai has its own incubator in the form of the Shanghai Nanotechnology Promotion Center (SNPC), which is funded largely by government initiative, particularly the Shanghai municipal government as well as the NDRC, although local enterprises have also contributed.[18] It was founded in July 2000, with the center's formal activities starting in 2001. SNPC is subordinate to the Science and Technology Commission, the lead government agency in Shanghai concerned with advancing the city's high-tech profile. The SNPC provides training for scientists and engineers on the specialized instruments used in nanoscale research and has several university-affiliated industrialization bases for the purpose of transferring research on nanomaterials and nanoparticles to the estimated 100–200 SMEs reportedly engaged in nano-related R&D in the Shanghai area. Roughly a third of its twenty-five-person staff members are science and engineering professionals.

The center's main focus is to promote commercialization. This is achieved in various ways: by funding basic application research;[19] through a research platform designed to help with the commercialization process; through the provision of nano materials testing; through the hosting of workshops and international conferences on nanotechnology; and through education (including a certificate program) and outreach to raise public awareness about nanotechnology. As an incubator, the SNPC provides services for start-ups before and as they enter the market—services that include legal advice for establishing a company, a variety of technology-related services, and help with marketing products.[20] The center also loans out lab and office space as well as a testing center that provides the costly equipment required for nanomaterials characterization—equipment that most start-ups could not afford. It currently supports some seventy to eighty companies, of which perhaps half are nano-related, with grants ranging from RMB50,000 for smaller projects to RMB1 million for large ones.

While there is some private industry investment in nanotechnology (local examples include limited investments by Baosteel and Shanghai Electronics), local government funding plays a key role in China. During our visit to the SNPC, we saw a number of examples of such support—private firms housed within the center's complex that receive public funding as well as access to center support and services.

Three examples are illustrative. The Shanghai Sunrise Chemical Company, which employs about eighty people making nanocoatings and nanophoto catalysts, received two-fifths of its initial capitalization of RMB5 million ($721,000) from government sources. The Shanghai NML Nanotechnology Company develops antibacterial and photo catalysts for use in textiles and plastics. Last year they began exporting the final products employing their materials (such as coffee cups that use nanopowders) to the United States and Australia. While the company has not received money from SNPC, it does have access to the center's training and information services. One final example is the Shanghai AJ Nano-Science Development Company, which manufactures atomic and scanning tunneling microscopes, two key instruments used in nanotechnology. AJ Nanoscience's principal funding comes from the Shanghai Aijian Trust Investment Company, a Chinese firm with significant Hong Kong ownership that invests in SMEs.[21] The company gets public support as well: it receives funding from the

Shanghai municipal government for R&D, relies on technology developed initially in the CAS Institute of Applied Physics, and has some projects with the Shanghai branch of CAS.[22] AJ Nanoscience, which was established in 2001, reportedly has 60 percent of the domestic market in its area of instrumentation—although the market is dominated by international players such as the U.S.-based Veeco Instruments.[23]

Shanghai's city government also supports the Climbing Mountain (*Dengshan*) Action Plan, which provides dedicated funding for joint projects that must be led by companies in collaboration with an academic partner. Within the plan, most work is contracted between university researchers and engineers/business partners from companies. The plan specifically earmarks funding for nanotechnology, with projects divided between basic and applied research intended for nanotechnology commercialization (Jia 2006). In Shanghai, as is typical of funding at the local level, the government provides funding for local players and for local collaboration with foreign companies such as Unilever (Li and Wang 2006). At the provincial and local levels, government funding is trying to make up for the weakness of funding from private capital (Li, Shi, and Min 2006).

Conclusion: China's Developmental State

China's dedication to high-tech growth is evident in its policies supporting efforts to leapfrog development through targeted science megaprojects in nanotechnology, development and reproductive biology, protein science, and quantum research. As we have shown, China's approach to nanotechnology is heavily state centered, with public investment originating at all levels of government, and ranging from support for basic research to funding intended to promote commercialization. Given China's relative lack of private business funding for commercialization, government at various levels has sought to pick up the slack, providing funding to get technological breakthroughs into the marketplace.

The Chinese model represents a complex mixture of centralized and decentralized elements. For example, the Chinese Academy of Sciences Knowledge Innovation Program (KIP, which is funded largely through the 973 Program) is typically treated as an example of decentralized influence of the scientific community, but it involves a significant amount of centralized targeting within the academy. The existence of multiple and overlapping funding sources introduces a significant element of decentralization where multiple agencies are reviewing the efforts of key scientists and institutes. Finally, we have seen that local and provincial governments and decentralized incubators play a central role in supporting the commercialization process.

Whether China's efforts to achieve first-mover status in nanotechnology are successful remains to be seen. Whether there will be any large-scale payoff also remains an outstanding issue in the future development of nanotechnology-enabled market applications. But one thing seems to be clear: nanotechnology in China is still largely in the stage of basic research, as is the case with most nanotechnology research outside of China as well. However, China has clearly shown itself to be very committed to adding high-tech initiatives like nanotechnology to its top national priorities, thereby showing the dynamism of its contemporary developmental state.

Notes

This material is based on work supported by the National Science Foundation grant no. SES 0531184. Any opinions, findings, and conclusions or recommendations expressed in this material are those of the authors and do not necessarily reflect the views of the National Science Foundation. It was conducted under the auspices of the UCSB Center for Nanotechnology in Society (www.cns.ucsb.edu).

   1. In 2004, SBIR and STTR awards totaled $61.4 million; in 2005 the amount was $63.1 million; in 2006, $86.6 million; and in 2007, $82.7 million. While funding in 2007 came from nine agencies (DOD, NSF, DOE, NIH, NASA, NIST, EPA, NIOSH, and USDA), 81 percent came from the first five in this list (U.S. NNI 2008f, 12).

   2. The principal vehicle for NSF funding (as of October 2008) has been fifteen nanoscale science and engineering centers (NSECs) on fifteen university campuses, and twenty-two university-based materials research science and engineering centers (MRSECs), four of which are fully dedicated to nanotechnology research, with eighteen having one or more nanotechnology research groups. The DOE has nanoscale science research centers at five national laboratories (Argonne, Lawrence Berkeley, Sandia/Los Alamos, Brookhaven, and Oak Ridge). For a complete listing (and websites) of NNI centers, networks, and facilities, see www.nano.gov/html/centers/nnicenters.html.

   3. According to the report, "critical barriers to nanotechnology commercialization include the ten year cycle time from science results in a laboratory to a commercial product … the gap between researcher and applied scientists; the gap in funding between basic research and applied research; a lack of understanding that for every dollar invested in basic research almost $100 is required for a commercially viable product, and a list of constraints including, time to patent, uncertainty of potential regulations by EPA, OSHA, FDA; and the high risk of new scientific results becoming commercially viable…. It appears that start-up nanotechnology related companies are struggling to realize revenues and most are not at the breakeven point" (McNeil et al. 2007, 10–11).

   4. Cong Cao (2004); Cao and Simon (2009); Suttmeier, Cao, and Simon (2006b).

   5. While the 1995 conference did not formally use the term "indigenous innovation," it did call for an increased capacity "to create technology indigenously and master key industrial technologies and systems design technologies" (section 4, as reported in U.S. 1996). At the same time it also stated that "while developing scientific and technological capabilities primarily on our indigenous efforts, adequate attention should also be assigned to the acquisition and assimilation of foreign technology. On the basis of equality and mutual benefit, a significantly greater level of international S & T cooperation and exchange through official, non-governmental, bilateral and multilateral channels should be vigorously assumed" (PRC 2003).

   6. This theme was taken from the then CCP general secretary Jiang Zemin's report to the fifteenth CCP Congress in 1997, which reads, "We should formulate a long-term plan for the development of science from the needs of long-range development of the country, taking a panoramic view of the situation, emphasizing key points, *doing what we need and attempting nothing where we do not*, strengthening fundamental research, and accelerating the transformation of achievements from high-tech research into industrialization" (emphasis added). This was in turn adapted from the May 1995 decision of the CCP and the State Council to push

forward China's S&T progress, although the wording was slight different: "catching up what we need and attempting nothing where we do not" (*you suo gan, you suo bu gan*).

7. The 863 Program was seen as a key vehicle for improving China's high-tech competitiveness, through the development of six advanced technologies selected as central to promoting economic growth: electronics, supercomputers, telecommunications, avionics, GPS, and nanotechnology (MOST-863 2001; Larson 2004).

8. The 973 Program sought "to strengthen the original innovations and to address the important scientific issues concerning the national economic and social development at a deeper level and in a wider scope, so as to improve China's capabilities of independent innovations and to provide scientific support for the future development of the country" (MOST-973 2004).

9. In recent years, MOST has been criticized for its inaction in handling misconduct in scientific research in China. The appointment of Wan Gang, a non-CCP member, as the minister of science and technology in April 2007, bypassing another non-CCP member high-ranking vice minister, seems to signal the importance of non-CCP members in government and indicate that the government may not be satisfied with MOST leadership, and in turn the progress of Chinese science, in spite of the large sums of money going into it. They may want someone with no previous relations with the ministry to bring in new ways of thinking and management.

10. Nanotubes are a form of carbon with unusual tensile strength that gives it potential for a variety of industrial uses. Nanopowders are extremely fine forms of elements such as iron that are believed to have considerable potential as a catalytic agent in fuel cells.

11. Many CAS members privately report that this is a "top design" (*ding ceng she ji*) approach, originating under the initiative of Lu Yongxiang, who was president of CAS in 1998 (for a discussion of CAS and the Knowledge Innovation Program, see Suttmeier, Cao, and Simon 2006a, b).

12. Bai, executive vice president of CAS with the rank of a full minister, is in line to succeed Lu Yongxiang as president. But Bai, an alternate member of the CCP Central Committee since the fifteenth CCP Congress in 1997, was not promoted to full member in the seventeenth CCP Congress, concluded in 2007, while Lu not only kept his full membership (which is rare as he is over 65, the age limit for being a full member) but also started his third term as CAS president in March 2008.

13. The Torch Program is intended to produce high-tech products involving new materials, biotechnology, electronic information, integrative mechanical-electrical technology, and advanced and energy-saving technology—products that have commercial potential for both Chinese and foreign markets. It involves, among other things, the creation of high-tech industrial development zones.

14. Why should we consider international collaboration as a form of market investment in high-tech development? If we view nanotechnology as a value chain that has distinctive governance structures, then international collaborations may be a form of relational governance, which has different characteristics than hierarchies (vertical firms) and markets (entrepreneurial start-ups). "Captive" and "modular" forms of governance, which complete the fivefold global value chains typology, may also have analogs in nanotechnology (Gereffi et al. 2005).

15. OECD, *Policy Brief: China's Governance in Transition* (September) (www.oecd.org/dataoecd/49/13/35312075.pdf). In 1997 President Jiang Zemin called for privatization (*feigongyou,* or "nonpublic ownership") of state-owned enterprises (SOEs), a plan that was ratified by the ninth National People's Congress the following year.

16. Gao is one of the founders of membrane technology in China. He introduced the term "nanofiltration" to China in 1993.

17. Handout from NIBC, August 3, 2006.

18. Information was obtained during interviews at the SNPC with Li Xiaoli (project manager), Shi Liyi, and Min Guoquan (August 7, 2006), and with Zhu Simon (SNPC Chinese Industry Association for Antimicrobial Materials & Products; Shanghai NML Nanotechnology Co.), Zhang Bo (Shanghai AJ Nano-Science Development Co.), and Fu Lefeng (Shanghai Sunrise Chemical Co.), (August 3, 2007).

19. For example, we were told that SNPC helped fund and manage a project involving the use of atomic force microscope tips to locate DNA molecules that involved CAS and Shanghai Jiao Tong University, which was featured on the cover of *Nano Letters*.

20. The SNPC has three incubators, each associated with a university: one affiliated with Shanghai University, and two with the Hua Dong Science and Technology University (East China University of Science and Technology).

21. Hong Kong Mingli Co. bought more than 40 percent of Shanghai Aijian Trust Co. in 2004, signaling greater openness to foreign investors on the part of Chinese trust companies. See Zhao 2005.

22. We were told that when profits are realized, they are shared with CAS members who created the technology.

23. AJ Nano-Science's instruments typically sell for roughly one-quarter the price of their foreign counterparts. Interview with Zhang Bo, manager of Research and Production Department, Shanghai AJ Nano-Science Development Co., August 3, 2007.

CHAPTER 12

Everyone an Innovator

John A. Alic

To prosper in this century as it did in the last, the United States will have to maintain its innovation lead. Too often in policy discussions, innovation is taken to mean technological innovation stemming from research and development, or even from scientific research alone. In fact, many economically significant innovations have little or nothing to do with R&D or even with technology as usually pictured. Rather than unidirectional progression from origins in invention or discovery, the general process is multidirectional and multidimensional. Large numbers of people contribute, not just engineers, scientists, and entrepreneurs, especially to the multitude of improvements in product performance and reductions in cost that, for many goods and services, make all the difference between commercial success and marketplace failure. Radical innovations too sometimes emerge, not from singular acts of invention or discovery but from complex social processes that, in effect, integrate large numbers of incremental contributions, as illustrated so dramatically by the Internet. Because innovation bubbles up through organizations, often from deep within them, with heterogeneous contributions from heterogeneous employees, almost everyone is a prospective innovator. Thus by broadening and deepening the pool of workers prepared to contribute, the United States can expand its innovative capacity.

The chapter explores these themes with the aid of a considerable range of examples, many drawn from digital electronics and systems (e.g., the microprocessor, business information processing) and also from health care, which exemplifies service production in postindustrial economies. Discussion begins with a survey of innovation as a process. The second section turns to comparison between radical innovations, those with notably large impacts on society and the economy, and incremental innovation, the steady stream of more predictable improvements that characterizes the evolutionary development of goods and services of all types. This section makes three essential points. First, radical innovations typically appear as such only in hindsight, the Internet again illustrating. This means, second, that distinctions between incremental and radical innovation have limited usefulness for purposes of forward-looking decision making. Third, in seeking breakthroughs, governments have relatively few policies from which to choose, chiefly support for research and protection for intellectual property (e.g., through patents). Both policies have uncertain outcomes, and intellectual property protection sometimes hinders ongoing innovation. In contrast, governments can draw from a much longer list of policies to foster continuous incremental innovation and can expect continuing gains in productivity from such policies, as illustrated by agriculture during the first half of the twentieth century.

The focus in the next two sections narrows to human capital as a building block—like innovation itself a slippery subject, hard to identify much less measure—beginning with a brief survey of skills and knowledge. While much innovation springs from tacit sources, vaguely apprehended, many innovation skills seem relatively generic, hence broadly distributed. Preconceptions and policies that assume innovations stem from a small number of preternaturally talented or specially trained individuals detract from the broad-based support for learning that is essential if the United States is to continue registering high levels of economic performance.

Since the skills that contribute to innovation remain murky, it is no surprise that their sources do as well. Some originate in education, as pointed out in the fourth section, but much learning is experiential. During the twentieth century, formal education expanded dramatically, becoming the common route to occupational entry. Meanwhile, support structures for informal learning atrophied. Given the rapid accumulation of codified knowledge in fields including engineering and medicine, the transformation in occupational preparation is easy enough to understand. But the consequences of this shift have not been fully appreciated. Continuous learning feeds continuous innovation. Yet institutions for supporting such learning, despite lip service to knowledge-based firms and a knowledge-based economy, are sparse and underdeveloped, in the United States as in other nations. Continuing medical education, a telling example, has been found almost totally ineffectual.

The next half century, the approximate working life of young people in school today, will almost certainly bring changes at least as revolutionary as those of the past half century, when millions of people found themselves learning to use innovations in computing and information technology, the subject of the fifth section of the chapter. Until recently, academic education and training could not hope to keep up with demand for computer specialists, and millions of people learned on their own and on the job to work with IT systems, many of them contributing along the way to innovation. The conclusion follows in straightforward fashion: institutions for supporting informal, experiential learning should be strengthened to foster innovation, international competitiveness, and a future of good jobs for more people. How to accomplish this remains an open question, since the needs are only beginning to be recognized. The first step is to accept that formal education cannot be expected to keep pace with technological, economic, and societal change, and must be supplemented.

Innovation: More Than Technology

After "an employee at Costco Wholesale … noticed that most supermarkets were selling 2¾-pound rotisserie chickens for $7.99," recalled one of the firm's executives, "'we *[handwritten margin notes: "Why innovation matters → Productivity↑", "Schumpeter (20th century)", "economic transaction ← introduction → production"]*

thought we could do better.'" In 2007 Costco sold more than 40 million 3¼-pound chickens at $4.99 each. "State-of-the-art bioengineering?" the executive was asked. "No. You just let them live longer" (Fisher 2008, 66). This may seem a trivial innovation, or no innovation at all, or simply an innovation in marketing. No matter; it points to a principal reason why innovation matters: productivity rises (less labor per pound is needed to raise, slaughter, process, distribute, and market bigger chickens) and consumers get more of what they want for less money. As this example suggests, economically significant innovations have diverse sources, not all of which can or should be characterized as scientific or technological. Within the organizations, private and public, and the networks of organizations that are responsible for innovation, people with many different backgrounds and occupations—sales and marketing personnel, production workers and customer service representatives, technicians and troubleshooters—make wide-ranging contributions.

The perspective of this chapter is fundamentally evolutionary and Schumpeterian. Schumpeter's insights, developed over the first several decades of the twentieth century, have proved remarkably robust. The archetypal Schumpeterian entrepreneur pushes ahead where others hesitate, undeterred by the disruptive or destructive impacts of innovation, which may endanger existing stocks of physical and human capital (adding machines, skills in shorthand), environmental resources (fisheries), or life itself (nuclear weapons). Schumpeter distinguished the entrepreneurial function sharply from invention. "To carry any improvement into effect is a task entirely different from the invention of it…. Although entrepreneurs of course *may* be inventors … they are inventors not by nature of their function but by coincidence and vice versa" (Schumpeter 1934, 88–89). Perhaps more than he recognized, the two functions, at least in the United States, have often been combined in the same person, as in the early years of the auto industry and in Silicon Valley more recently. In any event, commercialization remains the critical step—introducing the innovation into economic transactions, whether an improvement of the innovator's own devising or one bought, borrowed, or stolen from others.

Since the 1950s the Schumpeterian panorama has been almost endlessly elaborated. Many quantitative studies have related measures of economic output (gross domestic product, income per capita, labor productivity) to inputs such as R&D, capital investment, and average levels of education. Although technology and innovation cannot be measured directly, they emerge as high-octane fuel for the economic engine. Variables that can be measured, such as investments in physical capital, explain only a fraction of increases in output, and economists conventionally associate the unexplained residual with technological change. Attributing 35 percent of the increase in labor productivity for the U.S. nonfarm business sector over the period 1959–2006 to growth in total factor productivity, Jorgenson, Ho, and Stiroh (2008, 8) explain that this variable "is defined as the output per unit of both capital and labor inputs and primarily reflects innovations in both products and processes." Of course technology also enters through capital and labor as improvements in production systems and advances in human knowledge and skill.

While such calculations establish the primacy of innovation in economic growth, they reveal little or nothing about the processes through which new technologies emerge and diffuse. Other large literatures address these questions from many perspectives. Two findings have particular relevance for this chapter: feedback from users to innovators strongly affects the pace and direction of technical change, especially incremental change. Less established empirically but also significant: the expansion of service-producing economic sectors attenuates relationships between innovation and R&D spending.

Many types of feedback channels link innovating organizations with immediate customers and end users (Rosenberg 1982; von Hippel 1988). Firms survey consumers, pay attention to evaluations such as those in *Consumer Reports* and to Internet chatter. Customers provide one form of feedback when they defect to rival products, another through warranty claims. After backyard hot-rodders put big engines from big cars in lightweight Fords and Chevrolets during the 1950s, automakers began doing it for them in the 1960s. Airline employees contributed to improvements in jet engine performance by diagnosing in-service failures and devising maintenance and repair methods that extended "time on wing." Employees of the Japanese firm Busicom, the initial customer for Intel's first microprocessor in 1971, contributed to the design of the new chip (Aspray 1997). User groups have long had prominence in computing, users sometimes become innovators themselves (e.g., in development and diffusion of the Linux operating system), and on occasion start their own firms.

In business computing, IBM built a dominant market position by keeping close to customers and tying them to IBM products. IBM sales and service employees learned what firms wanted and often could tell customers what they needed even if they didn't. In the mid-1950s, for instance, IBM commercialized the hard disk drive (HDD) to provide the digital equivalent of storage for business records. The first HDDs sold for around $50,000 and held roughly fifty megabits of data (50 x 106 binary bits) on an assemblage of fifty disks, each two feet in diameter, housed in an enclosure the size of a jukebox. Today the majority of the 500 million HDDs sold each year cost $10 or less and store 100 gigabits (1012 bits) or more on a disk slightly over an inch in diameter. In terms of storage density (bits per square inch), performance has increased by 100 million times over five decades. In terms of cost or price per unit of storage capacity, the improvement has been still greater.

Rapid continuing gains in HDD performance, which have made possible new classes of semidisposable products such as MP3 players, resulted from ongoing incremental gains interspersed with occasional episodes of more radical change, as illustrated by giant magnetoresistance (GMR), a phenomenon discovered in the 1980s and applied to HDDs in the 1990s (Cho 2007). Depending on vantage point, HDDs incorporating GMR can be considered either a radical or an incremental innovation. GMR appears radical in the sense that a previously unknown magnetic phenomenon led to microstructures that replaced earlier, less dense storage media. It appears incremental in that GMR was simply one more in a fifty-year sequence of technical improvements underlying enormous gains in HDD price-performance ratio. Similar stories can be told about other families of products that depend in one way or another on microelectronics, such as the digital cameras that, in a classic Schumpeterian gale, swept away firms supplying photographic film, cameras, and processing services.

Technological innovations combine preexisting knowledge and precedents with creative insight and, sometimes, new knowledge from R&D. The demanding nature of the U.S. market for high-tech goods and services and the high density of feedback links between innovating firms and "smart customers" is part of the conventional explanation for U.S. advantages in industries such as digital electronics and also for inward direct investment by foreign-owned firms, which expect to learn by competing in the American market. Many observers have taken high U.S. levels of R&D spending, now around $400 billion annually, to be another part of the explanation. It is, but the significance of R&D, a loosely defined accounting category that includes a broad range of activities, not all of which are closely associated with either research and science or with product/process design and development, must be kept in perspective. A longtime observer of managerial practices notes, for example, that "I have seen cases where corporations include in R&D maintenance of equipment ... or quality control expenses ... because it's nice to have large R&D figures on your income statement and auditors are not going to argue with you" (Lev 2005, 564). Whatever firms choose to call R&D ends up in the national statistics, which are based on surveys, and what they don't—including a good deal of technical activity in the very large service sector of the U.S. economy—the surveys necessarily miss.

When a pharmaceutical firm introduces a new drug, the work may have begun many years earlier with the screening of thousands or millions of synthesized compounds, chosen based on some science-based heuristic, followed by laboratory testing of the more promising, and subsequent clinical trials. This is R&D by anyone's definition. When a cosmetics manufacturer introduces a new perfume, it will be a mixture of hundreds or thousands of compounds selected through a process more akin to alchemy than science. That too is counted as R&D. In the United States, automakers and their suppliers spend around $16 billion per year on R&D. Most of this pays for design, development, and testing of new models moving along the product pipeline, and much of the work is pedestrian—designing brackets to hold the catalytic converter in place, writing software for controlling power seats, piling up mileage on test tracks. Automakers and suppliers also do research. In recent years they have spent hundreds of millions of dollars, perhaps billions, on fuel cells. Even so, basic research (as defined by the National Science Foundation, NSF, keeper of the nation's R&D statistics) makes up a small fraction of R&D spending in this as in most industries.[1]

As an accounting category, R&D has relatively recent origins. Although Schumpeter would have been familiar with industrial research as pioneered in the latter part of the nineteenth century by German chemical firms and later by large U.S. manufacturing firms such as DuPont and General Electric, R&D as an umbrella category had not come into common use at the time of his death in 1950. That same year, Congress established NSF, and the new agency shortly began to collect and publish figures on R&D. These soon became the most watched indicators of national technical activity.

Sometimes innovation sprouts directly from research, as with GMR or drugs based on newly synthesized molecules. Other innovations, like Costco's heavyweight chickens, have little or nothing to do with science. The Toyota production system, credited with gains in efficiency and output quality since the 1960s and a part of the template for lean production, works by capturing large numbers of small improvements, many of them devised by factory workers. In effect, Toyota collects and codifies the myriad of shop floor process changes recognized since the 1930s by engineers, managers, and economists as a major source of productivity gains (e.g., as represented by learning curves or experience curves showing the decline in direct labor hours or production costs with cumulative output). Toyota's overarching innovation was to systematize procedures for turning informal, localized knowledge into codified practices that could be transferred to the firm's other factories, whereas the learning earlier inferred as occurring in aircraft plants and shipyards remained tacit and rarely spread beyond the immediate production group. This made Toyota's innovation "radical" and helped make lean production an integral part of what Womack, Jones, and Roos (1991) called "the machine that changed the world."

Similar to the Toyota production system, no new research was required to commercialize the microprocessor. Intel did not even originate the concept. One of the codevelopers recalled, "The idea of a 'CPU [central processing unit] on a chip' had been around since the mid-1960s" (Faggin 1992, 146). Intel's essential task was design: to determine and define product attributes. Design is the core technical activity in the manufacturing sector of the economy. Once attributes have been specified, the job on the production side is to fabricate the product exactly as intended. That is not the case in the service-producing sector.

In contrast to manufactured goods, most service products have no fixed, predetermined identity. With exceptions including fast foods and standardized products in industries such as banking (e.g., money market accounts), attributes are determined during the course of production. They emerge from dialog between the service provider's employees and customers. The dialog is sometimes perfunctory and sometimes entails much interpretation and iteration. Health care, now half again as large as all of U.S. manufacturing, exhibits nearly the entire range of features of service delivery. In psychotherapy, dialog itself is arguably the product. Hospital food service, at an opposite pole, is prepared according to "blueprints" not unlike those in chain restaurants. Clinical care delivery illustrates an elaborated form of what my colleagues and I termed the "interpretive model" of service production (Herzenberg, Alic, and Wial 1998, 85–94). Diagnosis and treatment normally begin with a physician (perhaps preceded by a nurse) querying the patient about his or her medical history, which may be recalled imperfectly, and current symptoms, which may be described vaguely. A competent physician listens with care, perhaps does some coaxing. A good patient will try to be responsive, alert to volunteer information for which the physician fails to ask. Laboratory tests may be ordered, perhaps consultation with specialists. With a diagnosis pointing to some preliminary set of conclusions, the physician devises a plan of treatment. This is subject to modification; an unexpected response may lead to an altered diagnosis. For chronic conditions, monitoring by the physician and reporting by the patient may continue indefinitely, with periodic adjustments in treatment regimen. Production is a microcosm of learning, on both sides. The physician who fails to understand the patient's symptoms may not prescribe appropriate treatment; the patient who fails to understand the physician's diagnosis, hence the reasons for the prescribed regimen, may not follow that regimen. Repeated millions of times, data and information from diagnosis and treatment feed the accumulating steams of knowledge from which flow advances in medical practice labeled as innovations, whether flu remedies or neurosurgery.

Because product definition and production in most parts of the service economy differ fundamentally from goods-producing industries, service-producing enterprises plan, budget, and manage their R&D (or other technical activity; not all service firms employ the term R&D) differently than do manufacturing firms. When NSF began collecting R&D data in the early 1950s, manufacturing's share of U.S. output and employment were at a peak and the big manufacturing firms so prominent in the nation's economy were widely assumed to be the primary driving force for innovation. For many years thereafter both service-producing firms and smaller manufacturing enterprises, only later acclaimed as wellsprings of innovation and job creation, were undersampled in NSF's R&D surveys (since 1957 conducted for the agency by the Census Bureau), while large manufacturing firms were oversampled. Until the 1990s, as a result, NSF reported that nonmanufacturing enterprises (including agriculture and construction along with services) accounted for less than 5 percent of industrial R&D. As the agency began to revise its estimates based on more representative surveys and reclassification of some firms from manufacturing to service-producing industries, estimated R&D by nonmanufacturing firms rose. NSF now puts it at slightly over 30 percent of the total (Wolfe 2008, table 2). Even so, the recent figures attribute most nonmanufacturing R&D to the information and technical services industries, a relatively small part of the service sector; they report only minor contributions from other service industries, which suggests that a good deal of business activity fitting NSF's definitions of R&D continues to be missed. Underestimates of R&D (or its equivalent) in the service sector have helped keep alive the idea that innovation is necessarily associated with science and research of the sort conducted by manufacturing firms.

As Figure 12.1 summarizes, R&D is but one input among many. Innovators are eclectic—hunters and gatherers of information and insights—and make use of knowledge from many other sources too. (As drawn, Figure 12.1 applies only to the manufacturing sector; it would be busier still if expanded to include services.) Innovating organizations may need skills in engineering design or industrial design (not the same thing), in conceiving an advertising campaign, in divining the unexpressed desires of teenagers or corporate purchasing agents. R&D statistics provide a useful indicator, but complementary measures are needed for mapping any sort of knowledge economy. To this point, development of such indicators has not advanced very far, though more so in Europe than in the United States (Metcalfe and Miles 2000).

Continuous Innovation and Radical Change

Despite Schumpeter's stress on creative destruction and the many studies it inspired, little more is known about the sources of radical innovation today than when he wrote. While discrete inventions (the telephone) and scientific discoveries (nuclear fission)

Figure 12.1 Knowledge Sources and Flows in Innovation, Manufacturing Industries

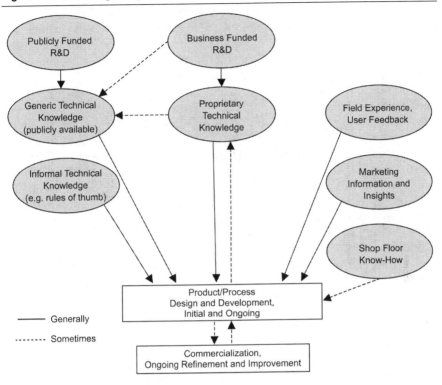

sometimes initiate major bursts of technological and societal change, in other cases radical innovations spring from incremental advances. Rather than being sparked by an immediately precipitating event, continuous incremental innovations coalesce, like ice crystallizing from water, to yield something fundamentally new and different. That is how the Internet came to be, as three distinct and largely independent technological streams came together, in microelectronics, software, and fiber-optic communications.

Digital computers themselves arose through the combination of multiple innovations; the closest thing to a discrete act of invention was perhaps von Neumann's 1945 exposition of stored program logic. On the other hand, highly touted breakthroughs sometimes lead to little. High-temperature superconductivity, discovered in 1986 and widely expected to revolutionize electric power technologies, has yet to exit the laboratory except for small-scale demonstrations. Lasers found early niche applications, such as eye surgery, but did not break out until the commercialization of semiconductor diode lasers nearly two decades after early demonstrations of lasing. Video phones flopped when introduced in the 1960s, while mobile telephony found acceptance beyond all expectations from the very beginning. As these examples suggest, uncertainty is endemic to innovation. In the early days of computing, IBM managers failed to anticipate rates of technical improvement and the scope of prospective applications; they expected worldwide demand to total a few dozen machines. Intel technical and marketing personnel were a little more optimistic about their newly commercialized microprocessor, projecting sales of only a few thousand units per year.

Hoping for the next breakthrough, critics of government and commentators on business sometimes dismiss incremental policies and strategies, portraying them as stodgy and unimaginative—a matter of small bets on small innovations. Instead, they urge bold spending on projects that promise huge rewards if they pay off. Those who urge taking on more risk in national R&D portfolios argue, based on opinion (and the complaints of scientists who can't get funding for their ideas) more than evidence (there isn't much), that existing portfolios are excessively conservative. The proposition cannot be tested, even retrospectively. There is also a more fundamental concern: the collection of available technology and innovation policies includes few measures that target radical innovation—chiefly basic research and patent protection (Table 12.1). Basic research usually results in incremental advances. And while an invention must demonstrate novelty to be awarded a patent, that is no promise of significance: most patents end up protecting minor variations on existing themes. Patent policy, furthermore, aims to balance the harm caused by a grant of monopoly rights to the inventor, an imponderable, against the spur to further innovation stemming from public disclosure of the invention, intended to encourage others to invent around the patent, another imponderable. The effects of patent policy are thus equivocal as well as uncertain: strong patent protection can deter further innovation. In any case, the United States already provides far more government funding for basic research than other nations and strong protection for intellectual property. It is the other policy categories, intended to encourage incremental innovation, that have been neglected.

The middle columns in Table 12.1 indicate whether each of sixteen policy tools is suited to fostering radical innovation, incremental innovation, or both. Only one policy, prizes (number 11 in the table), targets major innovations exclusively and it is new, untried, and limited to innovations that are not too radical to be envisioned. Many policies, conversely—the table lists nine—are available for encouraging incremental innovation. Such policies can be deployed with considerable confidence, since incremental innovations occur continuously and in large numbers. Although they cannot promise big gains through breakthroughs, these policies can be counted on to yield substantial benefits over time, as for the Internet at the end of the twentieth century and agriculture earlier.

At the beginning of the twentieth century, farm families lived isolated, impoverished lives. With limited schooling and little access to information, small farmers relied on traditional practices. Even if unable to produce enough to support their own families, many were reluctant to embrace "scientific agriculture," perceived as untried and risky. Over the next few decades, agriculture underwent a revolutionary transformation, the result of research funded by the U.S. Department of Agriculture (USDA) and by state governments and disseminated to farmers by federal-state agricultural extension services. Productivity rose and the number of Americans working on farms fell, even as output increased to supply an expanding population. Over the first half of the twentieth century, yields and productivity in growing potatoes nearly tripled; labor productivity in raising turkeys increased even more (Bureau of the Census 1975, series K 445–485). Higher productivity did not result simply from research (or mechanization), although there were many discoveries, such as hybrid corn. The key was balance between research and diffusion (Alic 2008a). Without extension, inherently incremental—county-based extension agents functioned as teachers and mentors, helping farmers understand and adapt new agricultural technologies to local conditions—diffusion would have been slower and might in some cases have stalled.

Before World War II, USDA had been the largest source of federal R&D funds. (As late as 1940, Congress appropriated more money for agricultural than for military research.) After the war, the artificially simple account in Vannevar Bush's 1945 report *Science: The Endless Frontier* (Bush 1945) imprinted in the minds of policymakers and the public a false image of innovation as flowing inexorably from research. Bush, wartime czar of military R&D as head of the Office of Scientific Research and Development (OSRD), saw that his report, prepared for the White House, got widespread publicity (including condensation as a supplement to *Fortune* magazine). *Science: The Endless Frontier* argued that Washington should continue to channel generous support to research even though the wartime emergency was at an end. Bush knew how far the United States had been behind Germany and Britain in military technologies such as jet propulsion in the 1930s and was determined that the nation be better prepared in the future. His report said little about sources of innovation other than science, or about diffusion, even though Bush himself had often been frustrated by the reluctance of the armed forces to move forward with weapons based on OSRD projects. Over the next few years Bush's argument, although not the specifics of his proposal, found broad acceptance. The diffusion-oriented USDA approach did not spread. Unlike agriculture, with its population of small farmers, policymakers assumed that business firms would readily exploit government-sponsored research in the physical sciences and engineering. Diffusion and applications would follow more or less automatically. Sometimes they did, but not always.

The Skills of Innovation: Not So Different

Innovators may do science. They may do R&D. Or they may not. The discussion so far has underscored three points central to the chapter. First, not all innovations depend on R&D or science in any direct or immediate way. This means, second, that almost anyone may turn out to be an innovator—the Costco employee who recognized a new product opportunity, factory workers at Toyota (or the many firms that have adopted some of Toyota's methods), the nurses we interviewed at a community hospital who, as users, adapted a vendor-supplied shell program to automate medical records (Keystone Research Center 1997, 116–125). Third, radical innovations cannot always be disentangled from incremental. This section looks more closely at the human capacities that enter into innovation—knowledge and skills, judgment and decision

Table 12.1 Technology Policies for Fostering Radical vs. Incremental Innovation[a]

Policy	Radical Innovation	Incremental Innovation	Both	Comments
I. Direct Government Funding of R&D				
1. R&D contracts with private firms.			√	Normally tied to government missions, such as defense.
2. R&D contracts and grants with nonprofits.			√	Mostly basic research.
3. Intramural R&D in government laboratories.			√	Wide range of activities, depending on agency.
4. R&D contracts with consortia or collaborations.		√		Proprietary interests of participating firms generally limit R&D to generic, pre-competitive work.
II. Direct or Indirect Support for Commercialization				
5. R&D tax credits.		√		Unlikely to alter firms' risk/reward choices.
6. Patents.			√	Powerful stimulus, but can also retard innovation.
7. Tax credits or other subsidies for firms bringing new technologies to market.	√	.		Policymakers cannot be expected to anticipate or to achieve consensus on prospects for radical innovation.
8. Tax credits or rebates for purchasers.		√		As above.
9. Procurement.			√	Defense agencies, somewhat more insulated from politics by national security concerns than other agencies, have fostered radical innovation.
10. Demonstration projects.		√		Political risks discourage demonstrations of radical technologies.
11. Monetary prizes.	√			Limited experience. Appropriate rules and reward levels may be difficult to define. Contestants must have own access to funding.

III. Diffusion and Learning

12. Education and training.	√	No one knows how to educate and train for radical innovation.
13. Codification and diffusion of technical knowledge (e.g., screening, interpretation, and validation of R&D results, support for databases).		Codification presumes certainty, little risk within accepted domain of application.
14. Technical standards.	√	Standards depend on consensus.
15. Technology and/or industrial extension.	√	Low risk by intent.
16. Publicity, persuasion, consumer information.	√	Presumes consensus.

a. The list in this table is restricted to measures with some level of political legitimacy in the United States. It excludes non-technology policies such as regulatory measures, some of which serve as powerful inducements to innovation.

making. It finds them not greatly different from other capacities that people call upon in the workplace and in their personal lives. But because such skills are heavily tacit, difficult to assess or even to observe, it has been easy to assume that a relatively small number of creative people are responsible for most innovations.

Applied to the nineteenth century, the claim that "anyone may turn out to be an innovator" would excite little dissent. Michael Chevalier, a Frenchman who toured the United States at about the same time as Tocqueville, wrote that "there is not a laborer who has not invented a machine or a tool" (Bledstein 1976, 18). Studies based on antebellum patent records found prolific innovators to be "experienced and committed, rather than uniquely gifted, individuals" (Khan and Sokoloff 1993, 290), "not exceptionally well endowed in terms of formal education or technical skills" (295). Since then, innovation has come to depend far more heavily on science and codified technical knowledge. Yet we have already seen that the dependence is far from uniformly high.

All innovations trace in one way or another to human ingenuity, which is no more measurable than innovation itself. The meanings assigned to intelligence remain controversial, and creativity seems still harder to come to grips with. Bunge (1962, 68), for instance, writes that "intuition is ... where we place all the intellectual mechanisms which we do not know how to analyze or even name with precision." Lacking better indicators, economists often fall back on educational attainment as a proxy for human capital, despite inadequacies that led analysts for the Organization for Economic Cooperation and Development (2008, 10) to conclude, a bit forlornly, "Human capital relates to the knowledge, skills, and know-how that employees 'take with them when they leave at night.'"

Skill comes with experience, although just how experience translates into lessons extracted, absorbed, and retained in each individual's personal storehouse remains a considerable mystery. Innovators and entrepreneurs, for example, often fail before they succeed. "Although [Henry Ford] was able to design two cars that performed well enough to attract backers, he was not able to develop an organization that could manufacture either car at a competitive cost" (Klepper 2007, 102). On the next try he managed to keep going and then introduced the Model T, which revolutionized the industry. And in Silicon Valley today it would be no surprise to hear that "entrepreneurial ability is thus a form of human capital" (Meier 2001, 4).

Knowledge itself has two fundamental dimensions, declarative and procedural, "knowing that" and "knowing how."[2] Declarative knowledge includes facts and theories, such as currently accepted principles of engineering and science. Procedural know-how ranges from the motor skills of bicycle riding to the mental skills of chess players and the diagnostic skills of physicians. Occupational skills mix the declarative and the procedural. Surgeons must know where to cut and how to cut, jazz musicians chord changes and how to improvise on them. Although most declarative knowledge is codified and widely available (some is proprietary, held closely by firms), no innovator can expect to locate all the knowledge that seems needed. The engineers who designed the first Mars lander in the early 1970s knew almost nothing about the surface on which Viking was to touch down. Would it be more like the Mojave or a boulder field in the Rockies? Might the lander sink into six feet of dust? They had to weigh risks and make choices. The two companies, Texas Instruments (TI) and Fairchild Semiconductor, that commercialized the integrated circuit (IC) in 1958–1959, took quite different paths (Wolff 1976)—in large part because the people involved knew different things, drew on contrasting stocks of declarative knowledge (and procedural knowledge, though probably to a lesser extent). Jack Kilby, an electrical engineer with a master's degree, was primarily responsible for the work at TI. At Fairchild, Robert Noyce led a group heavy with Ph.D.'s in physics and chemistry. The transistor had been invented only a decade earlier, and both Kilby (who initially worked alone) and those at Fairchild had practical experience going back to the early years. Kilby was first to build a working IC, but the Fairchild group drew more immediately and more heavily on research in solid-state physics and their approach pointed more directly to later advances.

The procedural aspects of innovation—making sense of poorly apprehended situations, exercising foresight based on imperfect knowledge, revisiting decisions when knowledge expands or when what had been thought true is withdrawn from the stockpile of accepted facts, theories, rules, and procedures—seem relatively generic compared with domain-dependent declarative knowledge requirements (carrier mobility in semiconductors, the geomorphology of Mars). As illustrated by the familiar example of bicycle riding, procedural skills are heavily tacit, easier to demonstrate than to analyze and explain. We observe that performance on many sorts of tasks, in many domains—playing chess, designing injection-molded plastic parts or nuclear weapons—improves over time with practice, but we cannot necessarily say just how or why. For a surprisingly wide range of skills, competence requires something like eight or ten years of experiential knowledge accumulation (Ericsson 1996), regardless of educational prerequisites, which are high for nuclear weapons design but not for chess. Through experience, physicians develop heuristics—patterned but implicit problem-solving strategies—that they call on when confronting inconclusive symptoms or conditions. Chess masters fall back on heuristics when they cannot see a clear path ahead, scientists when searching for regularities in their data, engineers in open-ended design tasks with uncountable numbers of alternatives. Where these heuristics come from, how they are formulated, under what circumstances experts decide to trust or distrust them remain largely unknown.

Many years ago Frank Knight, recognized for contributions to economics including the distinction between risk, which can be statistically estimated based on empirical data (the simple example being insurance), and uncertainty, which is incalculable, recognized the value of decision-making skills when he wrote that "the capacity for forming correct judgments (in a more or less extended or restricted field) is ... the most important endowment for which wages are received" (1964 [1921], 229). If a future situation can be characterized fully in terms of risk, prediction is possible in principle, although it may be difficult in practice. Otherwise, "the capacity for forming correct judgments" resides in the tacit realm. Making such judgments is a core skill in innovation and a necessity for competence in many occupations. When labeled common sense, almost everyone calls, almost every day, on problem-solving methods and decision-making capacities—in navigating traffic, cooking dinner, dealing with family or workplace conflicts, choosing a physician and interpreting her diagnosis—that seem not unlike those used in narrower domains by experts (Sternberg 2003). There seems no reason why vehicles for enhancing these sorts of skills could not be developed, although it does not promise to be quick or easy. Indeed, it seems likely that a good deal of rethinking of education and training will be needed.

Learning: More Than Education

All learning, individual and social, is in some sense experiential. (Social learning refers to processes through which individuals learn from one another.) Infants, lacking language, experiment on their surroundings: they are scientists in embryo. Children trade information and opinions, listen to teachers or ignore them. Occupational peers trade information too, sometimes with employees of rival establishments. Through unmediated experience and through dialog, coaching, and practice, people develop the skills and formulate the heuristics relied on by welders and entrepreneurs, surgeons and IT system designers. Over time, novices become experts. Or some of them do, for experiential learning is erratic and error prone. For one physician, thirty years of practice may yield deep insights into the interpretation of patients' symptoms; for another, it may simply mark the degree of obsolescence of whatever knowledge he or she retains from medical school.

Despite the self-evident importance of experiential skill acquisition, institutional supports for less formal modes of learning eroded over the last century as formal education expanded—high schools initially, colleges and universities later. That is not too surprising. For most people, self-study is no way to master chemistry or calculus, while employers were happy to see schools teach vocational skills. Still, education produces novices, not experts, and society has made little effort to reinvent, supplement, and replace the institutional mechanisms through which people continue to learn after leaving school. Even in professions such as medicine, continuing education and training have been pro forma undertakings.

Without too much oversimplification, we can say that the often inchoate amalgams of schooling, apprenticeship, and on-the-job learning that once preceded and accompanied occupational entry, skill acquisition, and advancement have been replaced by largely sequential patterns in which schooling comes first and is followed by largely unmediated workplace experience. Little more than a century ago, when few except relative handfuls of young people bound for college stayed in school past the eighth grade, occupational entry seldom depended on educational credentials. Engineers picked up know-how and competencies in machine shops, ironworks, through planning and constructing civil works. The early business journalist Henry Varnum Poor called the Baltimore and Ohio "the Railroad University of the United States" (Goodrich 1960, 79). Proprietary profit-seeking ventures provided training in professions such as medicine. This made little difference for occupational competence since medical schools had little to teach, given the primitive state of biomedical science. Almost anyone could enroll, no college degree required (being white and male sufficed), and graduates had only a marginally better chance of curing the sick than local clergy who sometimes provided bodily care too. When clerks were male, an entry-level position might be the initial step on the path to partnership or management, perhaps a business of one's own. For other young men, legal experience as a clerk in the local lawyer's office preceded enrollment in night law school. Basic literacy was enough for a start down the path to skills, expertise, and a career.

By the end of the nineteenth century, these patterns were changing quickly. Between 1900 and 1920, white-collar employment doubled, from 5 million to over 10 million, and the proportion of clerical employees within the white-collar workforce also doubled, to one-third of the total (Bureau of the Census 1975, series D 182–232). Young people had begun seeking "an education that would lead directly to employment, not college" (Goldin 1998, 353). High school enrollments rose from 520,000 to 2.2 million over the first two decades of the century; more students elected courses such as bookkeeping, and a declining proportion chose college-preparatory courses such as algebra (National Center for Education Statistics 1993, 34 and 50). A second shift followed World War II, in postsecondary education. College-level enrollments climbed from 2.4 million in 1950 to 8 million in 1970. Most of the nation's 1,100 community colleges were established during these same years. Young people, like their parents before the war, continued to migrate from academic to occupational curriculums and employers could now hire degree holders for jobs earlier filled by high school graduates, who found themselves headed for factory work, which began to disappear. Today, nearly two-thirds of the 15 million undergraduates enrolled in American colleges and universities opt for what the Department of Education considers a career program (National Center for Education Statistics 2004).

In engineering and medicine, rapidly accumulating knowledge, declarative knowledge especially, but also procedural knowledge in the form of new methods, began to replace the experiential predecessors of formal education and training. Rules of thumb that had evolved over centuries of construction with wood and masonry provided little guidance for engineers designing iron and steel structures. Nearly one in four early iron railway bridges collapsed; others sagged so much under the weight of passing trains that they had to be abandoned or rebuilt (Day 1984). Politicians and the public, not to mention the financiers who put up investment capital, demanded better. Manufacturing firms in emerging industries such as electrical equipment were relatively quick to adopt new methods based on mathematical models validated by systematic experimental research, later to be known as engineering science. Many companies in older industries, conversely, busy churning out low-cost goods in high volume—clocks and watches, cigarettes and shoes—continued to prefer "practical men" familiar with standard industrial practices. Heterogeneous employers and heterogeneous occupational specialties, and conflicts between faculty who favored engineering science and traditionalists, meant that the transformation of engineering extended over nearly a century (Calvert 1967; Servos 1980). Following World War II, a conflict widely portrayed as won by scientists with only secondary contributions from engineers, few of whom commanded the knowledge of underlying sciences and skills in applied mathematics needed to do more, universities infused undergraduate coursework with engineering science, boosted graduate enrollments, and built research programs with dollars from the Pentagon. Even so, entry into engineering remained relatively easy because employers wanted it that way. As late as 1950, only three-fifths of American engineers claimed a four-year degree (Blank and Stigler 1957, 74); while the proportion now approaches four-fifths, one-quarter of those degrees are outside of engineering fields (and relatively few in related disciplines such as science or mathematics) (Tsapogas 2004).

By contrast, the transformation in medical practice took barely a generation. Dread diseases such as typhoid and cholera that had long spread unchecked, their causes unknown or misunderstood, receded as elected officials, public health professionals, and engineers pushed for, planned, and built water purification and sewerage systems. Spurred by discoveries in anesthetics and anesthesiology, "In a burst of creative excitement, the amount, scope, and daring of surgery enormously increased" (Starr 1982, 156). Recognizably modern medical schools replaced diploma mills, hospitals took the place of private homes as sites for care delivery, and those hospitals, needing nurses, began to train them in large numbers. "By 1912 there were more than 1100 nursing schools, virtually all set up and run by hospitals, with 30,000 students" (Stevens 1989, 23). While the 1900 census found only 12,000 professional nurses, by 1920 the total had reached 150,000 (Bureau of the Census 1975, series D 233–682).

Gains in knowledge of the biomedical sciences and the engineering sciences were real enough, and deficient standards of practice can do grievous harm if misdiagnosis of disease leads to serious illness or bridges fall down because of faulty design. Societies are right to insist that professional expertise be built on a base of codified knowledge mastered through academic study and verified through licensing (for medicine, less commonly for engineering), imperfect though these may be as guarantors of competence. For other occupations and industries, less dependent on science-based technologies, the decline of structured forms of experiential learning has sometimes had unfortunate consequences. Construction apprenticeships financed through collective bargaining agreements, for instance, have shrunk with expansion on the nonunion side of the industry. Nonunion contractors hire graduates of apprentice programs without contributing to their support. As they pushed down wages, skilled workers left for other occupations. Productivity deteriorated (Gullickson and Harper 2002), inflating the costs of homes and highways relative to other goods and services.

Educators have not ignored tacit skills. But the teaching is time-consuming and expensive, relying as it does on models derived from apprenticeship—with learners working alongside or under the supervision of those whose competence has come to be accepted—and the simulated practice of workshops, laboratories, and internships. When graduate students in molecular biology struggle to interpret confusing results from experiments they might conduct a bit differently if they could begin again, they are apprenticing as working scientists. Today as in the past, training in the fine arts and in applied arts such as architecture relies on studio practice: both practitioners and connoisseurs need an eye trained to distinguish what is likely to be considered good or valuable or lasting from what is meretricious—in Knight's words, "the capacity for forming correct judgments." Community colleges train students in cosmetology or auto repair much as high schools trained bookkeepers. Shortcuts have been devised where possible. Pilots practice in simulators that cost less than airplanes and skirt the penalties accompanying lapses of judgment at 10,000 feet. Graduate business schools create artificial experience through case studies intended to speed learning through peer competition and cooperation, rapid feedback, and, in some instances, comparison of learners' solutions with actual outcomes. So far, however, neither society as a whole nor particular occupational groups have found dependable means for ensuring that practitioners keep up with the evolving state of knowledge and practice. Although employers sometimes provide continuing education and training, some forms of this have become less common than in the past.

With more young people staying in school longer, employers now expect to hire entry level workers with ready-made skills. Internal labor markets have contracted. Firms that once provided structured career paths along which employees could advance through on-the-job learning now limit many of these opportunities to carefully selected cohorts of managerial and professional employees—selected in considerable part based on educational credentials. For employers, education serves as a convenient screening device (Arkes 1999). Employers assume that educational attainment predicts potential contributions to group productivity and the firm's goals, correlates at least roughly with reasoning, problem-solving, and decision-making abilities, believe that workers with more (and more elite) education are likely to be smarter, more motivated, and more broadly socialized than those with less education, hence more likely to behave in ways consistent with organizational preferences.

Today, most employer-provided training aims simply to introduce employees to the organization and its expectations. Programs cover mandated health and safety proce-dures, scripts to be followed in dealing with customers, the workings of the corporate information system. At JetBlue University, new hires get "a brief history of the airline ..., a thorough immersion in its core values (safety, integrity, caring, passion, and fun), a sobering analysis of industry economics ..., and mundane sessions on uniforms and employee benefits" (Gunther 2009, 114). (By emphasizing the perilous economics of the industry, JetBlue seeks to motivate its employees, hoping they will work hard to keep the company going and protect their jobs; employee attachment to the firm and its goals is likewise an integral part of lean production in the auto industry.) In indus-tries that employ IT specialists, "most companies have neither the time nor the money for on-the-job training. They'd prefer that universities incorporate more training for real-world IT roles into their curricula so that graduates are ready to start contributing their first day on the job. 'The problem is that universities don't train people to take jobs,' says Michael Gabriel, CIO [chief information officer] at Home Box Office in New York" (King 2009). Not including informal on-the-job training, which, despite its extent and importance, few companies track, employers in the United States provide an average of around three days per employee year of training (Frazis, Gittleman, and Joyce 1998; Lerman, McKernan, and Riegg 2004).

Americans have long believed in self-improvement through adult education (Kett 1994). In recent years, something over one-quarter of the adult population reports some form of participation (National Center for Education Statistics 2008, 191–215). Much of this, however, is recreational or avocational, loosely connected at best to the labor market. And even when the intent is to ensure that professionals maintain their skills, many programs seem ineffective, as for continuing medical education (CME). A common licensing requirement and the object of much study, CME has almost universally been found to have little or no influence on clinical practice (Grimshaw et al. 2001), even though many physicians are known to fall far short of delivering care in accord with accepted standards, and bringing them up to those standards has been a major CME goal. Federal, state, and local agencies, finally, do support some work-related education and training, including skills training as part of incentive packages assembled by states to attract or retain employment. Nonetheless, most government programs (leaving aside military training) aim to put people to work, or back to work, leading to an emphasis on job search and interviewing more than substantive skills.

Although the picture sketched above is clouded, particularly as concerns training, more and better education and training remains the usual, indeed reflexive prescription by pundits and policymakers for adjusting to technological change and globalization. At best, training and retraining seems a glass half full. Education, its many virtues notwithstanding, is no panacea. As average levels of education rise, employers respond by ramping up job entry requirements. That has been the pattern for a century and there is no reason to expect it to change. Moreover, the deficiencies of America's public schools and the problematic nature of reform attempts, always under way and never seeming to accomplish much, coupled with the enormous range in quality of postsecondary education, mean that millions of people will enter the labor force in coming decades poorly prepared for fast-paced and potentially disruptive change in jobs and technology, society and the economy. Of course, many Americans will manage quite well, as demonstrated over six decades of evolution in computer technologies. During much of this period, academic education and training lagged well behind demand, and large numbers of people mastered IT skills on the job or on their own. Even in high technology, self-education can still be effective. But that does not make it ideal, or even broadly satisfactory. More structure would promise better results, for individuals and for society.

Computers and Systems

This penultimate section illustrates the continuing importance of informal skill acquisition. It also touches on aspects of the computer revolution, mostly concerning business applications before the Internet boom of the 1990s, providing further examples of how innovation takes place and why it is so demanding of everyone's skills, not just those of experts.

The revolution was hardly that, in any literal sense. Rather, many different companies tried over many years, with varying success and often inconclusively, to marry advancing technological capabilities with poorly understood business processes embedded in messy if not dysfunctional organizational settings. From the beginning, large-scale information systems proved difficult and costly to implement. Surveys have found as many as half of business IT projects canceled before completion or abandoned soon after (Strassmann 1997)—failures in innovation. Over time, nonetheless, some projects succeed, other firms emulate them, IT applications continue to evolve and diffuse, and economy-wide productivity rises, through both automation of existing paperwork-intensive processes (accounting, payroll) and entirely new applications such as dynamic pricing of airline tickets (replacement of fixed fares by prices more or less constantly adjusted to minimize empty seats and maximize revenues).

In 1965 nearly all of the 5,600 computers sold in the United States were mainframes. The minicomputer had just been commercialized (260 were sold), the PC was still a decade ahead, and the handful of universities offering programs in computer science and engineering (CSE) granted a few dozen degrees. Large corporations, universities, and government bought many of the mainframes for scientific and technical calculations. Some companies also installed them to automate "back office" records processing. For decades, paper-based corporate information systems had kept legions of clerical employees—those high school graduates mentioned earlier—busy entering data and information, searching out errors and correcting them, assembling files and losing them. Computers promised fewer clerks, fewer errors, lower overhead. While none of this was especially straightforward, by 1980, "a paycheck in almost any company of 100 or more employees in the United States was prepared by a computer" (Cortada 1996, 21). Specialized firms such as EDS performed much of the work under contract. Movement of computers to the front office had barely begun.

In the 1980s, both PC manufacturers and firms such as Intel that supplied them with microprocessors were taken by surprise as businesses began purchasing PCs to replace adding machines and typewriters—another illustration of how difficult it can be to anticipate the direction of innovation. For the microprocessor and the microcomputer, the 1970s had been a decade of learning by both producers (what did customers want?) and users (what could this new class of products do?). Much uncertainty surrounded both questions. Minicomputers had taken over many industrial process control tasks (e.g., in chemical plants), enabling adjustments via software. Microprocessor-based controllers now began to invade those niches. In the auto industry, microprocessors likewise replaced hard-wired circuitry in a widening range of applications (today's vehicles incorporate as many as 100 microprocessors to control engines, air bags, entertainment systems, and much else). Such markets were at least somewhat predictable. That was not true of general-purpose PCs. At first, it was not at all clear who might buy these. Since hobbyists had purchased many of the early machines (you could build a Heathkit), speculation centered on household applications. Would PCs be used for keeping address books and kitchen recipes? Around 1980, some observers were predicting that demand would resemble that for fancy cars and swimming pools, fueled by conspicuous consumption. Office automation got little attention until the appearance of low-cost, easy-to-use software for spreadsheets and word processing. Businesses recognized that inexpensive general-purpose machines could replace more costly dedicated word processing equipment (which in many offices had just begun to supplant electric typewriters), and PCs began to appear on desktops. Only then did the retail market boom, as people who had learned to use them at work bought PCs for their homes. Recalling these events reminds us that the spread of even the most radical-seeming innovations may be paced by meandering search processes as users uncover and explore applications initially unforeseen.

By the mid-1990s, PCs were everywhere and could be linked through the Internet; the computer had come to be seen as a universal tool. To combine front office PCs with back office information systems, organizations had to untangle and dissect their business processes, decide on some sort of system architecture, evaluate hardware, purchase or develop software to replicate or replace existing processes, get those many pieces of software installed and debugged, and teach their employees to use it—all without disrupting ongoing operations. Not many companies had the internal resources to attempt all this. Consultants and vendors might promise expertise in designing software, writing code, testing and debugging it. But the contracts under which they worked seldom provided resources and incentives sufficient for learning how the client's business actually functioned. Indeed, many enterprises did not understand their own processes, which had often grown up piecemeal over several decades. Paper flowed from here to there, up and down chains of authorization and approval, inward from field and divisional offices to headquarters and back out again. Copies were made, forms stamped, records filed away, perhaps never to be seen again. Few process maps existed. Organization charts omitted the host of informal arrangements that kept things going. Many companies found themselves with large and incompatible inventories of hardware and software bought over the years at the initiative of local or divisional managers. Now the enterprise might find itself with multiple systems for similar or identical tasks—in the case of more than one bank following a series of mergers, dozens of software packages just for auto loans or home mortgages. Employees might have to master fifty or even one hundred applications and switch quickly among them when responding to inquiries from customers or the boss. Understanding what people in various parts of the organization actually did might have to start with something like an anthropological study, and understanding *why* they did it could be even more puzzling, if the original reasons had vanished.

At an insurance company we studied in the 1990s, Mt. Washington Mutual (a pseudonym), "reengineering" to replace the existing system, consisting of mostly stand-alone computers in field offices and at headquarters, began with "process walk-throughs" conducted by teams of longtime employees pulled from many parts of the company (Keystone Research Center 1997, 82–85). Mt. Washington Mutual sold products including group disability policies to some 70,000 mostly small firms and professional partnerships through both independent agents and its own offices. The reengineering teams began by puzzling out existing processes, "stapling themselves to a policy" to observe each step at first hand. They started at the customer end, as information was gathered and the sale nailed down, then moved to headquarters for underwriting and rate setting (among other objectives, the reengineering project was intended to move underwriting from headquarters to the field offices), policy preparation (including specially prepared explanatory materials, needed because Mt. Washington Mutual's core marketing strategy was to let each and every customer "have it their way") and then back to the field, ending with payments (e.g., on a schedule requested by the customer). Eventually Mt. Washington Mutual came to view reengineering as a success, but similar projects elsewhere sometimes failed or proved technically satisfactory while registering little or no improvement on measures of organizational performance. The usual reason was that the new system automated processes that were inefficient or out of control to begin with (a common problem in factory automation too). While advances in hardware and software made many innovations in business IT possible, outcomes often hinged on factors other than technology.

That lesson might have been extracted from the first documented business application of computing, around 1950 at a small firm, Lyons, that supplied tea shops in and around London (Arris 2000). Lyons set out to computerize its system for tracking orders, production (in the firm's own bakeries and those of suppliers), inventory, and delivery, which the firm depended on each morning to guide its employees as they prepared and delivered fresh-baked goods and other perishables and nonperishables (ice cream, chocolate) in accordance with orders submitted the previous afternoon by some 200 shops. Lyons had been fine-tuning its procedures for several decades. They were well understood, designed from the beginning to be efficient and reliable and continuously refined (e.g., to compete effectively under rationing, still in force). It was this preexisting system that enabled Lyons to succeed, even though computers were so new at the time that the company had to design and fabricate its own (the company later began making IT hardware for sale).

Lyons employees also had to write their own software, as did everyone who was then applying computers for any purpose. Most of those purposes involved complicated mathematical problems, and the engineers and scientists working on them wrote and debugged their own code just as they labored over differential equations solved analytically. In so doing, they built the early foundations for academic CSE programs, which began to appear in the mid-1960s (Figure 12.2). For many years thereafter, despite several rapid growth spurts, these programs could not come close to keeping up with expanding labor market demand, and self-education remained a major route into skilled IT occupations (e.g., as programmers, systems analysts, and software designers). Only over the past decade or so have enrollments and graduation rates caught up to and begun to move roughly in parallel with employment.[3] Current employment is more than twice the cumulative number of CSE graduates since the 1960s (including all electrical engineering graduates; of course not all CSE graduates, much less all electrical engineers, work in computer-related occupations). This implies that many people in CSE-related jobs even today have had little or no formal training. Lateral (and upward) movement remains common, and career pathways remain relatively easy to negotiate because software development, given a lack of codified methods, remains a craft more than a science. As legions of hackers attest, with no large body of accepted technical knowledge to master, learning by doing remains a viable route to high levels of practical skill, much as in engineering more broadly a century ago. Whatever technological "revolution" next sweeps through wealthy economies like that of the United States, many of those who participate will probably pick up skills much as did the pioneers of IT innovation from the 1950s into the 1990s.

Figure 12.2 Bachelor's Degrees in Computer-Related Disciplines

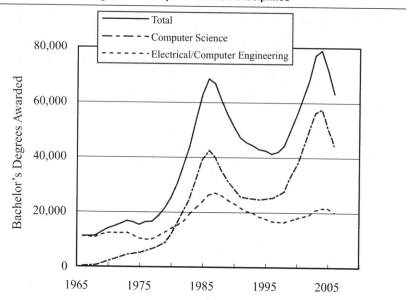

Note: Not all electrical engineering students specialize in computer-related subjects; because no breakdown is available, the total overestimates potential supply.
Source: National Science Foundation 2008a, tables 34 and 51.

Conclusion

This chapter has argued that innovation is often misconceived, viewed as flowing unidirectionally from singular acts of discovery or invention, after which incremental improvements and applications follow more or less spontaneously. In the alternative view presented here, innovation is distributed over organizations and over time. Incremental improvements are not incidental but essential for adoption and impact, and almost anyone and everyone may end up contributing, in small ways or large. Because major innovations become evident only in hindsight, efforts to anticipate them have limited utility, and public policy should support small-scale contributions as well as high-risk undertakings, through means including institutions for experiential learning. Such policies would promise substantial gains in the rate of innovation and in the resulting societal benefits.

The argument has proceeded along two lines. The first consisted of a depiction of the process of innovation itself, stressing its irreducible uncertainty, the multifaceted nature of contributing activities (e.g., those of users), and the growing significance of the service sector, which now makes up some four-fifths of the U.S. economy and depends less directly on science and research than does the goods-producing sector. Because no sharp separation exists between the determination of product attributes and production processes in much of the service sector, and because many direct production workers in service industries can be considered knowledge workers (nurses, insurance underwriters), a large and still growing proportion of the workforce is positioned to contribute to continuous incremental innovation.

The second line of argument was based on the skills and capabilities that enter into innovation. To the extent that these can be understood and analyzed, which is modest, they seem relatively generic—unlike, for example, the domain-specific procedural know-how and declarative knowledge of engineers and scientists. There is no reason to suppose good ideas will come exclusively from those with education and credentials in one of the professions or quasi-professions. And there is much reason to believe that innovators learn through experience many of the lessons vital to success.

The United States, like other countries, provides little in the way of an institutional framework for experiential learning. As a result, untapped potential exists for fostering innovation, productivity growth, and international competitiveness. Many of the 35 million or so young people currently enrolled in American high schools and colleges will still be working a half century from now. No one entering the labor force at the end of World War II, when the world's first and only electronic digital computer was put to work on top-secret calculations concerning the feasibility of a hydrogen bomb, could have imagined the changes she would see over the rest of the twentieth century. Does anyone believe the twenty-first century will see less change? Yet because experiential learning, as a process, is poorly understood and seemingly haphazard, it has been left to depend on self-motivation and self-monitoring. A new framework will have to be invented. That is a task for the future. Employers would benefit through greater access to capable employees. Employees with valued skills would benefit through better jobs. And if good enough at what they do, employees can sometimes force managerial or strategy shifts in firms for which they work; if unable to do so, some of those employees may go on to start their own firms.

No one can anticipate the future with confidence. What we can say is that tomorrow's technologies and industries will be built by those equipped to learn by doing. That is how people and societies adapt, adjust, and innovate. It is how computers and information technology spread through the economy in the past and how the disciplinary foundations for computer science and engineering were built. The decades to come will necessarily unfold in similar fashion, with plenty of blind alleys and mistakes, from which some people—those prepared to learn—will draw appropriate lessons and do better when they next try.

Everyone an innovator? Well, we all invent our own lives, just as we collectively invent the future.

Notes

1. While basic research accounts for 17–18 percent of all U.S. R&D spending, most of the money comes from federal agencies and pays for work in universities and the government's own laboratories. For autos and many other industries, NSF suppresses breakdowns of basic research,

applied research, and development, citing business confidentiality. On average, however, business firms classify no more than about 3 percent of internally funded R&D as basic (Boroush 2008, table 2).

2. The remainder of this section, and parts of the next, draw on Alic 2008b and Alic 2004.

3. From 2000 to 2007, CSE programs graduated about 550,000 people, while employment in CSE-related occupations rose by about 600,000. Some 3.7 million people now work in computer-related occupations—the figure at the end of 2008 for the Labor Department's category "computer and mathematical occupations," which includes programmers, systems administrators, and computer scientists and software engineers (*Employment & Earnings,* January 2009, table 11.)

CHAPTER 13

The Paradox of the Weak State Revisited

*Industrial Policy, Network Governance,
and Political Decentralization*

Josh Whitford and Andrew Schrank

As the chapters in this volume make clear, industrial policy is back in vogue. This is not to say that the much maligned practice of "picking winners" has been rehabilitated, nor is our point that otherwise timid governments intervene more frequently when depression strikes. We mean rather that this volume both draws on and adds to an incipient literature showing that state actors across the developed and the developing worlds have increasingly been looking for—and finding—useful ways to intervene in the industrial economy.

In this chapter, we take stock of industrial policy's return to favor with a contribution that—like the others in this volume—challenges the market fundamentalist agenda. But our chapter is also more explicitly programmatic than most of the others. We argue that the current framing that underpins most progressive calls for a new industrial policy premised on the strategic collaboration between government and private sector suffers from a major—but correctible—flaw: it represents industrial policy as a response only to *market* failure.

Why is this a problem? We believe that framing the case for industrial policy in the United States in terms of market failures unnecessarily leads us into some of the same despairing traps that undid calls for industrial policy in the 1980s because it does not sufficiently recognize that the decentralization of production and the advent of open innovation have created new spaces for useful and welfare-creating cooperation between government agencies, public institutions, and private actors.

Recall that contributors to the long and contentious body of literature on the alleged merits and putative preconditions of strategic industrial policy were ultimately skeptical of the possibilities of state intervention in the United States. They held that the resolution of market failures presupposed political centralization and authoritative decision making, and that government action was therefore undercut by federalism and the separation of powers. Indeed, in their classic 1982 call for government intervention designed to combat the "deindustrialization of America," Barry Bluestone and Bennett Harrison portrayed decentralization as an inveterate obstacle to their goal

(Bluestone and Harrison 1982, 180–188; Goodman 1979). And they were not alone. In more or less the same time period Ira Magaziner and Robert Reich (1982, 378) found it hard to fathom "a coherent industrial policy in a non-parliamentary system in which power is divided between Congress and the President, and shared with an array of commissions, agencies, boards, and administrations." Frank Dobbin (1994, 93, 90) traced the fact that "Washington's knee-jerk reaction to industrial policies of all varieties has been to enforce market competition" not only to the "administrative incapacities" of the American state but to the culture that reinforced them. And Mel Dubnick (1984, 25) worried that efforts to introduce a national industrial policy would provoke "intense programmatic and constitutional confrontations between national and state governments over policy jurisdictions and the nature of federalism."

While separation of powers and federalism—which we'll collectively refer to as *political decentralization*—may well have constituted an obstacle to industrial policy in the old world of vertical integration and Fordism when the original "industrial policy debate" began (Johnson 1984), they need not prove so problematic in the current era (variously labeled "post-Fordist," "flexible," "networked," etc.). Leaving aside the question of whether the shift has been fully realized or not, few doubt the fact that decentralized production networks—or what we will term *organizational decentralization*—have come to play at least as important a role in industrial governance as do vertically integrated firms and markets. They loom especially large in the rapid, innovation-based industries that industrial policies are designed to promote.

This decentralization reopens the question and design of industrial policy, for it is hardly obvious that decentralized interventions to make those networks function are inferior to a "one size fits all" effort to prop up ailing hierarchies or ensure their replacement with adequately functioning markets. By implication, industrial policymakers and planners should be at least as concerned with what we have elsewhere termed "network failures" as they are with market failure (Schrank and Whitford 2009). But we fear that, in practice, the case for industrial policy continues to be framed in terms of market failures and their correction.

Our point is not so much to find fault with the authors making that case as it is to argue that they have been misled by a more general gap in the governance literature: even those authors most concerned to show that networks represent a distinct mode of governance have paid little systematic attention to just what it means for a network to "fail."[1] This leaves better-developed theories of market and organizational failure to dominate the discussion, and thus to serve as the working theories that public and private officials use to direct their interventions. As a result, almost by definition, those policymakers are driven to look for ways in which markets can be made to function, or in which they can be supplanted by hierarchies, rather than to create or improve the functioning of decentralized production networks.

This flies in the face of considerable research showing that when an organizational field is characterized by volatile demand, rapid innovation, or chronic uncertainty more generally, production and distribution are often best governed by networks rather than by markets or hierarchies (Powell 1990; Smith-Doerr and Powell 2005). The problem, in short, is to ensure that those networks function effectively. The propensity of networks to fail has been recognized implicitly in the literature on network governance (Podolny and Page 1998). There is also evidence that the relative propensity of firms to govern their affairs through networks rather than markets is amenable to policy intervention (Whitford and Zeitlin 2004; Whitford 2005). But these interventions have been explored in an ad hoc manner if they have been studied at all, and industrial policymakers have therefore been left to defend their efforts not as correctives to network failure but as correctives to market failure (Schrank and Whitford 2009).

What are the likely consequences of the oversight? If industrial policies were framed as correctives to network failure, they would be able to exploit the synergies between decentralized political institutions and decentralized production. Insofar as they are framed in terms of market failure they are likely to fall prey to sophisticated forms of market fundamentalism. By misdiagnosing network failures as market failures, one implicitly advocates interventionist market making or hierarchy construction even where interventionist network-making might work better. There is therefore reason to abandon the framing that brought us to a dead end during the original industrial policy debate. We need a new framing that takes the extant socioeconomic landscape as well as U.S. political institutions on their own terms.

In this chapter, we offer just such a framing. We argue that the decentralization of production and the spread of a "new logic of organizing" (Powell 2001) gives reason to think explicitly about network failure, its causes, and the remedies that those causes imply. When we distinguish between problems that are due to failed networks and those that are products of failed markets, we are forced to reexamine the state's role in economic development more generally.

In particular, we argue that the ensuing emphasis on experimentation, local knowledge, and flexibility that characterizes network governance means that political decentralization, which has traditionally been perceived as an impediment to industrial policy, has features as well as bugs.

The remainder of the chapter is divided in three sections. In the second section, we examine recent formulations of the case for industrial policy and show that their framing in terms of market failure—absent a parallel discussion of network failure—leaves that case murkier than it should be. In the third section, we argue that this absence mirrors a gap in the governance literature more generally. We therefore provide a working definition of "network failure" to generate a preliminary typology which, along with examples drawn from recent analyses of innovative industrial policy, we use to show that state interventions can in fact do something about network failures. In the fourth and concluding section, we reconstruct the case for industrial policy by showing (1) that there is good reason to believe that the contemporary economy is as rife with network failures as it is with market and government failures; (2) that solutions to network failure demand experimentation, local knowledge, and flexibility and are therefore facilitated, rather than undercut, by political decentralization; and (3) that such solutions are already being pursed by technologists and policymakers throughout the United States and deserve far more attention than they've received to date.

The Case for a New Industrial Policy

To show that the case for a new industrial policy tends to be formulated in terms of market failure—when in our view it should be framed in terms of network failure—we rely on a pair of recent articles that have made the case for a new industrial policy particularly well: Fred Block's (2008) "Swimming Against the Current: The Rise of a Hidden Developmental State in the United States"; and Dani Rodrik's (2004) "Industrial Policy for the Twenty-First Century."

We rely on these papers for three reasons. First, they are well-known and self-consciously programmatic statements. Block's article—a very clear and recent synthesis of the case for a revamped industrial policy in the North American context—has of course inspired the project that gave birth to this volume. And Rodrik's (2004, 2) paper is very widely cited and similarly argues that the "softening of convictions" between proponents of strong state leadership on the one side, and unbridled liberalization on the other, represents a "rare historic opportunity ... to fashion an agenda for economic policies that takes an intelligent intermediate stand."

Second, both papers make clear that renewed calls for industrial policy do not represent a return to a bygone ideology. Those calls are driven rather by real changes in the organization of industry in both the developed and developing worlds. In Rodrik's words (2004, 1), "it is increasingly recognized that developing societies need to embed private initiative in a framework of public action that encourages restructuring, diversification, and technological dynamism." Block (2008, 170) notes that there may be many differences between the United States and Europe in terms of policy, but they are alike in at least one key respect: "governments have played an increasingly important role in underwriting and encouraging the advance of new technologies in the business economy."

Third, and most importantly, while Rodrik is talking about the developing world and Block about the United States, both make clear that global changes in the organization of industry have changed the industrial policy game for *everyone*. They agree, as Rodrik (2004, 38) writes, that "it is pointless to obsess, as is common in many discussions of industrial policy, about policy instruments and modalities of interventions. What is much more important is to have a process in place which helps reveal areas of desirable interventions. Governments that understand this will be constantly on the lookout for ways in which they can facilitate structural change and collaboration with the private sector." Or as Block (2008, 171) explains, the United States and Europe are no longer trying to distill and translate lessons from the experiences of developmental bureaucratic states in Japan and South Korea that were "designed to help domestic firms catch up and challenge foreign competitors." Rather, the big new thing is "something very different called a Developmental Network State" (DNS) that "involves public sector officials working closely with firms to identify and support the most promising avenues for innovation."

There are, of course, differences in the details of Rodrik's and Block's agendas for a new industrial policy. But similarities in the underlying logic mean that they can reasonably be taken to represent the essence of the contemporary case for industrial policy. Moreover, from the point of view of our argument, neither Block nor Rodrik is a "straw man." While we argue that the positions as they frame them remain overly wedded to the need to correct market failures, both are openly aware of the limits of that framing and are searching for something better.

The Case

The case—in Rodrik's (2004, 38) words—for a "twenty-first century industrial policy" breaks with the idea that effective industrial policy requires "an autonomous government applying Pigovian taxes or subsidies," carefully measuring those outcomes and then adjusting the subsidies. Rather, particularly for a world in which production is increasingly decentralized, the idea is an industrial policy based on "strategic collaboration between the private sector and government with the aim of uncovering where the most significant obstacles to restructuring lie and what types of interventions are most likely to remove them" (Rodrik 2004, 38).

As Block (2008, 172) explains, this means an industrial policy defined by "four distinct but overlapping tasks—targeted resourcing, opening windows, brokering, and facilitation."[2] Such an approach to industrial policy means that government officials consult with technologists in both business and academia to identify technological challenges "the solution of which is expected to open up important economic possibilities." At the same time, they must also recognize that "many good ideas for innovation will bubble up from below and might not fit with targeted priorities being pursued by particular agencies," and must thus make sure these do not get lost. Brokering and facilitation come to the fore because the real constraints on innovation tend to be on the demand side (Rodrik 2004, 4). Industrial policymakers thus find themselves spending time and resources helping new entrepreneurs "make the business connections that they need to create an effective organization … and helping them find potential customers for a product" (Block 2008, 173). Or they seek to clear obstacles to the creation of viable markets including, for example, establishing standards and regulatory frameworks so that potential purchasers know that a "product actually does what is promised and will work effectively" (Block 2008, 173).

Note that all of these tasks are premised on the belief that a fast-changing world requires the encouragement of *activities*—"a new technology, a particular kind of training, a new good or service" (Rodrik 2004, 14)—rather than the encouragement of *sectors* per se. The point is to move beyond a principal-agent model designed to "align the agents' behavior with the principal's objectives at least cost" and to instead forge a "more flexible form of strategic collaboration between public and private sectors, designed to elicit information about objectives, distribute responsibilities for solutions, and evaluate outcomes as they appear" (Rodrik 2004, 18). It is to make clear that industrial policy ought to be about *self-discovery* and thus to take the sting out of the traditional objection that governments have imperfect information by pointing out that the private sector *also* has imperfect information. It is, Block (2008, 170) writes, to reject market fundamentalism and to fight the "current of a hostile political philosophy" which accepts that markets fail but holds that government failures are in general more pernicious.[3]

Where the market fundamentalists cry that liberalization and privatization are necessary because regulators cannot be trusted, Block and Rodrik argue that government autonomy from private interests is not an unalloyed good, with Rodrik (2004, 37) observing that in many countries it is not industrial policy but rather "privatization [that] has turned out to be a boon for insiders or government cronies." The real question is simply whether the state is able to connect otherwise disconnected groups—say, technologists and capitalists. And it cannot do this unless it "can elicit useful information from the private sector" which it can do "only when it is engaged in an ongoing relationship with it" (Rodrik 2004, 4). They thus fear that market fundamentalist opposition to such relationships—since they can enable regulatory capture—might ironically lead instead to government failure. Private actors are unlikely to undertake joint investments with politically or financially vulnerable public agencies. And public agencies therefore hide their vulnerabilities from their private sector interlocutors. Yet this generates a "democratic deficit" that allows "certain entrenched corporate interests … to put their needs ahead of the public interest" (Block 2008, 194).[4]

Drawing on this insight, Block and Rodrik build on Peter Evans's (1995) studies of the developmental state to argue that industrial policy is well served by "embedded autonomy." That is, they hold that it depends on an "apparently contradictory combination of corporate coherence and connectedness" in which elements of Weberian bureaucracy with its sense of professionalism and attachment to meritocratic advancement are combined with an embedding of state actors in a "concrete set of social ties that bind the state to society and provide institutionalized channels for the continual negotiation and renegotiation of goals and policies" (Evans 1995, 59).

But they also build on Evans's original formulation by emphasizing two additional points that in our view form the core of the contemporary case for industrial policy. First, they underscore that neither business nor the state is a monolith. The best industrial policy in a given locale depends on the *actual* institutional setting. Not only is there no particular sector to be privileged a priori, but there is no particular state agency that ought to administer industrial policy in all cases. Block centers his discussion of effective industrial policy in the United States on DARPA and the NIH not because they have been the only or even the most natural centers for administering strategic collaboration with the private sector. His point is simply that they *were* highly competent agencies that *were* engaged in strategic collaboration with the private sector. As a result, they were able to develop measures to nurture new industries and thus "to translate the nation's scientific and technological leadership into commercially viable products that would be produced in the United States" (Block 2008, 179). Rodrik (2004, 22–24) writes that while it is "common to complain about incompetence and corruption in government bureaucracies," in fact "bureaucratic competence varies greatly among different agencies even within the same country." Industrial policy should openly take this into account and vest authority for the encouragement of desirable activities in "agencies with demonstrated competence," even if this has implications for "the tools of industrial policy that can be used."[5]

Second, decentralization favors—rather than inhibits—the exploitation of "embedded autonomy" and encouragement of activities rather than sectors by unleashing the efforts of competent agencies. Block (2008, 174) makes the point that "for opening windows and brokerage to be most effective, it is desirable to have some redundancy." Otherwise, "a single small office [perhaps one that is insufficiently embedded with the sector in question] might be able to completely shut down a promising line of investigation by denying funding." But with "multiple windows and multiple potential brokers, an idea might be able to survive and ultimately flourish despite initial negative responses."[6] Certainly there is still a need for coordination between elements of such a new industrial policy. But it ought not to be in principal-agent mode. The point is to be able to discover potentialities in existing resources, relations, and competencies. As Rodrik (2004, 31) writes, "the challenge is not to reinstitute industrial policy, but to redeploy the machinery that is already in place in a more productive manner." It is to recognize that "a first-best policy in the wrong institutional setting will do considerably less good than a second-best policy in an appropriate institutional setting" (Rodrik 2004, 17).

Block and Rodrik, in short, outline a powerful case for a new model of industrial policy that combats the market fundamentalists by pointing out that the *actual* obstacles to economic development are often different from those hypothesized ex ante. They thus locate responsibility for administering industrial policy in decentralized centers of competence within the state apparatus, and emphasize that those centers must be freed to build relationships with the private sector.

We accept in the main the case that Block and Rodrik lay out. But we believe there is still something missing. The case is pitched on the one hand in terms of the *limits* of markets, and on the other in terms of the *possibilities* of collaborative networks that bring together public and private actors to "solve problems in the productive sphere, each side learning about the opportunities and constraints faced by the other" in ways that make state interventions in markets more likely to succeed (Rodrik 2004, 21). The *possibilities* of markets are, of course, well-known. There is no need for Block and Rodrik to discuss them further, nor need we. But the *limits* of networks are less well-known and should be much more explicitly incorporated into the case for a new industrial policy. Insofar as a new industrial policy demands the replacement of failed markets with functioning networks, there should be much more attention to real-world limitations in those networks. Without this sensitivity, the case for a new industrial policy remains vulnerable to a sophisticated form of market fundamentalism, albeit through a back door.

Failed Markets or Failed Networks?

It is typical for discussions of the relative merits of state intervention in market functioning to be framed in terms of the prevalence of market failures and the possibility of public solutions—objections to the assumptions of perfect markets and imperfect governments. Existing theories of market and government failure dominate the contemporary discussion. They do so because they self-consciously serve to diagnose problems and thereby direct public and private officials toward meaningful solutions.

But, as noted at the outset of the chapter, efforts to stimulate industrial policy in the 1980s foundered when framed in these terms. So it is refreshing that Block and Rodrik look to networks and "strategic collaboration" for novel solutions to previously vexing governance problems. Their work here usefully parallels a broader shift in a governance literature that has been profoundly reshaped by portrayals of "networks that are neither market nor hierarchy" (Powell 1990) and of the "networked polity" (Ansell 2000) as distinctive—and not hybrid—modes of coordination and governance.

This parallel literature has a number of laudable aspects. Not only has network governance been shown to be quite common, its characterization as a "distinctive form of coordinating economic activity" (Powell 1990, 301) has also been roundly shown to accord with the beliefs and practices of actors who are party to the transactions themselves (Uzzi 1996, 677; Lorenzoni and Lipparini 1999; Shane and Cable 2002; Schrank 2004; Whitford 2005).

Because it has also been shown that network governance can in some situations foster learning, investment, and joint problem solving far better than can alternative modes of governance, we are generally pleased that the industrial policy debate has begun to import insights from analyses of network organizational governance. However, we remain worried that the case for a new industrial policy may import not merely the main insights of the literature on network governance, but also its main flaw: a tendency to focus on network success to the exclusion of network failure.

We do not mean to say that the literature on network governance has paid no attention to network failure. To the contrary, it has revealed that many—perhaps most—network relationships go belly up or underperform and that many more that would be desirable in theory nonetheless fail to get off the ground (Podolny and Page 1998). But attention to such failures has not been systematically incorporated into an analysis of network functioning (or nonfunctioning) in a literature that has sought instead simply to understand why the propensity to form collaborative arrangements varies across firms, regions, sectors, and time periods. Failures are taken only as evidence that the network is the fragile exception in need of explanation rather than as a possible rule from which deviations might occur. Such a presumption is at best unwarranted and at worst inconsistent with the fundamental organizing principle of economic sociology—economic transactions are "always embedded" in social relations (Granovetter 1985; Krippner 2001; Block 2003; Polanyi 2001 [1944]).

An implausible assumption of omnipresent networks is by no means superior to the ahistorical fiction of universal markets. Networks are neither more nor less obvious forms of governance than markets—or, for that matter, hierarchies—and their failure should therefore be theorized rather than assumed.

To do otherwise is to confirm rather than challenge the idea "that markets are the starting point" (Powell 1990, 298). This idea is reinforced by the existence of a well developed literature on market failure replete with distinctions between "absolute" failures that are attributable to externalities and "relative" failures that are associated with transaction costs (Arrow 1970; Papandreou 1994). And it is seconded by the view that the only—and generally inferior—alternative is hierarchy. This view has given birth to a sophisticated literature on failure populated not just by studies in organizational ecology of the causes of organizational disappearance (absolute failure), but also by an institutional literature attentive to the "ubiquity of problems in organized activity" (Perrow 1981) that has thus theorized what Meyer and Zucker (1989) refer to as the "permanently failing organization."[7]

By way of contrast, the literature on decentralized production networks includes no corresponding theory of their failure (Schrank and Whitford 2009b), an absence that is particularly glaring when the stimulation of network governance is put forth as a policy aim. Hence, while it is beyond the scope of this chapter to offer a general theory of network failures, we provide a working definition that we can use to distinguish between their different sources. We do so to illuminate the strengths and weaknesses of framing the call for a new industrial policy in terms that call for an alleviation not just of market failures but also of network failures.[8]

We define network failures as situations in which network governance is either absent or compromised but would be desirable were it to obtain. The existing literature highlights conditions of unstable demand, and/or complex interdependencies in production. And, based on our reading of that literature, as well as our own empirical work, we posit that such failures tend to occur when social, cultural, or institutional control mechanisms do not adequately squelch *opportunism* and/or have not ensured contracting parties access to and knowledge of appropriate *competencies*. These control mechanisms underpin the ethics of exchange that allow economic relations to emerge and endure in the absence of legitimate or formal organizational authority.

We represent network failures in this way for two reasons. First, we want to underscore that there are many transactions which simply should not be pursued through networks. Evidence that networks can succeed where both markets and hierarchies fail need not imply that network governance should be pursued in all instances. Sociological triumphalism notwithstanding, some (perhaps most) production and distribution is more efficiently pursued in either markets or hierarchies. We thus invoke "desirability" as a scope condition for network governance and failure. If network governance is not desirable in the first place, we cannot speak of a network failure.

We recognize, of course, that what is (and is not) desirable is subject to debate. But the extant literature provides direction. Network governance tends to be desirable for the production or distribution of goods and services characterized by volatile demand conditions, complex interdependencies on the supply side, or rapid technological changes.[9] We neither need nor want networked organizations to get us our toilet paper, nor do we want them to get us our home telephones. We may, however, want networked actors to get us our environmentally friendly pulping mills (Kivimaa and Mickwitz 2004) or our next generation cellular phones.

Second, our invocation of an ethic of exchange that squelches opportunism and directs actors toward appropriate competencies is consistent with prevailing definitions of network governance but simultaneously suggests that these features have *distinct* "flip sides." Network failures can derive from *either* opportunistic behavior *or* honest ignorance on the part of one or more transacting parties. To paraphrase Tolstoy, functional instances of network governance are in a sense alike; it's the dysfunctional ones that differ. In other words, we can speak generally of the network as a distinct mode to be counterposed to the market and to the hierarchy, but it does not follow that when networks fail, these failures are of a piece. And we highlight the difference between opportunism and incompetence in order to correct a widespread tendency in the literature to simultaneously distinguish between and conflate the two.

The issue, as Charles Sabel's (1993; 1994; 2006; Helper, MacDuffie, and Sabel 2000) work on "studied trust" and "learning by monitoring" has shown, is that ideal-typical network governance is fundamentally underpinned by a sort of virtuous interplay of safeguards against opportunism and the search for relevant competencies. However, writing elsewhere with Michael Dorf (1998, 308; emphasis added), even Sabel portrays "the fear of engaging an *incompetent or unreliable* partner" as the biggest obstacle to the emergence of decentralized production without drawing a distinction between the two. Similarly, when Gerrit Rooks (2000, 127; emphasis added) and his collaborators look at "how inter-firm co-operation depends on embeddedness," they manage simultaneously to be attentive to and to conflate the distinction—writing that a firm will "tend to exit from a relation with a partner who turns out to be *incompetent or unreliable*" in the same manner.

Such conflation is relatively unproblematic when we are talking about network functioning. But when things break down—which can happen when *either* is lacking—the distinction is of greater import. This first became clear to us when we jointly reflected on our independent interviews with buyers and suppliers in the decentralized production of durable and nondurable goods like auto parts, machinery, and apparel.[10] When asked why their various relationships would underperform or go belly up, we realized, our respondents used colloquial expressions like "he screwed me" or "they screwed up." But there is an interesting, if subtle, difference between "screwing" your exchange partner and "screwing up." After all, the former necessarily implies opportunism and the latter need imply nothing more than a lack of competence or inability to solve a joint problem. When asked to clarify which of the two labels applied in which particular case, however, our respondents would often demur. They could not say with any certainty whether they had been victims of competency shortfalls or deliberate self-dealing, and in their eyes it didn't matter. Either way, they had to find new exchange partners.

However, while it may not matter to the victims of failure whether their problems are due to an inability or an unwillingness to live up to the terms of an agreement, when we look at those same failures from a public policy standpoint, we see a different picture. It is not enough to know that network failures are due to bounded rationality; we need to know the bounds. If we do not distinguish between failures that are fundamentally derivative of opportunism on the one side, and those that are ultimately rooted in the systemic ignorance of relevant competencies on the other, how are we to fix them? Certainly network governance fails when exchange partners screw each other, *and* it fails when they screw up. But partners screw each other more often when formal and informal institutions fail to inhibit opportunism; and they screw up more often when such institutions fail to facilitate the search for new information beyond the network.

This simple distinction underpins an initial typology of network failures (see Table 13.1) that can be used to guide policy interventions designed to address actually existing network failures—by which we mean instances in which the sorts of activities that should be governed by networks are governed by poorly performing networks—if they are governed by networks at all.[11]

Table 13.1 Varieties of Network Failure

		Opportunism [within the network]	
		Low	*High*
Isolation [from different networks or institutions]	*Low*	Ideal typical networks	Contested networks
	High	Involuted networks	Network stillbirth or breakdown

Source: Schrank and Whitford (2009b)

The concordant cells describe instances in which issues of opportunism and issues of competence reinforce each other. Ideal-typical networks like the ones identified in the northwest quadrant presuppose a search for new information and safeguards against opportunism among existing exchange partners. Examples would include Silicon Valley and the Italian industrial districts (Piore and Sabel 1984; Whitford 2001). In the southeastern quadrant, absolute network failures are products of a combination of isolation from new information and opportunism among existing exchange partners and are manifested in network stillbirth or breakdown. Examples of the former might include the high-tech cluster that failed to emerge around Rensselaer Polytechnic Institute in Troy, New York (Leslie 2001), and the breakdown of strategic alliances like the one between Fiat and General Motors (Whitford and Enrietti 2005).

The discordant cells represent situations in which formal and/or informal institutions tend either to mitigate opportunism or to facilitate search but not both, thus begetting "partial" network failures that are analogous to the "relative" market failures (Arrow 1970; Papandreou 1994) and "permanently failing organizations" (Meyer and Zucker 1989) studied by economists and organizational theorists respectively.

Take the southwest quadrant. We know that opportunism is mitigated where informal or formal institutions fail to nourish trust, confidence, and loyalty and is more likely to dissipate where norms of reciprocity and good faith are pervasive. This certainly occurs in places where kinship relations, ethnic networks, and religious communities serve as bulwarks of community and reciprocity, but it can also be driven by political parties, trade associations, and labor unions that are potentially more susceptible to policy intervention. However, such institutions may mitigate opportunism without assuaging competency gaps, in which case there is substantial risk of "involution" due to isolation from new information sources that occurs regardless (or perhaps because) of the level of trust or good faith in the network. And in fact, there are many well-documented case of just such partial network failures, including most notably Gernot Grabher's (1993) celebrated analysis of "the weakness of strong ties" in the Ruhr Valley. Grabher shows that the substantial industrial decline of the heartland of the German coal, iron, and steel complex in the 1970s and 1980s was fundamentally regional and thus only contingently sectoral. Despite—or perhaps because of—strong institutions to mitigate opportunism, the parties to the network became functionally, cognitively, and politically locked in to transacting with each other, and thus were caught off guard by a series of fundamental technological and market changes occurring elsewhere in the industry.

In the northeast quadrant, by contrast, we reference situations in which formal and informal institutions foster the growth of skill and technical capacity. This can of course be driven by the same organizations and institutions that build trust—trade associations and labor unions—but it may also be a consequence of public institutions like schools, vocational and training institutions, development banks, and industrial extension services. However, it is possible that such institutions may assuage competency shortfalls without adequately blocking opportunism. And there is again strong empirical evidence that this occurs, manifesting in what we label "contested networks" that fail due to patterns of contestation rooted in the intersection of organizational dynamics and institutional legacies. MacDuffie and Helper (2006) and Whitford (2005; Whitford and Zeitlin 2004), for example, conclude that such conflictual networks are common in American durable manufacturing and argue that they are a consequence of an interaction between low trust and high, but dispersed, competencies. These partially failed networks tend to be stable because partners have become locked into "task-level collaboration" due to an outsourcing of design that leaves no single party able to develop workable products alone, but tend also to perform poorly because companies remain imbued with legacies of exit and are enmeshed in a system of corporate governance that generates immense pressures to meet short-term targets (Hall and Soskice 2001).

When partial network failures obtain, the case for industrial policy to correct those failures is both strong and straightforward.[12] Partial network failures rooted in opportunism should push policymakers to create and take advantage of confidence-building measures and institutions, including trade associations, peak business associations, cartels and cooperatives, mediation services, and alternative dispute resolution procedures. For network failures rooted in ignorance or isolation, by contrast, policymakers ought to focus on building and exploiting educational and training institutions including not only vocational and technical schools but also industrial extension services, overseas marketing agencies, and supplier development programs.

The case for industrial policy to mitigate absolute network failures (network still-birth) is more complicated, and we caution that policymakers should think seriously about the opportunity costs of different policy options. Certainly there are sectors and activities in the economy that are favored by network governance; but it is a big world and there is no a priori reason to believe that policymakers should focus on those sectors and activities to the relative detriment of sectors favored by market or hierarchical governance. Once that case has been made, however, the good news from recent analyses of American industrial policy is that state actors have in some instances proven able not merely to bolster poorly performing networks but also to seed the emergence of networks de novo.

Moreover, those same studies suggest that once the decision is made to undertake policy to combat network stillbirth, the distinction between efforts to combat "screwing" and "screwing up" can help us understand how that can usefully be done. The key is to recognize that although state actors may not have much to work with when networks are stillborn (by definition), political decentralization still makes it easier for state actors to exploit what Schneiberg (2007, 2) refers to as institutional "flotsam and jetsam." Writing in response to an institutionalist literature that has historically been skeptical of the possibilities of agent-driven and endogenous institutional change, Schneiberg argues that the historical record gives reason to be mindful of the fact that while typologies are useful, and types can even be thought to exist, they are rarely totalizing. In fact, he writes, "agent-centered" institutional change can draw on "elements of alternative economic orders and abandoned or partly realized institutional projects" and can, in so doing, generate otherwise unrealized "possibilities of change and innovation" (Crouch and Farrell 2004; Crouch 2005).[13]

Applying this optic to Block's (2008) descriptions of a "hidden developmental state in the United States," and to other recent analyses in a similar vein by authors looking in greater detail at American policy interventions to favor technologies that are relatively new and well-suited to network production, we find that the "flotsam and jetsam" in question is represented by (1) highly connected technologists who were induced to search for, and then to acquire or incorporate, new competencies and skills through public action; or (2) untapped but disconnected reservoirs of competencies that were complemented by new institutions designed to mitigate fears of opportunism, thus uncorking improvements in network governance.

The first pattern is well exemplified in Matthew Keller's (2010) chapter on "The CIA's Pioneering Role in Public Venture Capital Initiatives." Recall that Keller analyzes the formation and development of In-Q-Tel, the CIA's not-for-profit venture capital wing, whose success in turn led to a "broad expansion of VC or quasi-VC models within other defense and technology-focused agencies, including the Department of Defense, the Army, the Navy, NASA, the National Technology Alliance, and additional agencies tied to the management of the Department of Energy laboratories."

For our purposes, two elements of Keller's story are particularly interesting. First, Keller makes clear that the "initial imperatives driving government agencies to adopt the model had little to do with stimulating economic growth" but was rather a response to the fact that while the CIA, like other government agencies, had very strong ties to key parts of the American corporate sector (the military-industrial complex), the "dispersed nature of the computer-related technology boom" meant that those ties were no longer the right ties. Rather, Keller writes, "agencies that contracted with the large firms and suppliers favored by traditional procurement and service contracts were automatically receiving 'second order' technologies that had been created by a small firm," leaving little room for "shaping innovations to specifically fit targeted agency needs." The response was novel. The CIA borrowed the VC model, not to make money but rather to "expand and strengthen the networks of experts at the disposal of federal agencies" with the ultimate aim of shaping the "promising and targeted technologies rather than designing them." It has achieved some success, but, as Keller makes clear, "the public VC model is not able to stimulate the development of new ideas conceived by government agents—at least in its current configurations, it is designed to access markets, not to create them."

Second, the model Keller describes is a product of political decentralization. Keller notes that the initial public VC efforts occurred at the state level and were then copied by the CIA, which was in turn borrowing ideas from the Energy Department's national labs, where greater connections to commercial technologists had proven fruitful. Thus the public VC model was protected from the market fundamentalists not only by the fact that it could be justified to Congress in terms of national security but by the fact that it was spawned subnationally, where the commitment to market fundamentalism is more variegated in the first place.

The broader lesson is that decentralization is a feature rather than a bug in the new world of industrial policymaking. There is space for experimentation within the U.S. state that, if successful, can diffuse to other parts of the policy apparatus. In-Q-Tel would not have been undertaken if the orders had to come from on high; it was undertaken at lower levels of government, trickled up, and then across other agencies similarly trapped by an older and relatively involuted model of procurement.

For the second pattern—that of institutions that mitigate issues of risk and opportunism—we turn again to the national labs, but this time to the chapter by Schrank (2010) documenting the growth of network governance in an emergent renewable energy cluster in New Mexico.[14] Schrank's story contains two elements of particular interest. First, like Keller, Schrank tells a story of institutional change in the interstices of the American state in which a remnant of Cold War policy was turned into an instrument of industrial policy almost by accident. New Mexico has historically been a bastion of "oil patch" politics. The state's political scene, even more so than the national political scene, is dominated by oil and gas interests that "have evinced little— if any—interest in renewable energy," electing instead to "[decry] efforts to develop alternatives to fossil fuels." However, as the national labs had somehow to reinvent themselves in the aftermath of the Cold War, Sandia lab in particular took advantage of the relatively decentralized nature of the American bureaucracy to exploit new freedoms granted them by changes in federal regulations. They, like other labs, were allowed to create cooperative agreements so long as they would "enhance their ability to pursue their 'core mission'"—which in their case was weapons development.

Schrank also shows that while "Sandia's private partners were for the most part foreign to Albuquerque ... the lab officials responsible for technology transfer believed that co-location and clustering were central to their long term success." And their efforts gained the support of state and local politicians. The region was obviously blessed with tremendous technical and technological competencies, precisely due to the presence of the labs and the many Ph.D. scientists they employed.

But competency alone does not make a cluster of network governance (if it did, every major university would be at the center of a cluster). How then to encourage spin-offs? Schrank argues that the key factor has been Sandia's effort to create a safety net for entrepreneurial scientists and engineers, primarily through a program that allows Sandia employees to take leave to bring their inventions to market, but also through consulting and brokerage services that help their fledgling companies find capital, develop business plans, and so on. These programs, Schrank argues, not only sheltered potential entrepreneurs from risk but led them to maintain ties to the labs and to each other, each more secure that should problems arise they were welcome to return to the labs.

The Case for a New Industrial Policy: Empirical or Normative?

We began this chapter by recognizing an emerging consensus that changes in the organization of industry have created new ways for states to stimulate economic restructuring and productivity growth. To outline this emerging consensus, we drew on recent programmatic statements by Dani Rodrik and Fred Block which make it clear that these calls for a new industrial policy no longer talk about helping particular firms catch up to foreign competitors, nor do they obsess about policies, instruments, and modalities of intervention. Rather, they seek to build bridges between the public and private sector, and to put a process in place that can identify and support the most promising avenues for innovation.

Like Block and Rodrik, we see new space for an industrial policy construed as a process of collective discovery able to usefully encourage the production of innovation. We are thus heartened by their dressing down of market fundamentalism. But we worry that their case as currently pitched does not properly challenge the strongest market fundamentalist case to be made against a new progressive industrial policy.

In particular, we think that the sort of market fundamentalist against whom Block, Rodrik, and others in their camp have largely made their arguments are for the most part what Jeffrey Henderson and Richard Applebaum (1992, 20) label "market ideological" in nature. Henderson and Applebaum's label was coined to fill in the empty cell of Chalmers Johnson's (1982) famous typology of political economies (see Table 13.2).

Johnson divided the industrial countries into three camps depending on the locus of decision making (plan or market) and the nature of decision making (rational or ideological). Where the United States was market rational and Japan was plan rational,

Table 13.2 A Typology of Industrial Political Economies

		Locus of Decision Making	
		Plan	*Market*
Nature of Decision Making	*Rational*	Postwar Japan	Postwar U.S.
	Ideological	USSR	Neoliberal U.S. (Reagan era onward)

Source: Derived from Johnson (1982) and Henderson and Appelbaum (1992)

the Soviet Union was plan ideological in that party leaders let their ideology trump their national interests.

Henderson and Applebaum's innovation was to fill in the empty fourth cell by recognizing that in the 1980s the United States had abandoned market rationality for market fundamentalism—an irrational, ideologically motivated commitment to deregulation, privatization, and liberalization. And it is against this version of market ideology that Block and Rodrik target their arguments.

Market fundamentalists (or ideologues) hold that he or she who governs least governs best. This relies on a tendentious reading of the historical record that is ever on the lookout for government (but not market) failure. But at least in these crisis-ridden times, it has been widely enough discredited that the more serious worry is another sort of market fundamentalist who is well aware that markets are social institutions that require copious regulation to function properly and who recognizes that much of what the state does is essentially market making (which requires much more than simply guaranteeing property rights).

Members of this second group, best represented by Peter Hall, David Soskice, and their collaborators (2001), are *market rational*. They claim that different "varieties of capitalism" are differently amenable to market-making and to network-making policy interventions and that the differences are in part due to national political institutions and cultures. Hall and Soskice emphasize coordination and "the kinds of institutions that alter the outcomes of strategic interaction" (Hall and Soskice 2001, 5–6), and focus particularly on "the quality of the relationships the firm is able to establish" with both internal and external actors. The implication is that "a firm encounters many coordination problems. Its success depends fundamentally on its ability to coordinate effectively with a wide range of actors." They also argue that interlocking complementarities between institutions mean that economies can be expected to cluster with relatively little hybridity into one of two types at a national level: liberal market economies (LMEs), with the United States and the United Kingdom as archetypes, and coordinated market economies (CMEs), with Germany as archetype (Hall and Soskice 2001, 8). They do so, Hall and Soskice argue, because firms have strong incentives to "gravitate toward the mode of coordination for which there is institutional support."

By implication, firm strategy and organization should vary systematically by country (Hall and Soskice 2001, 9). In LMEs, "firms coordinate their activities primarily via hierarchies and competitive market arrangements" and "invest more extensively in *switchable assets*" (Hall and Soskice 2001, 8, 17). LMEs provide institutional support largely for market and hierarchical coordination. CMEs, however, also require institutions that (1) allow for credible commitments and the exchange of information; (2) facilitate the monitoring of behavior and the sanctioning of defection; and (3) "provide actors potentially able to cooperate with one another with a capacity for deliberation" (Hall and Soskice 2001, 11). Examples include business associations, strong trade unions, cross-shareholding networks, and legal/regulatory systems that facilitate information sharing. That is, Hall and Soskice argue that the CME is distinguished from the LME precisely by its ability to support the sorts of process-focused institutions that we have pointed to as exemplary of state response to network failures.

Why does this matter? Because it has implications for industrial policy in the United States and beyond. We can divide attitudes toward industrial policy in the United States along two axes that loosely parallel the Johnson-Henderson and Applebaum framework referenced in Table 13.2: the institutional and the normative (see Table 13.3). The former is about the degree to which American political institutions allow policymakers to pursue an activist industrial policy. The latter asks about the nature of those policies: should a country with the American institutional endowment actively pursue industrial policies of the sort that Rodrik and Block outline?

Hall and Soskice would answer both questions in the negative. They don't think it is *good* that the United States is a liberal market economy. They simply argue that it is *true* the United State is a liberal market economy. There is a role for the state, but it differs from what one might see in a CME framework where governments can work together with business associations to police defection and credibly administer policies that favor implicit contracts and other forms of collaborative nonmarket coordination. Indeed, their theory predicts that such "network making" policies will fail in an LME. Soskice (1999, 128) argues that "effective business coordinating capacity cannot generally be built 'spontaneously' to service an institutional framework" because this would require that companies already "be engaged in long-term relational contracts" that can sustain "common shared understandings" and the "creation of expert communities across associations, research institutions, and companies." And this, Soskice argues, "can only take place over long periods." In LMEs, the argument goes, policymakers should instead recognize and embrace their own comparative institutional advantage in industries favored by freer market coordination, as these are more amenable to such "blunt" policy instruments as deregulation and market incentive policies that "do not put extensive demands on firms to form relational contracts with others." Such policies, which amount to market making in that they allow actors more easily to coordinate their activities with prices, are the only ones that are "*incentive compatible* [in an LME],

Table 13.3 Attitudes Toward Industrial Policy in the United States

		Institutional: Can industrial policy be pursued in the United States?	
		No	*Yes*
Normative: Should the American state do more than make markets?	*No*	Market rational: believes that industrial policy is incentive incompatible with U.S. institutions (e.g., Hall and Soskice).	Market fundamentalist: believes that industrial policy is possible (and perhaps even under way) but ill-advised in the U.S. (e.g., Milton Friedman, Cato Institute).
	Yes	Plan (or policy) irrational: commitment to industrial policy trumps recognition that it is ill suited to U.S. institutional context (e.g., Magaziner and Reich; Bluestone and Harrison).	Plan (or policy) rational: recognizes that industrial policy is not only desirable but is increasingly compatible with U.S. institutional structure given the decentralization of production.

namely, complementary to the incentive structures and coordinating capacities embedded in the existing political economy" (Hall and Soskice 2001, 46).

The upshot is that the market rational position—exemplified here by Hall and Soskice—holds that there is not a lot an LME state (like the United States) can do to foment reciprocity. It simply does not have the assemblage of associations and networks needed to police the many prisoner's dilemmas that occur when you ask people to share potentially valuable information without financial compensation and only the hope of learning something valuable down the road.

The market rational position differs from the market fundamentalist view in that its opposition to industrial policy in the United States derives not from doubts about human nature but from doubts about the nature of North American institutions. Market rationalists do not presume that markets simply happen, nor do they expect them to function effectively absent significant and active institutional intervention. But whatever the basis for their opposition, the fact remains that advocates of the market rational approach are unlikely to favor industrial policies that go beyond market making and market smoothing in LMEs. They thus present a particularly strong challenge to traditional liberal advocates of industrial policy in the United States like Magaziner, Reich, Bluestone, and Harrison. While liberals worry that the industrial policies impeded by American institutions are essential, and therefore defend government intervention despite recognizing its incentive incompatibility with U.S. institutions. Hall and Soskice (2001) believe that well-governed markets can lead to efficient and (with the appropriate safety net) socially just outcomes. They make clear, for example, that while each of the two types of capitalisms "has its partisans," they believe that each seems "capable of providing satisfactory levels of long-run economic performance." The differences lie in the sectoral specializations of different countries, and in the underlying economic policies that should be followed in order to ensure that countries maintain their "comparative institutional advantage."

There is a fourth perspective that shares the liberal commitment to industrial policy but questions its concerns about U.S. institutions. After all, U.S. institutions may well have been incompatible with an industrial policy designed to save a particular vertically integrated and geographically concentrated sector (e.g., steel, autos) from low-cost foreign competition. But these sectors are no longer the heart and soul of the industrial policy debate—and even where they are, they are no longer organized in such a concentrated fashion. The core of the productive economy today relies on decentralized production networks described by Powell, and these activities and governance mechanisms may well *benefit* from a decentralized polity that can ensure flexibility, experimentation, and local knowledge (Whitford 2005).

This undermines a key tenet of the varieties of capitalism position. Hall and Soskice (2001, 16) argue that the national-specific character of "so many of the institutional factors conditioning the behavior of firms" means that variation at the regional level is largely insignificant. We argue, by contrast, that it is a grave mistake to ignore the implications of federalism, the separation of powers, and other decentralized elements in the American polity. To do so too quickly dismisses viable options hidden in interstices and inconsistencies in an American national institutional framework that is not nearly so coherent as theory would have it be.

Indeed, if we look at Block's (2008) description of the hidden developmental state and at the chapters in this volume, we find examples of an industrial policy that (1) focuses as much on the construction and repair of network failures as it does on remedies for market failure; (2) is able to do so in no small part by capitalizing on decentralized elements in the American policy apparatus. Block makes quite clear, after all, that the DARPA model is not simply seed money to offset the many externalities that are known to bedevil private investment in basic research. The agency's offices are "proactive rather than reactive and work to set an agenda for researchers in the field." More importantly, the agency recognizes as part of its task the responsibility to "use its oversight role to make constructive linkages of ideas, resources, and people across different research and development sites" (Block 2008, 176). As regards the salience of political decentralization, Block (2008, 181) notes that while the initiatives he describes "began at the Federal level, ... many of them were designed to coordinate with state and local initiatives" able to provide technical assistance and to "educate the firms about different types of assistance available."

Moreover, if we look at the programs analyzed by Block, Keller, Schrank, and the many others in this volume who have documented the seeds of a new industrial policy in American technology policy, we find that those seeds are located across a wide range of agencies, often with relatively little central oversight and thus with ample space for "institutional entrepreneurship." The Department of Energy, for example, recognized that the protection of its budget "required establishing the commercial value of the federal laboratories" and thus "embraced the ARPA model of industrial policy" in order to "accelerate the discovery of commercially viable products" (Block 2008, 182). Other labs pursue distinct missions in conjunction with different local partners using different policy tools—and it's not clear to us that a uniform approach would be superior. Indeed, in a world increasingly dominated by a new logic of organizing, in which the vagaries of technology and the uncertainties of ever shorter product cycles favor production networks as much as they do the stimulation of new markets, decentralization seems more virtue than necessity because it allows industrial policymakers who are close to the source to exploit local knowledge, experiment, and build redundancy into the system. In so doing, they not only raise the competitiveness of the American economy but lay the ideological as well as material groundwork for efforts to forge "wholly new pathways within the womb of the old order" (Schneiberg 2007, 70).

Frank Dobbin (1993, 49) has argued that "policy revolutions that are generated by crises—as policy revolutions tend to be—may be unlikely to persist due to the conditions of their origins," and by that logic the hidden industrial policy described by Block may turn out to be a fleeting experiment—or a footnote to U.S. economic history. But Dobbin (1994, 92, 57) has elsewhere noted that state governments pursued mercantilist policies with abandon in the United States until "market rational" federal intervention put a stop to their "rivalistic activism" in the nineteenth century.

The question before us is therefore whether market rationality is America's natural state, in which case today's decentralized industrial policies will in all likelihood wither once the crisis is over, or whether market rationality was itself a policy revolution that has now advanced through a reign of neoliberal terror into a Thermidorian Reaction that could well give way to the construction of a sustainable pathway out of the womb of the old order. There is certainly no guarantee that such a pathway will be forged, let alone that it will lead to a more just or peaceful world. And it would be ironic indeed to find a sustainable twenty-first century economy built with the "flotsam and jetsam" of the twentieth-century military-industrial complex and early-nineteenth-century "rivalistic statism" (Dobbin 1994, 58). But swords have been turned into plowshares at the behest of industrial policymakers before (Johnson 1982). And scientists have at times agreed to "study war no more" (Moore 2008). New pathways have been forged from old orders. And nowhere would such moves have more profound consequences—and thus be worth fighting for—than in the contemporary United States.

Notes

1. See Schrank and Whitford (2009a) for an extended discussion of the American polity and our initial call for a theory of network failure. And see Schrank and Whitford (2009a) for an extended discussion of the theoretical gap in the governance literature.

2. On the concept of the developmental network state, see especially Ó Riain (2004a).

3. To invoke Donald Mackenzie's apt metaphor (2006), Block holds that the theory underlying market fundamentalism is "an engine, not a camera." By decrying all but the market, he argues, they force government policy underground. But when government policy is underground, it is put at greater risk of regulatory capture. Market fundamentalism, insofar as it is the faith of the land, tends to *enact* its scope conditions (a world in which government failure is endemic).

4. It is perhaps worth noting that industrial policies are almost always hidden. The relevant question is, hidden from whom? As Chalmers Johnson (1999, 42–45) has argued, Japanese bureaucrats hide their industrial policies from prying Western eyes for fear of trade retaliation. U.S. officials, by way of contrast, hide their industrial policies from their own citizens.

5. For example, "If the development bank is in good shape but tax administration is a mess, promotion may need to be done through directed credit rather than tax incentives" (Rodrik 2004, 24).

6. Rodrik (2004, 25) argues emphatically that "an optimal strategy of discovering the productive potential of a country will necessarily" entail picking some "losers." The "objective should be not to minimize the chances that mistakes will occur, which would result in no self-discovery at all, but to minimize the costs of mistakes when they do occur." Decentralization widens the range of promoted activities, generating perhaps more successes but also more failures. Rodrik's point here is that industrial policymakers are in a situation akin to that of private loan officers who are told to thread the needle between a nonpayment (or failure) rate that is too high, in which case they are losing money to default, and a nonpayment rate that is too low, in which case they are losing money to foregone opportunities. A failure rate of zero implies an overly conservative loan officer—or industrial policymaker.

7. Others focus on the failure of public hierarchies or states. In so doing, however, they too

treat failure as a continuous variable. So-called government failures (Krueger 1990) range from misallocation to outright "state collapse" (Milliken 2002).

8. We have written at length elsewhere on the "anatomy of network failure" (Schrank and Whitford 2009b) and refer the reader there for a detailed discussion of the concept of the network failure and its broader theoretical implications. Here we reference the elements of that argument that are most relevant for the industrial policy debate. See especially Schrank (2004; 2005) and Whitford (2005) for empirical analyses of what we have since come to think of as "network failure."

9. Others may want to add other scope conditions under the rubric of desirability. In our focus on efficiency—implied in our reference to volatile demand and other interdependencies—we have left aside distributional issues that might follow from particular patterns of governance. For example, it might be the case that network governance in the biotechnology industry is profoundly productive of innovation but also underpins an oligopoly that ultimately generates high consumer prices. Our view is that the innovative parts of the value chain should still be governed in networks and that superprofits should simply be taxed away; but we do not dispute that one might plausibly take a different position on the grounds that superprofits seem never to be taxed away.

10. Whitford (2005) and Schrank (2004; 2005).

11. Some readers may feel that it is not enough to simply invoke "should" as our scope condition here (or, for that matter, our use of "desirability" in our initial definition). Space limitations prevent us from delving as deeply as we might like into the larger question of what is and is not desirable, and we thus draw on established findings and conventions in the literature on network governance. The finding, as referenced in the previous section, is that network governance tends to lead to more product and process innovation in sectors characterized by volatile demand conditions, by complex interdependencies on the supply side, or by rapid technological changes. The conventional assumption is that increasing the likelihood of either product or process innovation is likely to lead to better outcomes. We are open to the possibility in the real world that it may not, but do not consider this a failure of network governance per se.

12. See Schrank and Whitford (2009b) for detailed examples of industrial policy to correct partial network failures, with reference to cases in the United States, Europe, and Latin America.

13. Put another way, the United States is a variegated place. Political decentralization can allow states potentially to act on what might be thought of as otherwise "latent" partial networks that can be stimulated and strengthened through appropriate policy intervention in a move that is roughly akin to taking seriously Rodrik's (2004) claim that industrial policy ought essentially to be about creating the conditions for industrial "self-discovery" and applying it to network formation.

14. While we present Schrank's chapter as our exemplar here (since we are obviously familiar with it), we might for example as easily have selected Fuchs's chapter on DARPA (Chapter 7). It describes the ways that agency has solved classic moral hazard problems in emerging technology fields. She describes DARPA as an organization that formally draws on interpersonal relationships between technologists in academia and industry, many of whom are otherwise disconnected, to assess the viability of an array of new technologies and then to use those assessments to seed start-up companies.

CHAPTER 14

Avoiding Network Failure
The Case of the National Nanotechnology Initiative
Christopher Newfield

Several decades of research have established that markets often shortchange long-range research, especially in high-risk technologies whose calculable value to a given firm is far smaller than their eventual social value. The common term for this problem is "market failure," and the shared perspective of most of the contributors to this volume is that government agencies need to correct market failure, particularly by being an investor of last resort for valuable research that may take years or decades to come to fruition. The developmental state can aim at types of scientific, economic, and social progress that are well over the horizon of any individual firm or consortium. Taken as a whole, this volume encourages federal, state, and other U.S. governments to embrace their proper role as long-term investors, procurers, and enlightened, flexible, decentralized, problem-solving managers in relation to the colossal technical and economic challenges the United States currently confronts.

At the same time, many of the chapters point out that science and economic policy cannot in a straightforward way supplement markets with government action, much less replace markets with governments. The details of the linkages between economic, political, and institutional factors vary from one industry to another, from one time and place to another (e.g., Henderson and Newell 2009). What worked in the 1970s for agriculture did not work in the 1970s for electronics, and 1970s agricultural solutions cannot be applied to agriculture in the 2010s without great empirical and analytical effort of identifying differences and transforming previous models to fit new conditions and goals.

I will assume that recent research of the type that is described in this volume allows us to avoid the simplistic contrast between markets and governments that claimed innate differences of structure and effect (markets are open while governments are closed, markets allow free choice while governments coerce, etc.). Researchers can take as their starting point the idea that state-market interactions can better be described as networks (Powell 1990), and more specifically as public-private partnerships in which complicated organizations of different types have to work out intricate exchanges of information, authority, and activities. Industry and government interact as contrasting but related elements in heterogeneous networks whose details and variations need careful description.

That said, can we make any generalizations about the elements that need to be in place for these partnerships to work? Here I will argue that heterogeneous networks—valuably analyzed in this volume under various rubrics—should be seen as depending on both good *internal* relations and good *external* relations with various publics. In fact, we need to go one step farther and drop this contrast between internal relations among experts and external relations with publics: a large literature on the role of "lead users" as well as sociologies and histories of technology have been revealing for some time the involvement of different publics with research and development (Latour 1987; Latour 2005). Public interest in technology development is a major factor in the success of that development over both the short and the long term. I will discuss the National Nanotechnology Initiative (NNI) and more specifically its reporting of nanoscale research to that research's potentially interested public. I show how the NNI does not address its publics in the narrative mode most likely to interest those publics. This demonstration does not constitute proof that effective technology narratives would allow the NNI to offer better technological outcomes or arouse greater public interest. But the nonexistence of developmental narratives within the major R&D agency I look at here casts doubt on the scientific development itself. Public readers of agency records would also note this absence, and elsewhere I have sketched a scenario in which a citizen-reader tries and fails to identify federally funded nanoscale research with public impact (Newfield 2009). This failure could only suppress public interest, as well as public financial support. At the ten-year mark for the National Nanotechnology Initiative, the development of narratives that would help public participate in the development process (Irwin 1995; Bucchi and Neresini 2008) could well create more intensive and more equitable public-private partnerships.

Avoiding Network Failure

In their contribution to this volume, Josh Whitford and Andrew Schrank (Chapter 13) make the important point that a focus on market failure should not eclipse the equally important problem of "network failure." The NNI explicitly aimed at creating national network effects, and they need to be assessed and, where necessary, improved.

The same goes for Erica Fuchs's analysis of the Defense Advance Research Projects Agency (DARPA) (Chapter 7), which my analysis of DARPA's nanoscale research reporting complements. Fuchs shows that DARPA plays an important networking function, and given its distinguished history of sponsorship in computer science and other areas would seem well suited to serve as one of the major federal cures for market failure (Greenstein 2009). And yet in Fuchs's account, DARPA requires researchers to team up in collaborations in which major industry players served as prime contractors. Networks do improve on markets through their superior powers of coordination. Networks do improve on hierarchies through more efficient and more equitable distribution. But if a network is nepotistic or elitist, and in effect allows the rich to get richer while ignoring innovations that come from the research "poor" (including younger or outlier researchers), then it simply replicates the weaknesses of both hierarchies and concentrated markets.

Network analysis has made major contributions to understanding the institutional complexities of contemporary R&D. And yet it often understates the ease with which networks can replicate the features of both of these other forms—the hierarchy and the concentrated or monopolistic market (Roelofs 2009). One example is an important recent study of collaboration in the life sciences by a team that included one of the field's leading practitioners, Walter W. Powell. After the authors of this sophisticated study claim that accumulative advantage has the "weakest support" among their various explanations for the shape of the industry, and reject the possibility of excessive concentration, they note that "a very small core of perhaps one or two dozen organizations are routinely placed in the center, and their node size grows somewhat over the period" (Powell et al. 2005). They then associate centrality and advantage with "multiconnectivity," and conclude, "The key story, in our view, is less the issue of the nature and distribution of resources and more how these institutional features promoted dense webs of connection that, once in place, influenced both subsequent decisions and the trajectory of the field." But the authors' contrast between distribution of resources and multiconnectivity is artificial: in collaborations, "dense web of connections" function as an accumulative advantage. They can form the basis of a quasi-monopoly on knowledge and other resources that raises barriers to entry and forces innovators to work with established players or face marginalization. "Webs of connection" are often designed to do this in conformity with a given firm's business model, which is likely to target the *most* innovative entrants (since these are the most threatening). With this in mind, we can note that while DARPA may operate as an example of the *developmental network state*, it may (and at the same time) operate as a *bureaucratic market state*, in which firms or laboratories with either large market resources or special network placement or both have incumbent advantages that reduce overall innovation.

The third of this subset of four chapters is by John A. Alic (Chapter 12), who makes the crucial point that "innovation bubbles up through organizations, often from deep within them, with heterogeneous contributions from heterogeneous employees." He makes similar points about the importance of end users for technological development. We could wrench Alic into our network terminology and say that he insists on the full-spectrum network, one whose bit players, edges, bottoms, and outer limits are as important as the central players to the overall health of the innovation system.

Finally, this injunction to look at the entirety of an innovation system is put into practice by Chris Knight's chapter on photovoltaic (PV) development (Chapter 9). Knight examines R&D policy and practice but spends much of his time on implementations at the municipal level. His investigation shows that rates of PV adoption depend on fixing problems that exist far from the research centers of a technology's R&D networks. For example, U.S. installation costs are a higher percentage of overall PV system costs than they are in Europe in large part because of the absence of standardized building and electrical codes. PV innovation that leads to massively increased use depends on R&D at the high-end centers like Stanford and various University of

California campuses, but equally on the actions of innovative local actors like the Sacramento Municipal Utility District and county planning and development officials.

Thus the business of "creating and bolstering networks" (Whitford and Schrank, Chapter 13) needs to be seen as creating and bolstering complete and internally nonprejudicial networks. This is an ideal type (never attained in practice) in which "top" versus "bottom" and "core" versus "periphery" are not allowed to skew, distort, or interrupt the exchange of both information and resources. Networks are continuously evolving entities that must be reanalyzed and redesigned in perpetuity and whose hierarchical skews need persistent attention. While hierarchy and concentration can never be eliminated—and some beneficial forms of concentration should in fact be retained—an acknowledgment of the issues posed by hierarchy is the prerequisite to successful management of it. Much recent commentary stresses the extent to which technology development networks need to be inclusive, that is, need to involve lead customers or engage the public (von Hippel 2006). Effective networks are those whose parts are of sufficiently similar status to communicate, interact, and collaborate on the basis of mutual interest and consent—where status and resource differences do not present a preestablished barrier. To overstate only somewhat, *open networks must be egalitarian or they are not open.*

Knight's case study reminds us that without functional equality, heterogeneous networks do not work. At the same time, heterogeneous networks are exactly the type that are essential to the actual use of advanced technology to address urgent social needs. Most truly urgent social needs became urgent because the complexity of combined sociotechnical problems have prevented their timely solution for years or decades. Renewable energy is a case in point, and Knight's work on photovoltaic implementation indicates the need for good communication and collaboration among groups with diverse interests and social positions—Stanford electrical engineers, UC Davis contracts and grants officers, the Sacramento utility's project managers, county planners, contractors in the field, and homeowners who buy a PV module for their residence. To accomplish this within a heterogeneous network, networked actors must be *equal enough* to be taken seriously by one another, and to be truly addressed.

The goal here is *sufficient equality—equality sufficient for open exchange.* It cannot be measured by formal network analysis in itself or with quantitative measures of output. Both of these focus on actors who are central, dominant, and/or quantitatively the most productive, but do not account for the history or the dynamics of an innovation system even though they are major determinants of its overall results. We also need qualitative studies to account for the outcomes of heterogeneous systems. A crucial form of heterogeneity is that which links expert researchers and their institutions to the publics who fund, use, and judge that research. In the third part of this chapter I will analyze DARPA's form of address to that broader public, and I will suggest how improved functioning of the innovation system—which includes major public inputs—might improve interactions between agencies like DARPA and the public. Before I turn to this issue, however, I will elaborate further on the importance of the public to sustainable technological development—and to the fuller network dispersal of innovation as such.

The Centrality of the Peripheral Public

Evidence for the role of the public can be found in an important recent history of technology by British historian David Edgerton, *The Shock of the Old* (2007). Edgerton's core theme is the pervasive and profound social impact of old technology and low technology long after they supposedly peaked. One ghastly example is Rwanda's "spectacularly fast genocide" in 1994, which Edgerton traces in part to the machetes stockpiled in advance: "most victims were killed by machete (38 percent), clubs (17 percent) with firearms accounting for only 15 percent of deaths" (182). Edgerton seeks to explain our underestimation of the role of the old. He argues that we make the mistake of centering our histories of technology on laboratory innovation rather than on use. We date advancement and progress from the moment a technology appears or is first applied, and downplay the long and winding road of adoption, imitation, diffusion, improvement, recycling, and hybridization. And yet it is this long haul, he shows, that decides the impact of a technology on society, and not its exciting first revelation.

For example, steam power "was not only absolutely but relatively more important in 1900 than in 1800." Similarly, "the world consumed more coal in 2000 than in 1950 or 1900." If we date steam power from its earlier appearances in Britain in the 1700s, we will identify it with the "dawn of the industrial revolution," wrongly see its importance as ended by other energy forms (oil, electricity), and miss steam's long and influential presence in later decades. If we look at use rather than invention or first adoption, we can, to take another case, recognize the continuing importance of coal to China's current round of spectacular industrialization and appreciate the extent to which China may "win" at new technologies like nanotechnologies precisely by using the old.

A more familiar feature of U.S. R&D is also crucial to the post–World War II period: the United States benefited from massive Cold War military investment and from its long industrial experience with the highly skilled coordination of large-scale engineering projects (Shapin 2008). The most famous of these was the "Manhattan Engineering District," which produced the atomic bomb during World War II. As Edgerton points out, this "buil[t] on decades of experience in large-scale research and development" (199). The federal government provided network coordination, but the elements to be coordinated came from all over and arrived in large part through the processes of borrowing, imitation, and the adaptation of existing work. The same combination of adaptation and coordination helps explain the important role of very large firms in the innovation process. Major advances have continuously come from companies like BASF, Hoechst, Bayer, AGFA, General Electric, AT&T, IBM, DuPont, and Eastman Kodak: "all these firms were already very large, innovative in 'science-based' technologies, and employed an abundance of scientists and engineers" (193). They created internal R&D operations that generally remained productive for decades at a time. "At least fifteen out of the twenty-three firms listed as the top R&D spenders in 1997 (and 2003) were formed before 1914" (194).

Looking at the old and the new side by side and over time suggests that there has never been such a thing as "closed innovation," in which development took place inside one institution or cluster. Analysts like AnnaLee Saxenian in *Regional Advantage*, Clayton Christensen in *The Innovator's Dilemma,* and Henry Chesbrough in *Open Innovation* have made much of a new dependence on networks that no company or nation can control. The history of technology suggests that there is nothing new about the sheer dispersal, the boundary crossing, the complex coordination, the institutional mixing and sharing, or the global scale of invention. A whole range of motives, participants, organizations, and sectors are always involved in any major technological wave.

Most crucially for our purposes, however, is that Edgerton's accumulated examples confirm the view that the most effective innovation networks are those that are rooted in the everyday practice of the invention. It has always been true, he argues, that "most invention has taken place in the world of use (including many radical inventions) and furthermore has been under the direct control of users" (187). A full history of technology puts practitioners of every kind at the center of innovation throughout history. It puts use at the center of invention. It puts the street and the shop next to the state-of-the-art academic lab. It puts imitation at the heart of invention. It truly displaces the "linear model" (from bench to bedside, from lab to market, from specialist to customer, from agent to recipient, from producer to consumer, from smart to dumb). It discredits the basic categorical distinctions on which that model generally rests. It concludes that in the deepest sense, the history of technology is the history of everybody—of all public uses of it, which create continuous extension, adaptation, and innovation.

What this means in turn is that there is no "downstream" (public) to try to push "upstream" (scientific laboratories), because in the history of technology, there is no "upstream." In other words, the upstream consists, at different points in a technology's history, of *all* of a technology's active users. Technology develops variously all over a global field, a network of networks that mixes technique, infrastructure, know-how, facilities, social frameworks, and social needs. Where we do see a discrete "upstream," it is a generally temporary imposition on a multilateral innovation system, one imposed through intellectual property rights and trade secrets as in today's pharmaceutical industry. These upstreams can be powerful and stable for years or even decades, but they remain special circumstances, not essential conditions of innovation in general. Histories of technology like Edgerton's require that we take networks *seriously—in all their dispersal and complexity.* A given technology has multiple origins and ongoing variations: the lab-based starting point is often duplicated elsewhere and is in the majority of cases not governed by rigid intellectual property rights sooner or later overshadowed by multiple developments. Software is the contemporary industry that best exemplifies what happens when there are low artificial barriers to entry: innovation is everywhere (Chesbrough 2003).

Technological innovation is a fundamentally sociocultural process, which of course means that the study of the history of technology must become as radically interdisciplinary as technology itself. Economists and historians need to work together regularly. Institutional sociologists need to be there too. So do specialists in cultural and artistic change, which are part of the same process. The intellectual task needs to be seen in all its profound difficulty before it can be resized and broken down enough for progress to be made on its parts, correctly interrelated to one another. Social choice would also be part of this analysis. As Edgerton puts it, "the twentieth century was awash with inventions and innovations ... we are free to oppose technologies we do not like." We are free "to research, develop, innovate, even in areas which are considered out of date by those stuck in passé futuristic ways of thinking."

If we admit, then, the power of the old, grant the importance of networks, accept the major role of various governments in coordinating those networks, agree that use is inseparably linked with invention, and then embrace not just the extension but also the multiple *origins* of use that include a vast public that is creating and innovating routinely with whatever is at hand, we are ready to ask an important question about a vital federal government initiative like the National Nanotechnology Initiative: How are the country's various publics being involved in the new waves of nanoscale research?

An Unprepared Partner: The U.S. Government's Nanotechnology Strategy

There is no question that, in spite of decades-old political controversies, the U.S. government has long had the world's biggest program of technology development funding. Although the federal government funds only about 28 percent of all R&D, about 70 percent of this total is D—product development organized by corporations (National Science Foundation 2008b). Commentators often note that 60 percent of basic research in the United States is funded by the federal government (National Science Foundation 2008b). Importantly, most of this federal research is *not* explicitly trying to compensate for market failure by supporting basic research that will fill market niches that happen to be a long way down the road. Most federal research seeks to address the government's own missions, particularly military missions, which in turn account for 60 percent of the federal R&D budget (Mowery 2009a). Rather than being the servant of market forces often criticized on the left, or demanded on the right, the federal government is a leader in setting the agendas of basic research in continuous collaboration with the relevant scientific communities. This leads to the following questions: Are federal agencies focused on creating and sustaining networked partnerships that include science's various publics in the network? Did the NNI advance this cause?

Nanotechnology is something of an ideal case. In the 1990s, it was a domain of scientific research that had great momentum and major potential for good social impacts. The field had seen a remarkable boom in publications, and one of its major scientific spokespersons, Richard C. Smalley, had received a Nobel Prize (Chemistry 1996) for his codiscovery of the fullerene molecule and was popularizing such soon-to-be defining "nano" characteristics as self-assembly and such nanophenomena as molecular electronics (Bennett and Sarewitz 2005; Smalley 1996).

By the late 1990s, nano seemed poised for a major acceleration through better funding and national coordination. A 1997 meeting of major scientists in the field led to a report claiming that nanotechnology's "application areas include the pharmaceutical and chemical industries, nanoelectronics, space exploration, metallurgy, biotechnology, cosmetics, the food industry, optics, nanomedicine, metrology and measurement, and ultraprecision engineering—there are practically no unaffected fields." It added, "efficient conversion of energy, materials, and other resources into products of high performance will be a strategic necessity in the next century" (Roco 1997). Two years later, an overlapping group of science and policy figures conducted a similar workshop, this time sponsored by the White House's National Science and Technology Council, and was prepared to issue much stronger conclusions. They called for the creation of a grand coalition, "a cooperative national program involving universities, industry, government agencies at all levels, and the government/national laboratories." This coalition would be embodied in "a national nanotechnology initiative in fiscal year 2001 that will approximately double the current Government annual investment of about $255 million (in fiscal year 1999) in R&D supporting nanoscience, engineering and technology" (Interagency Working Group on Nanoscience 1999; Roco 2008).

The National Nanotechnology Initiative (NNI) was drafted, passed, announced by President Bill Clinton at Cal Tech in January 2000, and put into effect later that year.[1] An important step in its passage was the communication to policymakers of nanotechnology's broader social impacts. Some of these appeared when the House of Representatives Committee on Science heard testimony about the value of nanotechnology, including Smalley's claim that nanoscience was "about to enter a golden new era" (McCray 2005).[2] The committee's report, *Unlocking the Future*, has a long section on "science for society," which sang the praises of publicly funded science with practical benefits.[3] In 2002, NNI leaders issued a 500-page report on nanotechnology's impact on "human performance" that included an eloquent call for large government nano funding with high social benefits from none other than the former Republican Speaker of the House and "small government" activist Newt Gingrich (Roco et al. 2002). Discussions of nanotechnology's social benefits were essential to garnering political support. The harmonization of scientific, economic, and social impacts was something of a policy marvel, and a tribute to the institutional skill of its leading advocates, M. C. Roco and his colleagues.

And yet for all the focus on public outcomes, the public was not present for the genesis of the NNI. Societal impacts were generally reduced to economic impacts, and the leading rationale for the NNI was economic competition with other countries.[4] The agenda-setting hearings and meetings did not include testimony from members of the public who had knowledge or experience of the effects of technology policy, or desires for technology. The pool of experts in attendance did not include experts on societal implications. As science scholars Ira Bennett and Daniel Sarewitz put it, "social scientists and humanists had little if any engagement with nanotechnology during the 1980s and 1990s, leaving the consideration of societal implications to technologists like [Eric] Drexler, [Ray] Kurzweil, and [Bill] Joy, to activists like Pat Roy Mooney, and to science fiction authors." In addition to this limited cultural range, the NNI came into being through a top-down process (Bennett and Sarewitz 2005). The public did not appear as an active character in official discussions but as a recipient: an audience to be persuaded, students to be educated, reactors to risk events to be managed, and beneficiaries of the hard work of scientists and businesspeople.

When society did appear, it was in a distanced and attenuated form. Striking examples can be culled from the NNI Human Performance conference, which covered promising topics such as "Expanding Human Cognition and Communication" and "Enhancing Group and Societal Outcomes." While there is no doubting the participants' commitment to enhancing human abilities, the presentations uniformly subordinated human factors to technological developments. Society itself, social life, is all but nonexistent in the report, and always improvable if not largely replaceable by computer networks and other forms of associative technology.[5]

One particularly striking example occurs in a statement expressing a desire to use nanotechnology "to help overcome inequality between people, isolation of the individual from the environment, injustice and deprivation, personal and cultural biases, misunderstanding, and unnecessary conflict." In the broadest sense, the report continues, it will powerfully enhance communication and creativity, potentially of great economic and social benefit. But the imagined enhancer is called the "Communicator." I quote part of its description at length in an attempt to convey correctly the tone as well as the idea. The Communicator will consist of:

> nano/info technologies that let individuals carry with them information about themselves and their work that can be easily shared in group situations. Thus, each individual participant will have the option to add information to the common pool of knowledge, across all domains of human experience—from practical facts about a joint task, to personal feelings about the issues faced by the group, to the goals that motivate the individual's participation.
>
> The Communicator will also be a facilitator for group communication, an educator or trainer, and/or a translator, with the ability to tailor its personal appearance, presentation style, and activities to group and individual needs. It will be able to operate in a variety of modes, including instructor-to-group and peer-to-peer interaction, with adaptive avatars that are able to change their affective behavior to fit not only individuals and groups, but also varying situations. It will operate in multiple modalities, such as sight and sound, statistics and text, real and virtual circumstances, which can be selected and combined as needed in different ways by different participants. Improving group interactions via brain-to-brain and brain-machine-brain interactions will also be explored.[6]

The authors seem unaware of the Orwellian structure of this idea, of its hive-mind overtones, or of its potential for domestic surveillance. The closest thing to the Communicator in my own recent reading appears in John Scalzi's remarkable science fiction novel *Old Man's War* (2005), where a Communicator-style mind mesh is called the BrainPal. But Scalzi presents the BrainPal as a military device that enhances soldiers through their controlled coordination, thus underwriting Earth's Colonial Defense Forces' more-or-less permanent aggression against every other species in the universe. The BrainPal offers absolutely no capacity to improve or enhance social relationships, with the exception of enabling new levels of group sex. All nonmilitary and nonsexual understanding continues in Scalzi's correct assessment to depend on sociocultural factors (identifications, power relations, divergent economic interests, romantic attachments, communal experience, etc.) that cannot be resolved through enhanced communication alone. Something like the Communicator will not begin to be even a tolerable idea until its authors can concretely describe social settings and factors that exist independently of technological enhancements.

This report's discourse is marked at all points by asociality. Society is remote, weak, and receptive rather than present, involved, active, and intrinsic—both to problems and to their solutions. The nano-based enhancement projects do *not* start from or refer to people or social groups who live out and articulate individual or social needs that they would like nanotechnology to address and *then* offer technological expertise in applying nanotechnology to those social needs. Such articulations are often incomplete and in process, but that does not explain why the reports leave these social conditions as abstract, remote, and underdescribed; the people who comprise those conditions are not even present.

What about a fallback position? This would be less than public participation and deliberation; rather, a kind of communication in which governmental agencies can establish the conditions of equitable private-public partnerships by at least acknowledging and presenting the results of public funding to various publics. This would mean conveying the impact of the presence—if not of the public voice and will—of public money. The public pays for a lot of research, and its contribution could be granted, explained, and narrated as a progress story in which social actors play an important role in the improvement of their own society.

Our research group looked for these kinds of narratives of public contribution, ones that linked the public to developments with major public impact. We looked for a nanoscale technology that was in use and had been funded by the NNI, and then sought records that tracked development through the following sequence showing which parties received funding or recorded gains at each stage:

a. NNI funding
b. A federal agency (e.g., NSF)
c. Funding program and calls
d. Funded research
e. Disclosures of inventions and publications
f. Patents
g. Licenses
h. Development and products

This list is more linear than development ever is. Another problem with our list is that once the money arrives at (a), the public contribution disappears.[7] But we used this sequence as the baseline for our search for public documents that would explain "science progress" to interested members of the public by showing where public funds had wound up and what they had done.

We started with the Defense Department's Advanced Research Projects Agency (DARPA). The Department of Defense receives about a third of NNI's annual funding,[8] and DARPA, widely credited with creating the ARPANET that led to the Internet, is arguably a leading government agency in taking on high-risk projects that might be total losses or, on the other hand, might lead to something like the post-1960s revolution in information technology.[9]

No public documentation of DARPA nanoscale progress exists. What we found by spending many hours searching systematically on the DARPA site is a series of lists of topic areas tied to reported accomplishments. Looking at any given year's budget estimates reveals separate items of interesting but unrelated subjects that are scattered throughout the report.[10]

Typical copy reads as follows: "electronically controlled microinstruments offer the possibility of nanometer-scale probing, sensing and manipulation for ultra-high density information storage 'on-a-chip', for nanometer-scale patterning, and for molecular level analysis and synthesis. These microinstruments for nanometer-scale mechanical, electrical and fluidic analysis offer new approaches to integration, testing, controlling, manipulating and manufacturing nanometer-scale structures, molecules and devices."[11] Nonspecialists could not guess from this kind of reporting that the research in question is actually tied to a natural phenomenon—giant magnetoresistance or GMR—that led to massive improvements in hard disk storage that transformed the PC industry in the late 1990s, resulted in a Nobel Prize in 2007, and has been turned by at least one historian into a very interesting true story of discovery (McCray 2009).

We switched gears and sought to follow one subject area through several years of DARPA reporting. We selected "nanoscale/bio-molecular and metamaterials" for the first decade of the 2000s. Each of the early years offers a summary that takes up a few lines of text. Each description says very little about the actual research, and nothing about potential applications. The report on FY 1999 did anchor a major theme of nanoscale research in which materials are designed in the hope of replicating the capacity of biological systems to self-assemble: "Exploited recent advances in materials design and processing to demonstrate nanostructural control of materials properties with an emphasis on emulating the complex microstructure and scale of biological materials." From 2000 to 2003, there is some overlap in topics related to this idea but no sequencing, accumulation, general tendency, or systematic mutual referencing. The level of nonspecificity omits the stakes, the value, the financial sources, and the potential implications of possibly groundbreaking work. Reading through the entries offers a combination of overlap and disconnection that is not easy to describe.[12]

For 2004, the reporting adds additional components, and at the same time starts to repeat itself in an unsettling pattern of cutting and pasting. From one year to the next, large sections of the summaries appear to have been block-copied from the year before.[13] The reports do not link funded laboratory activity to the formal reporting. The text conveys a lack of interest in convincing the reader that public finance is being used for clearly articulated ends. It also conveys a surprising absence of advancement and learning.

Finally, in the estimate for FY 2009, a series of accomplishments can be gleaned from various pages of text.[14] But no cluster of goals, patterns, systematic developments, or public objectives appears. There is no way for a nonspecialist—and probably not for a specialist outside the subdiscipline in question—to understand the interconnection among the projects. Even more fundamentally, there is no granting of the contribution or the reporting of the effects of a major public effort like the NNI. Which projects were funded with nano-specific money, how was the money used, what areas were developed, and what were the outcomes? No one is saying that nano-enabled "personalized energy" applications (Nocera 2009) should already be on the market, and yet nearly ten years after the NNI began, there is no way of answering the question of the impact of the NNI on project development, research, and discovery as they converge toward platforms and products with promised public impacts.

Rather than creating coherent development narratives, nanotechnology analysts tend to use standardized forms of output metrics—publication and patent counts, coupled with impact quantifications based on citation analysis. These methods demonstrate significant growth curves and are often used to suggest that the promise of a field like nanotechnology to transform society is on its way to being fulfilled (Hu et al. 2007).[15] Sometimes international comparisons are made, and such comparisons have clear policy uses in encouraging politicians to improve the funding of a competition in which the United States may be losing ground to rivals (Youtie et al. 2008). Statistical growth curves convey the clear impression of progress and acceleration, and nearly all areas of nanoscale research have seen major increases in activity in the United States and elsewhere over the past two decades.

But publications and patents do not equal development, production, and use. Statistics are an imperfect and in some cases a misleading measure of social impacts and development (Godin 2009a, b). Publications signify scientific research activity rather than economic impact and social adoption and are almost always valuable primarily for further scientific research. Patent activity is similarly ambiguous: most patents do not recoup the cost of their filing and prosecution with the Patent Office, most patents go unused, only a few patents earn the vast majority of royalty revenues, and patents can be used to block innovation as well as stimulate it (Lemley 2005; Mowery 2009b; Newfield 2008; Scotchmer 2004). The construction of patent claims often expresses business strategies toward rivals as well as research results. At the same time, patents do not solve problems of technology development: they do not in themselves address component integration, manufacturing cost, and a hundred other problems that must be solved before an invention is released into society. A growth curve in publications and patents reflects activity and has *symbolic* value: it operates successfully as a *sign* of funded activity—actually, as a displaced and veiled index of scientific and related types of administrative labor. A growth curve can *represent* the growth of knowledge that arises from relationships among society, government, and corporations. But a growth curve does not in a literal way reflect or directly express the stages of that development, or suggest, before its realization, where development will lead, or what society will get out of it. The gap between a signifier and its "signified," or a sign and what it denotes, can only be addressed through acts of interpretation (Saussure 2002; Rorty 1979), or what I am discussing here as narrative analysis. Narrative analysis has been eclipsed in the statistical and measurement literature that surrounds science.

This situation recalls the question asked above: Can a government help create the conditions of an equitable network that includes the general public? In principle, of course, it can. But in the case of this well-developed, high-quality initiative, the NNI, my current answer is no, for three reasons. First, the NNI does not facilitate society's direct *participation* in this initiative, either "upstream" or "downstream." Second, the government, as represented here by the NNI, does not *communicate* to various publics the role those publics play in funding, shaping, or interacting with the development of nanoscale technology. Finally, the NNI does not *involve* and *learn from* its potential publics through inclusive public narratives, but uses measurement discourse as a nonrobust proxy. The NNI can do much better than this, but it will need to transform its relationship to the public in large part by transforming its modes of discourse and representation.

Conclusion

The chapters in this volume describe the U.S. innovation system as a complex matrix of heterogeneous institutions. The system depends on interconnections among private and public entities with a remarkable array of goals and missions. Many of these entities are mixtures of private and public elements with similarly mixed goals: they seek economic success and social impact at the same time. The volume's contributors generally agree that the dependence of private entities on government action has been eclipsed, in large part because the central role of the developmental state did not fit with the orthodox model of free enterprise that has dominated Washington politics and policy for over thirty years. Hence Bill Clinton's administration (1993–2001) did want the federal government to take an economic leadership role but felt compelled to keep its coordinating mechanisms in the dark. Science and economic policymakers understandably feared the kind of backlash that Republicans dished out not only on cultural issues like gays in the military but on economic development issues, as in the case of the attacks on the Advanced Technology Program noted in the introduction. For businesses to acknowledge their government partners was to invite criticism. For a federal agency to claim economic impact was to endanger funding. Hence the full extent of the innovation system was denied, and important public parts of it were buried under the political and discursive equivalent of a concrete bunker.

The introduction correctly notes that the Obama administration has not "yet advanced an alternative governing philosophy" to that of the Reagan-Bush continuum. This is true even on a flagship Obama issue like technological innovation. Without an inspiring explanation of the role of public infrastructure in supporting economic development—without the true stories that propelled Obama into the White House in the first place—government activity will continue to be regarded as tampering with the market. This remains true even as the market no longer strikes many Americans as an honest broker, and even as they look to government to not only control abuses but redevelop the parts of both the economy and the society that have fallen into disrepair. The valuable work of federal agencies is diminished by the silence on the full extent of the innovation system, particularly in its complex public dimensions. Another major victim is the developmental role played by various publics themselves, which for ideological and political reasons are hidden from those publics.

The most impressive feature of the Obama presidential campaign was its ability to scale up a community-organizing approach to politics—an appreciation of the intelligence of ordinary people and of their right and their ability to coauthor the rules of the institutions through which they conduct their daily lives. The Obama campaign combined national scope and sophistication with deep organizational connections to communities of every kind all over the country. This campaign vision rejected the idea that the country's publics are outside looking in, whether in regard to health care, foreign affairs, financial governance, or innovation policy. This vision was far more prominent during the Obama campaign than during the Obama administration, but it did imply the principle that has been important to my discussion in this chapter: an *egalitarian* partnership among government, industry, and various publics. Equality allows collaboration to be open, complete, and rapid, and to take place among the full complement of actors and insights, including those that appear from the policy center to be beyond the pale.

Policymakers are more interested than ever in public engagement, and they have some standard mechanisms that aim at creating partnerships between the public and the government. Government agencies try to communicate with society through procedures such as "public comment" that can include hearings and invitations from citizens groups, community organizers, activists, and various nongovernmental agencies. Science studies scholars have created focus groups and other mechanisms of structured feedback that involve up-front education. Though these can lay the groundwork for social partnerships, they are labor-intensive, highly localized, expensive, and not scalable to society as a whole (Pidgeon et al. 2009). These mechanisms are less common on technical subjects where most of the public lacks the background to participate equitably or even feel interested in the first place.

A more effective mode through which government agencies could reconnect with the public is by telling accurate stories of the trail "from bench to bedside." This would mean narrating the actual trails of scientific development that the government makes possible. In such stories, obstacles, conflicts, crises, and breakthroughs would not be buried under thick coats of varnish. These stories would also encompass society itself, including, in the world of the laboratory, the graduate students, staff, technicians, and private and public funders that populate this world. The social actors would not be subordinated to, but would be in the narrative *equal partners with* the university laboratories, government research centers, and corporations that manufacture and sell the eventual product.

Such stories would overcome the national tendency—which long predates the NNI—to treat laboratories as black boxes, scientists and businesspeople as the prime movers, innovation as a mysterious group process, and society as a backward but ultimately grateful recipient of technical knowledge. The story would move from public funding through laboratory research, and dwell on the intellectual and physical labor involved. The cruel irony of the habituation of the scientific community to quantitative and yet symbolic indexes of science progress is that they eclipse the effort, the amazement, the astonishing and tireless labor of scientists, technicians, students, and staffers—the very thing that links science to every other kind of familiar work all over the world. These stories would feature the consistent effort, the everyday teamwork, the up-and-down efforts at communication, the discoveries large and small, the gradual transfer of these discoveries into a development process, and the eventual emergence of the good or service in society at large.[16] All the actors, inside and outside formal R&D structures, would exist together inside a larger process of social self-governance, in which aims and means are collaboratively established and managed.

Such networks are not easy to sustain, precisely because of the institutional variety and perceived status differences that need to be negotiated. But the first step is creating narratives about the interactions that take place within the knowledge creation processes as they actually exist. These require new efforts of social imagination inside the government agencies that have so much influence over public interests, new levels of reporting of actual lab life (Toumey 2009), new histories of the present engagement of the publics of the United States and elsewhere with the terms of their technological future.

These innovation narratives are in science's self-interest, since a public that can read and appreciate its own long-term historical role in the creation, use, recreation, and adaptation of transformative technology will more effectively improve that technology by linking it to the public's long-term needs. They are also in the general interest of society as a whole, improving technology's address to society's deeply considered, long-term needs.

Notes

This material is based on work supported by the National Science Foundation under Cooperative Agreement no. 0531184. Any opinions, findings, and conclusions or recommendations expressed in this material are those of the author and do not necessarily reflect the views of the National Science Foundation. Special thanks to John Munro of the History Department at UCSB for providing excellent research assistance for this section and the next. Thanks as well the UCSB Faculty Senate Council on Research.

1. The White House press release on the NNI is available at http://clinton4.nara.gov/WH/New/html/20000121_4.html.

2. House of Representatives Committee on Science, 105th Congress. My understanding of the NNI's origins has benefited from the excellent history of the NNI written by my CNS colleague W. Patrick McCray (2005) "Will Small Be Beautiful? Making Policies for Our Nanotech Future." Smalley citation from McCray.

3. "Unlocking Our Future: Toward a New National Science Policy," September 1998, www.access.gpo.gov/congress/house/science/cp105-b/science105b.pdf.

4. McCray, "Will Small Be Beautiful?" Gingrich offers the *Human Performance* report's best summary of the consensus position: "If we want this economy to grow, we have to be the leading scientific country in the world. If we want to be physically safe for the next 30 years, we have to be the leading scientific country in the world. If we want to be healthy as we age, we have to be the leading scientific country in the world" (Roco and Bainbridge 2002, 39).

5. In Roco and Bainbridge 2002, see, for example, "Theme B Summary," 97–101, "Theme D Summary," 275–277; Turkle (2002). .

6. Roco and Bainbridge 2002, 276.

7. The linear model of R&D has been soundly critiqued in science and technology studies and among various specialists but remains important in communication with policymakers. For an influential account of the inadequacy of the linear model and a description of a better alternative, see Stokes (1997).

8. National Nanotechnology Initiative: FY 2009 Budget & Highlights, www.nano.gov/NNI_FY09_budget_summary.pdf.

9. Among the many works on this topic, see, for example, Fong 2001 (criticizing orthodox market-based explanations of technological and economic progress); Greenstein 2009.

10. Our primary grouping was:

DoD FY 2000/2001 Budget Estimates, February 1999: www.darpa.mil/Docs/DARPAFY20002001PB2–991.pdf

DoD FY 2001 Budget Estimates, February 2000: www.darpa.mil/Docs/FY2001BudgetEstimates.pdf

DoD FY 2002 Amended Budget Submission, February 2001: www.darpa.mil/Docs/pres_bud_fy02.pdf

DoD FY 2003 Budget Estimates, February 2002: www.darpa.mil/Docs/pres_bud_fy03.pdf

DoD FY 2004/2005 Budget Estimates, February 2003: www.darpa.mil/Docs/FY04PresBud.pdf

DoD FY 2005 Budget Estimates, February 2004: http://www.darpa.mil/Docs/DoDFY2005BdgtEstFeb04.pdf

DoD FY 2006/2007 Budget Estimates, February 2005: www.darpa.mil/Docs/DescriptiveSummaryFebruary2005.pdf

DoD FY 2007 Budget Estimates, February 2006: www.darpa.mil/Docs/FY07_Final.pdf

DoD FY 2008/2009 Budget Estimates, February 2007: www.darpa.mil/Docs/FY08_budg_est.pdf

DoD FY 2009 Budget Estimates, February 2008: www.darpa.mil/Docs/DARPAPB09February2008.pdf

11. DoD FY 2001 Budget Estimates, February 2000, p 14. www.darpa.mil/Docs/FY2001BudgetEstimates.pdf

12. DoD FY 2000/2001 Budget Estimates, February 1999: www.darpa.mil/Docs/DARPAFY20002001PB2–991.pdf. From page 16, under "FY 1999 Accomplishments": "Nanoscale/Biomolecular Materials. ($1.350 Million). Exploited recent advances in materials design and processing to demonstrate nanostructural control of materials properties with an emphasis on emulating the complex microstructure and scale of biological materials."

- DoD FY 2001 Budget Estimates, February 2000: www.darpa.mil/Docs/FY2001BudgetEstimates.pdf

  From page 18 under "FY 1999 Accomplishments":

  Nanoscale/Biomolecular Materials. ($6.306 Million)

  Demonstrated the applicability of nanostructural materials in defense applications such as armor, high strength fibers, coatings and electronics.

  Explored novel concepts in biomolecular materials and interfaces.

  Developed single molecules and nanoparticles that exhibit electronic functionality and measured their intrinsic electronic properties

- DoD FY 2002 Amended Budget Submission, February 2001: www.darpa.mil/Docs/pres_bud_fy02.pdf
  From page 19, under "FY 2000 Accomplishments":
  Nanoscale/Biomolecular Materials. ($9.233 Million)
  Explored novel processing schemes for the formation of nanoscale/biomolecular and spin-dependent materials, interfaces, and devices.
  Explored the capabilities of quasi-crystals, amorphous metals, metamaterials, carbon nanotubes, quantum dots, and other nanostructured/biomolecular materials for enhancing the structural and functional performance of DoD systems
- DoD FY 2003 Budget Estimates, February 2002: www.darpa.mil/Docs/pres_bud_fy03.pdf
  From page 32, under "FY 2001 Accomplishments":
  Nanoscale/ Biomolecular Materials ($6.574 Million)
  Demonstrated enhanced performance from materials and processes incorporating nanostructured components.
  Demonstrated the use of quantum chemistry for the theoretical design of new nanoscale/biomolecular/multifunctional materials and structures.

13. See Appendix B (pages 302–306) for examples of Budget Estimates 2003-2008 showing sections of summaries copied from year to year.
14. Our synthetic list reads as follows:
The development of nanochannel glass recording devices is mentioned under "Nanostructure in Biology" (13).
   - In a section on electronic sciences, nanoaperture vertical cavity surface emitting lasers are mentioned (27).
   - The next page mentions fabrication technologies for nanometer scaled transistors.
   - The Advanced Materials Research Institute records the development and demonstration of sensors made from metal oxide nanoparticles and nanowires (43).
   - Unconventional therapeutics demonstrated that engineered organic nanoparticles elicit an immune response (109).
   - A later section on materials processing and manufacturing mentions the establishment of digital representation of microstructure across the nano-mirco and meso scales to effectively and quantitatively describe structures and features of interest, as well as the demonstration of carbon nanotube filaments from electrospun precursor polymer fibers, and composite fibers incorporating carbon nanotubes in graphite derived via commercially scalable fiber production methodologies (206–207).
   - Multifunctional Materials and Structures mentions having demonstrated an ability to control period nano features in alumina for warm forming of polymers (209).
   - Reconfigurable Structures demonstrated >100 cycles of dry nanoadhesion to glass at approximately 30 psi (normal) (213).
   - Functional Materials and Devices demonstrated nanomaterial architectures that are calculated to significantly improve the energy product of magnets, power density of batteries, and figure of merit for high temperature thermoelectric. They also demonstrated two optimized nanophase mixed oxides for anodes in lithium ion batteries (216).
   - Cognitively Augmented Design for Quantum Technology investigated the exploitation of new fields of nanophotonics and plasmonics in which metal nanostructures converted electromagnetic radiation into charge density waves (281).

- The National Security Foundry Initiative pursued research concepts for shrinking semiconductor devices to the nanoscale and explored applications to integrated microsystems (295).
- RAD Hard by Design developed a standard cell application-specific integrated circuit (AISC) library in commercial 90 nanometer (nm) complementary metal oxide semiconductor (CMOS) processes (323).
- Nano-Electro-Mechanical-Computers (NEMS) developed nanomechanical switch-based logic in semiconductors, metals, and insulators (351).
- Laser-Photoacoustic Spectroscopy (L-PAS) developed tuned lasers with a range of ± 40 nanometers (nm) (363).
- Deep Ultraviolet Avalanche Photodetectors (DUVAP) demonstrated Geiger mode operation at 280 nanometers (373).
- Ultra-Low Power Electronics for Special Purpose Computers developed nanoscale now power electronics for defense applications (385).
- Persistent Ocean Surveillance demonstrated feasibility of using nanofluidic technology with moving magnets in a linear generator to harvest wave energy (453).

15. For a high-quality version of this argument, see Daning Hu et al. 2007: "The number of patents and article citations in patent documents has increased faster in this interval for the [Nanoscale Science and Engineering] area as compared to all areas together.... The number of academic article citations per journal and year for the top 10 most cited journals has increased about 50 times in the interval (2000–2004) as compared to the interval (1976–1989)" (541).

16. Newt Gingrich said, "When you lay out the potential positive improvements for the nation, for the individual, for the society, you then have to communicate that in relatively vivid language," drawing his vivid language from science fiction authors Isaac Asimov and Arthur C. Clarke, and the SF-like science popularizer Carl Sagan (Roco and Bainbridge 2002, 37).

Appendix A
Composition of R&D Magazine *100 Award Winners*

	1971	1975	1979	1982	1984	1988	1991	1995	1997	2002	2004	2006
Total Awards	**102**	**98**	**100**	**100**	**100**	**100**	**98**	**101**	**100**	**97**	**94**	**100**
Total Foreign	5	12	10	14	14	11	13	12	12	14	10	12
Total Domestic	97	86	90	86	86	89	85	89	88	83	84	88
					Of Domestic Award Winners[i]							
Private												
1. Fortune 500 Alone	38	40	29	37	26	14	9	11	7	5	5	2
2. Other Firms Alone	42	25	28	18	23	18	20	20	15	34	24	20
3. Private Consortia	3	8	6	4	3	5	4	7	3	11	1	5
Includes F-500 Firm	1	2	4	3	1	4	1	4	1	7	1	0
Sub-Total	**83**	**73**	**63**	**59**	**52**	**37**	**33**	**38**	**25**	**50**	**30**	**27**
Public or Quasi-Public												
4. Supported Spin-offs	4	1	2	1	1	5	4	5	8	4	8	11
5. Government Labs	4	8	15	15	24	38	44[ii]	38	42	26	38	42
Solo Credit	1	2	10	15	18	25	28	25	11	7	16	23
w/F-500	1	5	2	0	3	4	4	3	5	1	2	3
w/University	0	0	0	0	1	2	4	2	3	2	5	7
w/others	2	1	3	0	2	7	9	8	23	16	15	9
6. Universities	3	0	4	4	1	1	1	5	6	2	4	2
Solo Credit	1	0	4	1	1	1	1	1	2	0	1	0
w/F-500	1	0	0	0	0	0	0	0	0	0	0	0
w/others	1	0	0	3	0	0	0	4	4	2	3	2
7. Other Public	3	4	6	7	8	8	3	3	7	1	4	6
w/F-500	0	0	0	1	1	0	0	0	2	0	1	1
Sub-Total	**14**	**13**	**27**	**27**	**34**	**52**	**52**	**51**	**63**	**33**	**54**	**61**
Total F-500	41	47	35	41	31	22	14	18	15	13	9	6

i. As noted, if a single firm won multiple R&D 100 awards in a given year, it is counted one time for each award.
ii. The number of sub-categorizations exceeds 44 because one collaboration involved both a Fortune 500 firm and a university.

Appendix B
Examples of Budget Estimates, 2003-2008

A. DoD FY 2004/2005 Budget Estimates, February 2003: www.darpa.mil/Docs/
FY04PresBud.pdf
   - *This year the format and wording changed...*
   - From page 30 (which those cited in Budget Estimates A-D, deals with Materials Sciences), under "Program Accomplishments/ Planned Programs":
     o Nanoscale/Biomolecular and Metamaterials
       - FY 2002   5.028
       - FY 2003   12.881
       - FY 2004   8.907
       - FY 2005   5.051
       - The research in this thrust area exploits advances in nanoscale and biomolecular materials, including computationally based materials science, in order to develop unique microstructures and properties of materials. This includes efforts to develop the underlying physics for the behavior of materials whose properties have been engineered at the nanoscale (Metamaterials) level.
       - Program Plans:
         • Develop theoretical understanding and modeling tools for predicting novel metamaterial structures that exhibit superior microwave and magnetic properties for DoD electric drive and propulsion, power electronics, antenna, and radar applications.
         • Develop algorithmic approaches for predicting properties and structure of nanoscale and metamaterials using first principles/ quantum mechanical methods with higher accuracy and reduced computational complexity.
         • Couple the algorithmic approaches to methods that extract parameters for simulation of materials at larger spatial scales while conducting experiments to verify/validate the predicted properties at all spatial scales.
         • Explore the mechanisms of phonon engineering for enhancing transport properties in organics.
         • Develop advanced image detector materials to instantly and simultaneously detect one structural (computed tomography) and two

functional (position emission tomography and single photon emission tomography) images of medical and life science interest.

B. DoD FY 2005 Budget Estimates, February 2004: www.darpa.mil/Docs/ DoDFY2005BdgtEstFeb04.pdf
 - From page 21, under "Program Accomplishments/ Planned Programs":
   o Nanoscale/Biomolecular and Metamaterials
     ■ FY 2003   7.912
     ■ FY 2004   8.486
     ■ FY 2005   14.051
     ■ The research in this thrust area exploits advances in nanoscale and bio-molecular materials, including computationally based materials science, in order to develop unique microstructures and properties of materials. This includes efforts to develop the underlying physics for the behavior of materials whose properties have been engineered at the nanoscale (metamaterials) level.
     ■ Program Plans:
       • Develop theoretical understanding and modeling tools for predicting novel metamaterial structures that exhibit superior microwave and magnetic properties for DoD electric drive and propulsion, power electronics, antenna, and radar applications.
       • Develop algorithmic approaches for predicting properties and structure of nanoscale and metamaterials using first principles/ quantum mechanical methods with higher accuracy and reduced computational complexity.
       • Couple the algorithmic approaches to methods that extract parameters for simulation of materials at larger spatial scales while conducting experiments to verify/validate the predicted properties at all spatial scales.
       • Explore fundamental behavior of nanostructured materials that display quantum and/or nonequilibrium behavior.
       • Exploit an understanding of properties that are dominated by surface behavior to develop materials with increased thermal conductivity, biocidal properties, and phonon capture.
 - *This time, last year's vague description of accomplishments has merely been reasserted verbatim.*

C. DoD FY 2006/2007 Budget Estimates, February 2005: www.darpa.mil/Docs/ DescriptiveSummaryFebruary2005.pdf
 - From page 34, under "Program Accomplishments/Planned Programs":
   o Nanoscale/Biomolecular and Metamaterials
     ■ FY 2004   7.845
     ■ FY 2005   14.051
     ■ FY 2006   11.450
     ■ The research in this thrust area exploits advances in nanoscale and biomolecular materials, including computationally based materials

science, in order to develop unique microstructures and properties of materials. This includes efforts to develop the underlying physics for the behavior of materials whose properties have been engineered at the nanoscale (metamaterials) level.

- Program Plans:
  - Develop theoretical understanding and modeling tools for predicting novel metamaterial structures that exhibit superior microwave and magnetic properties for DoD electric drive and propulsion, power electronics, antenna, and radar applications.
  - Develop algorithmic approaches for predicting properties and structure of nanoscale and metamaterials using first principles/ quantum mechanical methods with higher accuracy and reduced computational complexity.
  - Couple the algorithmic approaches to methods that extract parameters for simulation of materials at larger spatial scales while conducting experiments to verify/validate the predicted properties at all spatial scales.
  - Explore fundamental behavior of nanostructured materials that display quantum and/or nonequilibrium behavior.

D. DoD FY 2007 Budget Estimates, February 2006: www.darpa.mil/Docs/ FY07_Final.pdf
  - From page 36, under "Program Accomplishments/Planned Programs":
    - o Nanoscale/Biomolecular and Metamaterials
      - FY 2005   14.826
      - FY 2006   11.000
      - FY 2007   15.450
      - The research in this thrust area exploits advances in nanoscale and biomolecular materials, including computationally based materials science, in order to develop unique microstructures and properties of materials. This includes efforts to develop the underlying physics for the behavior of materials whose properties have been engineered at the nanoscale (metamaterials) level.
      - Program Plans:
        - Develop algorithmic approaches for predicting properties and structure of nanoscale and metamaterials using first principles/ quantum mechanical methods with higher accuracy and reduced computational complexity.
        - Couple the algorithmic approaches to methods that extract parameters for simulation of materials at larger spatial scales while conducting experiments to verify/validate the predicted properties at all spatial scales.
        - Explore and exploit the underlying dualities between discrete and continuous computational methods to dramatically improve DoD computational abilities.

- Apply ideas from non-Euclidean geometry to obtain fast optimization methods for certain problems in robotics, including pursuit evasion, optimal path planning, and reconfiguration.
- Explore fundamental behavior of nanostructured materials that display quantum and/or nonequilibrium behavior.

E. DoD FY 2008/2009 Budget Estimates, February 2007: www.darpa.mil/Docs/FY08_budg_est.pdf
   - From page 32, under "Program Accomplishments/ Planned Programs":
     o Nanoscale/Biomolecular and Metamaterials
        - FY 2006   11.000
        - FY 2007   12.000
        - FY 2008   15.057
        - FY 2009   17.500
        - The research in this thrust area exploits advances in nanoscale and biomolecular materials, including computationally based materials science, in order to develop unique microstructures and properties of materials. This includes efforts to develop the underlying physics for the behavior of materials whose properties have been engineered at the nanoscale (metamaterials) level.
        - Program Plans:
          - Develop algorithmic approaches for predicting properties and structure of nanoscale and metamaterials using first principles/quantum mechanical methods with higher accuracy and reduced computational complexity.
          - Couple the algorithmic approaches to methods that extract parameters for simulation of materials at larger spatial scales while conducting experiments to verify/validate the predicted properties at all spatial scales.
          - Explore and exploit the underlying dualities between discrete and continuous computational methods to dramatically improve DoD computational abilities.
          - Develop theoretical advances to characterize the propagation of random effects through differential equation models of electromagnetic material systems to allow interpolation, extrapolation, and hybridization of solutions to known systems to closely related "perturbed" systems.

F. DoD FY 2009 Budget Estimates, February 2008: www.darpa.mil/Docs/DARPAPB09February2008.pdf
   - From page 38, under "Program Accomplishments/Planned Programs":
     o Nanoscale/Biomolecular and Metamaterials
        - FY 2007   12.029
        - FY 2008   16.500
        - FY 2009   17.500
        - The research in this thrust area exploits advances in nanoscale and

biomolecular materials, including computationally based materials science, in order to develop unique microstructures and material properties. This includes efforts to develop the underlying physics for the behavior of materials whose properties have been engineered at the nanoscale (metamaterials).

■ Program Plans:
  • FY 2007 Accomplishments
    o Developed a cluster expansion method for materials properties that achieved 106 reduction in the number of calculations
    o Developed a substantiation for quantum monte carlo calculations linear in the number of particles
    o Developed a new method for predicting material properties based on linear combinations of atomic potentials
    o Demonstrated a laser driven, 1 billion electron volt electron beam
    o Designed composite nanomaterial structures and demonstrated processing capabilities for achieving improved optical and mechanical properties over existing infrared windows
    o Developed and applied new theory for multiple input multiple array radar systems that lead to 10x improvement in missed target detection while providing 10x reduction in search volume

References

Books, Book Chapters, and Academic Articles

Abir-Am, Pnina Geraldine. 2001. Molecular Biology in the Context of British, French, and American Cultures. *International Social Science Journal* 175: 187–199.

Acemoglu, Daron, et al. 2001. The Colonial Origins of Comparative Development. *American Economic Review* 91 (5): 1369–1401.

Adams, Sean. 2004. *Old Dominion, Industrial Commonwealth: Coal, Politics, and Economy in Antebellum America.* Baltimore: Johns Hopkins University Press.

Aglietta, Michel. 1979. *A Theory of Capitalist Regulation.* London: New Left.

Agrawal, Madhu. 1999. *Global Competitiveness in the Pharmaceutical Industry: The Effect of National Regulatory, Economic, and Market Factors.* New York: Haworth.

Alic, John A. 2004. Technology and Labor in the New U.S. Economy. *Technology in Society* 26: 327–341.

———. 2007. *Trillions for Military Technology: How the Pentagon Innovates and Why It Costs So Much.* New York: Palgrave.

———. 2008a. A Weakness in Diffusion: U.S. Technology and Science Policy After World War II. *Technology in Society* 30: 17–29.

———. 2008b. Technical Knowledge and Experiential Learning: What People Know and Can Do. *Technology Analysis & Strategic Management* 20: 427–442.

Allen, Robert H., and Ram D. Sriram. 2000. The Role of Standards in Innovation. *Technological Forecasting and Social Change* 64: 171–181.

Ambrose, Stephen E. 2000. *Nothing Like It in the World: The Men Who Built the Transcontinental Railroad, 1863–1869.* New York: Simon & Schuster.

Amsden, Alice H. 1992. A Theory of Government Intervention in Late Industrialization. In *State and Market in Development: Synergy or Rivalry?* edited by D. Rueschemeyer and L. G. Putterman. Boulder: Lynne Rienner.

Andrews, James. 2001. A Tale of Three Cities. *Planning* 67 (7): 18–22.

Angevine, Robert. 2004. *The Railroad and the State: War, Politics, and Technology in Nineteenth-Century America.* Palo Alto: Stanford University Press.

Ansell, Chris. 2000. The Networked Polity: Regional Development in Western Europe. *Governance* 13 (3): 303–333.

Appel, Toby A. 2000. *Shaping Biology: The National Science Foundation and American Biological Research, 1945–1975.* Baltimore: Johns Hopkins University Press.

Arkes, Jeremy. 1999. What Do Educational Credentials Signal and Why Do Employers Value Credentials? *Economics of Education Review* 18: 133–141.

Arrighi, Giovanni. 2007. *Adam Smith in Beijing: Lineages of the 21st Century.* London: Verso.

Arris, John. 2000. Inventing Systems Engineering. *IEEE Annals of the History of Computing* 22 (3): 4–15.

Arrow, Kenneth. 1970. The Organization of Economic Activity: Issues Pertinent to the Choice of Market Versus Nonmarket Allocation. In *Public Expenditures and Policy Analysis*, edited by R. Haveman and J. Margolis. Chicago: Markham.

Asanovic, K., et al. 2006. *The Landscape of Parallel Computing Research: A View from Berkeley.* Berkeley: University of California Press.

Aspray, William. 1997. The Intel 4004 Microprocessor: What Constituted Invention? *IEEE Annals of the History of Computing* 19 (3): 4–15.

Auerswald, Philip E., and Lewis M. Branscomb. 2003. Valleys of Death and Darwinian Seas: Financing the Invention to Innovation Transition in the United States. *Journal of Technology Transfer* 28 (3–4): 227–239.

Bai Chunli. 2005. Ascent of Nanoscience in China. *Science*, July 1.

Bai Chunli and Chen Wang 2007. Nanotechnology Research in China. In *Innovation with Chinese Characteristics: High-Tech Research in China*, edited by Linda Jakobsen. New York: Palgrave Macmillan

Balutis, Alan P., and Barbara Lambis. 2001. The ATP Competition Structure. In *The Advanced Technology Program: Assessing Outcomes*, edited by C. W. Wessner. Washington, D.C.: National Academy Press.

Battelle, John. 2005. *The Search*. New York: Penguin.

Bell, Daniel. 1973. *The Coming of Post-Industrial Society: A Venture in Social Forecasting.* New York: Basic.

Belsie, Laurent. 1994. Federal Labs Hustling to Find New Roles. *Christian Science Monitor* (September 16): 3.

Bennis, Warren, and Philip Slater. 1968. *The Temporary Society.* New York: Harper & Row.

Berger, John J. 1997. *Charging Ahead: The Business of Renewable Energy and What It Means for America.* Berkeley: University of California Press.

Berk, Gerald. 2009. *Louis D. Brandeis and the Making of Regulated Competition, 1900–1932.* New York: Cambridge University Press.

Berman, Elizabeth Popp. 2008. Why Did Universities Start Patenting? Institution-Building and the Road to the Bayh-Dole Act. *Social Studies of Science* 38 (6): 835–871.

Bingham, Richard. 1998. *Industrial Policy American Style: From Hamilton to HDTV.* Armonk, NY: Sharpe.

Bingham, Tayler H. 2001. Estimating Economic Benefits from ATP Funding of New Medical Technologies. In *The Advanced Technology Program: Assessing Outcomes*, edited by C. W. Wessner. Washington, D.C.: National Academy Press.

Biscotti, Dina, et al. 2009. The "Independent" Investigator: How Academic Scientists Construct Their Professional Identity in University-Industry Agricultural Biotechnology Research Collaborations. *Research in the Sociology of Work* 18: 261–285.

Blank, David M., and George J. Stigler. 1957. *The Demand and Supply of Scientific Personnel.* New York: National Bureau of Economic Research.

Bledstein, Burton J. 1976. *The Culture of Professionalism: The Middle Class and the Development of Higher Education in America.* New York: Norton.

Block, Fred. 1977. *The Origins of International Economic Disorder: A Study of United States International Monetary Policy from World War II to the Present.* Berkeley: University of California Press.

———. 1990. *Postindustrial Possibilities.* Berkeley: University of California Press.

———. 1996. *The Vampire State.* New York: New Press.

———. 2003. Karl Polanyi and the Writing of *The Great Transformation*. *Theory and Society* 32 (3): 275–306.

———. 2007. Understanding the Diverging Trajectories of the United States and Western Europe: A Neo-Polanyian Analysis. *Politics & Society* 35 (1): 3–33.

———. 2008. "Swimming Against the Current": The Rise of a Hidden Developmental State in the United States. *Politics & Society* 36 (2): 169–206.

Block, Fred, and Matthew R. Keller. 2009. Where Do Innovations Come From? Transformations in the U.S. Economy, 1970–2006. *Socio-Economic Review* 7 (3): 459–483.

Bluestone, Barry, and Bennett Harrison. 1982. *Deindustrialization of America: Plant Closings, Community Abandonment, and the Dismantling of Basic Industry.* New York: Basic.

Boli, J., and G. Thomas. 1997. World Culture in the World Polity: A Century of International Non-Governmental Organization. *American Sociological Review* 62 (2): 171–190.

Bonvillian, William R. 2009. The Connected Science Model for Innovation: The DARPA Role. In *Twenty-First Century Innovation Systems for Japan and the United States,* edited by Committee on Comparative Innovation Policy, National Research Council. Washington, D.C.: National Academies Press.

Bourdieu, Pierre. 1984. *Distinction: A Social Critique of the Judgment of Taste.* Translated by Richard Nice. Cambridge: Harvard University Press.

Bourgin, Frank. 1989. *The Great Challenge: The Myth of Laissez-Faire in the Early Republic.* New York: George Braziller.

Boyer, Robert, and Yves Saillard. 2002. *Regulation Theory: The State of the Art.* London: Routledge.

Branscomb, Lewis M., and Richard Florida. 1998. Challenges to Technology Policy in a Changing World Economy. In *Investing in Innovation: Creating a Research and Innovation Policy That Works,* edited by L. M. Branscomb and J. H. Keller. Cambridge: MIT Press.

Brenner, Robert. 1972. The Social Bases of English Commercial Expansion. *Journal of Economic History* 32 (1): 361–384.

———. 2006. *The Economics of Global Turbulence.* London: Verso.

Bresnahan, T. F., and S. Greenstein. 1999. Technological Competition and the Structure of the Computer Industry. *Journal of Industrial Economics* 47 (1): 1–40.

Breznitz, Dan. 2007. *Innovation and the State: Political Choice and Strategies for Growth in Israel, Taiwan, and Ireland.* New Haven: Yale University Press.

Brick, Howard. 2006. *Transcending Capitalism: Visions of a New Society in Modern American Thought.* Ithaca: Cornell University Press.

Brint, Steven. 2001. Professionals and the "Knowledge Economy": Rethinking the Theory of Postindustrial Society. *Current Sociology* 49 (4): 101–132.

Brown, Kenneth. 1998. Sandia's Science Park: A New Concept in Technology Transfer. *Issues in Science & Technology* 15 (2): 67–70.

Bucchi, Massimiano, and Federico Neresini. 2008. Science and Public Participation. In *The Handbook of Science and Technology Studies.* 3rd ed. Cambridge: MIT Press.

Buderi, Robert, and Gregory T. Huang. 2006. *Guanxi: Microsoft, China, and Bill Gates's Plan to Win the Road Ahead.* New York: Simon & Schuster.

Bunge, Mario. 1962. *Intuition and Science.* Englewood Cliffs, NJ: Prentice-Hall.

Burger, Edward, Jr. 1980. *Science at the White House: A Political Liability.* Baltimore: Johns Hopkins University Press.

Burns, Tom, and G. M. Stalker. 1961. *The Management of Innovation.* London: Tavistock.

Bush, Vannevar. 1945. *Science: The Endless Frontier: A Report to the President on a Program for Postwar Scientific Research.* Washington, D.C.: Government Printing Office.

————. 1971. Dictation to Science by Laymen. *Science,* October 1.

Calvert, Monte A. 1967. *The Mechanical Engineer in America, 1830–1910: Professional Cultures in Conflict.* Baltimore, MD: Johns Hopkins Press, 1967.

Cao, Cong. 2004. *China's Scientific Elite.* London: Routledge.

Cao, Cong, and Denis Fred Simon. 2009. *Talent and China's Technological Edge.* Cambridge: Cambridge University Press.

Cao, Cong, Richard P. Suttmeier, and Denis Fred Simon. 2006b. China's 15-Year Science and Technology Plan. *Physics Today* (December): 38–43.

Carr, P. 1998. The Cultural Production of Enterprise: Understanding Selectivity as Cultural Policy. *Economic and Social Review* 29 (2): 133–155.

Casadesus-Masanell, R., and D. B. Yoffie. 2005. Wintel: Cooperation and Conflict. *Management Science* 53 (4): 584–598.

Casper, S., M. Lehrer, and D. Soskice. 1999. Can High-Technology Industries Prosper in Germany: Institutional Frameworks and the Evolution of the German Software and Biotechnology Industries. *Industry and Innovation* 1 (6): 6–23.

Castells, Manuel. 1996. *The Rise of the Network Society.* Oxford: Blackwell.

Casten, Thomas R., and Philip F. Schewe. 2009. Getting the Most from Energy. *American Scientist* 97 (1): 26–33.

Cerny, P. 1995. Globalization and the Changing Logic of Collective Action. *International Organization* 49: 595–625.

Chang, Connie K. N. 1998. A New Lexicon and Framework for Analyzing the Internal Structures of the U.S. Advanced Technology Program and its Analogues Around the World. *Journal of Technology Transfer* 23 (2): 67–73.

Chang, Connie K. N., Stephanie S. Shipp, and Andrew J. Wang. 2002. The Advanced Technology Program: A Public-Private Partnership for Early Stage Technology Development. *Venture Capital* 4 (4): 363–370.

Chang, Ha-Joon. 2008. *Bad Samaritans.* New York: Bloomsbury.

Charles, Daniel. 1988. Labs Struggle to Promote Spin-Offs. *Science,* n.s., 240 (4854): 874–876.

Chesbrough, Henry William. 2003. *Open Innovation: The New Imperative for Creating and Profiting from Technology.* Cambridge: Harvard Business School Press.

Chesbrough, Henry William, Wim Vanhaverbeke, and Joel West, eds. 2006. *Open Innovation: Researching a New Paradigm.* Oxford: Oxford University Press.

Chibber, Vivek. 2002. Bureaucratic Rationality and the Developmental State. *American Journal of Sociology* 107 (4): 951–989.

Cho, Adrian. 2007. Effect That Revolutionized Hard Drives Nets a Nobel. *Science* (October 12): 179.

Christensen, Clayton M. 1997. *The Innovator's Dilemma: When New Technologies Cause Great Firms to Fail.* Cambridge: Harvard Business School Press.

Cohen, Linda. 1998. Dual-Use and the Technology Reinvestment Project. In *Investing in Innovation: Creating a Research and Innovation Policy That Works,* edited by Lewis M. Branscomb and James H. Keller. Cambridge: MIT Press.

Collins, Steven. 2004. *The Race to Commercialize Biotechnology: Markets and the State in the U.S. and Japan.* New York: Routledge Curzon.

Colyvas, Jeannette A., and Walter W. Powell. 2006. Roads to Institutionalization: The Remaking of Boundaries Between Public and Private Science. *Research in Organizational Behavior* 27: 305–333.

Coriat, Benjamin. 1997. Globalization, Variety, and Mass Production: The Metamorphosis of

Mass Production in the New Competitive Age. In *Contemporary Capitalism: The Embeddedness of Institutions,* edited by J. R. Hollingsworth and R. Boyer. Cambridge: Cambridge University Press.

Cortada, James W. 1996. Commercial Applications of the Digital Computer in American Corporations, 1945–1995. *IEEE Annals of the History of Computing* 18 (2): 18–29.

Crouch, Colin. 2005. *Capitalist Diversity and Change: Recombinant Governance and Institutional Entrepreneurs.* Oxford: Oxford University Press.

Crouch, Colin, and Henry Farrell. 2004. Breaking the Path of Institutional Development? Alternatives to the New Determinism. *Rationality and Society* 16 (1): 5–43.

Crouch, Colin, and Wolfgang Streeck. 1997. *The Political Economy of Modern Capitalism.* Thousand Oaks, CA: Sage.

Crow, Michael, and Barry Bozeman. 1998. *Limited by Design: R&D Laboratories in the U.S. National Innovation System.* New York, Columbia University Press.

Cumings, Bruce. 1984. The Legacy of Japanese Colonialism in Korea. In *The Japanese Colonial Empire,* edited by R. Hawley et al. Princeton: Princeton University Press.

Darby, Michael R., Lynne G. Zucker, and Andrew Wang. 2004. Joint Ventures, Universities, and Success in the Advanced Technology Program. *Contemporary Economic Policy* 22 (2): 145–161.

David, Edward E., Jr. 1980. Current State of White House Science Advising. In *Science Advice to the President,* edited by William T. Golden, 55. New York: Pergamon.

Day, Thomas. 1984. Samuel Brown: His Influence on the Design of Suspension Bridges. In *History of Technology,* edited by Norman Smith, 8. London: Mansell.

Dobbin, Frank. 1993. The Social Construction of the Great Depression: Industrial Policy During the 1930s in the United States, Britain, and France. *Theory and Society* 22 (1): 1–56.

———. 1994. *Forging Industrial Policy: The United States, Britain, and France in the Railway Age.* New York: Cambridge University Press.

Dorf, Michael, and Charles Sabel. 1998. A Constitution of Democratic Experimentalism. *Columbia Law Review* 98 (2): 267–473.

Dubnick, Mel. 1984. American States and the Industrial Policy Debate. *Review of Policy Research* 4 (1): 22–27.

DuBridge, Lee A. 1971. The Role of Government Enterprise. *Proceedings of the American Philosophical Society,* February 17.

Edgerton, David. 2007. *The Shock of the Old: Technology and Global History Since 1900.* Oxford: Oxford University Press.

Eisenger, Peter. 1990. Do the American States Do Industrial Policy? *British Journal of Political Science* 20 (4): 509–535.

Ericsson, K. Anders, ed. 1996. *The Road to Excellence: The Acquisition of Expert Performance in the Arts and Sciences, Sports, and Games.* Mahwah, NJ: Erlbaum.

Estrin, Judy. 2009. *Closing the Innovation Gap: Reigniting the Spark of Creativity in a Global Economy.* New York: McGraw-Hill.

Etzkowitz, Henry. 2003. Innovation in Innovation: The Triple Helix of University-Industry-Government Relations. *Social Science Information* 42: 293–337.

Evans, Peter. 1995. *Embedded Autonomy: States and Industrial Transformation.* Princeton: Princeton University Press.

———. 2008. Is an Alternative Globalization Possible? *Politics & Society* 36 (2): 271–305.

Feldman, Maryann, and Richard Florida. 1994. The Geographic Sources of Innovation: Technological Infrastructure and Product Innovation in the United States. *Journal of the Association of American Geographers* 84 (2): 210–229.

Feldman, Maryann P., and Maryellen R. Kelley. 2001. Leveraging Research and Development: The Impact of the Advanced Technology Program. In *The Advanced Technology Program: Assessing Outcomes,* edited by C. W. Wessner. Washington, D.C.: National Academy Press.

Flamm, K. 1987. *Targeting the Computer: Government Support and International Competition.* Washington, D.C.: Brookings Institute.

———. 1988. *Creating the Computer: Government, Industry, and High Technology.* Washington, D.C.: Brookings Institution.

Fligstein, Neil. 1990. *The Transformation of Corporate Control.* Cambridge: Harvard University Press.

Florida, Richard, and Martin Kenney. 1991. Transplanted Organizations: The Transfer of Japanese Industrial Organization to the U.S. *American Sociological Review* 56 (3): 381–398.

Fong, Glenn R. 2000. Breaking New Ground or Breaking the Rules: Strategic Reorientation in U.S. Industrial Policy. *International Security* (August): 152–186.

———. 2001. ARPA Does Windows: The Defense Underpinnings of the PC Revolution. *Business and Politics* 3 (3): 213–237.

Freidberg, Aaron. 2000. *In the Shadow of the Garrison State: America's Anti-Statism and Its Cold War Grand Strategy.* Princeton: Princeton University Press.

Frickel, Scott, and Kelly Moore. 2006. Introduction to *The New Political Sociology of Science: Institutions, Networks, and Power.* Madison: University of Wisconsin Press.

Frieden, Jeffry A. 2006. *Global Capitalism: Its Fall and Rise in the Twentieth Century.* New York: Norton.

Friedman, Milton, and Rose Friedman. 1990 [1980]. *Free to Choose: A Personal Statement.* Orlando, FL: Harcourt.

Friedman, Thomas L. 2006. *The World Is Flat: A Brief History of the 21st Century.* Release 2.0. New York: Farrar, Straus & Giroux.

Fuchs, Erica, et al. 2006. Process-Based Cost Modeling of Photonics Manufacture: The Cost-Competitiveness of Monolithic Integration of a 1550nm DFB Laser and an Electro-Absorptive Modulator on an InP Platform. *Journal of Lightwave Technology* 24 (8).

Fujimura, Joan. 1988. The Molecular Biological Bandwagon in Cancer Research: Where Social Worlds Meet. *Social Problems* 35: 261–283.

Furman, Necah Stewart. 1990. *Sandia National Laboratories: The Postwar Decade.* Albuquerque: University of New Mexico Press.

Gawer, A., and M. A. Cusumano. 2002. *Platform Leadership: How Intel, Microsoft, and Cisco Drive Industry Innovation.* Boston: Harvard Business School Press.

Geiger, Roger, and Creso Sa. 2008. *Tapping the Riches of Science: Universities and the Promise of Economic Growth.* Cambridge: Harvard University Press.

Gereffi, Gary, John Humphrey, and Timothy Sturgeon. 2005. The Governance of Global Value Chains. *Review of International Political Economy* 12 (1): 78–104.

Gerschenkron, Alexander. 1962. *Economic Backwardness in Historical Perspective: A Book of Essays.* Cambridge: Belknap Press/Harvard University Press.

Girma, S., et al. 2008. Creating Jobs Through Public Subsidies: An Empirical Analysis. *Labour Economics* 15 (6): 1179–1199.

Goldhaber, Samuel Z. 1970. CBW: Interagency Conflicts Stall Administration Action. *Science* (July 31): 454.

Goldin, Claudia. 1998. America's Graduation from High School: The Evolution and Spread of Secondary Schooling in the Twentieth Century. *Journal of Economic History* 58: 345–374.

Gompers, Paul Alan, and Josh Lerner. 2004. *The Venture Capital Cycle.* 2nd ed. Cambridge: MIT Press.

Goodman, Robert. 1979. *The Last Entrepreneurs: America's Regional Wars for Jobs and Dollars.* New York: Simon & Schuster.

Goodrich, Carter. 1960. *Government Promotion of American Canals and Railroads, 1800–1890.* New York: Columbia University Press.

Goodstein, Eban. 1995. The Economic Roots of Environmental Decline. *Journal of Economic Issues* 29 (4): 1029–1043.

Gordon, David, Richard Edwards, and Michael Reich. 1982. *Segmented Work, Divided Workers: The Historical Transformation of Labor in the United States.* New York: Cambridge University Press.

Grabher, Gernot. 1993. The Weakness of Strong Ties: The Lock-In of Regional Development in the Ruhr Area. In *The Embedded Firm: On the Socioeconomics of Industrial Networks,* edited by G. Grabher. New York: Routledge.

Graham, Otis, Jr. 1992. *Losing Ground: The Industrial Policy Debate.* Cambridge: Harvard University Press.

Granovetter, Mark. 1985. Economic Action and Social Structure: The Problem of Embeddedness. *American Journal of Sociology* 91 (3): 481–510.

Greene, K. 2007. Illuminating Silicon. *Technology Review.* Cambridge: MIT Press.

Greider, William. 1987. *Secrets of the Temple: How the Federal Reserve Runs the Country.* New York: Simon & Schuster.

Grimshaw, Jeremy M., et al. 2001. Changing Provider Behavior: An Overview of Systematic Reviews of Interventions. *Medical Care* Supplement 2, 39 (8): II-2–II-45.

Guillemin, Jeanne. 2005. *Biological Weapons: From the Invention of State-Sponsored Programs to Contemporary Bioterrorism.* New York: Columbia University Press.

Gullickson, William, and Michael J. Harper. 2002. Bias in Aggregate Productivity Trends Revisited. *Monthly Labor Review* (March): 32–40.

Gunnigle, P., and D. McGuire. 2001. Why Ireland? A Qualitative Review of the Factors Influencing the Location of U.S. Multinationals in Ireland with Particular Reference to the Impact of Labour Issues. *Economic and Social Review* 32 (1): 43–68.

Hagstrom, Warren O. 1964. *The Scientific Community.* New York: Basic.

Hall, Peter, and David Soskice, eds. 2001. *Varieties of Capitalism: The Institutional Foundations of Comparative Advantage.* Oxford: Oxford University Press.

Hallacher, Paul M. 2005. *Why Policy Issue Networks Matter: The Advanced Technology Program and the Manufacturing Extension Program.* Lanham, MD: Rowman & Littlefield.

Harding, T. Swann. 1947. *Two Blades of Grass: A History of Scientific Development in the U.S. Department of Agriculture.* Norman: University of Oklahoma Press.

Hargadon, Andrew. 2003. *How Breakthroughs Happen: The Surprising Truth About How Corporations Innovate.* Boston: Harvard Business School Press.

Harris, Richard. 2001. The Knowledge-Based Economy: Intellectual Origins and New Economic Perspectives. *International Journal of Management Reviews* 3 (March): 21–40.

Hartley, Dan. 1999. Laboratory Partnerships with Industry. In *New Vistas in Transatlantic Science and Technology Cooperation,* edited by C. W. Wessner. Washington: National Academies Press.

Hartung, William D. 1996. Saint Augustine's Rules: Norman Augustine and the Future of the Defense Industry. *World Policy Journal* 13 (2): 65–73.

Heiman, Michael K., and Barry D. Solomon. 2004. Power to the People: Electric Utility

Restructuring and the Commitment to Renewable Energy. *Annals of the Association of American Geographers* 94 (1): 94–116.

Helper, Susan, John Paul MacDuffie, and Charles Sabel. 2000. Pragmatic Collaborations: Advancing Knowledge While Controlling Opportunism. *Industrial and Corporate Change* 9 (3): 443–483.

Henderson, Jeffrey, and Richard Appelbaum. 1992. Situating the State in the East Asian Development Process. In *States and Economic Development in the Asian Pacific Rim,* edited by R. Appelbaum and J. Henderson. New York: Sage.

Henderson, R., L. Orsenigo, and G. Pisano. 1999. The Pharmaceutical Industry and the Revolution in Molecular Biology: Interactions Among Scientific, Institutional, and Organizational Change. In *Sources of Industrial Leadership: Studies of Seven Industries,* edited by David Mowery and Richard R. Nelson. Cambridge: Cambridge University Press.

Henderson, Rebecca, Adam Jaffe, and Manuel Trajtenberg. 1998. University Patenting Amid Changing Incentives for Commercialization. In *Creation and Transfer of Knowledge,* edited by G. Barba Navaretti et al. New York: Springer.

Hennessy, J., and D. Patterson. 2007. *Computer Architecture: A Quantitative Approach.* San Francisco: Elsevier.

Hersh, Seymour. 1968. *Chemical and Biological Warfare: America's Hidden Arsenal.* New York: Bobbs-Merrill.

Herzenberg, Stephen A., John A. Alic, and Howard Wial. 1998. *New Rules for a New Economy: Employment and Opportunity in Postindustrial America.* Ithaca, NY: Cornell University Press.

Hill, Christopher T. 1998. The Advanced Technology Program: Opportunities for Enhancement. In *Investing in Innovation: Creating a Research and Innovation Policy That Works,* edited by L. M. Branscomb and J. H. Keller. Cambridge: MIT Press.

———. 1999. An Overview of the Program's History and Objectives. In *Advanced Technology Program: Challenges and Opportunities,* edited by C. Wessner. Washington, D.C.: National Academy Press.

Hilts, Philip. 2003. *Protecting America's Health: The FDA, Business, and One Hundred Years of Regulation.* New York: Knopf.

Hobsbawm, Eric J. 1999. *Industry and Empire: From 1750 to the Present Day.* New York: New Press.

Hollingsworth, J. Rogers, and Robert Boyer. 1997. *Contemporary Capitalism: The Embeddedness of Institutions.* New York: Cambridge University Press.

Holman, Michael, et al. 2007. *The Nanotech Report.* 5th ed. New York: Lux Research.

Hooks, Gregory. 1990. The Rise of the Pentagon and U.S. State Building: The Defense Program as Industrial Policy. *American Journal of Sociology* 96 (2): 358–404.

———. 1991. *Forging the Military-Industrial Complex.* Urbana: University of Illinois Press.

Hounshell, David. 1984. *From the American System to Mass Production, 1800–1932.* Baltimore: Johns Hopkins University Press.

———. 1996. The Evolution of Industrial Research in the United States. In *Engines of Innovation,* edited by Richard Rosenbloom and William Spencer. Boston: Harvard Business School Press.

Hu, Daning, et al. 2007. Longitudinal Study on Patent Citations to Academic Research Articles in Nanotechnology (1976–2004). *Journal of Nanoparticle Research* 9: 529–542.

Huber, E., and J. Stephens. 2001. *Development and Crisis of the Welfare State: Parties and Policies in Global Markets.* Chicago: University of Chicago Press.

Hyde, Alan. 2003. *Working in Silicon Valley.* Armonk, NY: Sharpe.

Iansiti, M., and R. Levien. 2004. *The Keystone Advantage: What the New Dynamics of Business Ecosystems Mean for Strategy, Innovation, and Sustainability.* Boston: Harvard Business School Press.

Irwin, Alan. 1995. *Citizen Science: A Study of People, Expertise, and Sustainable Development.* London: Routledge.

Jaffe, Adam B. 1998. The Importance of "Spillovers" in the Policy Mission of the Advanced Technology Program. *Journal of Technology Transfer* 23 (2): 11–19.

Jaffe, Adam B., Michael S. Fogarty, and Bruce A. Banks. 1998. Evidence from Patents and Patent Citations on the Impact of NASA and Other Federal Labs on Commercial Innovation. *Journal of Industrial Economics* 46 (2): 183–205.

Jaffe, Adam, and Josh Lerner. 2001. Reinventing Public R&D: Patent Policy and the Commercialization of National Laboratory Technologies. *Rand Journal of Economics* 32 (1): 167–198.

Jasanoff, Sheila. 2005. *Designs on Nature: Science and Democracy in Europe and the United States.* Princeton: Princeton University Press.

Jenkins, J. Craig, and Kevin T. Leicht. 1996. Direct Intervention by the Subnational State: The Development of Public Venture Capital Programs in the American States. *Social Problems* 43 (3): 306–326.

———. 1998. Political Resources and Direct State Intervention: The Adoption of Public Venture Capital Programs in the American States, 1974–1990. *Social Forces* 76 (4): 1323–1345.

Jenkins, C., K. Leicht, and A. Jaynes, 2008. Creating High-Technology Growth: High-Tech Employment Growth in U.S. Metropolitan Areas, 1988–1998. *Social Science Quarterly* 89 (2): 456–481.

Jenkins, J. Craig, Kevin T. Leicht, and Heather Wendt. 2006. Class Forces, Political Institutions, and State Intervention: Subnational Economic Development Policy in the United States, 1971–1990. *American Journal of Sociology* 111 (4): 1122–1180.

Johnson, Chalmers. 1982. *MITI and the Japanese Miracle: The Growth of Industrial Policy, 1925–1975.* Palo Alto: Stanford University Press.

———. 1984. *The Industrial Policy Debate.* San Francisco: ICS Press.

———. 1999. The Developmental State: Odyssey of a Concept. In *The Developmental State,* edited by M. Woo-Cumings. Ithaca, NY: Cornell University Press.

Jorgenson, D. W., M. S. Ho, and K. J. Stiroh. 2005. *Productivity: Information Technology and the American Growth Resurgence.* Cambridge: MIT Press.

Jorgenson, Dale W., Mun S. Ho, and Kevin J. Stiroh. 2008. A Retrospective Look at the U.S. Productivity Growth Resurgence. *Journal of Economic Perspectives* 22 (1): 3–24.

Jorgenson, D. W., and K. Vu. 2005. Information Technology and the World Economy. *Scandinavian Journal of Economics* 107 (4): 631–650.

Kammen, Daniel M., and Gregory F. Nemet. 2005. Real Numbers: Reversing the Incredible Shrinking Energy R&D Budget. *Issues in Science & Technology,* September. http://rael.berkeley.edu/files/2005/Kammen-Nemet-ShrinkingRD-2005.pdf.

Katz, Michael B. 1986. *In the Shadow of the Poorhouse.* New York: Basic.

Kelly, Cynthia. 2006. *Oppenheimer and the Manhattan Project.* Hackensack: World Scientific.

Kenney, Martin. 1986a. *Biotechnology: The University-Industrial Complex.* New Haven: Yale University Press.

———. 1986b. Schumpeterian Innovation and Entrepreneurs in Capitalism: A Case Study of the U.S. Biotechnology Industry. *Research Policy* 15: 21–31.

Kenney, Martin, and Richard Florida. 1993. *Beyond Mass Production.* New York: Oxford University Press.

Kett, Joseph F. 1994. *The Pursuit of Knowledge Under Difficulties: From Self-Improvement to Adult Education in America, 1750–1990.* Stanford, CA: Stanford University Press.

Kevles, Daniel. 1987. *The Physicists: The History of a Scientific Community in Modern America.* Cambridge: Harvard University Press.

———. 1992. Out of Genetics: The Historical Politics of the Human Genome. In *The Code of Codes: Scientific and Social Issues in the Human Genome Project,* edited by Daniel Kevles and Leroy Hood. Cambridge: Harvard University Press.

Keyssar, Alexander. 1986. *Out of Work: The First Century of Unemployment in Massachusetts.* New York: Cambridge University Press.

Khan, Zorina, and Kenneth L. Sokoloff. 1993. "Schemes of Practical Utility": Entrepreneurship and Innovation Among "Great Inventors" in the United States, 1790–1865. *Journal of Economic History* 53: 289–307.

Kimerling, L. C. 2000. Photonics to the Rescue: Microelectronics Becomes Microphotonics. *Interface* 9 (2): 28–31.

———. 2004. Monolithic Silicon Microphotonics. In *Silicon Photonics,* edited by L. Pavesi and D. J. Lockwood. Berlin: Springer-Verlag.

Kingdon, John W. 1995. *Agendas, Alternatives, and Public Policies.* New York: HarperCollins College.

Kleinman, Daniel Lee. 1995. *Politics on the Endless Frontier: Postwar Research Policy in the United States.* Durham, NC: Duke University Press.

Kleinman, Daniel Lee, Jason Delborne, and Robyn Autry. 2008. Beyond the Precautionary Principle in Progressive Politics: Toward the Social Regulation of Genetically Engineered Organisms. In *Tailoring Biotechnologies* 4 (1/2): 41–54.

Kleinman, Daniel Lee, and Abby J. Kinchy. 2003. Why Ban Bovine Growth Hormone? Science, Social Welfare, and the Divergent Biotech Policy Landscapes in Europe and the United States. *Science as Culture* 12 (3): 375–414.

Klepper, Steven. 2007. The Organizing and Financing of Innovative Companies in the Evolution of the U.S. Automobile Industry. In *Financing Innovation in the United States, 1870 to the Present,* edited by Naomi R. Lamoreaux and Kenneth L. Sokoloff. Cambridge: MIT Press.

Knight, Frank H. 1964 [1921]. *Risk, Uncertainty, and Profit.* New York: Augustus M. Kelley.

Kotz, David M., Terence McDonough, and Michael Reich, eds. 1994. *Social Structures of Accumulation: The Political Economy of Growth and Crisis.* New York: Cambridge University Press.

Krippner, Greta. 2001. The Elusive Market: Embeddedness and the Paradigm of Economic Sociology. *Theory and Society* 30 (6):775–810.

———. 2005. The Financialization of the American Economy. *Socio-Economic Review* 3 (2): 173–208.

Krueger, Anne. 1990. Government Failures in Development. *Journal of Economic Perspectives* 4 (3): 9–23.

Laidlaw, Frances Jean. 1998. ATP's Impact on Accelerating Development and Commercialization of Advanced Technology. *Journal of Technology Transfer* 23 (2): 33–41.

Lamont, Lansing. 1965. *Day of Trinity.* New York: Scribner.

Lardy, Nicholas R. 2006. China: Towards a Consumption-Driven Growth Path. *Policy Briefs in International Economics,* October.

Larson, Magali Sarfatti. 1993. *Behind the Postmodern Façade.* Berkeley: University of California Press.

———. 1994. Architectural Competitions as Discursive Events. *Theory and Society* 23 (4): 469–504.

Lasswell, Harold D. 1970. Must Science Serve Political Power? *American Psychologist* 25: 117–125.

Latour, Bruno. 1987. *Science in Action: How to Follow Scientists and Engineers Through Society.* Cambridge: Harvard University Press.

———. 2005. From Realpolitik to Dingpolitik, Or How to Make Things Public. In *Making Things Public: Atmospheres of Democracy,* edited by Bruno Latour and Peter Weibel. Cambridge: MIT Press.

Lawler, Andrew. 1996. DOE to Industry: So Long, Partner. *Science* 274 (5284): 24–26.

Lazowska, E., and D. Patterson. 2005. An Endless Frontier Postponed. *Science* 308: 757.

Lecuyer, Christophe. 2006. *Making Silicon Valley.* Cambridge: MIT Press.

Leitenberg, Milton. 2003. Distinguishing Offensive from Defense Biological Weapons Research. *Critical Reviews in Microbiology* 29 (3): 223–257.

Lemley, Mark. 2005. Patenting Nanotechnology. *Stanford Law Review* 601.

Leopold, Les. 2009. *The Looting of America.* White River Junction, VT: Chelsea Green.

Lerman, Robert I., Signe-Mary McKernan, and Stephanie Riegg, 2004. The Scope of Employer-Provided Training in the United States: Who, What, Where, and How Much? In *Job Training Policy in the United States,* edited by Christopher J. O'Leary, Robert A. Straits, and Stephen A. Wandner. Kalamazoo, MI: Upjohn Institute for Employment Research.

Lerner, Josh. 1999a. When Bureaucrats Meet Entrepreneurs: The Design of Effective "Public Venture Capital" Programs. *Economic Journal* 112: F73–F84.

———. 1999b. The Government as Venture Capitalist: The Long-Run Impact of the SBIR Program. *Journal of Business* 72 (3): 285–318.

Leslie, Stuart W. 1994. *The Cold War and American Science: The Military-Industrial-Academic Complex at MIT and Stanford.* New York: Columbia University Press.

———. 2001. Regional Disadvantage: Replicating Silicon Valley in New York's Capital Region. *Technology and Culture* 42 (2): 236–264.

Lester, Richard, and Michael J. Piore. 2004. *Innovation: The Missing Dimension.* Cambridge: Harvard University Press.

Lev, Baruch. 2005. Remarks. In *Measuring Capital in the New Economy,* edited by Carol Corrado, John Haltiwanger, and Daniel Sichel. Chicago: University of Chicago Press.

Lieberson, Stanley. 1985. *Making It Count: The Improvement of Social Research and Theory.* Berkeley: University of California Press.

Logan, John, and Harvey Molotch. 1987. *Urban Fortunes: The Political Economy of Place.* Berkeley: University of California Press.

Lorenzoni, Gianni, and Andrea Lipparini. 1999. The Leveraging of Interfirm Relationships as a Distinctive Organizational Capability: A Longitudinal Study. *Strategic Management Journal* 20 (4): 317–338.

Lovins, Amory. 1976. Energy Strategy: The Road Not Taken? *Foreign Affairs* 55 (1): 65–96.

Lundvall, B.-A. 1992. *National Systems of Innovation: Towards a Theory of Innovation and Interactive Learning.* London: Pinter.

MacDuffie, John Paul, and Susan Helper. 2006. Collaboration in Supply Chains: With and Without Trust. In *Collaborative Community,* edited by C. Heckscher and P. Adler. Oxford: Oxford University Press.

Macher, J., D. Mowery, and D. Hodges. 2000. Semiconductors. In *U.S. Industry in 2000,* edited by D. C. Mowery. Washington, D.C.: National Academies Press.

MacKenzie, Donald. 2006. *An Engine, Not a Camera: How Financial Models Shape Markets.* Cambridge: MIT Press.

Magaziner, Ira C., and Robert B. Reich. 1982. *Minding America's Business: The Decline and Rise of the American Economy.* New York: Vintage.

Mandel, Ernest. 1980. *Long Waves of Capitalist Development.* Cambridge: Cambridge University Press.

Mann, Catherine L., and Katharina Pluck. 2007. Understanding the U.S. Trade Deficit: A Disaggregated Perspective. In *G7 Current Account Imbalances: Sustainability and Adjustment,* edited by Richard Clarida. Chicago: University of Chicago Press.

Mansfield, Edwin. 1991. Academic Research and Industrial Innovation. *Research Policy* 20 (1): 1–12.

Mansfield, Edwin, and J. Y. Lee. 1996. The Modern University: Contributor to Industrial Innovation and Recipient of Industrial R & D Support. *Research Policy* 25: 1047–1058.

Markusen, Ann, and Catherine Hill. 1992. *Converting the Cold War Economy: Investing in Industries, Workers, and Communities.* Washington, D.C.: Economic Policy Institute.

Markusen, Ann, and Michael Oden. 1996. National Laboratories as Business Incubators and Region Builders. *Journal of Technology Transfer* 21 (1–2): 93–108.

Markusen, Ann, et al. 1991. *The Rise of the Gunbelt: A Military Remapping of Industrial America.* Oxford: Oxford University Press.

Martin, Ron, and Peter Sunley. 2006. Path Dependence and Regional Economic Evolution. *Journal of Economic Geography* 6: 395–407.

Martin, Susan. 2002. The Role of Biological Weapons in International Politics: The Real Military Revolution. *Journal of Strategic Studies* (March): 63–98.

McCray, W. Patrick. 2005. Will Small Be Beautiful? Making Policies for Our Nanotech Future. *History and Technology* 21 (2): 177–203.

———. 2009. From Lab to iPod: A Story of Discovery and Commercialization in the Post-Cold War Era. *Technology and Culture* 50 (1): 58–81.

Meier, Gerald M. 2001. Introduction to *Frontiers of Development Economics: The Future in Perspective,* edited by Gerald M. Meier and Joseph E. Stiglitz. New York: Oxford University Press.

Mendelsohn, Everett. 1994. The Politics of Pessimism: Science and Technology Circa 1968. In *Technology, Pessimism, and Postmodernism,* edited by Yaron Ezrahi, Everett Mendelsohn, and Howard Segal. Boston: Kluwer Academic.

Merton, Robert K. 1973. The Normative Structure of Science. In *The Sociology of Science: Theoretical and Empirical Investigations,* edited by Robert K. Merton. Chicago: University of Chicago Press.

Metcalfe, J. Stanley, and Ian Miles, eds. 2000. *Innovation Systems in the Service Economy: Measurement and Case Study Analysis.* Boston: Kluwer Academic.

Metz, B., et al., eds. 2007. *Contribution of Working Group III to the Fourth Assessment Report of the Intergovernmental Panel on Climate Change.* Cambridge: Cambridge University Press.

Meyer, Marshall, and Lynne Zucker. 1989. *Permanently Failing Organizations.* Newbury Park, CA: Sage.

Milliken, Jennifer. 2002. State Failure, State Collapse, and State Reconstruction: Concepts, Lessons, and Strategies. *Development and Change* 33 (5):753–774.

Mirowski, Philip, and Esther-Mirjam Sent. 2002. Introduction to *Science, Bought and Sold: Essays in the Economics of Science.* Chicago: University of Chicago Press.

Molzahn, Wendy. 2003. The CIA's In-Q-Tel Model: Its Applicability. *Acquisition Review Quarterly* 32 (Winter): 47–61.

Moore, G. 1965. Cramming More Components onto Integrated Circuits. *Electronics* 38 (8).

Moore, Kelly. 2008. *Disrupting Science: Social Movements, American Scientists, and the Politics of the Military, 1945–1975.* Princeton: Princeton University Press.

Mowery, David C. 1999. America's Industrial Resurgence? An Overview. In *U.S. Industry in 2000: Studies in Competitive Performance.* Washington, D.C.: National Academy Press.

———. 2009a. *Plus ca change*: Industrial R&D in the "Third Industrial Revolution." *Industrial and Corporate Change* 18 (1): 1–50.

———. 2009b. What Does Economic Theory Tell Us About Mission-Oriented R&D? In *The New Economics of Technology Policy*, edited by D. Foray. Northhampton, MA: Edward Elgar.

Mowery, David C., and Nathan Rosenberg. 1993. The U.S. National Innovation System. In *National Systems of Innovation: A Comparative Study*, edited by Richard R. Nelson. Oxford: Oxford University Press.

Mowery, David C., et al. 2004. *Ivory Tower and Industrial Innovation: University-Industry Technology Transfer Before and After the Bayh-Dole Act in the United States.* Stanford: Stanford University Press.

Mulkay, Michael. 1979. *Science and the Sociology of Knowledge.* London: George Allen and Unwin.

NAS. 2004. *Biotechnology Research in an Age of Terrorism: Confronting the Dual-Use Dilemma.* Washington, D.C.: National Academy Press.

———. 2007. *Rising Above the Gathering Storm: Energizing and Employing America for a Brighter Economic Future.* Washington, D.C.: National Academies Press.

Nature Biotechnology. 2007. "Billion Dollar Babies: Biotech Drugs as Blockbusters." (April): 380–382.

Needell, Allan A. 2000. *Science, Cold War, and the American State: Lloyd V. Berkner and the Balance of Professional Ideals.* Washington: Smithsonian Institution.

Nelkin, Dorothy. 1987. *Science as Intellectual Property: Who Controls Research?* New York: Macmillan.

Nelson, Richard, ed. 1993. *National Innovation Systems: A Comparative Analysis.* New York: Oxford University Press.

Nemet, G. F. 2006. Beyond the Learning Curve: Factors Influencing Cost Reductions in Photovoltaics. *Energy Policy* 34 (17): 3218–3232.

Newfield, Christopher. 2008. *Unmaking the Public University: The Forty-Year Assault on the Middle Class.* Cambridge: Harvard University Press.

———. 2009. Why Public Is Losing Private in American Research. *Polygraph* 21: 77–95.

Nocera, Daniel G. 2009. Chemistry of Personalized Solar Energy. *Inorganic Chemistry* 48 (21): 10001–10017.

NRC. 1999. *Funding a Revolution: Government Support for Computing Research.* Washington, D.C.: Commission on Physical Sciences, Mathematics, and Applications.

O'Mara, Margaret Pugh. 2005. *Cities of Knowledge: Cold War Science and the Search for the Next Silicon Valley.* Princeton: Princeton University Press.

Ó Riain, Seán 2004a. *The Politics of High Tech Growth: Developmental Network States in the Global Economy.* Cambridge: Cambridge University Press.

———. 2004b. State, Competition, and Industrial Change in Ireland, 1991–1999. *Economic and Social Review* 35 (1): 27–54.

————. 2009. Addicted to Growth: Developmental Statism and Neoliberalism in the Celtic Tiger. In *The Nation-State in Transformation: The Governance, Growth, and Cohesion of Small States Under Globalisation*, edited by M. Bøss. Aarhus: Aarhus University Press.

Obstfeld, Maurice, and Kenneth Rogoff. 2007. The Unsustainable U.S. Current Account Position Revisited. In *G7 Current Account Imbalances: Sustainability and Adjustment*, edited by Richard Clarida. Chicago: University of Chicago Press.

Owen-Smith, Jason. 2003. From Separate Systems to a Hybrid Order. *Research Policy* 32: 1081–1104.

Owen-Smith, Jason, and Walter W. Powell. 2001. Careers and Contradictions: Faculty Responses to the Transformation of Knowledge and Its Uses in the Life Sciences. *Research in the Sociology of Work* 10: 109–140.

Owen-Smith, Jason, et al. 2002. A Comparison of U.S. and European University-Industry Relations in the Life Sciences. *Management Science* 48: 24–43.

P.M.B. 1971. Losing Our Nerve to Experiment? *Science* 171 (3974): 875.

Paarlberg, Robert L. 2004. Knowledge as Power: Science, Military Dominance, and U.S. Security. *International Security* 29, 1 (Summer): 122–151.

Papandreou, Andreas. 1994. *Externality and Institutions*. Oxford: Clarendon.

Peck, Jamie. 2005. Struggling with the Creative Class. *International Journal of Urban and Regional Research* 29 (4): 740–770.

Perlin, John. 1999. *From Space to Earth: The Story of Solar Electricity*. Ann Arbor, MI: AATEC Publications.

Perrow, Charles. 1981. Markets, Hierarchies, and Hegemony. In *Perspectives on Organization Design and Behavior*, edited by A. Van De Ven and W. Joyce. New York: Wiley.

Peterson, J., and M. Sharp. 1998. *Technology Policy in the European Union*. Basingstoke: Macmillan.

Pidgeon, Nick, et al. 2009. Deliberating the Risks of Nanotechnologies for Energy and Health Applications in the United States and United Kingdom. *Nature Nanotechnology* 4: 95–98. www.nature.com/nnano/journal/v4/n2/abs/nnano.2008.362.html.

Piore, Michael, and Charles Sabel. 1984. *The Second Industrial Divide: Possibilities for Prosperity*. New York: Basic.

Plein, L. Christopher. 1991. Popularizing Biotechnology: The Influence of Issue Definition. *Science, Technology & Human Values* 16 (4): 474–490.

Podolny, Joel, and Karen Page. 1998. Network Forms of Organization. *Annual Review of Sociology* 24: 57–76.

Polanyi, Karl. 2001 [1944]. *The Great Transformation: The Political and Economic Origins of Our Time*. Boston: Beacon.

Polanyi, M. 1962. The Republic of Science. *Minerva* 1: 54–73.

Powell, Jeanne W. 1998. Pathways to National Economic Benefits from ATP-Funded Technologies. *Journal of Technology Transfer* 23 (2): 21–32.

Powell, Walter W. 1990. Neither Market Nor Hierarchy: Network Forms of Organization. In *Research in Organizational Behavior*, edited by B. Staw and L. L. Cummings. Greenwich, CT: JAI Press.

————. 2001. The Capitalist Firm in the Twenty-First Century: Emerging Patterns in Western Enterprise. In *The Twenty-First-Century Firm: Changing Economic Organization in International Perspective*, edited by P. DiMaggio. Princeton: Princeton University Press.

Powell, W. W., and S. Grodal. 2005. Networks of Innovators. In *The Oxford Handbook of*

Innovation, edited by J. Fagerberg, D. Mowery, and R.R. Nelson. Oxford: Oxford University Press.

Powell, Walter W., Kenneth K. Koput, and Laurel Smith-Doerr. 1996. Interorganizational Collaboration and the Locus of Innovation: Networks of Learning in Technology. *Administrative Science Quarterly* 41: 116–145.

Powell, Walter W., and Jason Owen-Smith. 1998. Universities and the Market for Intellectual Property in the Life Sciences. *Journal of Policy Analysis and Management* 17 (2): 253–277.

———. 2002. The New World of Knowledge Production in the Life Sciences. In *The Future of the City of Intellect: The Changing American University,* edited by Steven Brint. Palo Alto: Stanford University Press.

Powell, Walter W., and Kaisa Snellman. 2004. The Knowledge Economy. *Annual Review of Sociology* 30: 199–220.

Powell, Walter W., et al. 2005. Network Dynamics and Field Evolution: The Growth of Interorganizational Collaboration in the Life Sciences. *American Journal of Sociology* 110 (4): 1132–1205.

Rabinow, Paul. 1996. *Making PCR: A Story of Biotechnology.* Chicago: University of Chicago Press.

Roelofs, Joan. 2009. Networks and Democracy: It Ain't Necessarily So. *American Behavioral Scientist* 52 (7): 990–1005.

Rohrbaugh, Mark L. 2005. Distribution of Data and Unique Material Resources Made with NIH Funding. *Journal of Commercial Biotechnology* 11: 249–262.

Roland, Alex. 2003. Science, Technology, and War. In *The Cambridge History of Science.* Vol. 5, *The Modern Physical and Mathematical Sciences,* edited by Mary Jo Nye. Cambridge: Cambridge University Press.

Roland, Alex, with Philip Shiman. 2002. *Strategic Computing: DARPA and the Quest for Machine Intelligence, 1983–1993.* Cambridge: MIT Press.

Rooks, Gerrit, et al. 2000. How Inter-firm Co-operation Depends on Social Embeddedness: A Vignette Study. *Acta Sociologica* 43 (2):123–137.

Rorty, Richard. 1979. *Philosophy and the Mirror of Nature.* Princeton: Princeton University Press.

Rosenberg, Nathan. 1963. Technological Change in the Machine Tool Industry, 1840–1910. *Journal of Economic History* 23 (4): 414–443.

———. 1982. *Inside the Black Box: Technology in Economics.* New York: Cambridge University Press.

Rostow, Walt W. 1971 [1960]. *The Stages of Economic Growth: A Non-Communist Manifesto.* 2nd ed. Cambridge: Cambridge University Press.

Ruttan, Vernon. 2001. *Technology, Growth, and Development: An Induced Innovation Perspective.* New York: Oxford University Press.

———. 2006. *Is War Necessary for Economic Growth?* Oxford: Oxford University Press.

Sabel, Charles. 1993. Studied Trust: Building New Forms of Cooperation in a Volatile Economy. *Human Relations* 46 (9).

———. 1994. Learning by Monitoring: The Institutions of Economic Development. In *The Handbook of Economic Sociology,* edited by N. Smelser and R. Swedberg. Princeton: Princeton University Press.

———. 2006. A Real-Time Revolution in Routines. In *The Firm as a Collaborative Community: The Reconstruction of Trust in the Knowledge Economy,* edited by P. Adler and C. Heckscher. Oxford: Oxford University Press.

Salazar, Andres. 2005. Albuquerque: Technology City of Contrasts. *Canadian Journal of Regional Science* 28 (2): 265–282.

Sarewitz, Daniel. 2000. Human Well-Being and Federal Science: What's the Connection? In *Science, Technology, and Democracy,* edited by Daniel Lee Kleinman. New York: SUNY Press.

Saussure, Ferdinand de. 2002 [1916]. *Écrits de linguistique générale.* Edited by Simon Bouquet and Rudolf Engler. Paris: Gallimard.

Saxenian, AnnaLee. 1994. *Regional Advantage: Culture and Competition in Silicon Valley and Route 128.* Cambridge: Harvard University Press.

———. 2006. *The New Argonauts.* Cambridge: Harvard University Press.

Schabel, M. J. 2005. Current State of the Photonics Industry. In *Microphotonics: Hardware for the Information Age,* edited by L. Kimerling. Cambridge: MIT Microphotonics Center.

Schneiberg, Marc. 2007. What's on the Path? Path Dependence, Organizational Diversity, and the Problem of Institutional Change in the U.S. Economy, 1900–1950. *Socio-Economic Review* 5 (1): 47–80.

Schrank, Andrew. 2004. Ready-to-Wear Development? Foreign Investment, Technology Transfer, and Learning-by-Watching in the Apparel Trade. *Social Forces* 83 (1): 123–156.

———. 2005. Entrepreneurship, Export Diversification, and Economic Reform: The Birth of a "Developmental Community" in the Dominican Republic. *Comparative Politics* 38 (1).

Schrank, Andrew, and Josh Whitford. 2009a. Industrial Policy in the United States: A Neo-Polanyian Interpretation. *Politics & Society* 37 (4): 521–553.

Schreurs, Miranda. 2002. *Environmental Politics in Japan, Germany, and the United States.* Cambridge: Cambridge University Press.

Schumpeter, Joseph A. 1934 [1911]. *The Theory of Economic Development.* Cambridge: Harvard University Press.

———. 1947. *Capitalism, Socialism, and Democracy.* 2nd ed. New York: Harper.

Sciberras, E. 1986. Indicators of Technical Intensity and International Competitiveness: A Case for Supplementing Quantitative Data with Qualitative Studies in Research. *R&D Management* (May): 3–14.

Scotchmer, Suzanne. 2004. *Innovation and Incentives.* Boston: MIT Press.

Seidel, Robert. 2001. The National Laboratories of the Atomic Energy Commission in the Early Cold War. *Historical Studies in the Physical and Biological Sciences* 32 (1): 145–162.

Serger, Sylvia Schwaag, and Magnus Breidne. 2007. China's Fifteen-Year Plan for Science and Technology: An Assessment. *Asia Policy* (July): 135–164.

Servos, John W. 1980. The Industrial Relations of Science: Chemical Engineering at MIT, 1900–1939. *Isis* 77: 531–549.

Shallat, Todd A. 1994. *Structures in the Stream: Water, Science, and the Rise of the U.S. Army Corps of Engineers.* Austin: University of Texas Press.

Shane, Scott, and Daniel Cable. 2002. Network Ties, Reputation, and the Financing of New Ventures. *Management Science* 48 (3): 364–381.

Shapin, Steven. 2008. *The Scientific Life: A Moral History of a Late Modern Vocation.* Chicago: University of Chicago Press.

Shum, Kwok L., and Chihiro Watanabe. 2007. Photovoltaic Deployment Strategy in Japan and the U.S.A: An Institutional Appraisal. *Energy Policy* 35: 1186–1195.

Slaughter, Sheila, and Gary Rhoades. 1996. The Emergence of a Competitiveness Coalition and the Commercialization of Academic Science and Technology. *Science, Technology, and Human Values* 21: 303–339.

———. 2002. The Emergence of a Competitiveness Research and Development Policy Coalition and the Commercialization of Academic Science and Technology. In *Science Bought and Sold: Essays in the Economics of Science*, edited by Philip Mirowski and Esther Mirjam Sent, 69–108. Chicago: University of Chicago Press.

———. 2004. *Academic Capitalism and the New Economy: Markets, State, and Higher Education.* Baltimore: Johns Hopkins University Press.

Smith, Merritt Roe. 1977. *Harpers Ferry Armory and the New Technology.* Ithaca, NY: Cornell University Press.

Smith-Doerr, Laurel, and Walter Powell. 2005. Networks and Economic Life. In *The Handbook of Economic Sociology*, 2nd ed., edited by N. Smelser and R. Swedberg. Princeton: Princeton University Press.

Soete, Luc. 1985. International Diffusion of Technology, Industrial Development, and Technological Leapfrogging. *World Development* 13 (3): 409–422.

Soskice, David. 1999. Divergent Production Regimes: Coordinated and Uncoordinated Market Economies in the 1980s and 1990s. In *Continuity and Change in Contemporary Capitalism*, edited by H. Kitschelt et al. New York: Cambridge University Press.

Sperling, Daniel. 2001. Public-Private Technology R&D Partnerships: Lesson from U.S. Partnership for a New Generation of Vehicles. *Technology Policy* 8: 247–256.

Starr, Paul. 1982. *The Social Transformation of American Medicine.* New York: Basic.

Sternberg, E. 1992. *Photonic Technology and Industrial Policy: U.S. Responses to Technological Change.* Albany: SUNY Press.

Sternberg, Robert J. 2003. *Wisdom, Intelligence, and Creativity Synthesized.* Cambridge: Cambridge University Press.

Stevens, Rosemary. 1989. *In Sickness and in Wealth: American Hospitals in the Twentieth Century.* New York: Basic.

Stiglitz, Joseph E., and Scott J. Wallsten. 1999. Public-Private Technology Partnerships: Promises and Pitfalls. *American Behavioral Scientist* 43 (1): 52–73.

Stokes, Donald. 1997. *Pasteur's Quadrant: Basic Science and Technological Innovation.* Washington: Brookings Institution.

Strassmann, Paul A. 1997. *The Squandered Computer: Evaluating the Business Alignment of Information Technologies.* New Canaan, CT: Information Economics Press.

Suttmeier, Richard P., Cong Cao, and Denis Fred Simon. 2006a. "Knowledge Innovation" and the Chinese Academy of Sciences. *Science* 312 (April): 58–59.

———. 2006b. China's Innovation Challenge and the Remaking of the Chinese Academy of Sciences. *Innovations* (Summer): 78–97.

Tassey, Gregory. 2007. *The Technology Imperative.* Cheltenham, UK: Edward Elgar.

Taylor, Mark Zachary. 2004. Empirical Evidence Against Variety of Capitalism's Theory of Technological Innovation. *International Organization* 58 (Summer): 601–631.

Thorpe, Charles, and Steven Shapin. 2000. Who Was J. Robert Oppenheimer? Charisma and Complex Organization. *Social Studies of Science* 30 (4): 545–590.

Toumey, Chris. 2009. Science from the Inside. *Nature Nanotechnology* 4 (September): 536–538.

Touraine, Alain. 1971. *The Post-Industrial Society.* Translated by Leonard Mayhew. New York: Random House.

Tucker, Jonathan B. 2002. Farewell to Germs: The U.S. Renunciation of Biological and Toxin Warfare, 1969–1970. *International Security* 27: 107–148.

Turner, James. 2006. The Next Innovation Revolution: Laying the Groundwork for the United States. *Innovations* (Spring): 123–144.

Unruh, Gregory C. 2000. Understanding Carbon Lock In. *Energy Policy* 28: 817–830.

Uzzi, Brian. 1996. The Sources and Consequences of Embeddedness for the Economic Performance of Organizations: The Network Effect. *American Sociological Review* 61: 674–698.

Vallas, S. P., and Daniel L. Kleinman. 2008. Contradiction, Convergence, and the Knowledge Economy: The Confluence of Academic and Industrial Biotechnology. *Socio-Economic Review* 6 (2): 283–311.

Vettel, Eric. 2006. *Biotech: The Countercultural Origins of an Industry.* Philadelphia: University of Pennsylvania Press.

Von Hippel, Eric. 1988. *The Sources of Innovation.* New York: Oxford University Press.

———. 2006. *Democratizing Innovation.* Cambridge: MIT Press.

Wade, Nicholas. 1971a. Nixon's New Economic Policy: Hints of a Resurgence for R&D. *Science* (August 27): 796.

———. 1971b. Magruder in White House: SST Man Plans New Technology Take-Off. *Science* (October 22): 386.

———. 1979. Recombinant DNA: Warming Up for Big Payoff. *Science* 206: 663–665.

Wade, Robert. 1990. *Governing the Market: Economic Theory and the Role of Government in East Asian Industrialization.* Princeton: Princeton University Press.

Waldrop, Mitchell. 2001. *The Dream Machine: J.C.R. Licklider and the Revolution That Made Computing Personal.* New York: Penguin.

Wallerstein, Immanuel. 2004. *World-Systems Analysis: An Introduction.* Durham, NC: Duke University Press.

Walsh, John. 1973. Federal Science: Filling the Blanks in Policy and Personnel. *Science* (February 2): 456.

Walsh, Vivien, and Jordan Goodman. 1999. Cancer Chemotherapy, Biodiversity, Public and Private Property: The Case of the Anti-Cancer Drug Taxol. *Social Science & Medicine* 49: 1215–1225.

Walzer, Michael. 1983. *Spheres of Justice: A Defense of Pluralism and Equality.* New York: Basic.

Weiss, Charles, and William B. Bonvillian. 2009. *Structuring an Energy Technology Revolution.* Cambridge: MIT Press.

Weiss, Marc A. 1987. *The Rise of the Community Builders.* New York: Columbia University Press.

Wessel, David. 2009. *In Fed We Trust.* New York: Crown.

Wessner, Charles W., ed. 1999. *The Small Business Innovation Research Program: Challenges and Opportunities.* Washington, D.C.: National Academies Press.

———. 2001. *The Advanced Technology Program: Assessing Outcomes.* Washington, D.C.: National Academy Press.

———. 2008a. *An Assessment of the Small Business Innovation Research Program.* Washington, D.C.: National Academies Press.

———. 2008b. *An Assessment of the Small Business Innovation Research Program in the Department of Defense.* Washington, D.C.: National Academies Press.

Westney, Eleanor. 1987. *Imitation and Innovation: The Transfer of Western Organizational Practices in Meiji Japan.* Cambridge: Harvard University Press.

Westwick, Peter J. 2003. *The National Labs: Science in an American System, 1947–1974.* Cambridge: Harvard University Press.

Whitford, Josh. 2001. The Decline of a Model? Challenge and Response in the Italian Industrial Districts. *Economy and Society* 30 (1): 38–65.

———. 2005. *The New Old Economy: Networks, Institutions, and the Organizational Transformation of American Manufacturing.* Oxford: Oxford University Press.

Whitford, Josh, and Aldo Enrietti. 2005. Surviving the Fall of a King: The Regional Institutional Implications of Crisis at Fiat Auto. *International Journal of Urban and Regional Research* 29 (4): 771–795.

Whitford, Josh, and Jonathan Zeitlin. 2004. Governing Decentralized Production: Institutions, Public Policy, and the Prospects for Inter-Firm Collaboration in U.S. Manufacturing. *Industry and Innovation* 11 (1–2): 11–44.

Wickham, J. 1989. The Over Educated Engineer? The Work, Education, and Careers of Irish Electronics Engineers. *IBAR: Journal of Irish Business and Administrative Research* 10: 19–33.

Wise, David. 2000. *Cassidy's Run: The Secret Spy War over Nerve Gas.* New York: Random House.

Wise, George. 1985. *Willis R. Whitney, General Electric, and the Origins of U.S. Industrial Research.* New York: Columbia University Press.

Wolff, Michael F. 1976. The Genesis of the Integrated Circuit: How a Pair of U.S. Innovators Brought into Reality a Concept That Was on Many Minds. *IEEE Spectrum,* August, 45–53.

Womack, James P., Daniel T. Jones, and Daniel Roos. 1991. *The Machine That Changed the World.* New York: Harper Perennial.

Wright, Gavin. 2008. Purchases of Computers, by Type: 1955–1995. In *Historical Statistics of the United States, Earliest Times to the Present: Millennial Edition,* edited by Susan B. Carter et al. New York: Cambridge University Press.

Wright, Susan. 1990a. Biotechnology and the Military. In *Agricultural Bioethics: Implications for Agricultural Biotechnology,* edited by Steven M. Gendel et al. Ames: Iowa State University Press.

———. 1990b. Evolution of Biological Warfare Policy: 1945–1990. In *Preventing a Biological Arms Race.* Cambridge: MIT Press.

———. 1994. *Molecular Biology: Developing American and British Regulatory Policy for Genetic Engineering, 1972–1982.* Chicago: University of Chicago Press.

———. 2001. Legitimating Genetic Engineering. *Dissent* (Winter): 62–69.

Yager, Loren, and Rachel Schmidt. 1997. *The Advanced Technology Program: A Case Study in Federal Technology Policy.* Washington, D.C.: AEI Press.

Yanuzzi, Rick E. 2000. In-Q-Tel: A New Partnership Between the CIA and the Private Sector. *Defense Intelligence Journal* 9 (1): 25–37.

Youtie, Jan, Philip Shapira, and Alan L. Porter. 2008. Nanotechnology Publications and Citations by Leading Countries and Blocs. *Journal of Nanoparticle Research* 10 (6): 981–986.

Zucker, Lynne G., Michael R. Darby, and Jeff S. Armstrong. 2002. Commercializing Knowledge: University Science, Knowledge Capture, and Firm Performance in Biotechnology. *Management Science* 48 (1): 138–153.

Zucker, Lynne G., Michael R. Darby, Marilynn B. Brewer. 1998. Intellectual Human Capital and the Birth of U.S. Biotechnology Enterprises. *American Economic Review* 88 (1): 290–306.

Zucker, Lynne G., et al. 2007. Minerva Unbound: Knowledge Stocks, Knowledge Flows, and New Knowledge Production. *Research Policy* 36: 850–863.

Other Sources: Reports from Public Agencies, Universities, and Policy Institutes; Newspaper and Magazine Articles; Interviews and Public Testimony; and Other Miscellaneous Sources

ACORE (American Council on Renewable Energy). 2009. An Overview of the U.S. Renewable Energy Field in 2009. www.acore.org/files/re_overview2009.pdf.

Aitken, Donald W., Warren Schirtzinger, and Steven Strong. 2000. *SMUD's PV Program: Past, Present, and Future.* Consultant report for SMUD. December. www.donaldaitkenassociates .com/smudpvprogram_daa.doc.

AKOYA. 2007. *Measuring ATP Impact: 2006 Report on Economic Progress.* Economic Assessment Office, Advanced Technology Program, GCR 06-899.

Albuquerque Journal. 2002. Keep Politics out of Sandia Lab Contract. March 15, A12.

———. 2008. Top Honor Goes to Local Science Park (December 22): 1.

Alic, John A., David C. Mowery, Edward S. Rubin. 2003. U.S. Technology and Innovation Policies: Lessons for Climate Change. Pew Center on Global Climate Change. www .pewclimate.org/docUploads/U.S.%20Technology%20&%20Innovation%20Policies% 20(pdf).pdf.

Arend, Mark. 2006. "New Mexico Spotlight: A Place in the Sun." *Site Selection,* March. www .siteselection.com/features/2006/mar/nm.

Armstrong, Robert E. 1999. Testimony by Robert E. Armstrong, former executive director of the AARCC, before the House Subcommittee on Agriculture, Rural Development, Food and Drug Administration, and Related Agencies (March 17zz0. www.rurdev.usda.gov/ rd/cong/2000/2000aarc.htm.

Armstrong, Robert E., and Jerry B. Warner. 2003. Biology and the Battlefield. *Defense Horizons* 25: 1–8.

ATP. 2003. *Miniature LCDs Enhance High-Definition Displays.* Advanced Technology Program Status Report 94-01-0304.

———. 2004. *Developing Structural Composites for Large Automotive Parts.* Advanced Technology Program Status Report 94-02-0027.

———. 2006a. *Flow-Control Machining.* Advanced Technology Program Status Report 95-02-0058.

———. 2006b. *Improving Biodegradable Plastics Manufactured from Corn.* Advanced Technology Program Status Report 94-01-0173.

Ayres, Robert. 2001. The Energy We Overlook. *World Watch* 14 (6): 30–40.

AZoNano. 2008. National Nanotechnology Initiative Facing Change. *AZoNano News,* April 28. www.azonano.com/news.asp?newsID=6333.

Barfield, Claude E. 1970. Science Report/Money Shortage Forces New Look at Federal Science Policy. *National Journal* (October 22): 1805.

———. 1972. Science Report/White House Views Intense Technology Hunt As Useful Exercise, Though Few Projects Emerge. *National Journal* (May 6): 756–765.

———. 1973a. Nixon Reorganization Raises Questions About Role of Science in Federal Policy Making. *National Journal* (March 3): 405–415.

———. 1973b. Presidential Revamping of Science Tasks Upgrade of National Science Foundation Role. *National Journal* (March 24): 460–466.

Bartholomew, Richard, Amit Bagchi, and Stephen Campbell. 2007. *Enhancing America's Manufacturing Competitiveness: A Review of the NIST Advanced Technology Program's Investments in Manufacturing Technologies.* National Institute of Standards and Technology Technical Report, January.

Battelle Memorial Institute. 2004. *Positioning Arizona for the Next Big Technology Wave: Investment Prospectus to Create a Sustainable Systems Industry in Arizona.* Cleveland: BMI.

Belko, Michael E. 2004. Government Venture Capital: A Case Study of the In-Q-Tel Model. M.A. thesis, Air Force Institute of Technology.

Bennett, Ira, and Daniel Sarewitz. 2005. *Too Little, Too Late? Research Policies on the Societal Implications of Nanotechnology in the United States.* Arizona State University, Consortium for Science, Policy, and Outcomes. Phoenix: Arizona State University. www.cspo.org/ourlibrary/documents/Sci as Cult2.pdf.

Bernanke, Ben. 2005. The Global Saving Glut and the U.S. Current Account Deficit. Speech given in Richmond Virginia, March 10. www.federalreserve.gov/boarddocs/speeches/2005/200503102/default.htm.

Biotechnology Industry Organization. www.bio.org.

Blakeslee, Sandra. 1970. 25 Form Council to Make Scientists Aware of Consequences of Their Work. *New York Times,* February 19.

Blustein, Paul. 2001. Corporate Subsidies Suffer Under Bush Plan; Business Leaders Especially Rankled by Proposed Cuts in Export-Import Bank Lending. *Washington Post,* March 1.

Boroush, Mark. 2008. *New Estimates of National Research and Development Expenditures Show 5.8% Growth in 2007.* NSF 08-317. Arlington, VA: National Science Foundation.

Boyd, Dan. 2009. N.M., Japan Team Up for Stimulus. *Albuquerque Journal* (May 2): C7.

Branscomb, Lewis M., and Philip E. Auerswald. 2002. *Between Invention and Innovation: An Analysis of Funding for Early Stage Technology Development.* NIST GCR 02-841. Gaithersburg, Maryland: National Institute for Standards and Technology.

Bremer, Howard W. 2001. The First Two Decades of the Bayh-Dole Act as Public Policy. Presentation to National Association of State Universities and Land Grant Colleges, Washington, D.C., November 11.

Bresnahan, T.F., and S. Greenstein. 1999. Technological Competition and the Structure of the Computer Industry. *Journal of Industrial Economics,* 47 (1): 1–40.

Broad, William. 1992. Defining the New Plowshares Those Old Swords Will Make. *New York Times,* February 5, A1.

Broehl, Jesse. 2005. Sharp and Sandia National Labs Secure Research Partnership. Renewable Energy Worlds.com, November 5. www.renewableenergyworld.com/rea/news/article/2005/11/sharp-and-sandia-national-labs-secure-research-partnership-38848.

Bromberg, Joan Lisa. 1991. *The Laser in America 1950–1970.* Cambridge, Mass.: MIT Press.

Brown, John Seely, and John Hagel III. 2005. Innovation Blowback: Disruptive Management Practices from Asia. *McKinsey Quarterly* 1: 35–45.

Brownlee, Shannon. 2004. Plunder Drugs: Why Americans Believe They Have to Put Up with Pharmaceutical Profiteering. *Washington Monthly,* March, 55–58.

Bruns, Adam. 2009. The Nationals. *Site Selection* (July-August): 491–494.

Bryon, Christopher. 2005. Penny Stock Spies: CIA Fund Insiders Lurked Behind Three Shaky Stocks. *New York Post,* April 25.

———. 2006a. CIA Inc. Stinks: The Spy Agency Should Close Its Venture Capital Arm. *New York Post,* May 15.

———. 2006b. Academic Disguise: A College Research Center Pushes the CIA's Agenda. *New York Post,* November 6.

Bureau of the Census. 1975. *Historical Statistics of the United States: Colonial Times to 1970.* Pt. 1. Washington, D.C.: Department of Commerce.

Burroughs, Chris. 2002. Sandia, Boeing Establish Partnership to Develop Mutually Beneficial Technologies. SNL news release, September 5. www.sandia.gov/news-center/news-releases/2002/renew-energy-batt/Boeing.html.

———. 2008a. Sandia, Stirling Energy Systems Set New World Record for Solar-to-Grid Conversion Efficiency. SNL news release, February 12. www.sandia.gov/news/resources/releases/2008/solargrid.html.

———. 2008b. Sandia's Entrepreneurial Program Is Back. *Sandia Lab News.* November 7, 8.

Business Executives for National Security. 2001. *Accelerating the Acquisition and Implementation of New Technologies for Intelligence: The Report of the Independent Panel on the Central Intelligence Agency In-Q-Tel Venture.* www.bens.org/mis_support/nqtel-panel-rpt.pdf.

Cao, Cong, Richard P. Suttmeier, and Denis Fred Simon. 2006. China's 15-Year Science and Technology Plan. *Physics Today* (December): 38–43.

Castaldi, Carolina, and Giovanni Dosi. 2004. *The Grip of History and the Quest for Novelty: Some Results and Open Questions on Path Dependence in Economic Processes.* Laboratory of Economics and Management, Sant'Anna School of Advanced Studies, Pisa, Italy.

Chamberlain, Lisa. 2007. Planned City Rises Within a City in the Southwest. *New York Times,* September 26, 7.

Chen, Christine, and Jessica Sung. 2001. Hughes Hasn't Been This Sexy Since…. *Fortune,* February 5, 18–24.

Cheng, Jiaan. 2007. Interview conducted at the Zhejiang University, Zhejiang–California International Nanosystems Institute, August 1.

Childress, Marjorie. 2008. The Nexus of Clean Energy and Green Jobs. *New Mexico Independent,* October 22. http://newmexicoindependent.com/5128/new-energy-and-green-jobs.

Clark, Katherine, et al. 2001. *Technology Transfer from Sandia National Laboratories and Technology Commercialization by MODE/Emcore.* Sandia Report. Albuquerque: SNL.

Clinton, William J. 1995. Remarks by the President to the Staff of the CIA and the Intelligence Community. Official press release, July 14. www.fas.org/irp/news/1995/950714cia.htm.

Cohn, Victor. 1970. Nation's "Scientific Estate" Decaying, Hill Panel Warns. *Washington Post* (November 1): 9.

Coleman, Michael. 2001. N.M. Has Key Role in Energy Production. *Albuquerque Journal,* May 18, A1.

———. 2008. A Setting Sun? N.M.'s Solar Power Future Faces Tax Credit Hurdle. *Albuquerque Journal,* April 4, A1.

Commission on the Roles and Capabilities of the United States Intelligence Community. 1996. *Preparing for the 21st Century: An Appraisal of U.S. Intelligence.* Washington, D.C.: Government Printing Office.

Connelly, Joanne. 1992. Sandia Without AT&T. *Electronic News* 38 (1911): 18.

Cooper, C., and M. Kanellos. 2005. The Secret Behind CIA's Venture Capital. *CNet News,* June 2.

Copeland, Larry. 1999. Oil Country Suffers Dry Spell. *U.S.A. Today,* February 19, 3A.

Cordtz, Dan. 1995. Bye, Bye, Dr. Strangelove: Threatened with Extinction by Politicians, U.S. Weapons Labs Are Dying to Help Business. *Financial World* 164 (2): 32–37.

Cory, Karlynn, Toby Couture, and Claire Kreycik. 2009. *Feed-In Tariff Policy: Design, Implementation, and RPS Policy Interactions.* National Renewable Energy Laboratory Technical Report. www.nrel.gov/docs/fy09osti/45549.pdf.

CSO. 2007. *National Accounts.* Dublin: CSO.

Culliton Report/Industrial Policy Review Group. 1992. *A Time for Change: Industrial Policy for the 1990s*. Dublin: Stationery Office.

Davies, Frank. 2008. Congress Fails to Extend Credits. *San Jose Mercury News*, June 11.

Defense Base Closure and Realignment Commission. 1995. *1995 Report to the President*, July. www.brac.gov/finalreport.html.

Defense Science Board. 2005. *High Performance Microchip Supply*. Washington, D.C.: National Academies Press.

Deutsch, Claudia. 1997. Drumming Up Business to Survive in a World Without Cold War. *New York Times*. August 23, 35.

DOE (Department of Energy). 2002. The History of Solar. Timeline prepared by the Energy Efficiency and Renewable Energy Division of DOE. www1.eere.energy.gov/solar/pdfs/solar_timeline.pdf.

———. 2006. Why PV Is Important. DOE Energy Efficiency and Renewable Energy Solar Technologies Program. www1.eere.energy.gov/solar/pv_important.html.

———. 2007. *Technology Transfer Report*. Washington, D.C.: Department of Energy.

DSIRE (Database of State Incentives for Renewables and Efficiency). State Rebates for Solar PV Projects, May 1. www.dsireusa.org/solar/comparisontables/?rpt=1.

Duke, Richard D. 2002. Clean Energy Technology Buydowns, Economic Theory, Analytic Tools, and the Photovoltaics Case. Ph.D. diss., Princeton University.

Energy Information Administration. 2005. *State Energy Data 2005*. Washington: EIA.

EPA (Environmental Protection Agency). 2009. Renewable Portfolio Standards Fact Sheet. www.epa.gov/chp/state-policy/renewable_fs.html.

Evans, Donald L. 2002. *The Advanced Technology Program: Reform with a Purpose*. U.S. Department of Commerce.

Executive Office of the President. 2009. A Strategy for American Innovation: Driving Towards Sustainable Growth and Quality Jobs. Office of Science and Technology Policy, September. www.ostp.gov/galleries/press_release_files/SEPT%2020%20%20Innovation%20Whitepaper_FINAL.PDF.

Faggin, Federico. 1992. The Birth of the Microprocessor. *BYTE* (March): 145–150.

Fan, Shoushan. 2007. Interview conducted at Tsinghua University, July 27.

Farley, Peter. 1996. Competitiveness Council Bemoans U.S. Policy Drift. *Chemical Week,* April 17.

Farquhar, Ned. 2008. U.S. Oil Addicts Deny Need to Change Energy Policy. *Albuquerque Journal* (May 1): A9.

Farrell, John. 2008. Minnesota Feed-in Tariff Could Lower Cost, Boost Renewables, and Expand Local Ownership. New Rules Project. www.newrules.org/energy/publications/minnesota-feedin-tariff-could-lower-cost-boost-renewables-and-expand-local-ownership.

Fisher, Anne. 2008. Innovation Pays Off. *Fortune*, March 17, 65–67.

Fleck, John. 2008a. Still Growing: While the Nation's Other Nuclear Weapons Labs Have Cut Jobs, Sandia Defies the Trend. *Albuquerque Journal* (September 15): 1.

———. 2008b. Developer Wants "Smart" Energy Use. *Albuquerque Journal* (December 4): 10.

Florida, Richard. 2002. The Rise of the Creative Class. *Washington Monthly* (May): 15–25.

Forfás, 2008. *The Science Budget 2007/8*. Dublin: Forfás.

Forsen, Harold K. 1995. Role of the Laboratory Programs of the National Institute of Standards and Technology. U.S. House of Representatives, Hearing. September 12.

Frazis, Harley, Maury Gittleman, and Mary Joyce. 1998. Results of the 1995 Survey of Employer-Provided Training. *Monthly Labor Review* (June): 3–13.

Fuchs, E. 2010. Rethinking the Role of the State in Technology Development: DARPA and the Case for Embedded Network Governance. Manuscript.

Fuchs, Erica R. H., and R. E. Kirchain. 2010. Design for Location: The Impact of Manufacturing Offshore on Technology Competitiveness. Manuscript.

Gao Congjie. 2006. Interview conducted in Hangzhou, August 13.

Garthoff, Raymond L. 2000. Polyakov's Run. *Bulletin of Atomic Scientists,* September-October, 37–40.

Gaul, Gilbert M., and Susan Q. Stranahan. 1995. The Price of Keeping Labs Busy. *Philadelphia Inquirer* (June 5): A1.

Gelbspan, Ross. 2005. "Snowed." *Mother Jones* (May-June): 42–44.

General Accounting Office. 1994. *National Laboratories: Are Their R&D Activities Related to Commercial Product Development?* Washington, D.C.: GAO.

———. 1996. *Measuring Performance: The Advanced Technology Program and Private-Sector Funding.* U.S. General Accounting Office GAO/RCED-96-47.

Gipe, Paul. 2009. SMUD Announces "Feed-In Tariffs"—But Can Program Deliver as Promised? *Renewable Energy World,* August 11. www.renewableenergyworld.com/rea/news/article/2009/08/smud-announces-feed-in-tariffs-but-can-program-deliver-as-promised.

Global Insight. 2008. *Current and Potential Green Jobs in the U.S. Economy.* Lexington: Global Insight for the U.S. Conference of Mayors.

Godin, Benoît. 2009a. Making Science, Technology, and Innovation Policy: Conceptual Frameworks as Narratives. *Review Innovation RICEC* 1 (1): 2009. http://ricec.info/images/stories/articlerevue/b_godin_3iricec_042009.pdf.

———. 2009b. *The Culture of Numbers: The Origins and Development of Statistics on Science.* Project on the History and Sociology of STI Statistics Working Paper no. 40. www.csiic.ca/PDF/Godin_40.pdf.

Goode, Darren, and Christina Bourge. 2007. Hoyer Says No Energy Vote Until December at the Earliest. *National Journal's Congress Daily,* November 14.

Government Accountability Office. 2009. *Technology Transfer: Clearer Priorities and Greater Use of Innovative Approaches Could Increase the Effectiveness of Technology Transfer at Department of Energy Laboratories.* GAO-09-548. Washington, D.C.: GAO.

Grant, Gene. 2008. N.M. Leads the Way in Green Tech. *Albuquerque Journal,* May 19, A4.

Greenstein, Shane. 2009. Nurturing the Accumulation of Innovations: Lessons from the Internet. Forthcoming in Accelerating Energy Innovation: Lessons from Multiple Sectors. Draft Manuscript. www.nber.org/~confer/2009/EIf09/greenstein.pdf. http://www.nber.org/~confer/2009/EIf09/greenstein.pdf.

Gunther, Marc. 2009. Nothing Blue About This Airline. *Fortune* (September 14): 114–118.

Haber, Carol. 1997. New Defense Giant Born. *Electronic News* 43 (2151): 1–2.

Hagel, John, III, and John Seely Brown. 2006. Creation Nets: Harnessing the Potential of Open Innovation. Manuscript.

Hagengruber, Roger. 2002. Sandia's Ethos: Senior VP Roger Hagengruber Talks About What It Means to Be a Sandian. *Sandia Lab News,* May 3, 10.

Hartranft, Michael. 2009a. Bright Ideas: Visible Light Solar Technologies Plans to Change "the Way We Light the World." *Albuquerque Journal* (June 29): 1.

———. 2009b. Advent Solar Cuts 55 Workers. *Albuquerque Journal* (January 17): C5.

HEA. 2006. *The Program for Research in Third Level Institutions: Transforming the Irish Research Landscape.* Dublin: HEA.

Henderson, Jennifer A., and John J. Smith. 2002. Academia, Industry, and the Bayh-Dole Act:

An Implied Duty to Commercialize. Center for the Integration of Medicine and Innovative Technology. www.cimit.org/news/regulatory/coi_part3.pdf.

Henderson, Rebecca, and Richard G. Newell. 2009. Accelerating Energy Innovation: Lessons from Multiple Sectors. Draft Manuscript. http://www.nber.org/chapters/c11746.pdf.

Heuser, Stephen. 2009. One Girl's Hope, A Nation's Dilemma. *Boston Globe,* June 14.

Holtzman, Clay. 2005. Entrepreneurial Transfer. *New Mexico Business Weekly,* September 15. http://albuquerque.bizjournals.com/albuquerque/stories/2005/09/19/focus1.html.

Homeland Security Institute. 2005. *Venture Capital Concept Analysis: Final Report.* HSI no. RP05-006b-01.

Horn, C. 2009. Not Letting Cuts Harm Our Export Potential. *Irish Times,* April 13. www .irishtimes.com/newspaper/innovation/2009/0413/1224244557481.html.

Hughes, Kent H. 2005. *Building the Next American Century: The Past and Future of American Economic Competitiveness.* Baltimore: Johns Hopkins University Press.

Hunt, Robert M., and Leonard I. Nakamura. 2006. *The Democratization of U.S. Research and Development After 1980.* 2006 Meeting Papers 121. Society for Economic Dynamics.

Hurt, Shelley L. 2009. Science, Power, and the State: United States Foreign Policy, Intellectual Property Law, and the Origins of Agricultural Biotechnology. Ph.D. diss., New School for Social Research.

IEA (International Energy Agency). 2000. *Trends in Photovoltaic Applications: Survey Report of Selected IEA Countries Between 1992 and 1999.* www.iea-pvps.org/products/download/rep1_08.pdf.

———. 2008. *Trends in Photovoltaic Applications: Survey Report of Selected IEA Countries Between 1992 and 2007.* www.iea-pvps.org/products/download/rep1_17.pdf.

———. 2009a. IEA R&D Statistics Database. www.iea.org/Textbase/stats/rd.asp.

———. 2009b. *National Survey Report of PV Power Applications in the United States, 2008.* Prepared by NREL. www.iea-pvps.org/countries/download/nsr08/NSR%20U.S.A% 202008.pdf.

———. 2009c. *Trends in Photovoltaic Applications: Survey Report of Selected IEA Countries Between 1992 and 2008.* www.iea-pvps.org/products/download/rep1_18.pdf.

Interagency Working Group on Nanoscience. 1999. Engineering and Technology. *Nanotechnology Research Directions: IWGN Workshop Report,* iii–iv, xix–xxiv. www.wtec.org/loyola/nano/ IWGN.Research.Directions/chapter00.pdf.

ITIF. 2008. 2008 ITIF Broadband Rankings. itif.org/files/2008BBRankings.pdf.

ITRS. 2001. *International Technology Road Map for Semiconductors.* Austin, TX: SEMATECH.

———. 2006. *International Technology Road Map for Semiconductors: 2006 Update.* Austin, TX: SEMATECH.

Jern, Jarrett. 2008. Director of business development and membership at Solartech, personal communication, July.

Jia Jinping. 2006. Interview conducted at Shanghai Jiao Tong University School of Environmental Science and Engineering, August 6.

Johnson, Leland. 1997. *Sandia National Laboratories: A History of Exceptional Service in the National Interest.* Albuquerque: SNL.

Joint Statement. 2005. Joint Statement of the Computing Research Community. House Science Committee Hearing on the Future of Computer Science Research in the U.S., Washington, D.C.

Jordan, D. 2009. Research. *Irish Times,* April 6.

Kahn, R. 1983. *New-Generation Technology: A Strategic Plan for Its Development and Application to Critical Problems in Defense.* Arlington, VA: Defense Advanced Research Projects Agency.

Kammen, Daniel M., Kamal Kapadia, and Matthias Fripp. 2004. *Putting Renewables to Work: How Many Jobs Can the Clean Energy Industry Generate?* UC Berkeley Energy and Resources Group/Goldman School of Public Policy. http://rael.berkeley.edu/old-site/renewables .jobs.2006.pdf.

Kammen, Daniel M., and Robert M. Margolis. 1999. Under-Investment: The Energy Technology and R&D Policy Challenge. *Deregulation Watch* 2 (15): 8–11. http://rael.berkeley.edu/ files/1999/Kammen-Margolis-RnDPolicy-1999.pdf.

Kennedy, K. A., E. O'Malley. and R. O'Donnell. 1991. Report to the Industrial Policy Review Group on the Impact of the Industrial Development Agencies. Dublin, Stationery Office.

Keystone Research Center. 1997. *Technology and Industrial Performance in the Service Sector.* Field Research Report. Harrisburg, PA.

King, Julia. 2009. CIOs Complain College Grads Aren't Ready for IT Work. *Computerworld,* September 21.

Kivimaa, Paula, and Per Mickwitz. 2004. Driving Forces for Environmentally Sounder Innovations: The Case of the Finnish Pulp and Paper Industry. In *Governance for Industrial Transformation: Proceedings of the 2003 Berlin Conference on the Human Dimensions of Global Environmental Change,* edited by K. Jacob, M. Binder, and A. Wieczorek. Berlin: Environmental Policy Research Center.

Kravetz, Alexandra. 2009. 2008 Global Solar Report Cards. Global Green and Green Cross U.S.A. http://globalgreen.org/docs/publication-96-1.pdf.

Kristensen, Peer Hull. 2009. The Co-Evolution of Experimentalist Business Systems and Enabling Welfare States: Nordic Countries in Transition. In *New Modes of Globalizing,* edited by P. H. Kristensen and K. Lilja. EU-funded Sixth Framework Program. http://project.hkkk.fi/translearn/Book/New%20Modes%20of%20Globalization_book% 20manus_final%20version_250209.pdf.

Larson, Charles F. 2004. Institutional Development in China's Science and Technology. Session Discussion for International Symposium on Transforming Institutions in Global China, University of Maryland Institute for Global Chinese Affairs. http://law.gmu.edu/nctl/stpp/ us_china_pubs/8.1_Institutional_Development_in_China_Sci_Tech.pdf.

Larson, Linda. 2009. Vermont Experiments with Feed-In Tariffs to Promote Renewable Energy Production. Marten Law Group, September 23. www.martenlaw.com/news/?20090923-vermont-feed-in-tariffs.

Laurent, Anne. 2002. Raising the Ante. *Government Executive,* June 1.

Lazonick, William, Edward March, and Öner Tulum. 2008. *Boston's Biotech Boom: A "New Massachusetts Miracle"?* IKD Working Paper 35. Open University Research Center on Innovation, Knowledge, and Development.

Lerner, Josh, et al. 2004. *In-Q-Tel.* Harvard Business School Publishing Case 9-804-146.

Levratto, Nadine, and Renaud Lestringant. 1999. Path-Dependence and Technological Competition in the PV Cells Industry: The Case of Crystalline and Amorphous Silicon. Working Paper, October 1. http://ssrn.com/abstract=185115 or doi:10.2139/ ssrn.185115.

Levy, Esther, ed. 2006. *Advanced Materials.* Interview conducted at International Mesostructured Materials Association Conference, Fudan University, Shanghai, August 6.

Li, Ming. 2007. Interview conducted in Beijing, August 8.

Li, Naihu, and Kelvin Wang. 2006. Interview conducted at a breakfast meeting of the American Chamber of Commerce, August 8.

Li, Xiaoli, Liyi Shi, and Guoquan Min. 2006. Interview conducted at the Shanghai Nanotechnology Promotion Center. August 8, 2006.

Liu, Dongsheng. 2006. Interview conducted in Beijing, July 31.

Liu, Zhongfan. 2006. Interview conducted at Peking University Institute of Physical Chemistry, August 1.

Lynn, Leonard, and Harold Salzman. 2007a. *"Innovation Shifts" to Emerging Economies: Cases from IT and Heavy Industries.* Sloan Industry Studies Working Papers. www.industry.sloan .org/industrystudies/workingpapers.

———. 2007b. The Real Global Technology Challenge. *Change* (July-August): 8–13.

Lyons, Richard D. 1970. Nixon Reorganizing Vast Federal Science Complex. *New York Times,* November 1, 1.

Mandel, Michael. 2009. Innovation Interrupted: How America's Failure to Capitalize on Innovation Hurt the Economy—and What Happens Next. *Business Week,* June 15.

Margolis, Robert M. 2002. Understanding Technological Innovation in the Energy Sector: The Case of Photovoltaics. Ph.D. diss., Princeton University.

Margolis, Robert, and J. Zuboy. 2006. *Nontechnical Barriers to Solar Energy Use: Review of Recent Literature.* National Renewable Energy Laboratory Technical Report. www.nrel.gov/docs/ fy07osti/40116.pdf.

Markoff, John. 2005. Pentagon Redirects Its Research Dollars. *New York Times,* April 2.

Matlock, Staci. 2008a. What Voters Want: Energy. *Santa Fe New Mexican,* November 2, A6.

———. 2008b. Harnessing the Sun's Rays. *Santa Fe New Mexican,* November 1, A1.

McCurry, John. 2008. Solar System: The State's Commitment to Renewable Energy Companies Pays Off. *Site Selection,* March. www.siteselection.com/features/2008/mar/ newMexico.

McNeil, Ronald, et al. 2007. *Barriers to Nanotechnology Commercialization.* Final Report Prepared for the U.S. Department of Commerce Office of Technology Assessment. Springfield, IL: College of Business and Management, University of Illinois.

Metcalf, Richard. 2005. Solar Business Heats Up. *Albuquerque Journal* (November 12): C1.

Mintz, John. 1992. AT&T to Cut Its Ties with Sandia Lab. *Washington Post,* May 6, F1.

Mintz, Morton. 1971. Patent Policy Aims at Flexibility. *Washington Post* (August 25): A9.

Mjoset, L. 1992. *The Irish Economy in a Comparative Institutional Perspective.* National Economic and Social Council Report 93. Dublin: NESC.

Moe, Ronald C., and Kevin R. Kosar. 2005. *The Quasi Government: Hybrid Organizations with Both Government and Private Sector Legal Characteristics.* CRS Report for Congress RL30533. Library of Congress Congressional Research Service.

Moore, Stephen. 1997. The Advanced Technology Program and Other Corporate Subsidies. Senate Hearing, June 3.

Moran, Susan. 2007. The New Bioplastics, More Than Just Forks. *New York Times,* March 7.

Mortensen, John. 2001. *Factors Associated with Photovoltaic System Costs.* National Renewable Energy Laboratory. www.nrel.gov/docs/fy01osti/29649.pdf.

MOST-863. 2001. *Annual Report 2001: Overview of 863 Program in the Tenth Five-Year Plan Period.* www.863.org.cn/english/annual_report/annual_repor_2001/200210090007.html.

MOST 973. 2004. Profile of 973 Program. www.973.gov.cn/English/Index.asp.

Mott, John. 2008. From the Lab to the Marketplace. *Innovation,* April-May. www.innovation-america.org/archive.php?articleID=416.

Nanotechwire.com. 2005. China: Moving from Laggard to Power Player in Nanotechnology, November 10. www.nanotechwire.com/news.asp?nid=2564&ntid=116&pg=12.

National Center for Education Statistics. 1993. *120 Years of Education: A Statistical Portrait.* Washington, D.C.: Department of Education.

National Center for Education Statistics. 2004. *Undergraduate Enrollments in Academic, Career, and Vocational Programs.* NCES 04-018. Washington, D.C.: Department of Education.

National Center for Education Statistics. 2008. *Career and Technical Education in the United States: 1990 to 2005.* NCES 2008-035. Washington, D.C.: Department of Education.

National Commission on Terrorist Attacks upon the United States. 2004. *The 9/11 Commission Report: Final Report of the National Commission on Terrorist Attacks upon the United States.* Washington, D.C.: Government Printing Office.

National Research Council, Committee on Innovations in Computing and Communications. 1999. *Funding a Revolution: Government Support for Computing Research.* Washington, D.C.: National Academies Press.

National Science Board. 2008. *Science & Engineering Indicators, 2008.* Arlington: National Science Foundation.

National Science Foundation. 2008a. *Science and Engineering Degrees: 1966–2006: Detailed Statistical Tables.* NSF 08-321. Arlington, VA.

———. 2008b. *Science and Engineering Indicators,* chap. 4. www.nsf.gov/statistics/seind08/c4/c4h.htm.

Navigant (Navigant Consulting). 2006. *A Review of PV Inverter Technology Cost and Performance Projections.* National Renewable Energy Laboratory Subcontract Report, January. www.nrel.gov/pv/pdfs/38771.pdf.

NESC. 1996. *Networking for Competitive Advantage.* Dublin: NESC.

New Mexico Business Journal. 1994. Labs Discover the Real World (September): 33–38.

———. 2006. Solar Power Lights Homes on Indian Reservations (February): 26–27.

New Scientist. 1970. Golden Dawn for Genetic Engineering? (June 18): 564.

NIBC. 2006. Brochure provided by the Nanotechnology Industrialization Base of China during interview, August 6.

NIH OTT. 2005. *Keratinocyte Growth Factor: Reducing Costs and Increasing the Quality of Life for Cancer Patients.*

Nixon, Richard M. 1973. Message to the Congress Transmitting Reorganization Plan no. 1 of 1973: Restructuring the Executive Office of the President, January 26. Public Papers.

NNEC (Network for New Energy Choices). 2008. *Freeing the Grid: Best and Worst Practices in State Net Metering Policies and Interconnection Requirements.* www.newenergychoices.org/uploads/FreeingTheGrid2008_report.pdf.

NREL (National Renewable Energy Laboratory). 2008. Record Makes Thin-Film Solar Cell Competitive with Silicon Efficiency, March 24. www.nrel.gov/news/press/2008/574.html.

O'Connell, Jock. 1999. Soft Figures on Software Exports. *Sacramento Bee,* August 15.

O'Leary, E. 2009. "Smart Economy" Plan Gambles with Taxpayers' Money. *Irish Times,* May 25. www.irishtimes.com/newspaper/innovation/2009/0525/1224247324770.html.

O'Malley, E. 1980. *Industrial Policy and Development: A Survey of Literature from the Early 1960s to the Present.* Dublin: NESC.

O'Malley, E., K.A. Kennedy, and R. O'Donnell. 1992. *Report to the Industrial Policy Review Group on the Impact of the Industrial Development Agencies.* Dublin: Stationery Office.

OECD (Organization for Economic Cooperation and Development). 1963. Science and Irish Economic Development OECD: Paris.

———. 1974. *Reviews of National Science Policy.* Paris: OECD.

———. 1978. *Policies for the Stimulation of Industrial Innovation.* Paris: OECD.

———. 1997. *Government Venture Capital for Technology Based Firms.* Paris: OECD.

———. 2007. *OECD Reviews of Innovation Policy: China: Synthesis Report.* Paris: OECD.

———. 2008. *Intellectual Assets and Value Creation: Synthesis Report.* Paris: OECD.

Office of Technology Assessment. 1981. Appendix III-A, History of the Recombinant DNA Debate. In *Impacts of Applied Genetics: Micro-Organisms, Plants, and Animals.*

———. 1984. *Commercial Biotechnology: An International Analysis.* Washington, D.C.: Government Printing Office.

———. 1992. *A New Technological Era for American Agriculture.* Washington, D.C.: Government Printing Office.

———. 1992a. *Federal and Private Roles in the Development and Provision of Alglucerase Therapy for Gaucher Disease.* Washington, D.C.: Government Printing Office.

Office of the Under Secretary of Defense. 2004. *Defense Industrial Base Capabilities Study: Force Application.* Washington, D.C.: Department of Defense.

Olukotun, K. 2007. A Conversation with John Hennessy and David Patterson. *ACM Queue* 4 (10).

Osama, Athar. 2008. *Washington Goes to Sand Hill Road: The Federal Government's Forays into the Venture Capital Industry.* Foresight and Governance Research Brief no. 1. Woodrow Wilson International Center for Scholars.

Osborn, David E. 2001. Sustained Orderly Development and Commercialization of Grid-Connected Photovoltaics: SMUD as a Case Example. Keynote Address, World Sustainable Energy Conference, March.

Osborne, Mark. 2009. First Solar's Market Share Set to Soar. *PV-tech.org Daily News*, September 7. www.pv-tech.org/ news/_a/first_solars_market_share_set_to_soar.

Palmer, Thomas C., Jr. 1992. Industrial Policy Inevitable for U.S.; It May Be a Dirty Phrase to Some, But Process Has Already Begun. *Boston Globe,* March 8.

Palmintera, Diane. 2003. *Partners on a Mission: Federal Laboratory Practices Contributing to Economic Development.* Washington: Department of Commerce.

Paskus, Laura. 2005. The City Renewable. *Alibi* (November): 24–30. http://alibi.com/index .php?story=13318&scn=feature.

PBS Frontline. 2000. Richard Cheney Interview. www.pbs.org/wgbh/pages/frontline/shows/ future/interviews/cheney.html.

Pollack, Andrew. 2002. Cities and States Clamor to Be Bio Town, U.S.A. *New York Times,* June 11, C1.

Pope, Carl. 2000. Fossil Fools. *Sierra* 85 (4): 14–15.

PRC. 2003. Science and Technology Policy. Press release from the Embassy of the PRC in the United Kingdom, Great Britain, and Northern Ireland, October 10. www.chinese-embassy .org.uk/eng/kjjl/t27122.htm.

Prescrire International. 2007. Prescrire Awards, April, 76.

Pugh, Lori. 1997. Entrepreneurs Live on Edge with Untested Spin-off Firms. *Albuquerque Journal,* May 12, 1.

Quigley, Winthrop. 2009. Solar Cluster: Local Officials Want Industry to Blossom Here. *Albuquerque Journal* (June 7): A1.

Ram, R., 2004. Discussion on Emerging Technology Alternatives. Erica Fuchs, Cambridge, MA (December 2).

Ramo, Simon. 1972. Technology and Resources for Business: Government-Industry-Science. Paper delivered at the White House Conference on the Industrial World Ahead: A Look at Business in 1990, Washington, D.C., February 7. Reprinted in *Vital Speeches of the Day* 38.

Rand Science and Technology Policy Institute. 2003. *Technology Transfer of Federally Funded R&D: Perspectives from a Forum.*

Rathmann, George B. 2004. Chairman, CEO, and President of Amgen, 1980–1988. An Oral History Conducted in 2003 by Sally Smith Hughes, Ph.D., Regional Oral History Office, the Bancroft Library, University of California–Berkeley.

Rauch, Jonathan. 2001. The New Old Economy: Oil, Computers, and the Reinvention of the Earth. *Atlantic* (January): 35–49.

Rayburn, Rosalie. 2006. Solar Start-up Plans Factory. *Albuquerque Journal* (July 19): B4.

Reese, April. 2006. New Mexico: The World's Biggest "Solar Farm." *E: The Environmental Magazine* 17 (4): 33.

Reinhold, Robert. 1984. Agrarian New Mexico Seeks a Silicon Harvest. *New York Times,* June 12, A16.

Rensberger, Boyce. 1993. For U.S. Manufacturing, a Champion of New Ways. *Washington Post,* September 2.

Rensselaer Magazine. 2002. DARPA Inside, June.

Rezendes, Victor. 1997. *Department of Energy: Clearer Missions and Better Management Are Needed at the National Labs.* Washington: GAO.

Robinson, C. Paul. 2001. Prepared Statement of Dr. C. Paul Robinson, Director, Sandia National Laboratories. Senate Committee on Energy and Natural Resources, June 5.

Robinson-Avila, Kevin. 2007. Let the Sun Shine: Solar Plants Are on NM Horizon. *New Mexico Business Weekly,* November 9. http://albuquerque.bizjournals.com/albuquerque/stories/2007/11/12/story10.html.

Roco, Mihail C. 1997. Introduction. *WTEC Workshop Report on R&D Status and Trends,* edited by Richard Siegel, Evelyn Hu, and M. Roco. www.wtec.org/loyola/nano/U.S.Review/01_01.htm.

———. 2008. Long View for Nanotechnology R&D. American Academy of Nanomedicine Symposium. www.nsf.gov/crssprgm/nano/reports/NNI_080906_Roco@Nanomedicine_LongViewU.S._50sl.pdf.

Roco, Mihail C., and William Sims Bainbridge, eds. 2002. *Converging Technologies for Improving Human Performance: Nanotechnology, Biotechnology, Information Technology, and Cognitive Science,* 36–55. Arlington: NSF. www.wtec.org/ConvergingTechnologies/1/NBIC_report.pdf.

Rodrik, Dani. 2004. Industrial Policy for the Twenty-First Century. Harvard University. Working Paper. http://ksghome.harvard.edu/~drodrik/UNIDOSep.pdf.

Roessner, David, et al. 1997. *The Role of NSF Support of Engineering in Enabling Technological Innovation.* Stanford: SRI Policy Division.

Romero, Simon. 2004. Family Gas Empire vs. Governor on a Mesa Out West. *New York Times* (April 16): C1.

Rong, H., et al. 2005. An All-Silicon Raman Laser. *Nature* 433: 292–294.

Sampat, Bhaven N., David C. Mowery, and Arvids A. Ziedonis. n.d. Changes in University Patent Quality After the Bayh-Dole Act: A Re-Examination. Manuscript.

Sandia Lab News. 2008. Sandia Entrepreneurs Take Wing Under Angels at TVC. September 26, 4.

Sandia National Laboratories. 1999. White Paper on Sandia National Laboratories and the Sandia Science and Technology Park. In *Industry-Laboratory Partnerships: A Review of the Sandia Science and Technology Park Initiative,* Appendix A, edited by C. Wessner. Washington: National Academies Press.

———. 2005. *Partnering for a Strong America: Annual Partnerships Report FY 2005.*

Sands, David R. 1993. Standards Chief Poised to Develop New Association with Private Sector. *Washington Times,* October 29.

Santa Fe New Mexican. 2008. Our View: Renewable Energy Part of Climate Equation (May 30): A9.

Saunders, G. 2004. *COTS in Military Systems: A Ten-Year Perspective.* Military and Aerospace Electronics Show, Baltimore, MD.

Sawin, Janet L. 2004. *Mainstreaming Renewable Energy in the 21st Century.* Worldwatch Paper 169. www.worldwatch.org/system/files/EWP169.pdf.

Saxenian, AnnaLee, and Charles Sabel. 2009. *A Fugitive Success: Finland's Economic Future.* Helsinki: SITRA. www.sitra.fi/julkaisut/raportti80.pdf.

Schacht, Wendy H. 2005. *Technology Transfer: Use of Federally Funded Research and Development.* Congressional Research Service Report IB85031, April 1.

Schmit, Russell. 2007. Reducing Barriers to Growth of Renewable Energy Technologies—Relationships Among Federal, State, and Local Governments. Testimony to the Senate Energy and Natural Resources, Oversight Hearing, August 7.

Schott Solar. 2008. SCHOTT Solar to Build Production Facility in Albuquerque, New Mexico. Press release, January 14.

Schrage, Michael. 1994. A Technocrat Faces the GOP Assault on Government's Role in Innovation. *Washington Post,* November 18.

Schrank, Andrew, and Josh Whitford. 2009b. *The Anatomy of Network Failure.* Working Paper. University of New Mexico/Columbia University.

Scott, William B. 1995. Technology Transfer Support Wavers. *Aviation Week and Space Technology* 143: 17.

SEIA (Solar Energy Industries Association). 2009. SEIA: The United States Has Some of the Best Untapped Solar Resources in the World. SEIA press release, February 10. www.seia .org/cs/news_detail?pressrelease.id=342.

SFI. 2007. *Annual Report 2007.* Dublin: SFI.

Shah, J. 2004. *Electronic and Photonic Integrated Circuits (EPIC).* Microsystems Technology Office. Arlington, VA: Defense Advanced Research Agency.

———. 2005. Moore's Law for Photonics and Beyond. In *DARPATech: Powered by Ideas,* 129–131. Microsystems Technology Office. Washington, D.C.: DARPA.

———. 2007. Ultraperformance Nanophotonic Intrachip Communication (UNIC). Microsystems Technology Office. Washington, D.C.: DARPA.

Shanahan, Eileen. 1972. Revisions Asked for Patent Laws. *New York Times* (September 28): 43.

Sherwood, Larry. 2009. *U.S. Solar Market: Trends 2008.* Interstate Renewable Energy Council. www.irecusa.org/fileadmin/user_upload/NationalOutreachDocs/SolarTrendsReports/ IREC_Solar_Market_Trends_Report_2008.pdf.

Siemens, Warren. 1997. Sandia: A New Approach to Partnerships. *New Mexico Business Journal* (June): 19–21.

Simmons, Jerry. 2007. Statement of Dr. Jerry A. Simmons Jr., solid state lighting program manager and acting codirector, Center for Integrated Nanotechnologies, Sandia National Laboratories. Testimony Before the Senate Committee on Energy and Natural Resources, June 7.

Smalley, Richard C. 1996. Discovering the Fullerenes. http://nobelprize.org/nobel_prizes/ chemistry/laureates/1996/smalley-lecture.pdf.

Solartech. 2007. *Solartech: Creating a Solar Center of Excellence.* White Paper, June. http:// solartech.org/images/stories/pdf/stwp_2007.pdf.

Solvig, Kim. 2008. My View: Oil and Gas Welcome to Play by the Same Rules. *Santa Fe New Mexican* (March 9): B3.

Spohn, Larry. 1996. Don't Tell Anybody—but Congratulations. *New Mexico Business Journal,* August, 59.

Strahs, G., and C. Tombari. 2006. *Laying the Foundation for a Solar America: The Million Solar Roofs Initiative.* National Renewable Energy Laboratory Report, October. www.nrel.gov/docs/fy07osti/40483.pdf.

Sullivan, Walter. 1973. Nixon to Revamp the Science Establishment. *New York Times* (January 31): 20.

Tatge, Mark. 2006. Ready for Takeoff. *Forbes* (May 22): 178–182.

Taylor, Margaret, et al. 2007. Government Actions and Innovation in Clean Energy Technologies: The Cases of Photovoltaic Cells, Solar Thermal Electric Power, and Solar Water Heating. Report to the California Energy Commission, October. http://gspp.berkeley.edu/academics/faculty/docs/mtaylor/CEC-500-2007-012.pdf.

Telesis Consultancy Group. 1982. *A Review of Industrial Policy.* NESC Report No. 64. Dublin: NESC.

Tether, T. 2003. Statement by Dr. Tony Tether, director, Defense Advanced Research Projects Agency. Subcommittee on Terrorism, Unconventional Threats, and Capabilities, House Armed Services Committee, Washington, D.C..

The Economist. 1990. The Competition Industry, July 7.

———. 1991. Will the Bangs End with a Whimper? (November 2): 79–82.

———. 1992. American Technology Policy: Settling the Frontier, July 25.

———. 2007. Something New Under the Sun: A Special Report on Innovation, October 13.

Tsapogas, John. 2004. *More Than One-Fifth of All Individuals Employed in Science and Engineering Occupations Have Less Than a Bachelor's Degree Education.* Info Brief NSF 04-333. Arlington, VA: National Science Foundation.

———. 2006. The Promise and Perils of Synthetic Biology. *New Atlantic* (Spring): 25–45.

Turkle, Sherry. 2002. Sociable Technologies: Enhancing Human Performance When the Computer is Not a Tool but a Companion. In *Converging Technologies for Improving Human Performance,* edited by Roco and Bainbridge. Arlington: NSF.

U.S. 1996. *PRC State Council Decision on Accelerating S&T Development.* www.fas.org/nuke/guide/china/doctrine/stdec2.htm.

U.S. NNI. 2006. *Research and Development Leading to a Revolution in Technology and Industry: Supplement to the President's FY 2007 Budget.* Washington, D.C.: NNI (July).

U.S. NNI. 2008a. FY 2008 Budget and Highlights. www.nano.gov/NNI_FY08_budget_summary-highlights.pdf.

U.S. NNI. 2008b. About the NNI: Goals of the NNI. www.nano.gov/html/about/home_about.html.

U.S. NNI. 2008c. NNI Research Centers. www.nano.gov/html/centers/home_centers.html.

U.S. NNI. 2008d. Funding Strategy: NNI Program Component Areas. www.nano.gov/html/about/fundingstrategy.html.

U.S. NNI. 2008e. FY 2009 Budget and Highlights. www.nano.gov/NNI_FY09_budget_summary.pdf.

U.S. NNI. 2009. Research and Development Leading to a Revolution in Technology and Industry: Supplement to the President's 2009 Budget. www.nano.gov/NNI_2010_budget_supplement.pdf.United States Census Bureau. 2000. *Census 2000 Summary File 1 (SF 1) 100-Percent Data.* Washington: Census Bureau.

Velasco, Diane. 2005. Mesa del Sol Plans Unveiled. *Albuquerque Journal* (July 4): B7.

Vorenberg, Sue. 2006. N.M. Universities Unite for the Love of Science. *Albuquerque Journal* (April 15): A1.

Wall, Dennis. 1995. Can New Mexico Really Become a World-Class Center for High-Tech? *New Mexico Business Journal,* June 23.

Washington Post. 1971. U.S. Patent Rein Loosened (August 24): A17.

Wasserman, Jim. 2008. SMUD Solar Deal with Woodside Homes. *Sacramento Bee,* Home Front, April 4. www.sacbee.com/static/weblogs/real_estate/archives/011648.html.

Webb, Andrew. 2004. Local Solar Energy Firm Gets $8 Million. *Albuquerque Journal* (December 10): A1.

———. 2008. Solar Firm Heads to Mesa del Sol. *Albuquerque Journal* (January 15): A1.

Weisman, Jonathan. 1995a. Even with the Republicans in Charge, the Labs' Future Is Murky. *New Mexico Business Journal,* February, 53–56.

———. 1995b. The Bloom Is Off Tech Transfer. *New Mexico Business Journal* (April): 61–62.

———. 1996. Strictly Business at Sandia. *New Mexico Business Journal* (March): 59.

Wilford, John Noble. 1971. Nixon Men Map New Aid to Technology. *New York Times,* October 31.

Willey, Tara, and Steve Hester. 2001. *TEAM-UP Final Reports.* Solar Electric Power Association. www.osti.gov/bridge/servlets/purl/794223-9v3sYT/webviewable/794223.pdf.

Wiser, Ryan, and Galen Barbose. 2008. *Renewables Portfolio Standards in the United States: A Status Report with Data Through 2007.* Lawrence Berkeley National Laboratory. http://eetd.lbl.gov/ea/ems/reports/lbnl-154e.pdf.

Wiser, Ryan, Galen Barbose, and Carla Peterman. 2009. *Tracking the Sun: The Installed Cost of Photovoltaics in the U.S. from 1998–2007.* Lawrence Berkeley National Laboratory. http://eetd.lbl.gov/EA/emp/reports/lbnl-1516e-web.pdf.

Wiser, Ryan, et al. 2006. *Letting the Sun Shine on Solar Costs: An Empirical Investigation of Photovoltaic Cost Trends in California.* Lawrence Berkeley National Laboratory. http://eetd.lbl.gov/ea/EMP/reports/59282.pdf.

Wolfe, Raymond M. 2008. *U.S. Business R&D Expenditures Increase in 2006; Companies' Own and Federal Contributions Rise.* NSF 08-313. Arlington, VA: National Science Foundation.

Woody, Todd. 2007. Big Solar's Day in the Sun. *Business 2.0,* June 1, http://money.cnn.com/magazines/business2/business2_archive/2007/06/01/100050990/index.htm.

Xie, Sishen. 2006. Interview conducted at conference of U.S. and China nanoscientists and engineers, National Science Foundation, Washington, D.C., March 6.

———. 2007a. Interview conducted at Institute of Physics, Beijing, July 24.

———. 2007b. Funding and Networks for Nanotechnology in China. Presentation given at the Institute for Physics, Beijing, July 17.

Xu Jianzhong. 2006. Interview conducted at China National Academy of Nanotechnology & Engineering, August 3.

Yang, D. J. 2000. On Moore's Law and Fishing: Gordon Moore Speaks Out. *U.S. News Online* (7/10/2000) http://www.usnews.com/usnews/transcripts/moore.htm.

Young, Kerry. 2009. Overdose of Influence in Epogen Debate. *CQ Weekly* (September 28): 2143–2147.

Zhao, Renfeng. 2005. Trust Sector Seeks Foreign Investments. *China Daily,* March 9. www.chinesetao.com/China%20Daily%20-%20March%207%202005.pdf.

About the Editors and Contributors

Fred Block is a sociologist at the University of California, Davis. His books include *The Origins of International Economic Disorder and Postindustrial Possibilities.* He is currently completing a manuscript called "Free Market Utopia" (with Margaret Somers) that elaborates an approach to economic sociology rooted in the writings of Karl Polanyi.

Matthew R. Keller is an Assistant Professor of Sociology at Southern Methodist University. His research explores shifts in intellectual and political trends and their relation to government organization and policy. Current research includes an investigation of U.S. federal policies designed to stimulate alternative energy technologies, and a cross-national comparative analysis of government commissions into collective violence.

John A. Alic worked for many years at the congressional Office of Technology Assessment, where he directed studies beginning with *U.S. Industrial Competitiveness: A Comparison of Steel, Electronics, and Automobiles,* published in 1981. Since OTA's closure, he has consulted for nonprofits and government. His book *Trillions for Military Technology: How the Pentagon Innovates and Why It Costs So Much* appeared in 2007. Alic has also taught at several universities.

Richard P. Appelbaum, Ph.D., is Professor of Sociology and Global and International Studies at the University of California at Santa Barbara. He currently serves as Director of the M.A. Program in Global & International Studies and is a co-PI of UCSB's Center for Nanotechnology in Society. He has previously served as chair of the Sociology Department and was founder and Acting Director of the UCSB Global & International Studies Program. He is presently engaged in a comparative study of the role of technology policy in fostering equitable development.

Dina Biscotti is a doctoral candidate in Sociology at the University of California, Davis. Her dissertation analyzes the institutional boundaries between academic and commercial science in U.S. university-industry agricultural biotechnology research collaborations. Her work explores the interdependencies between government, industry, and nonprofits. She is interested in how the public good is framed by states, experts, and other social actors to support particular knowledge regimes.

Cong Cao, Ph.D., is a researcher with the Levin Institute, State University of New York, where he directs the Center for Science, Technology, and Innovation in China. As one of the leading scholars in the studies of China's science and innovation, Dr. Cao is the author of *China's Scientific Elite* (RoutledgeCurzon, 2004), a study of those Chinese scientists holding the elite membership in the Chinese Academy of Sciences, and *China's Emerging Technological Edge: Assessing the Role of High-End Talent* (with Denis Fred Simon, Cambridge University Press, 2009). He has been involved in the study of development of nanotechnology in China and will embark on a project examining China's biotechnology policy, both supported by the U.S. National Science Foundation.

Peter Evans is Professor of Sociology and Marjorie Meyer Eliaser Professor of International Studies at the University of California, Berkeley. His work on the comparative political economy of national development is exemplified by his 1995 book *Embedded Autonomy: States and Industrial Transformation*. His continued interest in the role of the state is reflected in a recent series of articles on the "21st Century Developmental State." He is now working on "counter-hegemonic globalization" with a focus on the role of the global labor movement and other transnational social movements.

Erica Fuchs is an Assistant Professor in the Department of Engineering and Public Policy at Carnegie Mellon University. Her research focuses on the role of government in technology development and the effect of location on the competitiveness of new technologies. In 2008, she won the Oak Ridge Associated Universities Junior Faculty Enhancement Fellowship for her research on the impact of offshoring on technology directions. Her work has been published in *High Temperature Materials and Processes, Composite Science and Technology, International Journal of Vehicle Design, Journal of Lightwave Technology,* and *Issues in Science and Technology.*

Gary Gereffi is Professor of Sociology and Director of the Center on Globalization, Governance & Competitiveness at Duke University (www.cggc.duke.edu). He received his B.A. degree from the University of Notre Dame and his Ph.D. degree from Yale University. Gereffi has published numerous books and articles on globalization, industrial upgrading, and social and economic development, including *Manufacturing Miracles: Paths of Industrialization in Latin America and East Asia* (Princeton University Press, 1990); *Commodity Chains and Global Capitalism* (Praeger Publishers, 1994); and *The New Offshoring of Jobs and Global Development* (International Institute of Labor Studies, 2006). Gereffi's research interests deal with the competitive strategies of global firms, the governance of global value chains, economic and social upgrading, and the emerging global knowledge economy.

Shelley L. Hurt is Assistant Professor of Political Science at the California Polytechnic State University in San Luis Obispo. She recently completed her dissertation, "Science, Power, and the State: U.S. Foreign Policy, Intellectual Property Law, and the Origins of Agricultural Biotechnology, 1969-1994" at the New School for Social Research. She is currently working on a book-length project, "Public-Private Hybridization of the 21st Century State," with Professor Ronnie D. Lipschutz.

Daniel Lee Kleinman is professor and chair of the Department of Community and Environmental Sociology at the University of Wisconsin—Madison, where he is also the director of the Robert F. and Jean E. Holtz Center of Science and Technology Studies. For the past decade, his research has focused on three areas: the knowledge economy and the commercialization of the university, democracy and expertise, and the politics of agricultural biotechnology policy. Among his books are *Impure Cultures: University Biology and the World of Commerce* and *Controversies in Science and Technology: From Energy to Evolution* (edited with Jason Delborne, Karen Cloud-Hansen, and Jo Handelsman).

Chris Knight is an independent researcher living in Davis, California. He has previously worked with economist Skip Laitner at the American Council for an Energy-Efficient Economy in Washington, DC, and with sociologist Fred Block at the University of California Davis Institute of Governmental Affairs. He graduated from the University of California, Davis, in 2007 with a B.A. in economics.

Marian Negoita is a postdoctoral scholar at the Institute of Governmental Affairs at the University of California, Davis. His research primarily focuses on developmental states with an emphasis on the interplay between states and civil societies. His work has been published in *Socio-Economic Review* and *Politics and Society*. He is currently working on projects related to developmental state building and technology and innovation policy.

Christopher Newfield teaches American Studies in the English Department at the University of California, Santa Barbara. He is the author of *Ivy and Industry: Business and the Making of the American University, 1880-1980* (Duke University Press, 2003), and *Unmaking the Public University: The Forty Year Assault on the Middle Class* (Harvard University Press, 2008), chairs the Innovation Group at the NSF Center for Nanotechnology in Society, runs a blog on the current crisis in higher education, *Rethinking the University*, and is working on a book called *Lower Education: What to Do About Our Downsized Future*.

Seán Ó Riain is Professor of Sociology at the National University of Ireland, Maynooth. His research examines the politics of the information economy through studies of developmental network states, regional and national development strategies, and of the politics of high tech workplaces. He is the author of *The Politics of High Tech Growth: Developmental Network States in the Global Economy* (Cambridge, 2004). Current projects include studies of the dynamics and politics of the Silicon Valley–Ireland production system (with C.Benner) and a life history study of social change in twentieth century Ireland (with J. Gray and A.O'Carroll).

Rachel Parker is a Ph.D. candidate in Sociology at the University of California, Santa Barbara, and a Senior Research Fellow at the Center for Nanotechnology in Society, where she works with Richard Appelbaum on a comparative project investigating Nanotechnology Policy in China and the United States. Rachel's dissertation analyzes China's Science and Technology Policy using Nanotechnology as a case study. She is interested in nano and other emerging technologies that can be used for equitable development and environmental remediation. Rachel received an MSc in NGO Management from the London School of Economics, and a B.A. in sociology from Brandeis University.

Andrew Schrank received his Ph.D. from the University of Wisconsin in 2000 and is currently Associate Professor of Sociology at the University of New Mexico. He studies the organization, regulation, and performance of business.

Steven Vallas, Professor and Department Chair at Northeastern University, writes and teaches on the sociology of work and on sociological theory. He has studied a wide array of workplace settings, focusing on organizational change in deeply traditional manufacturing settings, institutions of higher education, and high tech, science-intensive industries. His work has appeared in the *American Journal of Sociology*, *American Sociological Review*, *Social Problems*, and *Sociological Theory*, among many other venues. He is currently working on the theoretical paradigms that inform the study of work and economic institutions.

Josh Whitford is an Assistant Professor of Sociology at Columbia University. He is the author of *The New Old Economy: Networks, Institutions and the Organizational Transformation of American Manufacturing* (Oxford University Press, 2005) as well as of several articles on the implications of decentralized production (outsourcing) for the governance of regional economies. In 2007, he was named an Industry Studies Fellow by the Alfred P. Sloan Foundation.

Index

ACM Queue, 136

Advanced Research Projects Agency (ARPA). *See* Defense Advanced Research Projects Agency (DARPA)

Advanced Technology Program (ATP): beginnings, 80–82; Bush (G.W.) administration, 85, 91–92; Clinton administration, 82–84; DARPA-emulating approach, 83; effectiveness evaluation, 86–87; funding, 84, 90; manufacturing extension program, 12, 13; political visibility and threats to survival, 13, 77–78, 85–86, 90–91, 129, 294; post-1994 decline, 84–85; program competitions, 82, 83–84, 85; purpose, 12, 14, 77, 80, 86; substantive contribution, 87–89

Advent Solar, 104

AEC. *See* Atomic Energy Commission (AEC)

agriculture, 5–6, 74, 245

Agriculture Department, U.S. (USDA), 5, 7, 20, 21, 244–245

Ahern, Bertie, 213

Alternative Agricultural Research and Commercialization Corporation (AARCC), 111–112

AMD, 136, 144

America Competes Act, 85

American Recovery and Reinvestment Act, 2, 14–15

Ames, Aldrich, 118

Amgen, 68

antitrust legislation, 12

Appel, Toby, 46

Apple, 11, 141, 160

Applebaum, Richard, 275–276

Aranesp, 68

arms control, Nixon administration, 35–36

Army Corps of Engineers, 7

ARPA-E, 14

ARPANET, 139, 292

Aspin-Brown Commission, 118

AT&T, 102–103, 106

Atomic Energy Commission (AEC), 101

Auerswald, Philip, 80

Augustine, Norman, 119

automobile industry: ATP programs focusing on, 88; Chrysler Motors bailout, 11; computerization in, 255; fuel-efficient vehicle development funding, 21–22; innovation in, 248; outsourcing, 157; U.S. domination of, 78

aviation industry, 88

Ayres, Robert, 98

Bai Chunli, 223, 226

Barriers to Nanotechnology Commercialization (DOC), 218

Batelle Ventures, 126

Battelle, 126, 169

Bayh-Dole Act, 32, 50–51, 61, 63–64, 69–70, 103

Bell, Daniel, 33, 155, 158

Bell, Gordon, 136

Bell Labs, 177

Bell Telephone Labs, 102, 106

Bennett, Ira, 289

Bennis, Warren, 155

Berg, Paul, 62, 70

Berk, Gerald, 6

Berkeley Scientific Laboratories, 62

Biogen, 68

biological warfare, 7, 35

biological warfare programs, converting to